FORMAL ISSUES IN LEXICAL-FUNCTIONAL GRAMMAR

T0345357

CSLI
Lecture Notes
No. 47

FORMAL ISSUES IN LEXICAL-FUNCTIONAL GRAMMAR

edited by
Mary Dalrymple, Ronald M. Kaplan,
John T. Maxwell III, Annie Zaenen

CSLI Publications
CENTER FOR THE STUDY OF
LANGUAGE AND INFORMATION
STANFORD, CALIFORNIA

Copyright ©1995
Center for the Study of Language and Information
Leland Stanford Junior University
Printed in the United States
99 98 97 96 95   5 4 3 2 1

Library of Congress Cataloging-in-Publication Data

Formal issues in lexical-functional grammar / edited by Mary Dalrymple, Ronald
M. Kaplan, John T. Maxwell III, Annie Zaenen.
    p.   cm. — (CSLI lecture notes ; no. 47)
Includes bibliographical references and index.
ISBN 1-881526-37-2. — ISBN 1-881526-36-4 (pbk.).
1. Lexical-functional grammar I. Dalrymple, Mary. II. Series.
P158.25.F67 1994
415 — dc20   94-26186
                                                CIP

CSLI was founded early in 1983 by researchers from Stanford University, SRI International, and Xerox PARC to further research and development of integrated theories of language, information, and computation. CSLI headquarters and CSLI Publications are located on the campus of Stanford University.

CSLI Lecture Notes report new developments in the study of language, information, and
computation. In addition to lecture notes, the series includes monographs, working papers, and conference proceedings. Our aim is to make new results, ideas, and approaches
available as quickly as possible.

Contents

Contributors

JOAN BRESNAN is Howard H. and Jesse T. Watkins University Professor at Stanford University. She co-designed the first formal theory of LFG in 1978 with Ron Kaplan. Her research interests have included lexicalist syntax, computational psycholinguistic modelling, and issues in universal grammar and natural language typology.

MARY DALRYMPLE is a researcher in the Natural Language Theory and Technology group at Xerox Palo Alto Research Center and a Consulting Assistant Professor in the Department of Linguistics at Stanford University. Her recent work focuses on the syntax-semantics interface.

PER-KRISTIAN HALVORSEN is a Principal Scientist and Laboratory Manager for the Information Sciences and Technologies Laboratory at Xerox Palo Alto Research Center. He holds appointments as consulting professor in the Department of Linguistics at Stanford University and as professor (II) at the University of Oslo. Dr. Halvorsen is a co-author of the book *Situations, Language and Logic* and has published widely in the areas of linguistics and natural language semantics.

MARK JOHNSON is Associate Professor in the Department of Cognitive and Linguistic Sciences at Brown University. He is interested in the computational properties of natural language syntax and semantics.

RONALD M. KAPLAN is a Research Fellow at the Xerox Palo Alto Research Center, where he heads the Natural Language Theory and Technology group. He is also a Consulting Professor of Linguistics at Stanford University and a Principal of the Center for the Study of Language and Information. He is a co-designer of the formal theory of Lexical-Functional Grammar and the creator of its initial computational implementation.

JOHN T. MAXWELL III is a researcher in the Natural Language Theory and Technology group at the Xerox Palo Alto Research Center. His work mostly focuses on formal complexity.

KLAUS NETTER is a computational linguist whose research concentrates on German syntax in constraint-based grammar formalisms, machine translation and the structure of the lexicon. He has worked at the Institute for Natural Language Processing at the University of Stuttgart and is currently working at the German AI Center in Saarbrücken.

JÜRGEN WEDEKIND is a researcher at the Institute for Natural Language Processing at the University of Stuttgart. His research mostly concentrates on algorithmic problems.

ANNIE ZAENEN is the director of the Multilingual Technology and Theory area in the Grenoble Laboratory of the Rank Xerox Research Centre, France and a Consulting Associate Professor of Linguistics at Stanford University. She works on natural language syntax and lexical issues.

Introduction

The year 1982 saw the publication of *The Mental Representation of Grammatical Relations*, the first collection of papers on the theory of Lexical-Functional Grammar. Since the publication of that volume, the growing body of work within the LFG framework has shown the advantages of an explicitly formulated, non-transformational approach to syntax, and the influence of this theory has been extensive. LFG is particularly distinguished by its use of formally different representations for linguistically different kinds of information, and we believe that this is one important factor that has enabled LFG to provide new insights into linguistic structure. These insights have in turn shaped the theory in both formal and substantive ways.

Unfortunately, however, many of the developments in the formal theory of LFG since the publication of the 1982 volume have not been readily available to a wide audience. Many papers elaborating new proposals have appeared only in conference proceedings or as technical reports, or have never been published at all. It has been difficult for the larger linguistic community to learn about and make use of the advances that have been made.

As a partial remedy to this situation, we have pulled together into a single volume a set of papers by ourselves and our colleagues that address some of the developments of the past years. This book outlines work in formal issues in LFG theory in the twelve year period from 1982 to 1994. We have included papers on a range of topics that have been central in LFG research during this period. In particular, we have tried to include those papers which have been most influential as well as those that have previously been most inaccessible.

Each section of this book contains papers that address a central issue in the development of the theory. We have provided an introduction to each section to give a sense of the historical context in which these papers were written and to make clear how the papers fit in with other work in LFG and other frameworks before and since they were written.

Part I of the book, "Formal Architecture", reproduces the Kaplan and Bresnan paper "Lexical-Functional Grammar: A Formal System for Grammatical Representation" from the original 1982 volume. Since that volume is now out of print, we thought it useful to include this paper, both as an overview of the original LFG theory and as a backdrop against which later developments can be viewed. The other paper in Part I, Kaplan's "The Formal Architecture of Lexical-Functional Grammar", gives an overview of the current state of LFG formal theory and provides a preview of the material covered in more detail in the remainder of the book.

Among the advances in the theory of functional structure since the publication of the 1982 volume is the ability to characterize nonlocal relations between f-structures, allowing for a formally well-defined treatment of long-distance dependencies and constraints on anaphoric binding. Part II of the book, "Nonlocal Dependencies", details the developments of this aspect of the theory, including an account of the interaction of coordination with long-distance relations. More recently, work on anaphoric binding by Strand (1992) and Culy, Kodio, and Togo (1995) and on the interpretation of wh-in-situ by Huang (1993) has built on these formal developments, applying them in new ways and to new sets of data.

Earlier work within LFG on the word order and constituency puzzles in Dutch and other Germanic languages (e.g., Bresnan et al. 1982) showed the success of an approach relying on the explicit separation of different kinds of syntactic information into distinct modules. The papers in Part III of this volume, "Word Order", chronicle more recent explorations of word order, constituent structure, and the constituent structure/functional structure interface. These papers examine word order constraints that are definable in terms of functional relations and the functional structure/constituent structure interface. A new formal device called *functional precedence* is proposed to characterize relatively minor interactions involving information that is expressed most naturally in these different representations.

Part IV of this volume, "Semantics and Translation", assembles work on the relation of syntactic structure to semantic form, representing and relating the various kinds of linguistic information by means of the projection architecture. The work presented in that section addresses issues that have also been raised by other researchers, in particular by Andrews and Manning in their 1993 paper "Information spreading and levels of representation in LFG".

From its inception, the theory of LFG has been concerned with psycholinguistic and computational issues of processing, and the original 1982 volume contained a number of papers addressing these topics. More recent developments concerning formal characterization, computational complexity, and processing strategies are treated in Part V of the book, "Mathematical and Computational Issues". These papers help to establish a deeper understanding of the LFG formalism and related systems and to outline a space of efficient implementation possibilities. Recent studies on psycholinguistics and language acquisition relying on LFG theory have also been conducted by Pinker and his colleagues (Pinker 1989a, Pinker 1989b, Gropen et al. 1991).

A large and varied body of linguistic work has grown up in the years since the introduction of the theory of LFG. In the following we will attempt to give brief mention of some of the research that is not described in detail elsewhere in this volume. It is of course impossible to do justice to all of this work in this small space, and so in doing this, we risk neglecting important contributions to the theory. We hope our readers will forgive us for the incompleteness of this summary.

One major focus of work in LFG theory in recent years is the study of the relation between syntactic structure and argument structure. Beginning with Levin's 1986 dissertation *Operations on lexical forms: Unaccusative rules in Germanic languages*, this research has focused on the connection between thematic argument structure and grammatical functions, and has attempted to discover the generalizations by which the two are related.

Bresnan and Kanerva continued this work in their 1989 paper "Locative inversion in Chicheŵa: a case study of factorization in grammar", in which they proposed a decomposition of the grammatical functions SUBJ, OBJ, OBL, and so on into a set of more basic features, analogous to the decomposition of phonemes into phonological features. Grammatical functions continue to be "primitives" of the theory in that they are not definable in terms of concepts from other levels of linguistic structure, such as phrase structure or thematic structure. However, grammatical functions are no longer seen as atomic entities, but instead are composed of more primitive elements which organize the grammatical functions into natural classes. On this view of mapping theory, the primitive features are associated with thematic roles, and the array of grammatical functions subcategorized by a predicate is deduced. A similar approach was followed by Alsina and Mchombo in their 1990 paper "The syntax of applicatives in Chicheŵa: Problems for a theta theoretic asymmetry" and by Bresnan and Moshi in their 1990 paper "Object asymmetries in comparative Bantu syntax", which outlined a theory of linking for "applied" arguments such as benefactives and instrumentals. Linking of causatives was treated by Alsina (1992), and a complete theory of predicate linking—similar to Bresnan and Kanerva's, but with important differences—was proposed by Alsina in his 1993 dissertation *Predicate composition: A Theory of Syntactic Function Alternations*. Other recent work on linking can be found in Mchombo (1993), drawing on Bantu languages, and in Austin (1995) on Australian.

The problem of linking between thematic roles and grammatical functions has been dealt with in various other ways, in particular in the analysis of complex predicates. These constructions seem to exhibit both monoclausal and biclausal properties. Butt, Isoda, and Sells discussed Urdu complex predicates in their 1990 paper "Complex predicates in LFG". They observed that complex predicates provide a challenge for most syntactic theories because they violate their basic architectural assumptions. Manning's 1992 paper "Romance is so complex" discussed formal issues in complex predicate linking in Romance languages. The analysis of Urdu complex predicates is dealt with more fully in Butt's 1993 dissertation *Complex predicates in Urdu*. She provides a theory of linking between grammatical functions and argument positions in a Jackendoff-style thematic role representation.

Research into the nature of unaccusativity has been presented in a series of papers by Zaenen. This work is summarized in her 1993 paper "Unaccusativity in Dutch: An integrated approach". Unaccusativity provides important insights into the nature of the relationship between thematic roles and grammatical functions, and in particular about how thematic roles can affect syntactic realization. In their 1990 paper "Deep unaccusativity in LFG", Bresnan and Zaenen propose a theory of linking that accounts for the phenomenon of deep unaccusativity in a principled way without relying on otherwise unmotivated levels of syntactic representation.

The phenomenon of locative inversion also provides clues as to how arguments with different thematic roles can be syntactically realized. Bresnan proposed a theory of locative inversion in her 1991 paper "Locative case vs. locative gender", showing among other things that a view on which grammatical functions are defined in terms of a thematic role hierarchy is untenable. Her 1994 paper "Locative inversion and the architecture of universal grammar" provides elaborations and extensions of that theory.

Other important research into linking theory has been conducted by Laczko in his 1994 dissertation *Predicates in the Hungarian Noun Phrase*, by Ackerman in his 1995 paper "Systemic patterns and lexical representations: analytic morphological words", and by Bodomo in his dissertation *Complex Verbal Predicates*, in preparation. Related work is presented in dissertations by Manning (1994) and by T. Mohanan (1990) and in work by Ackerman and LeSourd (1995) and Ackerman and Webelhuth (1995).

A major focus of work in LFG from the beginning has been lexical integrity and the various levels at which wordhood can be defined. Recent work on this topic includes Matsumoto (1992), Bresnan and Mchombo (1995), and Sells (1995).

Another line of investigation in LFG has dealt with the phenomena of agreement and apparent "null pronominals" cross-linguistically. The appearance of Bresnan and Mchombo's 1987 paper "Topic, pronoun, and agreement in Chicheŵa" constituted an important step in clarifying these issues; Bresnan and Mchombo showed that a clean account of pronominalization in Chicheŵa and other Bantu languages can be obtained by assuming that null pronominals are syntactically represented at functional structure but not in the constituent structure. Related work has been conducted by Demuth and Johnson (1989), Andrews (1990b), Uyechi (1991), and Nordlinger (1995b).

In recent years there has also been work exploring constituent structure and its independence from functional structure. Progress on these issues has been reported in recent dissertations by Kroeger (1991) and King (1993), by Austin and Bresnan in their 1995 paper "Non-configurationality in Australian Aboriginal languages", and by Bresnan in her 1995 paper "Morphology competes with syntax: Explaining typological variation in weak crossover effects".

Another new development in the formal theory of LFG came with the introduction of the restriction operator by Kaplan and Wedekind (1993). The restriction operator allows reference to subparts of f-structures by explicitly "removing" one or more attributes from an f-structure; for instance, it is possible to refer to an f-structure for a noun phrase with the CASE attribute and its value removed. Though the full range of potential uses for this operator is as yet not fully understood, some work—for example, work on type-driven semantic interpretation by Wedekind and Kaplan (1993)—has already begun to take advantage of its properties.

Other recent work explores semantic composition and the syntax-semantics interface. Dalrymple, Lamping, and Saraswat (1993) proposed a deductive approach to assembly of meanings that relies on the projection architecture to specify the correspondence between an f-structure and its meaning. The use of linear logic as a 'glue' for assembling meanings gives a clean treatment of a range of phenomena including modification, complex predicate formation (Dalrymple et al. 1993), and quantifier scoping, bound anaphora and their interactions with intensionality (Dalrymple et al. 1994).

In the years since its introduction, LFG theory has been applied to the description and analysis of a large variety of languages. Though the following is far from an exhaustive list, we would like to draw attention to some studies of languages that are not specifically mentioned elsewhere in this book: work on Arabic (Fassi-Fehri 1981, Wager 1983, Fassi-Fehri 1988), Bangla (Klaiman 1987a, Sengupta 1994), Basque (Abaitua 1988), Chinese (Her 1990, Tan 1991, Huang 1990, Huang 1991), Cree (Dahlstrom 1986), Finnish (Niño 1995), French (Hanson 1987, Schwarze 1988, Frank 1990), Icelandic (Andrews 1990a), Japanese (Ishikawa 1985, Saiki 1986, Saiki 1987, Iida 1987), Korean (Cho 1985, Hong 1991, Cho and Sells 1995), Malay (Alsagoff 1991), Malayalam (Mohanan 1983), Marathi (Joshi 1993), Modern Irish (Andrews 1990b), Norwegian (Rosén 1988, Lødrup 1991, Lødrup 1994, Kinn 1994), Old English (Allen 1995), Russian (Neidle 1988), Sanskrit (Klaiman 1987b), Serbo-Croatian (Zec 1987), Taiwanese (Huang 1992), Turkish (Güngördü and Oflazer 1994), Wambaya (Nordlinger 1995a), and Warlpiri (Simpson and Bresnan 1983, Simpson 1991).

This volume has been long in the making, and its existence is due to the hard work of many people. We are especially grateful to María-Eugenia Niño for her superb job of editing the volume and constructing the indexes. Chris Manning, Christian Rohrer, Jürgen Wedekind, and Paula Newman proofread and corrected several of the papers and introductions; they and Joan Bresnan also made valuable organizational suggestions. The cover art was produced at Xerox Palo Alto Research Center by Steve Wallgren. We are also grateful for the expert editorial advice and assistance of Dikran Karagueuzian, Tony Gee, and Emma Pease and for the unstinting support, technical and otherwise, of Jeanette Figueroa.

References

Abaitua, J. 1988. *Complex predicates in Basque: from lexical forms to functional structures.* Doctoral dissertation, University of Manchester, Department of Languages and Linguistics.

Ackerman, Farrell. 1995. Systemic patterns and lexical representations: analytic morphological words. In *Levels and Structures (Approaches to Hungarian, Vol. 5)*, ed. Istvan Kenesei. Szeged: JATE.

Ackerman, Farrell, and Phil LeSourd. To appear. Toward a lexical representation of phrasal predicates. In *Complex Predicates*, ed. Alex Alsina, Joan Bresnan, and Peter Sells. Stanford, CA: CSLI Publications.

Ackerman, Farrell, and Gert Webelhuth. 1995. Topicalization, Complex Predicates and Functional Uncertainty in German. MS.

Allen, Cynthia. 1995. *Case Marking and Reanalysis: Grammatical Relations from Old to Early Modern English.* Oxford: Clarendon Press.

Alsagoff, Lubna. 1991. *Topic in Malay: The Other Subject.* Doctoral dissertation, Stanford University.

Alsina, Alex. 1992. On the Argument Structure of Causatives. *Linguistic Inquiry* 23(4):517–555.

Alsina, Alex. 1993. *Predicate Composition: A Theory of Syntactic Function Alternations.* Doctoral dissertation, Stanford University.

Alsina, Alex, and Sam A. Mchombo. 1990. The Syntax of Applicatives in Chicheŵa: Problems for a Theta Theoretic Asymmetry. *Natural Language and Linguistic Theory* 8:493–506.

Andrews, Avery. 1990a. Case structures and control in Modern Icelandic. In *Modern Icelandic Syntax*, ed. Joan Maling and Annie Zaenen. 187–234. New York: Academic Press.

Andrews, Avery. 1990b. Unification and morphological blocking. *Natural Language and Linguistic Theory* 8(4):508–558.

Andrews, III, Avery, and Chris Manning. 1993. Information Spreading and Levels of Representation in LFG. Technical Report CSLI-93-176. Stanford University: Center for the Study of Language and Information.

Austin, Peter. 1995. Caustives and applicatives in Australian aboriginal languages. In untitled collection, ed. Kazuto Matsumura. Tokyo: Hitsuji Shobo. To appear.

Austin, Peter, and Joan Bresnan. 1995. Non-configurationality in Australian Aboriginal languages. *Natural Language and Linguistic Theory*, to appear.

Bodomo, Adams B. 1995. *Complex Verbal Predicates.* Doctoral dissertation, University of Trondheim, Norway. In preparation.

Bresnan, Joan (ed.). 1982. *The Mental Representation of Grammatical Relations.* Cambridge, MA: The MIT Press.

Bresnan, Joan. 1994. Locative Inversion and the Architecture of Universal Grammar. *Language* 70(1):72–131.

Bresnan, Joan. 1995. Morphology competes with syntax: Explaining typological variation in weak crossover effects. In *Proceedings of the MIT Workshop on Optimality in Syntax.* To appear. Invited paper presented at the MIT Workshop on Optimality in Syntax, May 1995.

Bresnan, Joan, and Jonni M. Kanerva. 1989. Locative Inversion in Chicheŵa: A Case Study of Factorization in Grammar. *Linguistic Inquiry* 20(1):1–50. Also in E. Wehrli and T. Stowell, eds., Syntax and Semantics 26: Syntax and the Lexicon. New York: Academic Press.

Bresnan, Joan, Ronald M. Kaplan, Stanley Peters, and Annie Zaenen. 1982. Cross-serial Dependencies in Dutch. *Linguistic Inquiry* 13:613–635.

Bresnan, Joan, and Sam A. Mchombo. 1987. Topic, pronoun, and agreement in Chicheŵa. *Language* 63(4):741–782.

Bresnan, Joan, and Sam A. Mchombo. 1995. The lexical integrity principle: evidence from Bantu. *Natural Language and Linguistic Theory* 13:181–254.

Bresnan, Joan, and Lioba Moshi. 1990. Object asymmetries in comparative Bantu syntax. *Linguistic Inquiry* 21(2):147–185. Reprinted in Sam A.

Mchombo (ed.) Theoretical Aspects of Bantu Grammar 1, 47–91. Stanford: CSLI Publications.

Bresnan, Joan, and Annie Zaenen. 1990. Deep Unaccusativity in LFG. In *Grammatical Relations. A Cross-Theoretical Perspective*, ed. Katarzyna Dziwirek, Patrick Farrell, and Errapel Mejías-Bikandi. 45–57. Stanford University: Center for the Study of Language and Information.

Butt, Miriam. 1993. *The Structure of Complex Predicates in Urdu*. Doctoral dissertation, Stanford University. Revised and corrected version published in the *Dissertations in Linguistics* series, CSLI Publications, Stanford, CA., 1995.

Butt, Miriam, Michio Isoda, and Peter Sells. 1990. Complex Predicates in LFG. MS, Stanford University.

Cho, Young-Mee Yu. 1985. An LFG analysis of the Korean reflexive caki. In *Harvard Studies on Korean Linguistics*, ed. Susumu Kuno et al. 3–13. Seoul: Hanshin.

Cho, Young-Mee Yu, and Peter Sells. 1995. A lexical account of inflectional suffixes in Korean. *Journal of East Asian Linguistics* 4(2):119–174.

Culy, Christopher D., Koungarma Kodio, and Patrice Togo. 1995. Dogon pronominal systems: their nature and evolution. *Studies in African Linguistics*. To appear.

Dahlstrom, Amy. 1986. *Plains Cree morphosyntax*. Doctoral dissertation, University of California, Berkeley.

Dalrymple, Mary, Angie Hinrichs, John Lamping, and Vijay Saraswat. 1993. The Resource Logic of Complex Predicate Interpretation. In *Proceedings of the 1993 Republic of China Computational Linguistics Conference (ROCLING)*. Hsitou National Park, Taiwan, September. Computational Linguistics Society of R.O.C.

Dalrymple, Mary, John Lamping, Fernando C. N. Pereira, and Vijay Saraswat. 1994. Quantifiers, Anaphora, and Intensionality. MS, Xerox PARC and AT&T Bell Laboratories.

Dalrymple, Mary, John Lamping, and Vijay Saraswat. 1993. LFG Semantics Via Constraints. In *Proceedings of the Sixth Meeting of the European ACL*. University of Utrecht, April. European Chapter of the Association for Computational Linguistics.

Demuth, Katherine, and Mark Johnson. 1989. Interactions between discourse functions and agreement in Setswana. *Journal of African Languages and Linguistics* 11:21–35.

Fassi-Fehri, Abdulkader. 1981. *Complémentation et Anaphore en Arabe Moderne: Une Approche Lexicale Fonctionelle*. Doctoral dissertation, Université de Paris III, Paris, France.

Fassi-Fehri, Abdulkader. 1988. Agreement in Arabic, Binding, and Coherence. In *Agreement in natural language: Approaches, theories, descriptions*, ed. Michael Barlow and Charles A. Ferguson. Stanford University: Center for the Study of Language and Information.

Frank, Anette. 1990. Eine LFG-analyse zur Kongruenz des Participe Passé – im Kontext von Auxiliarselektion, Reflexivierung, Subjektinversion und Clitic-Climbing in kohärenten Konstruktionen. Master's thesis, University of Stuttgart.

Gropen, Jess, Steven Pinker, Michelle Hollander, and Richard Goldberg. 1991. Affectedness and direct objects: The role of lexical semantics in the acquisition of verb argument structure. *Cognition* 41:153–195. Reprinted (1992) in B. Levin and S. Pinker (Eds.), *Lexical and conceptual semantics*. Cambridge, MA: Blackwell.

Güngördü, Zelal, and Kemal Oflazer. 1994. Parsing Turkish using the Lexical-Functional Grammar Formalism. In *Proceedings of the 15th International Conference on Computational Linguistics (COLING '94)*, 494–500. Kyoto.

Hanson, Kristen. 1987. Topic constructions in spoken French: some comparisons with Chicheŵa. In *Proceedings of BLS*, 105–116.

Her, One-Soon. 1990. *Grammatical Functions and Verb Subcategorization in Mandarin Chinese*. Doctoral dissertation, University of Hawaii. Also: Taipei: Crane Publishing Co., 1991.

Hong, Ki-Sun. 1991. *Argument selection and case marking in Korean*. Doctoral dissertation, Stanford University, Department of Linguistics.

Huang, Chu-Ren. 1990. A unification-based LFG analysis of lexical discontinuity. *Linguistics* 28:263–307.

Huang, Chu-Ren. 1991. Mandarin Chinese and the Lexical Mapping Theory – a study of the interaction of morphology and argument changing. *Bulletin of the Institute of History and Philology (BIHP)* 62(2):337–388.

Huang, Chu-Ren. 1992. Adjectival reduplication in Southern Min – a study of morpholexical rules with syntactic effects. In *Chinese Languages and Linguistics, Volume I, Chinese Dialects [Papers from the First International Symposium on Chinese Languages and Linguistics (ISCLL I)]*, 407–422. Taipei. Academia Sinica.

Huang, Chu-Ren. 1993. Reverse long-distance dependency and functional uncertainty: The interpretation of Mandarin questions. In *Language, Information, and Computing*, ed. Chungmin Lee and Boem-Mo Kang. 111–120. Seoul: Thaehaksa.

Iida, Masayo. 1987. Case-assignment by nominals in Japanese. In *Working Papers in Grammatical Theory and Discourse Structure, Vol. I: Interactions of Morphology, Syntax, and Discourse*, ed. Masayo Iida, Stephen Wechsler, and Draga Zec. 93–138. Stanford, CA: CSLI Publications. CSLI Lecture Notes, number 11.

Ishikawa, Akira. 1985. *Complex predicates and lexical operations in Japanese*. Doctoral dissertation, Stanford University.

Joshi, Smita. 1993. *Selection of Grammatical and Logical Functions in Marathi*. Doctoral dissertation, Stanford University, Department of Linguistics.

Kaplan, Ronald M. 1989. The Formal Architecture of Lexical-Functional Grammar. In *Proceedings of ROCLING II*, ed. Chu-Ren Huang and Keh-Jiann

Chen, 1–18.

Kaplan, Ronald M., and Joan Bresnan. 1982. Lexical-Functional Grammar: A Formal System for Grammatical Representation. In *The Mental Representation of Grammatical Relations*, ed. Joan Bresnan. 173–281. Cambridge, MA: The MIT Press.

Kaplan, Ronald M., and Jürgen Wedekind. 1993. Restriction and Correspondence-Based Translation. In *Proceedings of the Sixth Meeting of the European ACL*. University of Utrecht, April. European Chapter of the Association for Computational Linguistics.

King, Tracy H. 1993. *Configuring topic and focus in Russian*. Doctoral dissertation, Stanford University. Revised and corrected version published in the *Dissertations in Linguistics* series, CSLI Publications, Stanford, CA., 1995.

Kinn, Torodd. 1994. Prepositional phrases in Norwegian. Internal structure and external connections - an LFG analysis. Cand.philol. thesis, University of Bergen, Department of Linguistics and Phonetics. Skriftserie Nr. 45, serie B. ISBN 82-90381-54-9 ISSN 0800-6962.

Klaiman, Miriam H. 1987a. A lexical-functional analysis of Bengali inversive constructions. In *Pacific Linguistics Conference*.

Klaiman, Miriam H. 1987b. The Sanskrit passive in Lexical-Functional Grammar. In *Proceedings of CLS*.

Kroeger, Paul. 1991. *Phrase Structure and Grammatical Relations in Tagalog*. Doctoral dissertation, Stanford University. Revised and corrected version published in the *Dissertations in Linguistics* series, CSLI Publications, Stanford, CA., 1993.

Laczko, Tibor. 1994. *Predicates in the Hungarian Noun Phrase*. Doctoral dissertation, Hungarian Academy of Sciences. To appear as: A Lexical-Functional Approach to the Grammar of Hungarian Noun Phrases.

Levin, Lori S. 1986. *Operations on lexical forms: Unaccusative rules in Germanic languages*. Doctoral dissertation, MIT.

Lødrup, Helge. 1991. The Norwegian pseudopassive in lexical theory. In *Working Papers in Scandinavian Syntax, volume 47*. 118–129. Lund, Sweden: Department of Scandinavian Linguistics.

Lødrup, Helge. 1994. 'Surface proforms' in Norwegian and the definiteness effect. In *Proceedings of the North East Linguistic Society 24*, ed. M. Gonzalez, 303–315. Department of Linguistics, University of Massachusetts. North East Linguistic Society, GLSA.

Manning, Christopher D. 1992. Romance is So Complex. Technical Report CSLI-92-168. Stanford University: Center for the Study of Language and Information.

Manning, Christopher D. 1994. *Ergativity: Argument Structure and Grammatical Relations*. Doctoral dissertation, Stanford University.

Matsumoto, Yo. 1992. *On the wordhood of complex predicates in Japanese*. Doctoral dissertation, Stanford University, Department of Linguistics. To appear in the *Dissertations in Linguistics* series, CSLI Publications, Stanford, CA.

Mchombo, Sam A. (ed.). 1993. *Theoretical Aspects of Bantu Grammar*. Stanford, CA: CSLI Publications. CSLI Lecture Notes, number 38.

Mohanan, K. P. 1983. Functional and Anaphoric Control. *Linguistic Inquiry* 14(4):641–674.

Mohanan, Tara. 1990. *Arguments in Hindi*. Doctoral dissertation, Stanford University. Published in the *Dissertations in Linguistics* series, CSLI Publications, Stanford, CA., 1994.

Neidle, Carol. 1988. *The Role of Case in Russian Syntax*. Dordrecht: Kluwer Academic Publishers.

Niño, María-Eugenia. 1995. A Morphologically-Based Approach to Split Inflection in Finnish. MS, Stanford University.

Nordlinger, Rachel. 1995a. Split tense and imperative mood inflection in Wambaya. MS, Stanford University.

Nordlinger, Rachel. 1995b. Split tense and mood inflection in Wambaya. In *Proceedings of BLS*.

Pinker, Steven. 1989a. *Learnability and Cognition: The Acquisition of Argument Structure*. Cambridge, MA: The MIT Press.

Pinker, Steven. 1989b. Resolving a learnability paradox in the acquisition of the verb lexicon. In *The teachability of language*, ed. M. Rice and R. Schiefelbusch. Baltimore: Paul H. Brookes Publishing Co.

Rosén, Victoria. 1988. Norsk passiv: En LFG-analyse. *Norsk Lingvistisk Tidsskrift* 1/2:239–252.

Saiki, Mariko. 1986. A new look at Japanese relative clauses: A Lexical Functional Grammar approach. *Descriptive and Applied Linguistics* 19:219–230. Also in Bulletin of the ICU Summer Institute in Linguistics 19. International Christian University, Tokyo.

Saiki, Mariko. 1987. *On the Manifestations of Grammatical Functions in the Syntax of Japanese Nominals*. Doctoral dissertation, Stanford University, Department of Linguistics.

Schwarze, Christophe. 1988. The treatment of the French adjectif detache in Lexical Functional Grammar. In *Natural Language Parsing and Linguistic Theories*, ed. Uwe Reyle and Christian Rohrer. 262–288. Dordrecht: D. Reidel.

Sells, Peter. 1995. Korean and Japanese morphology from a lexical perspective. *Linguistic Inquiry* 26:277–325.

Sengupta, Probal. 1994. *On Lexical and Syntactic Processing of Bangla Language by Computer*. Doctoral dissertation, Indian Statistical Institute, Calcutta, India.

Simpson, Jane. 1991. *Warlpiri Morpho-Syntax: A Lexicalist Approach*. Dordrecht: Kluwer Academic Publishers.

Simpson, Jane, and Joan Bresnan. 1983. Control and Obviation in Warlpiri. *Natural Language and Linguistic Theory* 1(1):49–64.

Strand, Kjetil. 1992. Indeksering av nomenfraser i et textforstående system [Indexing of nominal phrases in a text understanding system]. Master's thesis, University of Oslo.

Tan, Fu. 1991. *Notion of subject in Chinese*. Doctoral dissertation, Stanford University, Department of Linguistics.

Uyechi, Linda. 1991. The functional structure of the Navajo third person alternation. In *Proceedings of CLS, Part One: The General Session*, ed. Lise M. Dobrin, Lynn Nichols, and Rosa M. Rodriguez, 434–446.

Wager, Janet. 1983. *Complementation in Moroccan Arabic*. Doctoral dissertation, MIT, Department of Linguistics and Philosophy.

Wedekind, Jürgen, and Ronald M. Kaplan. 1993. Type-driven Semantic Interpretation of F-Structures. In *Proceedings of the Sixth Meeting of the European ACL*. University of Utrecht, April. European Chapter of the Association for Computational Linguistics.

Zaenen, Annie. 1993. Unaccusativity in Dutch: An Integrated Approach. In *Semantics and the Lexicon*, ed. James Pustejovsky. Dordrecht: Kluwer Academic Publishers.

Zec, Draga. 1987. On Obligatory Control in Clausal Complements. In *Working Papers in Grammatical Theory and Discourse Structure*, ed. Masayo Iida, Stephen Wechsler, and Draga Zec. 139–168. CSLI Lecture Notes, No. 11. Stanford University: Center for the Study of Language and Information.

Part I

Formal Architecture

The formal architecture of Lexical-Functional Grammar developed in the late 1970s and was first described in detail by Kaplan and Bresnan (1982). The theory, which was motivated by psycholinguistic considerations, brought together several ideas that emerged from computational and linguistic investigations carried out in the early 1970s. As an introduction to the papers in this section, we provide a brief history of some formal notions that are most central to the LFG architecture. Some of these ideas have appeared in other modern syntactic theories and are now quite familiar, but their origin in the work leading up to LFG may not be so well known.

One set of concepts evolved from earlier work with the Augmented Transition Network (ATN) grammatical formalism (Woods 1970). Augmented transition networks had become a standard technology for constructing natural language analysis programs (e.g. Woods et al. 1972), and they had also served as a basis for the first computationally explicit models of human language performance (Kaplan 1972; Wanner and Maratsos 1978). In contrast to transformational grammar of the late 1960s, an ATN assigns only two levels of syntactic representation to a sentence, simulating the surface and deep phrase-structure trees without depending on the intermediate structures of a transformational derivation. The surface structure tree corresponds to a recursive sequence of transitions that traverses the string of words. Underlying information is accumulated during this traversal by arbitrary operations acting on the contents of a set of named 'registers', and this information is used at the end of the traversal to construct the deep structure tree. Kaplan, Wanner, and Maratsos argued that the ATN's surface-directed recovery of underlying relations could serve as a natural basis for competence-based models of psycholinguistic performance.

Kaplan observed that the ATN framework itself provided no particular motivation for encoding underlying grammatical relations in tree-shaped structures (Kaplan 1975a, 1975b). All the underlying information was already available in the hierarchy of register contents; tree construction was merely a complicated way of presenting that information in a form familiar to linguists. As a simpler and more convenient but theoretically sufficient alternative, Kaplan (1975a, 1975b) proposed reifying the hierarchy of register names and values and letting them serve directly as the underlying syntactic representation. These hierarchical attribute-value structures later became the functional structures of LFG and the feature structures of Functional Unification Grammar (Kay 1979) and other syntactic formalisms.

As the theoretical significance of the registers increased, the operations for setting and manipulating their contents required much closer examination. The register operations in the original ATN treated registers merely as temporary stores of useful information that could be modified at any moment, much like variables in ordinary programming languages. The ability to make arbitrary changes to register contents was a crucial aspect of some of the early ATN analyses (for example, of the English passive and dative alternations). But these analyses were later shown to miss certain linguistic generalizations, and the content-changing power made it difficult to give a restricted formal characterization of the system and made it difficult to implement certain processing strategies.

Taking these considerations into account, Kaplan (1976) suggested a strong limitation on the power of the register-setting operations: that they be allowed only to augment a given register with features that are consistent with information already stored there. This led to a new interpretation of the grammar's register-setting specifications: they could be viewed not as ordered sequences of operations to be performed but as sets of constraints on the values that the registers must have when an analysis is complete. Kaplan (1976) argued that well-formedness should be defined in terms of the satisfiability of descriptions, not in terms of the end-state of some sequence of computations. This idea shows up in LFG in the notions of functional description and the model-based interpretation of constraints. The restriction to only compatible feature assignments was also the basis of the unification operation in Kay's FUG and the theories that FUG influenced, although the value of model-based interpretation was more slowly recognized in the unification tradition.

Thus a number of important formal and computational advances had been made by the mid-1970s, but a coherent linguistic theory had not yet emerged. One problem was that the desirable limitations on register operations removed some of the power that had been essential to certain ATN analyses, and it was difficult to find alternative treatments using only the restricted machinery. The solution to this problem came from developments that had been taking place in the transformational tradition.

Bresnan and others had been studying a number of difficulties that had emerged in the transformational approach to certain linguistic phenomena (Bresnan 1976a, 1976b, 1977). She was also concerned that there was little or no connection between the formal aspects of transformational grammar and the observable properties of human language performance. Early experiments suggesting a direct link between competence and performance (e.g. Miller 1962) had been undermined both by theoretical revisions and by later experiments, and in the early 1970's the Derivational Theory of Complexity was largely abandoned (Fodor, Bever, and Garrett 1974). Bresnan felt that restricting the power of the transformational apparatus might resolve many outstanding linguistic issues while at the same time providing for a psychologically more realistic model of grammar (Bresnan 1977). As one step in this direction, she proposed using lexical redundancy rules to characterize certain kinds of systematic dependencies (such as the active/passive and dative alternations). That line of research came into contact with the ATN tradition in 1975 at an AT&T-sponsored workshop on language and cognitive processing organized at MIT by George Miller and Morris Halle. Bresnan and Kaplan each participated in that workshop, with Bresnan presenting her work on transformational grammar and lexical rules and Kaplan and Wanner presenting their work on ATN-based computational psycholinguistics.

Despite the different approaches they had been pursuing, it became apparent that Bresnan and Kaplan shared mutual goals. Bresnan's paper "A Realistic Transformational Grammar" outlined the first attempts at relating the two different traditions. This paper appeared in the volume *Linguistic theory and psychological reality*, which was an outgrowth of the workshop. From the computational side, Bresnan's work on lexical redundancy rules provided the missing ingredient for reestablishing the linguistic analyses that had been lost in the restriction of the ATN formalism. From the linguistic side, the ATN work showed that a coherent and psycholinguistically interesting formalism could be constructed even in the limit when all conventional transformations had been eliminated. From this initial encounter, Bresnan and Kaplan developed a sense of common interests and an enthusiasm for synthesizing the best features of the two different approaches.

In 1977, at the Fourth International Summer School in Computational Linguistics in Pisa, Bresnan and Kaplan continued their efforts to develop a mathematically precise theory that would provide for the statement of linguistically significant generalizations, support effective computational implementations, and serve in concrete models of human linguistic performance. This work came to fruition in 1978 at MIT, when Bresnan and Kaplan co-taught a course in computational psycholinguistics in which the theory of LFG was developed and presented in more or less its current form; it was in teaching this course that the real abstractions and generalizations emerged that still characterize the theory of LFG.

Over the course of the following year, Kaplan and Bresnan extended this work in a number of ways, producing as an overview paper the second paper in this section, "Lexical-Functional Grammar: A Formal System for Grammatical Representation". This paper appeared in the 1982 volume *The Mental Representation of Grammatical Relations*, edited by Bresnan; since the volume is now out of print, we have included this seminal paper in this collection. The 1982 volume included other papers, by Andrews, Bresnan, Grimshaw, Levin, Neidle, and Mohanan, that applied the newly defined formalism to a range of linguistic phenomena. Papers by Bresnan, Ford, Kaplan, and Pinker explored the theory's implications for the psycholinguistic processes of comprehension, production, and acquisition.

In the first paper in this section, "The Formal Architecture of Lexical-Functional Grammar", Kaplan reviews and states more explicitly the architectural principles that were first set forth in the 1982 paper. He also outlines how the formal architecture has evolved since the earlier publication. These developments are aimed at providing clean and intuitive treatments of a wide variety of linguistic phenomena.

References

Bresnan, Joan. 1976a. Evidence for a Theory of Unbounded Transformations. *Linguistic Analysis* 2:353–393.

Bresnan, Joan. 1976b. On the Form and Functioning of Transformations. *Linguistic Inquiry* 7(1):3–40.

Bresnan, Joan. 1977. Variables in the Theory of Transformations. In *Formal Syntax*, ed. Peter W. Culicover, Thomas Wasow, and Adrian Akmajian. 157–196. New York: Academic Press.

Bresnan, Joan. 1978. A realistic transformational grammar. In *Linguistic theory and psychological reality*, ed. Morris Halle, Joan Bresnan, and George A. Miller. Cambridge, MA: The MIT Press.

Bresnan, Joan (ed.). 1982. *The Mental Representation of Grammatical Relations*. Cambridge, MA: The MIT Press.

Fodor, Jerry A., Thomas G. Bever, and Merrill F. Garrett. 1975. *The Psychology of Language*. New York: McGraw-Hill.

Halle, Morris, Joan Bresnan, and George A. Miller (ed.). 1978. *Linguistic theory and psychological reality*. Cambridge, MA: The MIT Press.

Kaplan, Ronald M. 1972. Augmented transition networks as psychological models of sentence comprehension. *Artificial Intelligence* 3:77–100.

Kaplan, Ronald M. 1975a. On process models for sentence analysis. In *Explorations in cognition*, ed. Donald A. Norman and David E. Rumelhart. 117–135. San Francisco: W. H. Freeman.

Kaplan, Ronald M. 1975b. *Transient Processing Load in Relative Clauses*. Doctoral dissertation, Harvard University.

Kaplan, Ronald M. 1976. Models of comprehension based on augmented transition networks. Paper presented to the ATT-MIT Convocation on Communications, March 1976.

Kaplan, Ronald M., and Joan Bresnan. 1982. Lexical-Functional Grammar: A Formal System for Grammatical Representation. In *The Mental Representation of Grammatical Relations*, ed. Joan Bresnan. 173–281. Cambridge, MA: The MIT Press. Reprinted in Part I of this volume.

Kay, Martin. 1979. Functional Grammar. In *Proceedings of the Fifth Annual Meeting of the Berkeley Linguistic Society*, ed. Christine Chiarello, John Kingston, Eve E. Sweetser, James Collins, Haruko Kawasaki, John Manley-Buser, Dorothy W. Marschak, Catherine O'Connor, David Shaul, Marta Tobey, Henry Thompson, and Katherine Turner, 142–158. The University of California at Berkeley. Berkeley Linguistics Society.

Miller, George A. 1962. Some Psychological Studies of Grammar. *American Psychologist* 17:748–762.

Wanner, E., and M. Maratsos. 1978. An ATN Approach to Comprehension. In *Linguistic Theory and Psychological Reality*, ed. Morris Halle, Joan Bresnan, and George A. Miller. 119–161. Cambridge, MA: The MIT Press.

Woods, William A. 1970. Transition Network Grammars for Natural Language Analysis. *Communications of the ACM* 13(10):591–606.

Woods, William A., Ronald M. Kaplan, and Bonnie Nash-Webber. 1972. The Lunar Sciences Natural Language Information System: Final report. Technical Report 2378. Cambridge, MA: Bolt, Beranek, and Newman, Inc.

The Formal Architecture of Lexical-Functional Grammar

RONALD M. KAPLAN

Abstract. This paper describes the basic architectural concepts that underlie the formal theory of Lexical-Functional Grammar. The LFG formalism, which has evolved from previous computational, linguistic, and psycholinguistic research, provides a simple set of devices for describing the common properties of all human languages and the particular properties of individual languages. It postulates two levels of syntactic representation for a sentence, a constituent structure and a functional structure. These are related by a piecewise correspondence that permits the properties of the abstract functional structure to be defined in terms of configurations of constituent structure phrases. The basic architecture crucially separates the three notions of structure, structural description, and structural correspondence. This paper also outlines some recent extensions to the original LFG theory that enhance its ability to express certain kinds of linguistic generalizations while remaining compatible with the underlying architecture. These include formal variations in the elementary linguistic structures, in descriptive notation, and in the arrangement of correspondences.

1   Introduction

Since it was first introduced by Kaplan and Bresnan (1982), the formalism of Lexical-Functional Grammar has been applied in the description of a wide range of linguistic phenomena. The basic features of the formalism

Earlier versions of this paper appeared in *Proceedings of ROCLING II*, ed. C.-R. Huang and K.-J. Chen (Taipei, Republic of China, 1989), 1–18, and *Journal of Information Science and Engineering*, vol. 5, 1989, 305–322.

are quite simple: the theory assigns two levels of syntactic representation to a sentence, the constituent structure and functional structure. The c-structure is a phrase-structure tree that serves as the basis for phonological interpretation while the f-structure is a hierarchical attribute-value matrix that represents underlying grammatical relations. The c-structure is assigned by the rules of a context-free phrase structure grammar. Functional annotations on those rules are instantiated to provide a formal description of the f-structure, and the smallest structure satisfying those constraints is the grammatically appropriate f-structure.

This formal conception evolved in the mid-1970's from earlier work in computational and theoretical linguistics. Woods' (1970) Augmented Transition Networks demonstrated that a direct mapping between superficial and underlying structures was sufficient to encode the discrepancy between the external form of utterances and their internal predicate-argument relations. ATN grammars followed transformational grammar in using the same kind of mathematical structure, phrase-structure trees, as both surface and deep grammatical representations. Kaplan (1975) noticed that the strong transformational motivation for this commonality of representation did not exist in the ATN framework. Inputs and outputs of transformations had to be of the same formal type if rules were to feed each other in a derivational sequence, but a nonderivational approach imposed no such requirement. Thus, while hierarchical and ordered tree structures are suitable for representing the sequences of surface words and phrases, they are not particularly convenient for expressing more abstract relations among grammatical functions and features. Although the fact that *John* is the subject in *John saw Mary* can be formally represented in a tree in which *John* is the NP directly under the S node, there is no explanatory advantage in using such an indirect way of encoding this simple intuition. Kaplan (1975) proposed hierarchical attribute-value matrices, now familiar as f-structures, as a more natural way of representing underlying grammatical relations.

The ATN register setting operations enabled explicit reference to labels like Subject and Object. They were originally used to manipulate the temporary information that accumulated during the course of analyzing a sentence and which was reorganized at the end to form a traditional transformational deep structure. Kaplan (1975) saw no need for that reorganization, since the accumulated registers already contained all the significant grammatical information. But this change in register status from merely being a repository of necessary bookkeeping information to being the major target of linguistic analysis had far-reaching consequences. The exact nature of the register setting and accessing operations became issues of major theoretical importance, and theoretical commitments were also required for the particular configurations of register contents that the grammar associated with individual sentences. The LFG formalism emerged from a careful study of questions of this sort. The accumulated register information was formalized as monadic functions defined on the set of grammatical relation and feature names (SUBJ, OBJ, CASE), and the ATN computational operations for manipulating these functions evolved into the equational specifications in LFG's functional descriptions.

This formal machinery has served as backdrop for and has been refined by substantive investigations into the common properties of all human languages and the particular properties of individual languages. Early investigations established, for example, the universal character of grammatical functions like subject and object, general principles of control and agreement, and basic mechanisms for expressing and integrating lexical and syntactic information (see Bresnan 1982a,c; Bresnan and Kaplan 1982; Kaplan and Bresnan 1982; and other papers in Bresnan 1982b). These studies and more recent results have offered strong support for the general organization of the theory, but they have also uncovered problems that are difficult to handle in the theory as originally formulated. Thus, a number of extensions and revisions to LFG are currently under consideration, dealing with long-distance dependencies, coordination, word-order, and semantic and pragmatic interpretation. Some of these proposals may seem at first sight like radical departures from the details of traditional LFG. But the LFG formalism as presented by Kaplan and Bresnan (1982) was an expression of a general underlying architectural conception, and most recent proposals remain quite compatible with that basic perspective.

That underlying architecture is the focus of the present paper. In the first section I review and explicate the fundamental notions that guided the development of the LFG formalism. These ideas provide a general view of the way in which different properties of an utterance can be represented and interrelated, and how constraints on those representations can be expressed. The second section surveys some of the recently proposed extensions to LFG, suggesting that they can be regarded as variations on the basic architectural theme.

2 Fundamental notions: Structures, descriptions, and correspondences

LFG posits two levels of syntactic representation for a sentence, and, as indicated above, these are of different formal types. This is a fundamental architectural presupposition of LFG and is the main point of departure for understanding the theory's formal organization. These different representations reflect the fact that there are different kinds of informational dependencies among the parts of a sentence, and that these are best expressed using different formal structures. The goal is to account for significant linguistic generalizations in a factored and modular way by means of related but appropriately dissimilar representations.

Elementary structures. We start with the simplest mathematical notion of a structure as a set of elements with some defined relations and properties. The strings that make up a sentence such as (1) are a trivial example: the elements of the set are the words and immediate precedence is the only native relation. The looser nonimmediate precedence relation is specified indirectly, as the transitive closure of immediate precedence.

(1)   I saw the girl.

The phrase structure tree representing surface constituency configurations (2) is a slightly more complex example. The elements of this structure are nodes which are labeled by parts of speech and abstract phrasal categories and satisfy native relations of precedence (a partial order in this case) and immediate domination.

(2)

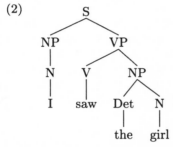

To put it in more explicit terms, a tree consists of a set of nodes N related by a labeling function λ that takes nodes into some other finite labeling set L, a mother function M that takes nodes into nodes, and a partial ordering $<$:

(3)   N: set of nodes, L: set of category labels
      M: N $\rightarrow$ N
      $< \subseteq$ N$\times$ N
      λ: N $\rightarrow$ L

LFG admits only nontangled trees: for any nodes n_1 and n_2, if $M(n_1) < M(n_2)$, then $n_1 < n_2$.

Our third example is the functional structure illustrated in (4), which explicitly represents the primitive grammatical relations of subject, predicate, and object, as well as various kinds of agreement features.

(4)

$$
\begin{bmatrix}
\text{SUBJ} & \begin{bmatrix} \text{PRED} & \text{`pro'} \\ \text{PERS} & 1 \\ \text{NUM} & \text{SG} \end{bmatrix} \\
\text{TENSE} & \text{PAST} \\
\text{PRED} & \text{`see}\langle(\uparrow \text{ SUBJ}), (\uparrow \text{ OBJ})\rangle\text{'} \\
\text{OBJ} & \begin{bmatrix} \text{PRED} & \text{`girl'} \\ \text{DEF} & + \\ \text{PERS} & 3 \\ \text{NUM} & \text{SG} \end{bmatrix}
\end{bmatrix}
$$

F-structures are defined recursively: they are hierarchical finite functions mapping from elements in a set of symbols to values which can be symbols, subsidiary f-structures, or semantic forms such as 'see<SUBJ, OBJ>'. The set of f-structures F is characterized by the following recursive domain equation:

(5) A: set of atomic symbols, S: set of semantic forms
$$F = (A \rightarrow_f F \cup A \cup S)$$

In effect, the only defining relation for f-structures is the argument-value relation of function application.

Descriptions of structures. Given a collection of well-defined structure-types whose defining relations can represent various kinds of linguistic dependencies, the problem of grammatical analysis is to ensure that all and only the appropriate structures are assigned to the sentences of the language. Structures can be assigned by *constructive* or *procedural* methods, by a set of operations that either analyze the properties of a string and build appropriate abstract representations that are consistent with these properties (as in the ATN approach) or that synthesize an abstract structure and systematically convert it to less abstract structures until the string is reached (the canonical interpretation of a transformational derivation). Alternatively, structures can be assigned by *descriptive, declarative,* or *model-based* methods. In this case, the properties of one structure (say, the string) are used to generate formal descriptions of other representations, in the form of a collection of constraints on the defining relations that those structures must possess. There are no operations for building more abstract or more concrete representations—any structures that satisfy all the propositions in the description are acceptable. These are the description's models.

The descriptive, model-based approach is, of course, the hallmark of LFG. This is motivated by the fact that particular properties of other representations are not neatly packaged within particular words or phrases. Rather, each word or phrase provides only some of the information that goes into defining an appropriate abstract representation. That information interacts with features of other words to uniquely identify what the abstract properties must be. The constraints on grammatical representations are distributed in partial and piecemeal form throughout a sentence—this is a second architectural presupposition of LFG theory. The descriptive method accommodates most naturally to this modular situation, since partial information can be assembled by a simple conjunction of constraints that can be verified by straightforward satisfiability tests.

We implement the descriptive approach in the most obvious way: a description of a structure can consist simply of a listing of its defining properties and relations. Taking a more formal example, we can write down a description of a tree such as (6) by introducing names (n_1, n_2 etc.) to stand for the various nodes and listing the propositions that those nodes satisfy. For this tree, the mother of n_2 is n_1, the label of n_1 is A, and so forth. A complete description of this tree is provided by the set of equations formulated in (7):

(6)

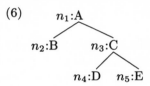

(7) $\begin{aligned} &M(n_2) = n_1 && M(n_4) = n_3 \\ &\lambda(n_1) = A && M(n_5) = n_3 \\ &\lambda(n_2) = B && \lambda(n_4) = D \\ &M(n_3) = n_1 && \lambda(n_5) = E \\ &\lambda(n_3) = C && n_4 < n_5 \\ &n_2 < n_3 \end{aligned}$

This description is presented in terms of the tree-defining properties and relations given in (3).

We can also write down a set of propositions that a given f-structure satisfies. For the f-structure in (8), where the names f_i are marked on the opening brackets, we note that f_1 applied to q is the value f_2, f_2 applied to s is t, and so forth.

(8) $f_1:\begin{bmatrix} q & f_2:\begin{bmatrix} s & t \\ u & v \end{bmatrix} \\ w & x \end{bmatrix}$

Using LFG's parenthetic notation for function application as defined in (9), the constraints in (10) give the properties of this f-structure.

(9) (f a) = v iff <a v> ∈ f, where f is an f-structure and a is an atomic symbol

(10) $(f_1 \text{ q}) = f_2$
     $(f_2 \text{ s}) = \text{t}$
     $(f_2 \text{ u}) = \text{v}$
     $(f_1 \text{ w}) = \text{x}$

Structures can thus be easily described by listing their properties and relations. Conversely, given a consistent description, the structures that satisfy it may be discovered—but not always. For the simple functional domain of f-structures, descriptions that involve only equality and function application can be solved by an attribute-value merging or unification operator, or other techniques that apply to the quantifier-free theory of equality (e.g. Kaplan and Bresnan 1982). But allowing more expressive predicates into the description language may lead to descriptions whose satisfiability cannot be determined. For example, I discuss below the proposal of Kaplan and Zaenen (1989b) to allow specifications of regular languages to appear in the attribute position of an LFG function-application expression. Their notion of *functional uncertainty* permits a better account of long-distance dependencies and other phenomena than the constituent-control theory of Kaplan and Bresnan (1982) provided. Kaplan and Maxwell (1988a) have shown that the satisfiability of uncertainty descriptions over the domain of acyclic f-structures is decidable, but the problem may be undecidable for certain types of cyclic f-structures (e.g. those that also satisfy constraints such as $(f \text{ x})=f$). This example indicates the need for caution when adding richer predicates to a descriptive formalism; so far, however, theoretically interesting description-language extensions have been well-behaved when applied in linguistically reasonable structural domains.

A set of propositions in a given structural description is usually satisfied by many structures. The description (7) is satisfied by the tree (6) but it is also satisfied by an infinite number of larger trees (e.g. (11)). It is true of this tree that the mother of n_2 is n_1 and, indeed, all the equations in (7) are true of it. But this tree has nodes beyond the ones described in (7) and it satisfies additional propositions that the tree in (6) does not satisfy.

(11)

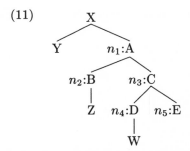

In general, structures that satisfy descriptions form a semi-lattice that is partially ordered by the amount of information they contain. The minimal structure satisfying the description may be unique if the description itself is determinate, if there are enough conditions specified and not too many unknowns. The notion of minimality figures in a number of different ways within the LFG theory, to capture some intuitions of default, restriction, and completeness.

LFG clearly distinguishes the mathematical structures that comprise linguistic representations from the propositions in a description language that characterize those structures, that those structures serve as models for. This is an important difference between LFG and other so-called "unification-based" theories of grammar, such as Kay's (1979, 1984) Functional Unification Grammar. If the only descriptions are simple conjunctions of defining properties and relations, then there is an isomorphic mapping between the descriptions and the objects being described. Further, combining two descriptions by a unification operation yields a resulting description that characterizes all objects satisfying both those descriptions. Thus, in simple situations the distinction between descriptions and objects can safely be ignored, as Kay proposed. But the conflation of these two notions leads to conceptual confusions when natural extensions to the description language do not correspond to primitive properties of domain objects. For example, there is no single primitive object that naturally represents the negation or disjunction of some collection of properties, yet it is natural to form descriptions of objects by means of such arbitrary Boolean combinations of defining propositions. Kay's FUG represents disjunctive constraints as sets of descriptions: a set of descriptions is satisfied if any of its member descriptions is satisfied. This contrasts with the equally plausible interpretation that a set of descriptions is satisfied by a collection of more basic structures, one satisfying each of the elements of the description set. The Kasper and Rounds (1986) logic for feature structures clarified this issue by effectively resurrecting for FUG the basic distinction between objects and their descriptions.

As another example of the importance of this distinction, no single object can represent the properties of long-distance dependencies that Kaplan and Zaenen (1989b) encode in specifications of functional uncertainty. As discussed below, they extend the description language to include constraints such as:

$$(f \text{ COMP}^*\{\text{SUBJ} \mid \text{OBJ}\}) = (f \text{ TOPIC})$$

The regular expression in this equation denotes an infinite set of alternative strings, and such a set does not exist in the domain of basic structures. The Kaplan/Zaenen approach to long-distance dependencies is thus incompatible with a strict structure/description isomorphism.

Structural correspondences. We have seen that structures of different types can be characterized in different kinds of description languages. It remains to correlate those structures that are properly associated with a particular sentence. Clearly, the words of the sentence and their grouping and ordering relationships carry information about (or supply constraints on) the linguistic dependencies that more abstract structures represent. In the LFG approach, this is accomplished by postulating the existence of other very simple formal devices, correspondence functions that map between the elements of one (usually more concrete) structure and those of another; the existence of structural correspondences is the third architectural presupposition of LFG. The diagram in (12) illustrates such an element-wise correspondence, a function ϕ that goes from the nodes of a tree into units of f-structure space.

(12)

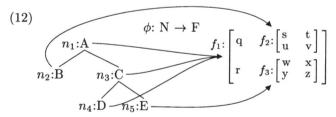

This function maps nodes n_1, n_3, and n_4 into the outer f-structure f_1, and nodes n_2 and n_5 to the subsidiary f-structures f_2 and f_3, respectively. A correspondence by itself only establishes a connection between the pieces of its domain and range structures, unlike a more conventional interpretation function that might also at the same time derive the desired formal properties of the range. But nothing more than these simple correspondence connections is needed to develop a description of those formal properties. Previously we described an f-structure by specifying only f-structure properties and elements, independent of any associated c-structure. The structural correspondence now permits descriptions of range f-structures to be formulated in terms of the elements and native relations of the tree. In other words, the element-wise structural correspondence allows the mother-daughter relationships in the tree to constrain the function-application properties in the f-structure, even though those formal properties are otherwise completely unrelated.

The f-structure in (12), for example, satisfies the condition that $(f_1\text{ q}){=}f_2$, a constraint in the f-structure description language. But f_1 and f_2 are the f-structures corresponding to n_1 and n_2, respectively, so this condition can be expressed by the equivalent $(\phi(n_1)\text{ q}) = \phi(n_2)$. Finally, noting that n_1 is the mother of n_2, we obtain the equation $(\phi(\text{M}(n_2))\text{ q}){=}\phi(n_2)$, which establishes a dependency between a node configuration in part of the tree and value of the q attribute in the corresponding f-structure. Systematically replacing the f_i identifiers in the usual description of the f-structure by the equivalent $\phi(n_i)$ expressions and making use of the mother-daughter tree relations leads to an alternative characterization of (12):

(13)
$$
\begin{array}{ll}
(\phi(\text{M}(n_2))\text{ q}) = \phi(n_2) & \text{M}(n_2) = n_1 \\
(\phi(n_2)\text{ s}) = \text{t} & (\phi(n_2)\text{ u}) = \text{v} \\
(\phi(n_5)\text{ w}) = \text{x} & (\phi(n_5)\text{ y}) = \text{z} \\
\phi(\text{M}(n_3)) = \phi(n_3) & \text{M}(n_3) = n_1 \\
\phi(\text{M}(n_4)) = \phi(n_4) & \text{M}(n_4) = n_3 \\
(\phi(\text{M}(n_5))\text{ r}) = \phi(n_5) & \text{M}(n_5) = n_3
\end{array}
$$

Thus, our notions of structural description and structural correspondence combine in this way so that the description of a range structure can involve not only its own native relations but also the properties of a corresponding domain structure.

We require a structural correspondence to be a function but it is not required to be one-to-one. As illustrated in (12), the correspondence ϕ maps the nodes n_1, n_3, and n_4 all onto the same f-structure f_1. When several nodes map onto the same f-structure, that f-structure can be loosely interpreted as the equivalence class or quotient of nodes induced by the correspondence. Conceptually, it represents the folding together or normalization of information carried jointly by the individual nodes that map onto it. Many-to-one configurations appear in many linguistic analyses. Lexical heads and their dominating phrasal categories, for example, usually map to the same f-structure, encoding the intuition that a phrase receives most of its functional properties from its head. Discontinuous constituents, functional units whose properties are carried by words in noncontiguous parts of the string, can be characterized in this way, as demonstrated by the Bresnan et al. (1982) analysis of Dutch cross-serial dependencies.

A structural correspondence also need not be onto. This is illustrated by (14), which shows the c-structure and f-structure that might be appropriate for a sentence containing a gerund with a missing subject.

(14)

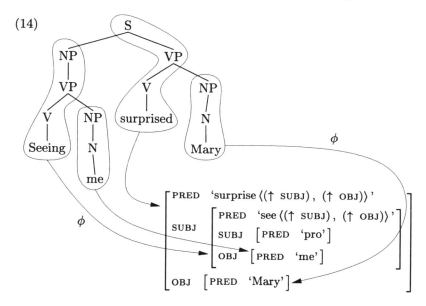

Phrasally-based theories typically postulate an empty node on the tree side in order to represent the fact that there is a dummy understood subject, because subjects (and predicate-argument relations) are represented in those theories by particular node configurations. In LFG, given that the notion of subject is defined in the range of the correspondence, we need not postulate empty nodes in the tree. Instead, the f-structure's description, derived from the tree relations of the gerund c-structure, can have an equation that specifies directly that the subject's predicate is an anaphoric pronoun, with no node in the tree that it corresponds to. This account of so-called null anaphors has interesting linguistic and mathematical properties, discussed below and in Kaplan and Zaenen (1989a).

In sum, the LFG formalism presented by Kaplan and Bresnan (1982) is based on the architectural notions of structure, structural description, and structural correspondence. Within this framework, particular notational conventions were chosen to suppress unnecessary detail and make it more convenient to express certain common patterns of description. Thus, the allowable c-structures for a sentence were specified by the rewriting rules of a context-free grammar (augmented by a Kleene-closure operator for repetitive expansions) rather than by what seemed to be a less perspicuous listing of dominance, precedence, and labeling relations. The description of an appropriate f-structure was derived from functional annotations attached to the c-structure rules. For interpreting these functional annotations, Kaplan and Bresnan defined a special instantiation procedure that relied implicitly on the c-structure to f-structure correspondence ϕ. To see that dependence more explicitly, consider the annotated rewriting rule in (15):

(15) S $\longrightarrow$ NP   VP

$\qquad\qquad\qquad (\phi(\mathrm{M}(n))\ \textsc{subj}) = \phi(n) \qquad \phi(\mathrm{M}(n)) = \phi(n)$

The context-free expansion is matched against nodes in a candidate c-structure to verify that the local [$_{\mathrm{S}}$ NP VP] configuration is acceptable. The symbol n in a constraint annotated to a category stands for the node that matches that particular category in the candidate tree. The annotations use that symbol, the mother function M, and the structural correspondence ϕ to express general propositions about the f-structures that correspond to the nodes that satisfy this rule. Thus, (15) specifies that the f-structure corresponding to the NP's mother applies to SUBJ to give the f-structure corresponding to the NP, and that the f-structure corresponding to the mother of the VP, namely the S node, is also the f-structure corresponding to the VP. The conjunction of these constraints across the whole c-structure, with actual nodes substituted for the generic n, is the desired f-structure description. Kaplan and Bresnan simplified to a more convenient notation. The symbol $\uparrow$ abbreviates the complex term $\phi(\mathrm{M}(n))$, the composition of the structural correspondence with the mother function, and $\downarrow$ stands for $\phi(n)$, the f-structure corresponding to the matching node. This reduces the annotation on the NP to the familiar form in (16):

(16) $(\uparrow \textsc{subj}) = \downarrow$

This can be read as 'the matching NP node's mother's f-structure's subject is the matching node's f-structure'. This method of generating range descriptions by analyzing and matching the properties of domain structures is what we call *description by analysis*. Halvorsen (1983) applied this technique to derive descriptions of semantic structures from an analysis of the f-structures they were assumed to correspond to.

LFG's store of basic underlying concepts is thus quite limited, yet it supports a notational system in which a variety of complex linguistic phenomena have been easy to characterize. Perhaps because of its simple architectural base, this system has remained remarkably stable in the years since it was introduced, particularly when compared to other formal frameworks that have undergone extensive revision over the same period of time. In continuing to explore the implications of this architecture, we have found some useful consequences that had previously gone unnoticed and have also seen the value of certain extensions and revisions. The remainder of this paper gives a brief survey of these more recent developments.

3   Extensions and variations

The tripartite division of structures, descriptions, and correspondences suggests three ways in which the theory might be modified. One way, of course, is to add to the catalog of structure-types that are used for linguistic representations. LFG currently acknowledges two syntactic structure-types beyond the string, and there may be grammatical phenomena that are best represented in terms of other native relations. Kaplan and Bresnan (1982) introduced one extension to the f-structure domain beyond the simple attribute-value properties that have been discussed here. They allowed the values of f-structure attributes to be sets of f-structures as well as individual f-structures, symbols, and semantic forms. Sets were used to represent grammatical relations such as adjuncts that can be independently realized in several positions in a clause and thus seemed to be immune to the functional uniqueness condition. The description language also was augmented with the membership operator $\in$, so that constraints on set elements could be stated.

A more recent example of how the properties of formal structures might usefully be extended can be seen in Bresnan and Kanerva's (1989) proposals for a natural-class organization of grammatical functions. They observe that many lexical redundancy rules can be eliminated in favor of general instantiation principles if lexical entries are marked with underspecified grammatical function labels (for example, a neutral objective function that subsumes (and can be instantiated as either) OBJ or OBJ2). In previous work, function labels were unanalyzable atomic symbols bearing no relation to one another. On this new suggestion, the functions are partially ordered in a subsumption lattice, and new principles of interpretation are required.

Beyond these relatively minor adjustments to the structural domain, there have been no proposals for substantially different ways of organizing linguistic information. By far the most interesting innovations have concerned the c-structure and f-structure description languages and the variety of attribute-value structures that can be related by structural correspondences.

Extending the description language. C-structures were described originally by context-free rewriting rules whose right-hand sides could contain the Kleene-closure operator and thus could denote arbitrary regular languages. The regular sets are closed not only under union and (Kleene) concatenation but also under intersection and complementation. Thus, the generative capacity of the c-structure component is unchanged if intersection and complementation are allowed as operators in c-structure rules. These operators permit many new ways of factoring c-structure generalizations, including but not limited to the ID/LP format that Pullum (1982) proposed for GPSG. Immediate dominance and linear precedence constraints can both be transformed into regular predicates using concatenation and complementation, and the combined effect of these constraints in a given rule can be obtained simply by intersecting that regular-set collection. For example, the unordered ID rule

(17)   S → [NP, VP]

can be translated to the equivalent but less revealing form

(18)   S → [VP* NP VP*] ∩ [NP* VP NP*]

This intersection will admit an S node if its string of daughter nodes satisfies two conditions: it must contain one NP with some unknown number of VP's around it, and it must also contain one VP surrounded by some unknown number of NP's. The only strings that simultaneously satisfy both conditions are those that contain exactly one NP and one VP appearing in either order, and this is precisely the requirement intended by the ID rule (17). As detailed by Kaplan and Zaenen (1989a), this translation goes through even with repetition factors attached to the categories and does not require a complex multi-set construction for its mathematical interpretation as Gazdar et al. (1985) proposed. Similarly, linear-precedence restrictions can also be translated to simple, intersectable regular predicates. The condition that NP's must come before VP's, for example, is satisfied by strings in the regular set

$$\overline{\Sigma^* \text{ VP } \Sigma^* \text{ NP } \Sigma^*}$$

where Σ denotes the set of all categories and the over-bar indicates complementation with respect to Σ^*.

Thus, compact notation for immediate domination and linear precedence, as well as for other regular predicates described by Kaplan and Maxwell (1993), can be freely introduced without changing the power of the context-free system. Some caution is required, however, for regular predicates defined over categories annotated with functional schemata.

Although the system of combined c-structure/f-structure constraints is closed under intersection (since the f-structure description language is closed under conjunction), it is not known whether it is closed under complementation of arbitrary regular expressions. The complement of a single annotated category can be translated to standard notation, however, by applying de Morgan's laws and using negated f-structure constraints. This more limited form of complementation is sufficient for the ID/LP specifications and for a number of other useful predicates.

Extensions to the c-structure description language provide one way of characterizing the kinds of ordering variations that appear across languages. The LFG architecture naturally provides for another way of expressing ordering dependencies, by defining an order-like relation (called f-precedence) on f-structures and including a precedence operator in the f-structure description language. The formal and empirical properties of f-precedence relation are explored at some length by Kaplan and Zaenen (1989a); here we give only a brief summary of their discussion. We first note that precedence is not a native relation on f-structure: f-structures are not distinguished by the order in which attributes and values appear. However, the native precedence relation in the c-structure (c-precedence to distinguish it from f-precedence) naturally induces a relation on f-structure by virtue of the c-structure to f-structure correspondence ϕ. For two f-structures f_1 and f_2 we say that f_1 f-precedes f_2 if and only if all nodes that ϕ maps into f_1 c-precede all nodes that ϕ maps into f_2. This can be formalized in terms of the inverse mapping ϕ^{-1}:

(19) $f_1 <_f f_2$ iff
        for all $n_1 \in \phi^{-1}(f_1)$ and for all $n_2 \in \phi^{-1}(f_2)$,
        $n_1 <_c n_2$

This relation has some peculiar and unexpected properties because of the fact that ϕ may be neither one-to-one nor onto. A null anaphor is not the image of any node, and therefore it vacuously both f-precedes and is f-preceded by every other element in the f-structure. Mathematically, this implies that f-precedence is neither transitive nor anti-symmetric—it is not really an ordering relation at all. But these characteristics appear to be just what is needed to given a systematic account of certain constraints on anaphoric relations (Bresnan 1984; Kameyama 1988; Kaplan and Zaenen 1989a). Kaplan and Zaenen also point out one other interesting property of f-precedence: it can be used to impose ordering restrictions on nodes that are not sisters in the c-structure tree and may in fact be quite removed from each other. This can happen when the correspondence ϕ maps these nodes to locally related units of f-structure.

Functional precedence illustrates the interplay of description and correspondence mechanisms in expressing interesting linguistic constraints. Native relations in a domain structure map into induced relations on the range; these relations are typically degraded in some way, for the same reason that the range structures are degraded images of the domain structures they correspond to. The structural correspondence collapses some distinctions and in some cases introduces new ones, as it picks out and represents a subset of the domain's information dependencies. The definition of functional precedence given in (19) is an example of what we call *description through inversion*.

Functional uncertainty is another example of new expressive power obtained by extending the description language without changing the collection of underlying formal objects. The original LFG theory provided a mechanism of *constituent control* to characterize the constraints on long-distance dependencies (Kaplan and Bresnan 1982). Constituent control was essentially a translation into LFG terms of traditional phrasal approaches to long-distance dependencies, and carried forward the claim that the various constraints on those constructions were best formulated in terms of phrase and category configurations. Kaplan and Bresnan (1982) had briefly considered a functional approach to these phenomena, but rejected it since it seemed to require grammatical specifications of infinite size. Kaplan and Zaenen (1989b) proposed functional uncertainty as a new descriptive technique for avoiding the problem of infinite specification, reexamined the constituent control account of island constraints in light of this new technique, and concluded that functional restrictions offered a clearer and more accurate characterization of long-distance dependencies and island constraints. Kaplan and Zaenen simply extended the LFG notation for expressing function application so that the attribute position could be realized as a regular set. Thus, in addition to ordinary equations such as $(\uparrow \text{SUBJ})=\downarrow$, it is possible to write in the grammar equations such as $(\uparrow \text{COMP}^* \ \text{SUBJ}|\text{OBJ})=\downarrow$. This equation expresses the uncertainty about what the within-clause functional role of an extraposed topic might be: it might be identified as either the subject or object of a clause embedded inside any number of complements. According to Kaplan and Zaenen, this constraint is satisfied by an f-structure if there is some string in the regular language COMP* SUBJ|OBJ such that the equation resulting from substituting that string for the regular expression is satisfied by that f-structure. In effect, the uncertainty expression provides a finite specification for what would otherwise be an infinite disjunction. Under this proposal, the constraints on when a long-distance dependency is permitted are embodied in restrictions on the regular expressions that appear in uncertainty equations, and are quite independent of categorial config-

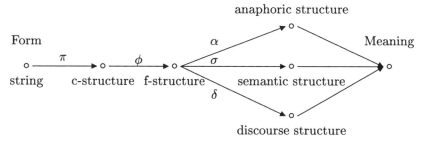

FIGURE 1 Decomposition of Γ

urations. Kaplan and Zaenen give a number of arguments in support of this functional approach, pointing out, for example, that subcategorized functions but not adjuncts can be extracted in Icelandic, even though these appear in identical phrase-structure positions.

Extending the configuration of correspondences. The LFG architecture was developed with only two syntactic structures set in correspondence, but the correspondence idea provides a general way of correlating many different kinds of linguistic information through modular specifications. Representations of anaphoric dependencies, discourse functions, and semantic predicate-argument and quantifier relations can all be connected in mutually constraining ways by establishing an appropriate set of structures and correspondences. One hypothetical configuration for mapping between the external form of an utterance and internal representations of its meaning (e.g., the claims that it makes about the world, speaker, discourse, etc.) is shown in Figure 1. Starting out with the word string, we assume a structural correspondence π that maps to the phrases of the constituent structure, which is then mapped by ϕ to the functional structure in the usual LFG way. We might postulate a further correspondence σ from f-structure to units of a semantic structure that explicitly marks predicate-argument relationships, quantifier scope ambiguities, and so forth—dependencies and properties that do not enter into syntactic generalizations but are important in characterizing the utterance's meaning. We might also include another correspondence α defined on f-structures that maps them onto anaphoric structures: two f-structure units map onto the same element of anaphoric structure just in case they are coreferential. The figure also shows a mapping δ from f-structure to a level of discourse structure to give a separate formal account of discourse notions such as topic and focus. The anaphoric and discourse structures, like the semantic structure, also contribute to meaning representations. By fitting these other systems of linguistic information into the same conceptual framework of description and correspondence, we can make use of already existing mathematical and computational techniques.

We note, however, that this arrangement suggests a new technique for generating abstract structure descriptions. In this diagram, the f-structure is both the range of ϕ and the domain of σ (and also α and δ). Thus the composition of σ and ϕ is implicitly a function that maps from the c-structure directly to the semantic structure, and this can also be regarded as a structural correspondence. This enables somewhat surprising descriptive possibilities. Since σ only maps between f-structure and semantic structure, it might seem that the semantic structure may only contain information that is derivable from attributes and values present in the f-structure. This would be expected if the correspondence σ were an interpretation function operating on the f-structure to produce the semantic structure. The semantic structure, for example, could not reflect category and precedence properties in the c-structure that do not have correlated features in the f-structure. But σ, as an element-wise correspondence, does not interpret the f-structure at all. It is merely a device for encoding descriptions of the semantic structure in terms of f-structure relations. And since the f-structure is described in terms of ϕ and c-structure properties, the composition $\sigma(\phi(n))$ can be used to assert properties of semantic structure also in terms of c-structure relations, even though there is no direct correspondence. Descriptions generated by the context-free grammar can use designators such as $\sigma \uparrow [=\sigma(\phi(M(n)))]$ along with $\uparrow$ to characterize f-structure and semantic structure simultaneously.

In general, a compositional arrangement of correspondences permits the *codescription* of separate levels of representation, yet another descriptive technique that has been applied to a number of problems. Halvorsen and Kaplan (1988) explore various uses of codescription in defining the syntax/semantics interface. Kaplan and Maxwell (1988b) exploit a codescription configuration in their account of constituent coordination in LFG. To deal with coordinate reduction, they interpreted function application on f-structure set-values as picking out a value from the mathematical generalization of the set elements. This properly distributes grammatical functions and predicates over the reduced clauses, but there is no place in the resulting f-structure to preserve the identity of the conjunction (*and* or *or*) which is required in the semantic structure to properly characterize the meaning. A codescriptive equation establishes the proper conjunction in the semantic structure even though there is no trace of it in the f-structure. As a final application, Kaplan et al. (1989) suggest using codescription as a means for relating source and target functional and semantic structures in a machine translation system.

4 Conclusion

The formal architecture of Lexical-Functional Grammar provides the theory with a simple conceptual foundation. These underlying principles have become better understood as the theory has been applied to a wide range of grammatical phenomena, but the principles themselves have remained essentially unchanged since their inception. The recent work surveyed in this paper has identified and explored a number of variations that this architecture allows, in an effort to find more natural and formally coherent ways of discovering and expressing linguistic generalizations. Promising new descriptive devices are being introduced and new correspondence configurations are being investigated. The success of these mechanisms in easily extending to new areas of grammatical representation indicates, perhaps, that this architecture mirrors and formalizes some fundamental aspects of human communication systems.

References

Bresnan, Joan. 1982a. Control and Complementation. In *The Mental Representation of Grammatical Relations*, ed. Joan Bresnan. 282–390. Cambridge, MA: The MIT Press.

Bresnan, Joan (ed.). 1982b. *The Mental Representation of Grammatical Relations*. Cambridge, MA: The MIT Press.

Bresnan, Joan. 1982c. The Passive in Lexical Theory. In *The Mental Representation of Grammatical Relations*, ed. Joan Bresnan. 3–86. Cambridge, MA: The MIT Press.

Bresnan, Joan, and Ronald M. Kaplan. 1982. Introduction: Grammars as Mental Representations of Language. In *The Mental Representation of Grammatical Relations*. xvii–lii. Cambridge, MA: The MIT Press.

Bresnan, Joan, Ronald M. Kaplan, Stanley Peters, and Annie Zaenen. 1982. Cross-serial Dependencies in Dutch. *Linguistic Inquiry* 13:613–635.

Bresnan, Joan. 1984. Bound Anaphora on Functional Structures. Presented at the Tenth Annual Meeting of the Berkeley Linguistics Society.

Bresnan, Joan, and Jonni M. Kanerva. 1989. Locative Inversion in Chicheŵa: A Case Study of Factorization in Grammar. *Linguistic Inquiry* 20(1):1–50. Also in E. Wehrli and T. Stowell, eds., Syntax and Semantics 26: Syntax and the Lexicon. New York: Academic Press.

Gazdar, Gerald, Ewan Klein, Geoffrey K. Pullum, and Ivan A. Sag. 1985. *Generalized Phrase Structure Grammar*. Cambridge, MA: Harvard University Press.

Halvorsen, Per-Kristian. 1983. Semantics for Lexical-Functional Grammar. *Linguistic Inquiry* 14(4):567–615.

Halvorsen, Per-Kristian, and Ronald M. Kaplan. 1988. Projections and Semantic Description in Lexical-Functional Grammar. In *Proceedings of the International Conference on Fifth Generation Computer Systems*, 1116–1122.

Tokyo, Japan. Institute for New Generation Systems. Reprinted in Part IV of this volume.

Kameyama, Megumi. 1988. Functional Precedence Conditions on Overt and Zero Pronominals. Unpublished MS, MCC, Austin, Texas.

Kaplan, Ronald M. 1975. On Process Models for Sentence Comprehension. In *Explorations in cognition*, ed. Donald A. Norman and David E. Rumelhart. San Francisco: W. H. Freeman.

Kaplan, Ronald M., and Joan Bresnan. 1982. Lexical-Functional Grammar: A Formal System for Grammatical Representation. In *The Mental Representation of Grammatical Relations*, ed. Joan Bresnan. 173–281. Cambridge, MA: The MIT Press. Reprinted in Part I of this volume.

Kaplan, Ronald M., and John T. Maxwell. 1988a. An Algorithm for Functional Uncertainty. In *Proceedings of COLING-88*, 297–302. Budapest. Reprinted in Part II of this volume.

Kaplan, Ronald M., and John T. Maxwell. 1988b. Constituent Coordination in Lexical-Functional Grammar. In *Proceedings of COLING-88*, 303–305. Budapest. Reprinted in Part II of this volume.

Kaplan, Ronald M., Klaus Netter, Jürgen Wedekind, and Annie Zaenen. 1989. Translation by Structural Correspondences. In *Proceedings of the Fourth Meeting of the European ACL*, 272–281. University of Manchester, April. European Chapter of the Association for Computational Linguistics. Reprinted in Part IV of this volume.

Kaplan, Ronald M., and Annie Zaenen. 1989a. Functional Precedence and Constituent Structure. In *Proceedings of ROCLING II*, ed. Chu-Ren Huang and Keh-Jiann Chen, 19–40. Taipei, Republic of China.

Kaplan, Ronald M., and Annie Zaenen. 1989b. Long-distance Dependencies, Constituent Structure, and Functional Uncertainty. In *Alternative Conceptions of Phrase Structure*, ed. Mark Baltin and Anthony Kroch. Chicago University Press. Reprinted in Part II of this volume.

Kaplan, Ronald M., and John T. Maxwell. 1993. LFG Grammar Writer's Workbench. Unpublished technical report. Xerox Palo Alto Research Center.

Kasper, Robert T., and William C. Rounds. 1986. A Logical Semantics for Feature Structures. In *Proceedings of the Twenty-Fourth Annual Meeting of the ACL*. New York. Association for Computational Linguistics.

Kay, Martin. 1979. Functional Grammar. In *Proceedings of the Fifth Annual Meeting of the Berkeley Linguistic Society*, ed. Christine Chiarello and others, 142–158. The University of California at Berkeley. Berkeley Linguistics Society.

Kay, Martin. 1984. Functional Unification Grammar: A Formalism for Machine Translation. In *Proceedings of COLING-84*, 75–78. Stanford, CA.

Pullum, Geoffrey K. 1982. Free Word Order and Phrase Structure Rules. In *Proceedings of the Twelfth Annual Meeting of the North Eastern Linguistic Society*, ed. James Pustejovsky and Peter Sells, 209–220. University of Massachusetts at Amherst.

Woods, William A. 1970. Transition Network Grammars for Natural Language Analysis. *Communications of the ACM* 13(10):591–606.

2

Lexical-Functional Grammar: A Formal System for Grammatical Representation

RONALD M. KAPLAN AND JOAN BRESNAN

In learning their native language, children develop a remarkable set of capabilities. They acquire knowledge and skills that enable them to produce and comprehend an indefinite number of novel utterances, and to make quite subtle judgments about certain of their properties. The major goal of psycholinguistic research is to devise an explanatory account of the mental operations that underlie these linguistic abilities.

In pursuing this goal, we have adopted what we call the *Competence Hypothesis* as a methodological principle. We assume that an explanatory model of human language performance will incorporate a theoretically justified representation of the native speaker's linguistic knowledge (a *grammar*) as a component separate both from the computational mechanisms that operate on it (a *processor*) and from other nongrammatical processing parameters that might influence the processor's behavior.[1] To a certain extent the various components that we postulate can be studied independently, guided where appropriate by the well-established methods and evaluation standards of linguistics, computer science, and experimental psychology. However, the requirement that the various components ultimately must fit together in a consistent and coherent model imposes even stronger constraints on their structure and operation.

This paper originally appeared in *The Mental Representation of Grammatical Relations*, ed. Joan Bresnan (Cambridge, MA: The MIT Press, 1982), 173–281.

[1] Kaplan (1975a,b) gives an early version of the Competence Hypothesis and discusses some ways in which the grammatical and processing components might interact. Also see Ford, Bresnan, and Kaplan (1982).

Formal Issues in Lexical-Functional Grammar
edited by
Mary Dalrymple
Ronald M. Kaplan
John T. Maxwell III
Annie Zaenen

This paper presents a formalism for representing the native speaker's syntactic knowledge. In keeping with the Competence Hypothesis, this formalism, called *lexical-functional grammar* (LFG), has been designed to serve as a medium for expressing and explaining important generalizations about the syntax of human languages and thus to serve as a vehicle for independent linguistic research. Of equal significance, it is a restricted, mathematically tractable notation for which simple, psychologically plausible processing mechanisms can be defined. Lexical-functional grammar has evolved both from previous research within the transformational framework (e.g., Bresnan 1978) and from earlier computational and psycholinguistic investigations (Woods 1970; Kaplan 1972, 1973, 1975a; Wanner and Maratsos 1978).

The fundamental problem for a theory of syntax is to characterize the mapping between semantic predicate-argument relationships and the surface word and phrase configurations by which they are expressed. This mapping is sufficiently complex that it cannot be characterized in a simple, unadorned phrase structure formalism: a single set of predicate-argument relations can be realized in many different phrase structures (e.g., active and passive constructions), and a single phrase structure can express several different semantic relations, as in cases of ambiguity. In lexical-functional grammar, this correspondence is defined in two stages. Lexical entries specify a direct mapping between semantic arguments and configurations of surface grammatical functions. Syntactic rules then identify these surface functions with particular morphological and constituent structure configurations. Alternative realizations may result from alternative specifications at either stage of the correspondence. Moreover, grammatical specifications impose well-formedness conditions on both the functional and constituent structures of sentences.

The present paper is concerned with the grammatical formalism itself; its linguistic, computational, and psychological motivation are dealt with in separate papers. In the next several sections we introduce the formal objects of our theory, discuss the relationships among them, and define the notation and operations for describing and manipulating them. Illustrations in these and later sections show possible LFG solutions to various problems of linguistic description. Section 5 considers the functional requirements that strings with valid constituent structures must satisfy. Section 6 summarizes arguments for the independence of the constituent, functional, and semantic levels of representation. In Section 7 we introduce and discuss the formal apparatus for characterizing long-distance grammatical dependencies. We leave to the end the question of our system's generative power. We prove in Section 8 that despite their linguistic expressiveness, lexical-functional grammars are *not* as powerful as unrestricted rewriting systems.

1 Constituent structures and functional structures

A lexical-functional grammar assigns two levels of syntactic description to every sentence of a language. Phrase structure configurations are represented in a *constituent structure*. A constituent structure (or 'c-structure') is a conventional phrase structure tree, a well-formed labeled bracketing that indicates the superficial arrangement of words and phrases in the sentence. This is the representation on which phonological interpretation operates to produce phonetic strings. Surface grammatical functions are represented explicitly at the other level of description, called *functional structure*. The functional structure ('f-structure') provides a precise characterization of such traditional syntactic notions as subject, "understood" subject, object, complement, and adjunct. The f-structure is the sole input to the semantic component, which may either translate the f-structure into the appropriate formulas in some logical language or provide an immediate model-theoretic interpretation for it.

Constituent structures are formally quite different from functional structures. C-structures are defined in terms of syntactic categories, terminal strings, and their dominance and precedence relationships, whereas f-structures are composed of grammatical function names, semantic forms, and feature symbols. F-structures (and c-structures) are also distinct from semantic translations and interpretations, in which, for example, quantifier-scope ambiguities are resolved. By formally distinguishing these levels of representation, our theory attempts to separate those grammatical phenomena that are purely syntactic (involving only c-structures and f-structures) from those that are purely lexical (involving lexical entries before they are inserted into c-structures and f-structures) or semantic (for example, involving logical inference). Our framework thus facilitates an empirically motivated division of labor between the lexical, syntactic, semantic, and phonological components of a grammar.

A c-structure is determined by a grammar that characterizes all possible surface structures for a language. This grammar is expressed in a slightly modified context-free formalism or a formally equivalent specification such as a recursive transition network (Woods 1970; Kaplan 1972). For example, the ordinary rewriting procedure for context-free grammars would assign the c-structure (3) to the sentence (2), given the rules in (1):

(1) a. S $\longrightarrow$ NP VP
    b. NP $\longrightarrow$ Det N
    c. VP $\longrightarrow$ V NP NP

(2) A girl handed the baby a toy.

(3)

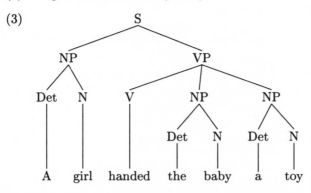

We emphasize that c-structure nodes can be derived only by phrase structure rules such as (1a,b,c). There are no deletion or movement operations which could, for example, form the double-NP sequence from a phrase structure with a *to* prepositional phrase. Such mechanisms are unnecessary in LFG because we do not map between semantically and phonologically interpretable levels of phrase structure. Semantic interpretation is defined on functional structure, not on the phrase structure representation that is the domain of phonological interpretation.

The functional structure for a sentence encodes its meaningful grammatical relations and provides sufficient information for the semantic component to determine the appropriate predicate-argument formulas. The f-structure for (2) would indicate that the *girl* noun phrase is the grammatical subject, *handed* conveys the semantic predicate, the *baby* NP is the grammatical object, and *toy* serves as the second grammatical object. The f-structure represents this information as a set of ordered pairs each of which consists of an *attribute* and a specification of that attribute's *value* for this sentence. An attribute is the name of a grammatical function or feature (SUBJ, PRED, OBJ, NUM, CASE, etc.). There are three primitive types of values:

(4) a. Simple *symbols*

b. *Semantic forms* that govern the process of semantic interpretation

c. Subsidiary *f-structures*, sets of ordered pairs representing complexes of internal functions.

A fourth type of value, *sets* of symbols, semantic forms, or f-structures, is also permitted. We will discuss this type when we consider the grammatical treatment of adjuncts.

Given possibility (4c), an f-structure is in effect a hierarchy of attribute/value pairs. We write an f-structure by arranging its pairs vertically inside square brackets with the attribute and value of a single pair placed on a horizontal line. The following is a plausible f-structure for sentence (2):

(5)

$$
\begin{bmatrix}
\text{SUBJ} & \begin{bmatrix} \text{SPEC} & \text{A} \\ \text{NUM} & \text{SG} \\ \text{PRED} & \text{`girl'} \end{bmatrix} \\
\text{TENSE} & \text{PAST} \\
\text{PRED} & \text{`hand} \langle (\uparrow \text{ SUBJ}), (\uparrow \text{ OBJ}), (\uparrow \text{ OBJ2}) \rangle \text{'} \\
\text{OBJ} & \begin{bmatrix} \text{SPEC} & \text{THE} \\ \text{NUM} & \text{SG} \\ \text{PRED} & \text{`baby'} \end{bmatrix} \\
\text{OBJ2} & \begin{bmatrix} \text{SPEC} & \text{A} \\ \text{NUM} & \text{SG} \\ \text{PRED} & \text{`toy'} \end{bmatrix}
\end{bmatrix}
$$

In this structure, the TENSE attribute has the simple symbol value PAST; pairs with this kind of value represent syntactic "features". Grammatical functions have subsidiary f-structure values, as illustrated by the subject function in this example:

(6)

$$
\begin{bmatrix}
\text{SPEC} & \text{A} \\
\text{NUM} & \text{SG} \\
\text{PRED} & \text{`girl'}
\end{bmatrix}
$$

The attributes SPEC (specifier) and NUM mark embedded features with the symbol values A and SG respectively.

The quoted values of the PRED attributes are semantic forms. Semantic forms usually arise in the lexicon[2] and are carried along by the syntactic component as unanalyzable atomic elements, just like simple symbols. When the f-structure is semantically interpreted, these forms are treated as patterns for composing the logical formulas encoding the meaning of the sentence. Thus, the semantic interpretation for this sentence is obtained from the value of its PRED attribute, the semantic form in (7):

(7) 'hand $\langle (\uparrow \text{ SUBJ}), (\uparrow \text{ OBJ}), (\uparrow \text{ OBJ2}) \rangle$'

This is a predicate-argument expression containing the semantic predicate name 'hand' followed by an argument-list specification enclosed in angle-

---

[2]Semantic forms with a lexical source are often called *lexical forms*. Less commonly, semantic forms are produced by syntactic rules, for example, to represent unexpressed pronouns; this will be illustrated in Section 6 in the discussion of English imperative subjects.

brackets.[3] The argument-list specification defines a mapping between the logical or thematic arguments of the three-place predicate 'hand' (e.g. agent, theme, and goal) and the grammatical functions of the f-structure. The parenthetic expressions signify that the first argument position of that predicate is filled by the formula that results from interpreting the SUBJ function of the sentence, the formula from the OBJ2 is substituted in the second argument position, and so on. The formula for the embedded SUBJ f-structure is determined by *its* PRED value, the semantic form 'girl'. 'Girl' does not have an argument-list because it does not apply to arguments specified by other grammatical functions. It is a predicate on individuals in the logical universe of discourse quantified by information derived from the SPEC feature.[4]

There are very strong compatibility requirements between a semantic form and the f-structure in which it appears. Loosely speaking, all the functions mentioned in the semantic form must be included in the f-structure, and all functions with subsidiary f-structure values must be mentioned in the semantic form. A given semantic form is in effect compatible with only one set of grammatical functions (although these may be associated with several different c-structures). Thus the semantic form in (8) is not compatible with the grammatical functions in (5) because it does not mention the OBJ2 function but does specify ($\uparrow$ TO OBJ), the object of the preposition *to*.

(8)   'hand $\langle(\uparrow$ SUBJ$), (\uparrow$ OBJ$), (\uparrow$ TO OBJ$)\rangle$'

This semantic form is compatible instead with the functions in the f-structure (9):

---

[3]The angle-brackets correspond to the parentheses in the logical language that would ordinarily be used to denote the application of a predicate to its arguments. We use angle-brackets in order to distinguish the semantic parentheses from the parentheses of our syntactic formalism.

[4]This paper is not concerned with the details of the semantic translation procedure for NP's, and the specifications for the SPEC and common noun PRED features are simplified accordingly. With more elaborate expressions for these features, NP's can also be translated into a higher-order intensional logic by a general substitution procedure. For instance, suppose that the symbol A is taken as an abbreviation for the semantic form

$$\text{'}\lambda Q.\lambda P.\exists x.\langle Q(x) \wedge P(x)\rangle\text{'}$$

which represents the meaning of an existential quantifier, and suppose that 'girl' is replaced by the expression '($\uparrow$ SPEC)$\langle girl'\rangle$'. Then the translation for the SUBJ f-structure would be a formula in which the quantifier is applied to the common noun meaning. See Halvorsen (1983) for an extensive discussion of f-structure translation and interpretation.

(9)

$$
\begin{bmatrix}
\text{SUBJ} & \begin{bmatrix} \text{SPEC} & \text{A} \\ \text{NUM} & \text{SG} \\ \text{PRED} & \text{`girl'} \end{bmatrix} \\
\text{TENSE} & \text{PAST} \\
\text{PRED} & \text{`hand}\langle(\uparrow \text{ SUBJ}), (\uparrow \text{ OBJ}), (\uparrow \text{ TO OBJ})\rangle\text{'} \\
\text{OBJ} & \begin{bmatrix} \text{SPEC} & \text{A} \\ \text{NUM} & \text{SG} \\ \text{PRED} & \text{`toy'} \end{bmatrix} \\
\text{TO} & \begin{bmatrix} \text{PCASE} & \text{TO} \\ \text{OBJ} & \begin{bmatrix} \text{SPEC} & \text{THE} \\ \text{NUM} & \text{SG} \\ \text{PRED} & \text{`baby'} \end{bmatrix} \end{bmatrix}
\end{bmatrix}
$$

We show in Section 4 how this f-structure is assigned to the NP–*to*–NP sentence (10):

(10)   A girl handed a toy to the baby.

This f-structure, with (8) as its PRED value, defines *girl*, *baby*, and *toy* as the agent, goal, and theme arguments of 'hand', just as in (5). The native speaker's paraphrase intuitions concerning (2) and (10) are thus accurately expressed. This account of the English dative alternation is possible because our grammatical functions SUBJ, OBJ, TO OBJ, etc., denote *surface* grammatical relationships, not the underlying, logical relationships commonly represented in transformational deep structures.

The semantic forms (7) and (8) are found in alternative entries of the lexical item *handed*, reflecting the fact that the predicate 'hand' permits the alternative surface realizations (2) and (10), among others. Of course, many other verbs in the lexicon are similar to *handed* in having separate entries along the lines of (7) and (8). Our theory captures the systematic connection between NP–NP and NP-*to*-NP constructions by means of a lexical redundancy rule of the sort suggested by Bresnan (1978, 1982c). The semantic form (7) results from applying the "dativizing" lexical rule shown in (11) to the semantic form in (8).

(11) $(\uparrow \text{ OBJ}) \mapsto (\uparrow \text{ OBJ2})$
       $(\uparrow \text{ TO OBJ}) \mapsto (\uparrow \text{ OBJ})$

According to this rule, a word with a lexical entry containing the specifications $(\uparrow \text{ OBJ})$ and $(\uparrow \text{ TO OBJ})$ may have another entry in which $(\uparrow \text{ OBJ2})$ appears in place of $(\uparrow \text{ OBJ})$ and $(\uparrow \text{ OBJ})$ appears in place of $(\uparrow \text{ TO OBJ})$.

It is important to note that these relation-changing rules are not applied in the syntactic derivation of individual sentences. They merely express patterns of redundancy that obtain among large but finite classes of lexical entries and presumably simplify the child's language-acquisition task (see Pinker 1982 for discussion). Indeed, just as our formalism admits no rules for transforming c-structures, it embodies a similar prohibition against syntactic manipulations of function assignments and function/argument mappings:

> (12) *Direct Syntactic Encoding*
> No rule of syntax may replace one function name by another.

This principle is an immediate consequence of the Uniqueness Condition, which is stated in the next section. The principle of direct syntactic encoding sharpens the distinction between two classes of rules: rules that change relations are lexical and range over finite sets, while syntactic rules that project onto an infinite set of sentences preserve grammatical relations.[5] Our restrictions on the expressive power of syntactic rules guarantee that a sentence's grammatical functions are "visible" directly in the surface structure and thus afford certain computational and psychological advantages.

2 Functional descriptions

A string's constituent structure is generated by a context-free c-structure grammar. That grammar is augmented so that it also produces a finite collection of statements specifying various properties of the string's f-structure. The set of such statements, called the *functional description* ('f-description') of the string, serves as an intermediary between the c-structure and the f-structure.

The statements of an f-description can be used in two ways. They can be applied to a particular f-structure to decide whether or not it has all the properties required by the grammar. If so, the candidate f-structure may be taken as the f-structure that the grammar assigns to the string. The f-description may also be used in a constructive mode: the statements support a set of inferences by which an f-structure satisfying the grammar's requirements may be synthesized. The f-description is thus analogous to a set of simultaneous equations in elementary algebra that express properties of certain unknown numbers. Such equations may be used to validate a proposed solution, or they may be solved by means of arithmetic inference rules (canceling, substitution of equals for equals, etc.) to discover the particular numbers for which the equations are true. In line with this analogy, this section presents an algebraic formalism for representing an f-description.

---

[5]This correlation of rule properties is a significant difference between lexical-functional grammar and Relational Grammar (see for example the papers in Perlmutter 1983). The two approaches are similar, however, in the emphasis they place on grammatical relations. Bell (1980) offers a more extensive comparison of the two theories.

The statements in an f-description and the inferences that may be drawn from them depend crucially on the following axiom:

(13)   *Uniqueness*
       In a given f-structure a particular attribute may have at most one value.

This condition makes it possible to describe an f-structure by specifying *the* (unique) values of the grammatical functions of which it is composed. Thus, if we let the variables f_1 and f_2 stand for unknown f-structures, the following statements have a clear interpretation:

(14)   a.   the SUBJ of $f_1 = f_2$
       b.   the SPEC of $f_2 = $ A
       c.   the NUM of $f_2 = $ SG
       d.   the PRED of $f_2 = $ 'girl'

In fact, these statements are true if f_1 and f_2 are the f-structures (5) and (6), and the statements in (14) may thus be considered a part of the f-description of sentence (2).

We have defined a functional structure as a set of ordered pairs satisfying the Uniqueness Condition (13). We now observe that this is precisely the standard definition of a *mathematical* function. There is a systematic ambiguity in our use of the word *function*: an f-structure is a mathematical function that represents the *grammatical* functions of a sentence. This coincidence provides a more conventional terminology for formulating the statements of an f-description. For example, statement (14c) can be paraphrased as (15a), and this can be stated more formally using the familiar parenthesis notation to indicate the application of a function to an argument, as in (15b):

(15)   a.   The function f_2 is such that applying it to the argument NUM yields the value SG.
       b. $f_2(\text{NUM}) = $ SG

Thus, the statements of an f-description are simply equations that describe the values obtained by various function applications. Unlike the typical functions of elementary algebra, an f-structure is a function with a finite domain and range and thus can be defined by a finite table of arguments and values, as represented in our square-bracket notation. Also, we do not draw a clear distinction between functions and their values. Algebraic equations commonly involve a known function that take on a given value when applied to some unknown argument; the problem is to determine that argument. In (15b), however, the argument and the corresponding value are *both* known, and the problem is to find the function![6] Moreover, applying an f-structure to an argument may produce a function that may be applied in turn to another argument. If (16a) is true, then the stipulations in (15b) and (16b) are equivalent.

(16) a. $f_1(\text{SUBJ}) = \begin{bmatrix} \text{SPEC} & \text{A} \\ \text{NUM} & \text{SG} \\ \text{PRED} & \text{`girl'} \end{bmatrix} = f_2$

  b. $f_1(\text{SUBJ})(\text{NUM}) = \text{SG}$

The form of function composition illustrated in equation (16b) occurs quite often in f-descriptions. We have found that a slight adaptation of the traditional notation improves the readability of such specifications. Thus, we denote a function application by writing the function name *inside* the parentheses next to the argument instead of putting it in front. In our modified notation, the stipulation (15b) is written as (17a) and the composition (16b) appears as (17b).

(17) a. $(f_2 \text{ NUM}) = \text{SG}$
  b. $((f_1 \text{ SUBJ}) \text{ NUM}) = \text{SG}$

We make one further simplification: since all f-structures are functions of one argument, parenthetic expressions with more than two elements (a function and its argument) do not normally occur. Thus, we introduce no ambiguity by defining our parenthetic notation to be left-associative, by means of the identity (18):

(18) $((f \ \alpha) \ \beta) = (f \ \alpha \ \beta)$

This allows any leftmost pair of parentheses to be removed (or inserted) when convenient, so that (17b) may be simplified to (19):

(19) $(f_1 \text{ SUBJ NUM}) = \text{SG}$

With this notation, there is a simple way of determining the value of a given function-application expression: we locate the f-structure denoted by the leftmost element in the expression and match the remaining elements from left to right against successive attributes in the f-structure

---

[6]There is an equivalent formulation in which the grammatical relation symbols SUBJ, OBJ, etc., are taken to be the names of functions that apply to f-structure arguments. We would then write SUBJ(f_1) instead of $f_1(\text{SUBJ})$, and the left- and right-hand elements of all our expressions would be systematically interchanged. Even with this alternative, however, there are still cases where the function is an unknown (see for example the discussion below of oblique objects). The conceptual consideration underlying our decision to treat f-structures as the formal functions is that only total, finite functions are then involved in the characterization of particular sentences. Otherwise, our conceptual framework would be populated with functions on infinite domains, when only their restriction to the sentence at hand would ever be grammatically relevant. Only this intuition would be affected if the alternative formulation were adopted.

hierarchy. Also, the English genitive construction provides a natural gloss for these expressions: (19) may be read as "f_1's SUBJ's NUM is SG".

3   From c-structures to f-descriptions

Having said what an f-description is, we now consider how the f-description for a string is produced from a grammar and lexicon. This is followed by a discussion of the inferences that lead from an f-description to the f-structure that it describes.

The statements in an f-description come from functional specifications that are associated with particular elements on the right-hand sides of c-structure rules and with particular categories in lexical entries. These specifications consist of templates from which the f-description statements are derived. A template, or statement *schema*, has the form of the statement to be derived from it except that in place of f-structure variables it contains special *metavariables*. If a rule is applied to generate a c-structure node or a lexical item is inserted under a preterminal category, the associated schemata are *instantiated* by replacing the metavariables with actual variables (f_1, f_2, ...). Which actual variables are used depends on which metavariables are in the schemata and what the node's relationship is to other nodes in the tree. The metavariables and grammatically significant tree relations are of just two types:

(20)   *Immediate domination*, with metavariables ↑ and ↓
       Bounded domination, with metavariables ⇑ and ⇓

Statements based on nonimmediate but bounded tree relations are needed to characterize the "long-distance" dependencies found in relative clauses, questions, and other constructions. We postpone our discussion of bounded domination to Section 7 since it is more complex than immediate domination.

Schemata involving immediate domination metavariables and relations yield f-description statements defining the local predicate-argument configurations of simple sentence patterns such as the dative. To illustrate, the c-structure rules (21a,b,c) are versions of (1a,b,c) with schemata written beneath the rule elements that they are associated with.

(21) a. S $\longrightarrow$ NP   VP

                         $(\uparrow \text{SUBJ}) = \downarrow$ $\uparrow = \downarrow$

    b. NP $\longrightarrow$ Det   N

                    $\uparrow = \downarrow$ $\uparrow = \downarrow$

    c. VP $\longrightarrow$ V   NP   NP

                     $(\uparrow \text{OBJ}) = \downarrow$ $(\uparrow \text{OBJ2}) = \downarrow$

According to the instantiation procedure described below, the SUBJ and OBJ schemata in this grammar indicate that the subject and object f-structures come from NP's immediately dominated by S and VP. While superficially similar to the standard transformational definitions of 'subject' and 'object' (Chomsky 1965), our specifications apply only to surface constituents and establish only a loose coupling between functions and phrase structure configurations. Given the OBJ2 schema, for example, an NP directly dominated by VP can also function as a second object. These schemata correspond more closely to the SETR operation of the augmented transition network notation (ATN) (Woods 1970): $(\uparrow \text{SUBJ}) = \downarrow$ has roughly the same effect as the ATN action (SETR SUBJ *). The direct equality on the VP category in (21a) has no ATN (or transformational) equivalent, however. It is an *identification* schema, indicating that a single f-structure is based on more than one constituent, and thus that the f-structure is somewhat "flatter" than the c-structure.

The syntactic features and semantic content of lexical items are determined by schemata in lexical entries. The entries for the vocabulary of sentence (2) are listed in (22):[7]

(22)   *a*   Det $(\uparrow \text{SPEC}) = \text{A}$

                       $(\uparrow \text{NUM}) = \text{SG}$

    girl   N $(\uparrow \text{NUM}) = \text{SG}$

                       $(\uparrow \text{PRED}) = \text{'girl'}$

    handed   V $(\uparrow \text{TENSE}) = \text{PAST}$

                       $(\uparrow \text{PRED}) = \text{'hand} \langle (\uparrow \text{SUBJ}), (\uparrow \text{OBJ}), (\uparrow \text{OBJ2}) \rangle\text{'}$

    the   Det $(\uparrow \text{SPEC}) = \text{THE}$

---

[7]This illustration ignores the morphological composition of lexical items, which makes a systematic contribution to the set of inflectional features represented in the schemata.

baby   N   (↑ NUM) = SG
              (↑ PRED) = 'baby'

toy   N   (↑ NUM) = SG
              (↑ PRED) = 'toy'

A lexical entry in LFG includes a categorial specification indicating the preterminal category under which the lexical item may be inserted, and a set of schemata to be instantiated. As shown in (22), schemata originating in the lexicon are not formally distinct from those coming from c-structure rules, and they are treated uniformly by the instantiation procedure.

Instantiation is carried out in three phases. The schemata are first attached to appropriate nodes in the c-structure tree, actual variables are then introduced at certain nodes, and finally those actual variables are substituted for metavariables to form valid f-description statements. In the first phase, schemata associated with a c-structure rule element are attached to the nodes generated by that element. Lexical schemata are considered to be associated with a lexical entry's categorial specification and are thus attached to the nodes of that category that dominate the lexical item.[8] Attaching the grammatical and lexical schemata in (21) and (22) to the c-structure for sentence (2) produces the result in (23). In this example we have written the schemata above the nodes they are attached to.

In the second phase of the instantiation procedure, a new actual variable is introduced for the root node of the tree and for each node where a schema contains the ↓ metavariable. Intuitively, the existence of ↓ at a node means that one component of the sentence's f-structure corresponds to that subconstituent. The new variable, called the '↓-variable' of the node, is a device for describing the internal properties of that f-structure (called the node's '↓ f-structure') and its role in larger structures. In (24) we have associated ↓-variables with the nodes as required by the schemata in (23).

With the schemata and variables laid out on the tree in this way, the substitution phase of instantiation is quite simple. Fully instantiated statements are formed by substituting a node's ↓-variable first for all the ↓'s at that node and then for all the ↑'s attached to the nodes it immediately dominates. Thus, arrows pointing toward each other across

---

[8] Another convention for lexical insertion is to attach the schemata directly to the terminal nodes. While the same functional relationships can be stated with either convention, this alternative requires additional identification schemata in the common case where the preterminal category does not correspond to a distinct functional unit. It is thus more cumbersome to work with.

(23)

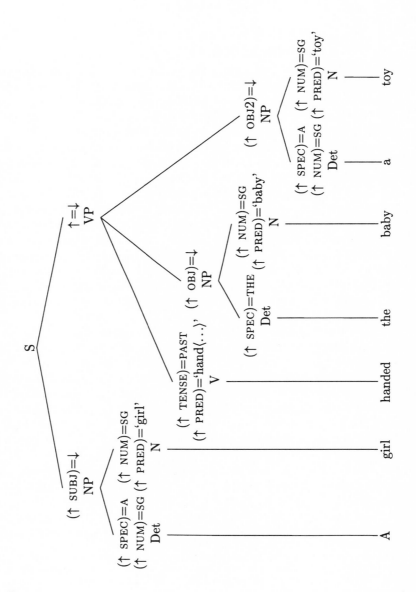

(24)

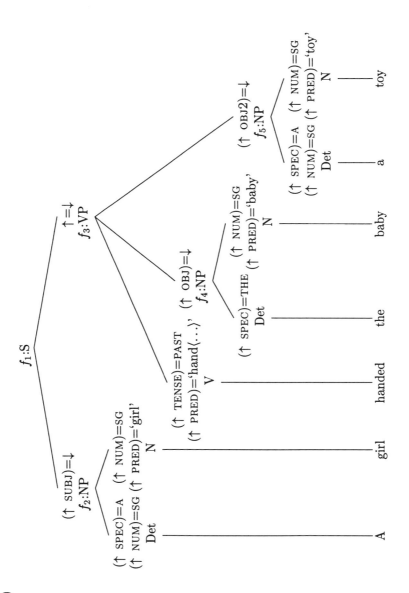

one line in the tree are instantiated with the same variable.[9] The $\uparrow$ is called the "mother" metavariable, since it is replaced by the $\downarrow$-variable of its mother node. From the point of view of the S-dominated NP node, the schema $(\uparrow \text{SUBJ}) = \downarrow$ may be read as 'My mother's f-structure's SUBJ is my f-structure'.[10] In this case, the mother's variable is the root node's $\downarrow$-variable and so represents the f-structure of the sentence as a whole.

When we perform the substitutions for the schemata and variables in (24), the schemata attached to the S-dominated NP and VP nodes yield the equations in (25), and the daughters of the VP cause the equations in (26) to be included in the sentence's f-description:

(25) a. $(f_1 \text{ SUBJ}) = f_2$
      b. $f_1 = f_3$

(26) a. $(f_3 \text{ OBJ}) = f_4$
      b. $(f_3 \text{ OBJ2}) = f_5$

The equations in (25–26) taken together constitute the syntactically determined statements of the sentence's functional description. The other equations in the f-description are derived from the schemata on the preterminal nodes:[11]

---

[9] If a schema containing $\uparrow$ is attached to a node whose mother has no $\downarrow$-variable, the $\uparrow$ cannot be properly instantiated and the string is marked ungrammatical. This situation is not likely to occur with immediate domination metavariables but provides an important well-formedness condition for bounded domination. This is discussed in Section 7.

[10] In effect, the instantiation procedure adds to the schemata information about the tree configurations in which they appear. As shown in Section 4, the f-structure for the sentence can then be inferred without further reference to the c-structure. An equivalent inference procedure can be defined that does not require the introduction of variables and instead takes into account the relative position of schemata in the tree. This alternative procedure searches the c-structure to obtain the information that we are encoding by variables in instantiated schemata. It essentially intermixes our instantiation operations among its other inferences and is thus more difficult to describe.

[11] For simplicity in this paper, we do not instantiate the $\uparrow$ metavariable when it appears within semantic forms. This is permissible because the internal structure of semantic forms is not accessible to syntactic rules. However, the semantic translation or interpretation procedure may depend on a full instantiation.

(27) a. $(f_2\ \text{SPEC}) = \text{A}$ from *a*
      b. $(f_2\ \text{NUM}) = \text{SG}$

      c. $(f_2\ \text{NUM}) = \text{SG}$ from *girl*
      d. $(f_2\ \text{PRED}) = \text{'girl'}$

      e. $(f_3\ \text{TENSE}) = \text{PAST}$ from *handed*
      f. $(f_3\ \text{PRED}) = \text{'hand}\,\langle(\uparrow\ \text{SUBJ}),\ (\uparrow\ \text{OBJ}),\ (\uparrow\ \text{OBJ2})\rangle\text{'}$

      g. $(f_4\ \text{SPEC}) = \text{THE}$ from *the*

      h. $(f_4\ \text{NUM}) = \text{SG}$ from *baby*
      i. $(f_4\ \text{PRED}) = \text{'baby'}$

      j. $(f_5\ \text{SPEC}) = \text{A}$ from *a*
      k. $(f_5\ \text{NUM}) = \text{SG}$

      l. $(f_5\ \text{NUM}) = \text{SG}$ from *toy*
      m. $(f_5\ \text{PRED}) = \text{'toy'}$

Adding these to the equations in (25–26) gives the complete f-description for sentence (2).

4 From f-descriptions to f-structures

Once an f-description has been produced for a given string, algebraic manipulations can be performed on its statements to make manifest certain implicit relationships that hold among the properties of that string's f-structure. These manipulations are justified by the left-associativity of the function-application notation (18) and by the substitution axiom for equality. To take an example, the value of the number feature of sentence (2)'s f-structure (that is, the value of $(f_1\ \text{OBJ NUM})$) can be inferred in the following steps:

(28) $(f_1\ \text{OBJ NUM})$ $= (f_3\ \text{OBJ NUM})$ Substitution using (25b)
                         $= ((f_3\ \text{OBJ})\ \text{NUM})$ Left-associativity
                         $= (f_4\ \text{NUM})$ Substitution using (26a)
                         $= \text{SG}$ Substitution using (27h)

An f-description also supports a more important set of inferences: the equations can be "solved" by means of a construction algorithm that actually builds the f-structure they describe.

An f-structure solution may not exist for every f-description, however. If the f-description stipulates two distinct values for a particular attribute, or if it implies that an attribute-name is an f-structure or semantic form instead of a symbol, then its statements are inconsistent with the basic axioms of our theory. In this case we classify the string as syntactically ill-formed, even though it has a valid c-structure. The functional well-formedness conditions of our theory thus account for many types of ungrammaticality. It is therefore essential that there be an algorithm for deciding whether or not an f-description is consistent, and for producing a consistent f-description's f-structure solution. Otherwise, our grammars would generate all but not *only* the sentences of a language.

Fortunately, f-descriptions are well-understood mathematical objects. The problem of determining whether or not a given f-description is satisfiable is equivalent to the decision problem of the quantifier-free theory of equality. Ackermann (1954) proved that this problem is solvable, and several efficient solution algorithms have been discovered (for example, the congruence closure algorithm of Nelson and Oppen 1980). In this section we outline a decision and construction algorithm whose operations are specially adapted to the linguistic representations of our theory.

We begin by giving a more precise interpretation for the formal expressions that appear in f-description statements. We imagine that there is a collection of entities (symbols, semantic forms, and f-structures) that an f-description characterizes, and that each of these entities has a variety of names, or *designators*, by which the f-description may refer to it. The character strings that we have used to represent symbols and semantic forms, the algebraic variables we introduce, and the function-application expressions are all designators. The entity denoted by a designator is called its *value*. The value of a symbol or semantic form character string is obviously the identified symbol or semantic form. The value of a variable designator is of course not obvious from the variable's spelling; it is defined by an assignment list of variable–entity pairs. A basic function-application expression is a parenthesized pair of designators, and its value is the entity, if any, obtained by applying the f-structure value of the left designator to the symbol value of the right designator.[12] This rule applies recursively if either expression is itself a function-application: to obtain the value of $((f_1 \text{ OBJ}) \text{ NUM})$ we must first obtain the value of $(f_1 \text{ OBJ})$ by applying the value of f_1 to the symbol OBJ.

Note that several different designators may refer to the same entity. The deduction in (28), for example, indicates that the designators $(f_1 \text{ OBJ NUM})$ and $(f_4 \text{ NUM})$ both have the same value, the symbol SG. Indeed, we interpret the equality relation between two designators as an explicit stipulation that those designators name the same entity. In

---

[12] An attribute in an f-structure is thus a special kind of designator, and the notion of a designator's value generalizes our use of the term *value*, which previously referred only to the entity paired with an attribute in an f-structure.

processing an f-description, our algorithm attempts to find a way of associating with designators values that are consistent with the synonymy relation implied by the equality statements and with the procedure just outlined for obtaining the values of different types of designators.

The algorithm works by successive approximation.[13] It goes through a sequence of steps, one for each equation in the f-description. At the beginning of each step, it has a collection of symbols, semantic forms, and f-structures that satisfy all the equations considered at preceding steps, together with an assignment of tentative values for the variables occurring in those equations. The algorithm revises the collection of entities and value assignments to satisfy in addition the requirements of one more equation from the f-description. The entities after the last equation is processed thus satisfy the f-description as a whole and provide a final value for the $\downarrow$-variable of the c-structure tree's root node. This is the f-structure that the grammar assigns to the string.

The processing of a single equation is carried out by means of two operators. One operator, called *Locate*, obtains the value for a given designator. The entities in the collection might be augmented by the Locate operator to ensure that a value exists for that designator. When the values for the equation's left-hand and right-hand designators have been located, the second operator, *Merge*, checks to see whether those values are the same and hence already satisfy the equality relation. If not, it constructs a new entity by combining the properties of the distinct values, provided those properties are compatible. The collection is revised so that this entity becomes the common value of the two designators and also of all previously encountered synonyms of these designators. Stated in more formal terms, if d_1 and d_2 are the designators in an equation $d_1 = d_2$, and if brackets represent the application of an operator to its arguments, then that equation is processed by performing Merge[Locate[d_1], Locate[d_2]].

A technical definition of these operators is given in the Appendix. In this section we present an intuitive description of the solution process, using as an example the f-description in (25–27). The final result does not depend on the order in which equations are considered, so we will simply take them as they appear above. We start with an empty collection of entities and consider equation (25a): $(f_1 \text{ SUBJ}) = f_2$. To locate the value

---

[13]This algorithm is designed to demonstrate that the various conditions imposed by our theory are formally decidable. It is unlikely that this particular algorithm will be incorporated intact into a psychologically plausible model of language performance or even into a computationally efficient parser or generator. For these other purposes, functional operations will presumably be interleaved with c-structure computations, and functional data representations will be chosen so as to minimize the combinatoric interactions with the nondeterministic uncertainty of the c-structure rules.

of $(f_1 \text{ SUBJ})$, we must first obtain the value of f_1. There is as yet no assignment for that variable, so the Locate operator creates a value out of whole cloth: it adds a special "place-holder" entity to our collection and assigns it as the value of f_1. A representation for the new entity and variable assignment is shown in (29):

(29) f_1——

A place-holder is represented by a blank line, indicating that it is an entity none of whose properties are known. The variable prefix signifies that whatever that entity is, it has been assigned as the tentative value of f_1. A place-holder is just a bookkeeping device for recording the relations between entities before we have discovered anything else about them.

With the value of f_1 in hand, we return to the larger designator $(f_1 \text{ SUBJ})$. This provides more specific information about the entity that the place-holder stands for: the value of f_1 must be an f-structure that has SUBJ as one of its attributes. We revise our collection again to take account of this new information:

(30) f_1:[SUBJ ——]

Knowing nothing about the value of SUBJ in the f_1 f-structure, we have represented it by another place-holder. This place-holder is the entity located for the designator $(f_1 \text{ SUBJ})$. We now turn to f_2, the second designator in the equation. This is a variable with no previous assignment, so our location procedure simply assigns it to another newly created place-holder:

(31) f_2——

This completes the location phase of the algorithm's first step: the equation's designators now denote the place-holders in (30) and (31).

The Merge operator changes the collection once more, so that the two designators denote the same entity. The two place-holders are distinct, but neither has any properties. Thus, a common value, also a place-holder with no properties, can be constructed. This place-holder appears as the value of SUBJ in the f_1 f-structure, but it is also assigned as the value of f_2, as shown in (32):

(32) f_1:[SUBJ f_2:——]

The structure (32) is now the only member of our entity collection. Notice that with this assignment of variables, the designators $(f_1 \text{ SUBJ})$ and f_2 have the same value, so the equation $(f_1 \text{ SUBJ}) = f_2$ is satisfied.

We move on to equation (25b), the identification $f_1 = f_3$. This means that the variables f_1 and f_3 are two different designators for a single entity. That entity will have all the properties ascribed via the designator f_1 and also all the properties ascribed to the synonymous f_3. The f-structure (32) is located as the value of f_1, and a new place-holder is assigned to f_3. Since the place-holder has no properties, the result of combining it with the f-structure is simply that f-structure again, with its variable prefixes modified to reflect the new equality. Thus, the result of the merge for the second equation is (33):

$$(33) \quad f_1, f_3 : [\text{SUBJ} \quad f_2 : \text{——}]$$

The variable assignments in (33) now satisfy the first two equations of the f-description.

The equation at the next step is (26a): $(f_3 \text{ OBJ}) = f_4$. f_3 already has an f-structure value in (33), but it does not include OBJ as one of its attributes. This is remedied by adding an appropriate place-holder:

$$(34) \quad f_1, f_3 : \begin{bmatrix} \text{SUBJ} & f_2 : \text{——} \\ \text{OBJ} & \text{——} \end{bmatrix}$$

This place-holder is merged with one created for the variable f_4, yielding (35):

$$(35) \quad f_1, f_3 : \begin{bmatrix} \text{SUBJ} & f_2 : \text{——} \\ \text{OBJ} & f_4 : \text{——} \end{bmatrix}$$

Equation (26b) is handled in a similar fashion and results in (36):

$$(36) \quad f_1, f_3 : \begin{bmatrix} \text{SUBJ} & f_2 : \text{——} \\ \text{OBJ} & f_4 : \text{——} \\ \text{OBJ2} & f_5 : \text{——} \end{bmatrix}$$

After we have processed these equations, our collection of entities and variable assignments satisfies all the syntactically determined equations of the f-description.

The lexically derived equations are now taken into account. These have the effect of adding new features to the outer f-structure and filling in the internal properties of the place-holders. Locating the value of the left-hand designator in equation (27a), $(f_2 \text{ SPEC}) = \text{A}$, converts the SUBJ place-holder to an f-structure with a SPEC feature whose value is a new place-holder:

$$(37) \quad f_1, f_3 : \begin{bmatrix} \text{SUBJ} & f_2 : [\text{SPEC} \quad \text{——}] \\ \text{OBJ} & f_4 : \text{——} \\ \text{OBJ2} & f_5 : \text{——} \end{bmatrix}$$

The value of the right-hand designator is just the symbol A. Merging this with the new SPEC place-holder yields (38):

(38)
$$f_1, f_3: \begin{bmatrix} \text{SUBJ} & f_2:[\text{SPEC} \quad \text{A}] \\ \text{OBJ} & f_4:\text{——} \\ \text{OBJ2} & f_5:\text{——} \end{bmatrix}$$

Note that this modification does not falsify any equations processed in previous steps.

Equation (27b) has the same form as (27a), and its effect is simply to add a NUM SG feature to the SUBJ f-structure, alongside the SPEC:

(39)
$$f_1, f_3: \begin{bmatrix} \text{SUBJ} & f_2:\begin{bmatrix} \text{SPEC} & \text{A} \\ \text{NUM} & \text{SG} \end{bmatrix} \\ \text{OBJ} & f_4:\text{——} \\ \text{OBJ2} & f_5:\text{——} \end{bmatrix}$$

Though derived from different lexical items, equation (27c) is an exact duplicate of (27b). Processing this equation therefore has no visible effects.

The remaining equations are quite straightforward. Equation (27d) causes the PRED function to be added to the SUBJ f-structure, (27e–27f) yield the TENSE and PRED functions in the f_1–f_3 structure, and (27g–27m) complete the OBJ and OBJ2 place-holders. Equation (27l) is similar to (27c) in that it duplicates another equation in the f-description and hence does not have an independent effect on the final result. After considering all the equations in (27), we arrive at the final f-structure (40):

(40)
$$f_1, f_3: \begin{bmatrix} \text{SUBJ} & f_2:\begin{bmatrix} \text{SPEC} & \text{A} \\ \text{NUM} & \text{SG} \\ \text{PRED} & \text{'girl'} \end{bmatrix} \\ \text{TENSE} & \text{PAST} \\ \text{PRED} & \text{'hand}\langle(\uparrow \text{ SUBJ}), (\uparrow \text{ OBJ}), (\uparrow \text{ OBJ2})\rangle\text{'} \\ \text{OBJ} & f_4:\begin{bmatrix} \text{SPEC} & \text{THE} \\ \text{NUM} & \text{SG} \\ \text{PRED} & \text{'baby'} \end{bmatrix} \\ \text{OBJ2} & f_5:\begin{bmatrix} \text{SPEC} & \text{A} \\ \text{NUM} & \text{SG} \\ \text{PRED} & \text{'toy'} \end{bmatrix} \end{bmatrix}$$

Since f_1 is the ↓-variable of the root node of the tree (24), the outer f-structure is what our simple grammar assigns to the string. This is just the structure in (5), if the variable prefixes and the order of pairs are ignored.

This example is special in that the argument positions of all the function-application designators are filled with symbol designators. Certain grammatical situations give rise to less restricted designators, where the argument position is filled with another function-application. This is possible because symbols have a dual status in our formalism: they can serve in an f-structure both as attributes and as values. These more general designators permit the grammatical relation assigned to the ↓ f-structure at a given node to be determined by internal features of that f-structure rather than by the position of that node in the c-structure. The arguments to a large number of English verbs, for instance, may appear as the objects of particular prepositions instead of as SUBJ, OBJ, or OBJ2 noun phrases. In our theory, the lexical entry for a "case-marking" preposition indicates that its object noun phrase may be treated as what has traditionally been called a verb's *oblique object*. The semantic form for the verb then specifies how to map that oblique object into the appropriate argument of the predicate.

The *to* alternative for the double-NP realization of *handed* provides a simple illustration. The contrasting sentence to our previous example (2) is (10), repeated here for convenience:

(41) A girl handed a toy to the baby.

The c-structure for this sentence with a set of ↓-variables for the functionally relevant nodes is shown in (42). It includes a prepositional phrase following the object NP, as permitted by the new c-structure rules (43):[14]

(42)

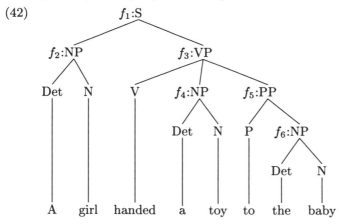

---

[14]We use the standard context-free abbreviation for optionality, parentheses that enclose categories and schemata. Thus, (43a) also derives intransitive and transitive verb phrases. Optionality parentheses should not be confused with the function-application parentheses within schemata. We also use braces in rules to indicate alternative c-structure expansions.

(43) a. VP $\longrightarrow$

$$V \quad \begin{pmatrix} NP \\ (\uparrow\ \text{OBJ})=\downarrow \end{pmatrix} \quad \begin{pmatrix} NP \\ (\uparrow\ \text{OBJ2})=\downarrow \end{pmatrix} \quad \begin{matrix} PP^* \\ (\uparrow\ (\downarrow\ \text{PCASE}))=\downarrow \end{matrix}$$

b. PP $\longrightarrow$ P   NP
(\uparrow OBJ)=\downarrow

The PP element in (43a) exhibits two new rule features. The asterisk on the PP category symbol is the Kleene-star operator; it indicates that that rule element may be repeated any number of times, including none.[15] The schema on the PP specifies that the value of the PCASE attribute in the PP's f-structure determines the functional role assigned to that structure. Because the lexical schemata from *to* are attached to the Prep node, that feature percolates up to the f-structure at the PP node. Suppose that *to* has the case-marking lexical entry shown in (44a)[16] and that *handed* has the entry (44b) as an alternative to the one given in (22). Then the PP f-structure serves the TO function, as shown in (45).

(44) a. *to*   P   ($\uparrow$ PCASE) = TO
b. *handed*   V   ($\uparrow$ TENSE) = PAST
($\uparrow$ PRED)='hand $\langle(\uparrow$ SUBJ$), (\uparrow$ OBJ$), (\uparrow$ TO OBJ$)\rangle$'

---

[15]Our c-structure rules thus diverge from a strict context-free formalism. We permit the right-hand sides of these rules to be regular expressions as in a recursive transition network, not just simply-ordered category sequences. The * is therefore not interpreted as an abbreviation for an infinite number of phrase structure rules. As our theory evolves, we might incorporate other modifications to the c-structure formalism. For example, in a formalism which, although oriented towards systemic grammar descriptions, is closely related to ours, Kay (1979) uses patterns of partially-ordered grammatical relations to map between a linear string and his equivalent to an f-structure. Such partial orderings might be particularly well-suited for free word-order languages.

[16]The case-marking entry is distinct from the entry for *to* when it serves as a predicate in its own right, as in prepositional complements or adjuncts.

(45)

$$
\begin{bmatrix}
\text{SUBJ} & \begin{bmatrix} \text{SPEC} & \text{A} \\ \text{NUM} & \text{SG} \\ \text{PRED} & \text{`girl'} \end{bmatrix} \\
\text{TENSE} & \text{PAST} \\
\text{PRED} & \text{`hand}\langle(\uparrow \text{ SUBJ}), (\uparrow \text{ OBJ}), (\uparrow \text{ TO OBJ})\rangle\text{'} \\
\text{OBJ} & \begin{bmatrix} \text{SPEC} & \text{A} \\ \text{NUM} & \text{SG} \\ \text{PRED} & \text{`toy'} \end{bmatrix} \\
\text{TO} & \begin{bmatrix} \text{PCASE} & \text{TO} \\ \text{OBJ} & \begin{bmatrix} \text{SPEC} & \text{THE} \\ \text{NUM} & \text{SG} \\ \text{PRED} & \text{`baby'} \end{bmatrix} \end{bmatrix}
\end{bmatrix}
$$

The 'baby' f-structure is accessible as the TO OBJ, and it is correctly mapped onto the goal argument of 'hand' by the semantic form for *handed* in (44b) and (45). As mentioned earlier, this is systematically related to the semantic form in (22) by a dative lexical redundancy rule, so that the generalization marking sentences (2) and (41) as paraphrases is not lost.

Most of the statements in the f-description for (41) are either the same as or very similar to the statements in (25–27). The statements most relevant to the issue at hand are instantiated inside the prepositional phrase and at the PP node in the verb phrase:

(46) a. $(f_3 \ (f_5 \ \text{PCASE})) = f_5$ from PP in (43a)
      b. $(f_5 \ \text{PCASE}) = \text{TO}$ from *to*

The designator on the left side of (46a) is of course the crucial one. This is processed by first locating the values of f_3 and $(f_5 \ \text{PCASE})$, and then applying the first of these values to the second. If (46b) is processed before (46a), then the value of $(f_5 \ \text{PCASE})$ will be the symbol TO, and (46a) will thus receive the same treatment as the more restricted equations we considered above.

We cannot insist that the f-description be processed in this or any other order, however. Since equality is an equivalence relation, whether or not an f-structure is a solution to a given f-description is not a property of any ordering on the f-description statements. An order dependency in our algorithm would simply be an artifact of its operation. Unless we could prove that an acceptable order can be determined for any set of statements, we would run the risk of ordering paradoxes whereby our algorithm does not produce a solution even though satisfactory f-structures do exist. A potential order dependency arises only when one equation establishes relationships between entities that have not yet been defined. Place-holders serve in our algorithm as temporary surrogates for those unknown entities. Our examples above illustrate their use in representing simple relationships. Changing the order in which equations (46) are processed demonstrates that the proper treatment of more complicated cooccurrence relationships does not depend on a particular sequence of statements.

Suppose that (46a) is processed before (46b). Then the value of $(f_5 \text{ PCASE})$ will be a place-holder as shown in (47a), and f_3 will be assigned an f-structure with place-holders in both attribute and value positions, as in (47b):

(47) a. $\quad f_5$:[PCASE ——]

   b. $\quad f_3$:[—— ——]

The value of the larger designator $(f_3 \ (f_5 \text{ PCASE}))$ will thus be the second place-holder in (47b). When this is merged with the f-structure assigned to f_5, the result is (48):

(48) $\quad f_3$:[—— f_5:[PCASE ——]]

It is not clear from (48) that the two blank lines stand for the same place-holder. One way of indicating this fact is to annotate blank lines with an identifying index whenever they represent occurrences of the same place-holder in multiple contexts, as shown in (49). An alternative and perhaps more perspicuous way of marking the important formal relationships is to display the blank line in just one of the place-holder's positions and then draw connecting lines to its other occurrences, as in (50):

(49) $\quad f_3$:[——₁ f_5:[PCASE ——₁]]

(50) $\quad f_3$:[—— f_5:[PCASE ——]]

This problem of representation arises because our hierarchical f-structures are in fact directed graphs, not trees, so all the connections cannot easily be displayed in textual form. With the cooccurrences explicitly represented, processing equation (46b) causes the symbol TO to be substituted for the place-holder in both positions:

(51) $\quad f_3$:[TO f_5:[PCASE TO]]

The index or connecting line is no longer needed, because the common spelling of symbols in two positions suffices to indicate their formal identity. The structure (51) is combined with the result of processing the remaining equations in the f-description, yielding the final structure (45).

The Kleene-star operator on the PP in (43a) allows for sentences having more than one oblique object:

(52)   The toy was given to the baby by the girl.

The f-structure of this sentence will have both a TO OBJ and a BY OBJ. Because of the functional well-formedness conditions discussed in the next section, these grammatical relations are compatible only with a semantic form that results from the passive lexical rule:

(53)   'hand ⟨(↑ BY OBJ), (↑ SUBJ), (↑ TO OBJ)⟩'

Although the c-structure rule suggests that any number of oblique objects are possible, they are in fact strictly limited by semantic form specifications. Moreover, if two prepositional phrases have the same preposition and hence the same PCASE feature, the Uniqueness Condition implies that only one of them can serve as an argument. If the sentence is to be grammatical, the other must be interpreted as some sort of adjunct. In (54), either *the policeman* or *the boy* must be a nonargument locative:

(54)   The baby was found by the boy by the policeman.

Thus, the PP element in rule (43a) derives the PP nodes for dative *to* phrases, agentive *by* phrases, and other, more idiosyncratic English oblique objects. Schemata similar to the one on the PP will be much more common in languages that make extensive use of lexically as opposed to structurally induced grammatical relations (e.g., heavily case-marked, nonconfigurational languages).

We have illustrated how our algorithm builds the f-structure for two grammatical sentences. However, as indicated above, f-descriptions which contradict the Uniqueness Condition are not solvable, and our algorithm must also inform us of this inconsistency. Consistency checking is carried out by both the Locate and the Merge operators. The Locate operator, for example, cannot succeed if a statement specifies that a symbol or semantic form is to be applied as a function or if a function is to be applied to an f-structure or semantic form argument. The string is marked ungrammatical if this happens. Similarly, a merger cannot be completed if the two entities to be merged are incompatible, either because they are of different types (a symbol and an f-structure, for example) or because they are otherwise in conflict (two distinct symbols or semantic forms, or two f-structures that assign distinct values to the same argument). Again, this means that the f-description is inconsistent.

Our algorithm thus produces *one* solution for an arbitrary consistent f-description, but it is not the *only* solution. If an f-structure F is a solution for a given f-description, then any f-structure formed from F by adding values for attributes not already present will also satisfy the f-description. Since the f-description does not mention those attributes or values, they cannot conflict with any of its statements. For example, we could add the arbitrary pairs X–Y and Z–W to the SUBJ f-structure of (40) to form (55):

(55)
$$f_2: \begin{bmatrix} \text{SPEC} & \text{A} \\ \text{NUM} & \text{SG} \\ \text{PRED} & \text{'girl'} \\ \text{X} & \text{Y} \\ \text{Z} & \text{W} \end{bmatrix}$$

Substituting this for the original SUBJ value yields another solution for (25–27). This addition procedure, which defines a partial ordering on the set of f-structures, can be repeated indefinitely. In general, if an f-description has one solution, it has an infinite number of "larger" solutions.

Of course, there is something counterintuitive about these larger solutions. The extra features they contain cannot conflict with those specifically required by the f-description. In that sense they are grammatically irrelevant and should not really count as f-structures that the grammar assigns to sentences. This intuition, that we only countenance f-structures with relevant attributes and values, can be formalized in a technical refinement to our previous definitions that makes "*the* f-structure of a sentence" a well-defined notion.

Looking at the partial ordering from the opposite direction, an f-description may also have solutions smaller than a given one. These are formed by removing various combinations of its pairs (for example, removing the X–Y, Z–W pairs from (55) produces the smaller original solution in (40). Some smaller f-structures are too small to be solutions of the f-description, in that they do not contain pairs that the f-description requires. For example, if the SPEC feature is removed from (55), the resulting structure will not satisfy equation (27a). We say that an f-structure F is a *minimal* solution for an f-description if it meets all of the f-description's requirements and if no smaller f-structure also meets those requirements.

A minimal solution exists for every consistent f-description. By definition, each has at least one solution. Either that one is minimal, or there is a smaller solution. If that one is also not minimal, there is another, still smaller, solution. Since an f-structure has only a finite number of pairs to begin with, there are only a finite number of smaller f-structures. This sequence will therefore stop at a minimal solution after a finite number of steps.

However, the minimal solution of an f-description is not necessarily unique. The fact that f-structures are partially but not totally ordered means that there can be two distinct solutions to an f-description both of which are minimal but neither of which is smaller than the other.

This would be the case for an f-description that contained the equation
(56), asserting that the subject and object have the same person, if other
equations were not included to specify that common feature's value.

(56) († SUBJ PERS) = († OBJ PERS)

Any f-structure that is a minimal solution for all other equations of the f-
description and contains any value at all for both the OBJ and SUBJ person
features will also be a minimal solution for the larger f-description that
includes (56). The values FIRST, SECOND, or THIRD, for instance, would
all satisfy (56), but an f-structure without *some* person value would not be
a solution. An f-description that does not have a unique minimal solution
is called *indeterminate*. In effect, such an f-description does not have
enough independent specifications for the number of unknown entities
that it mentions.

We can now formulate a precise condition on the well-formedness of a
string:

(57) *Condition on Grammaticality*
      A string is grammatical only if it has a valid c-structure with
      an associated f-description that is both consistent and determi-
      nate. The f-structure assigned to the string is the value in the
      f-description's unique minimal solution of the ↓-variable of the
      c-structure's root node.

This condition is necessary but not sufficient for grammaticality; we later
postulate additional requirements. As presented above, our solution algorithm decides whether or not the f-description is consistent and, if it is,
constructs one solution for it. We observe that if no place-holders remain
in that solution, it is the unique minimal solution: if any attribute or value
is changed or removed, the resulting structure is not a solution since it
no longer satisfies the equation the processing of which gave rise to that
attribute or value. On the other hand, if there are residual place-holders
in the f-structure produced by the algorithm, the f-description is indeterminate. Those place-holders can be replaced by any number of values to
yield minimal solutions. Our algorithm is thus a decision procedure for
all the functional conditions on grammaticality specified in (57).

5   Functional well-formedness

The functional well-formedness conditions of our theory cause strings with
otherwise valid c-structures to be marked ungrammatical. Our functional
component thus acts as a filter on the output of the c-structure component, but in a sense that is very different from the way surface structure
filtering has been used in transformational theory (e.g., Chomsky and

Lasnik 1977). We do not allow arbitrary predicates to be applied to the c-structure output. Rather, we expect that a substantive linguistic theory will make available a universal set of grammatical functions and features and indicate how these may be assigned to particular lexical items and particular c-structure configurations. The most important of our well-formedness conditions, the Uniqueness Condition,[17] merely ensures that these assignments for a particular sentence are globally consistent so that its f-structure exists. Other general well-formedness conditions, the Completeness and Coherence Conditions, guarantee that grammatical functions and lexical predicates appear in mutually compatible f-structure configurations.

Consider the string (58), which is ungrammatical because the numbers of the final determiner and noun disagree:

(58) *A girl handed the baby a toys.

The only f-description difference between this and our previous example is that the lexical entry for *toys* produces the equation (59) instead of (271):

(59) $(f_5 \text{ NUM}) = \text{PL}$

A conflict between the lexical specifications for *a* and *toys* arises because their schemata are attached to daughters of the same NP node. Some of the properties of that node's f-structure are specified by the determiner's lexical schemata and some by the noun's. According to the Uniqueness Condition, all properties attributed to it must be compatible if that f-structure is to exist. In the solution process for (58), f_5 will have the tentative value shown in (60) when equation (59) is encountered in place of (271). The value of the left-hand designator is the symbol SG, which is incompatible with the PL value of the right-hand designator. These two symbols cannot be merged.

(60) $f_5: \begin{bmatrix} \text{SPEC} & \text{A} \\ \text{NUM} & \text{SG} \end{bmatrix}$

The consistency requirement is a general mechanism for enforcing grammatical compatibilities among lexical items widely separated in the

---

[17]Our general Uniqueness Condition is also the most crucial of several differences between lexical-functional grammar and its augmented transition network precursor. ATN SETR operations can arbitrarily modify the f-structure values (or "register contents", in ATN terminology) as they are executed in a left-to-right scan of a rule or network. The register SUBJ can have one value at one point in a rule and a completely different value at a subsequent point. This revision of value assignments is not allowed in LFG. Equations at one point cannot override equations instantiated elsewhere—all equations must be simultaneously satisfied by the values in a single f-structure. As we have seen, the properties of that f-structure thus do not depend on the particular sequence of steps by which schemata are instantiated or the f-description is solved.

c-structure. The items and features that will enter into an agreement are determined by both lexical and grammatical schemata. Number agreement for English subjects and verbs illustrates a compatibility that operates over a somewhat wider scope than agreement for determiners and nouns. It accounts for the unacceptability of (61):

(61) *The girls hands the baby a toy.

The grammar fragment in (21) needs no further elaboration in order to reject this string. The identification on the VP in (21a) indicates that one f-structure corresponds to both the S and the VP nodes. This implies that any constraints imposed on a SUBJ function by the verb will in fact apply to the SUBJ of the sentence as a whole, the f-structure corresponding to the first NP. Thus, the following lexical entry for *hands* ensures that it will not cooccur with the plural subject *girls*:

(62) *hands* V $(\uparrow$ TENSE$) = $ PRES
$(\uparrow$ SUBJ NUM$) = $ SG
$(\uparrow$ PRED$) = $ 'hand $\langle(\uparrow$ SUBJ$),(\uparrow$ OBJ$),(\uparrow$ OBJ2$)\rangle$ '

The middle schema, which is contributed by the present tense morpheme, specifies the number of the verb's subject. It is instantiated as (63a), and this is inconsistent with (63b), which would be derived from the lexical entry for *girls*:

(63) a. $(f_3$ SUBJ NUM$) = $ SG
b. $(f_2$ NUM$) = $ PL

The conflict emerges because f_2 is the SUBJ of f_1, and f_1 is equal to f_3.

We rely on violations of the Uniqueness Condition to enforce many cooccurrence restrictions besides those that are normally thought of as agreements. For example, the restrictions among the elements in an English auxiliary sequence can be handled in this way, even though the matching of features does not at first seem to be involved. There is a natural way of coding the lexical features of auxiliaries, participles, and tensed verbs so that the "affix-hopping" phenomena follow as a consequence of the consistency requirement. Auxiliaries can be treated as main verbs that take embedded VP' complements. We expand our grammar as shown in (64) in order to derive the appropriate c-structures:[18]

---

[18]The optional *to* permitted by rule (64b), while necessary for other types of VP complements, does not appear with most auxiliary heads. This restriction could be imposed by an additional schema.

(64) a. VP $\longrightarrow$

$$V \quad \begin{pmatrix} NP \\ (\uparrow OBJ)=\downarrow \end{pmatrix} \quad \begin{pmatrix} NP \\ (\uparrow OBJ2)=\downarrow \end{pmatrix} \quad \begin{matrix} PP^* \\ (\uparrow (\downarrow PCASE))=\downarrow \end{matrix} \quad \begin{pmatrix} VP' \\ (\uparrow VCOMP)=\downarrow \end{pmatrix}$$

     b.   VP' $\longrightarrow$ (*to*)   VP
                                $\uparrow=\downarrow$

Rule (64a) allows an optional VP' following the other VP constituents. Of course, auxiliaries exclude all the VP possibilities except the VCOMP; this is enforced by general completeness and coherence conventions, as described below. For the moment, we focus on their affix cooccurrence restrictions, which are represented by schemata in the lexical entries for verbs. Each nonfinite verb will have a schema indicating that it is an infinitive or a participle of a particular type, and each auxiliary will have an equation stipulating the inflectional form of its VCOMP.[19] The lexical entries in (65–66) are for *handing* considered as a present participle (as opposed to a past tense or passive participle form) and for *is* as a progressive auxiliary:[20]

(65)   *handing*   V $(\uparrow$ PARTICIPLE$) =$ PRESENT
                      $(\uparrow$ PRED$) =$ 'hand $\langle(\uparrow$ SUBJ$),(\uparrow$ OBJ$),(\uparrow$ OBJ2$)\rangle$ '

(66)   *is*   V   a. $(\uparrow$ TENSE$) =$ PRES
                      b. $(\uparrow$ SUBJ NUM$) =$ SG
                      c. $(\uparrow$ PRED$) =$ 'prog$\langle(\uparrow$ VCOMP$)\rangle$'
                      d. $(\uparrow$ VCOMP PARTICIPLE$) =$ PRESENT
                      e. $(\uparrow$ VCOMP SUBJ$) = (\uparrow$ SUBJ$)$

Schema (66d) stipulates that the PARTICIPLE feature of the verb phrase complement must have the value PRESENT. The VCOMP is defined in (64a) as the $\downarrow$ f-structure of the VP' node, and this is identified with the $\downarrow$ f-structure of the VP node by the schema in (64b). This means that the PARTICIPLE stipulations for *handing* and *is* both hold of the same f-structure. Hence, sentence (67a) is accepted but (67b) is rejected because *has* demands of its VCOMP a non-PRESENT participle:

(67)   a.   A girl is handing the baby a toy.

---

[19]A small number of additional features are needed to account for the finer details of auxiliary ordering and for other cooccurrence restrictions, as noted for example by Akmajian, Steele, and Wasow (1979).
[20]In a more detailed treatment of morphology, the schemata for *handing* would be derived systematically by combining the schemata for *hand* (namely, the PRED schema in (65)) with *ing*'s schemata (the PARTICIPLE specification) as the word is formed by suffixation.

   b. *A girl has handing the baby a toy.

   Schemata (66c,e) deserve special comment. The semantic form for *is* specifies that the logical formula derived by interpreting the VCOMP function is the single argument of a predicate for progressiveness. Even though the f-structure for (67a) will include a SUBJ function at the level of the PROG predicate, that function does not serve as an argument of PROG. Instead, it is asserted by (66e) to be equivalent to the SUBJ at the *handing* level. This would not otherwise exist, because there is no subject NP in the VP' expansion. The effect is that *girl* is correctly interpreted as the first argument of 'hand'. (66e) is an example of a schema for *functional control*, which we will discuss more fully below.

   These illustrations of the filtering effect of the Uniqueness Condition have glossed over an important conceptual distinction. A schema is often included in a lexical entry or grammatical rule in order to *define* the value of some feature. That is, instantiations of that schema provide sufficient grounds for inserting the feature–value pair into the appropriate f-structure (assuming of course that there is no conflict with the value defined by other equations). However, sometimes the purpose of a schema is only to *constrain* a feature whose value is expected to be defined by a separate specification. The feature remains valueless when the f-description lacks that specification. Intuitively, the constraint is not satisfied in that case and the string is to be excluded. Constraints of this sort thus impose stronger well-formedness requirements than the definitional inconsistency discussed above.

   Let us reexamine the restriction that schema (66d) imposes on the participle of the VCOMP of *is*. We have seen how this schema conspires with the lexical entries for *handing* (65) and *has* to account for the facts in (67). Intuitively, it seems that the same present-participle restriction ought to account for the unacceptability of (68):

   (68) *A girl is hands the baby a toy.

This string will not be rejected, however, if *hands* has the lexical entry in (62) and (66d) is interpreted as a defining schema. The PARTICIPLE feature has no natural value for the finite verb *hands*, and (62) therefore has no specification at all for this feature. This permits (66d) to define the value PRESENT for that feature without risk of inconsistency, and the final f-structure corresponding to the *hands* VP will actually contain a PARTICIPLE–PRESENT pair. We have concluded that *hands* is a present participle just because *is* would like it to be that way! If, on the other hand, we interpret (66d) as a constraining schema, we are prevented from making this implausible inference and the string is appropriately rejected. The constraining interpretation is clearly preferable.

Introducing a special interpretation for f-description statements is not strictly necessary to account for these facts. We could allow only the defining interpretation of equations and still obtain the right pattern of results by means of additional feature specifications. For example, we could insist that there be a PARTICIPLE feature for every verbal form, even finite forms that are notionally not participles at all. The value for tensed forms might be NONE, and this would be distinct from and thus conflict with PRESENT and all other real values. The lexical entry for *hands* would become (69), and (68) would be ruled out even with a defining interpretation for (66d):

(69) *hands*   V   ($\uparrow$ PARTICIPLE) = NONE
                    ($\uparrow$ TENSE) = PRES
                    ($\uparrow$ SUBJ NUM) = SG
                    ($\uparrow$ PRED) = 'hand $\langle(\uparrow$ SUBJ$), (\uparrow$ OBJ$), (\uparrow$ OBJ2$)\rangle$ '

There are two objections to the presence of such otherwise unmotivated features: they make the formal system more cumbersome for linguists to work with and less plausible as a characterization of the linguistic generalizations that children acquire. Lexical redundancy rules in the form of marking conventions provide a partial answer to both objections. A redundancy rule, for example, could assign special no-value schemata to every lexical entry that is not already marked for certain syntactic features. Then the NONE schema would not appear in the entry for *hands* but would still be available for consistency checking.

Although we utilize lexical redundancy rules to express a variety of other generalizations, we have chosen an explicit notational device to highlight the conceptual distinction between definitions and constraints. The ordinary equal-sign that has appeared in all previous examples indicates that a schema is definitional, while an equal-sign with the letter "c" as a subscript indicates that a schema expresses a constraint. With this notation, the lexical entry for *is* can be formulated more properly as (70):

(70) *is*   V   ($\uparrow$ TENSE) = PRES
                 ($\uparrow$ SUBJ NUM) = SG
                 ($\uparrow$ PRED) = 'prog$\langle(\uparrow$ VCOMP$)\rangle$'
                 ($\uparrow$ VCOMP PARTICIPLE) $=_c$ PRESENT
                 ($\uparrow$ VCOMP SUBJ) = ($\uparrow$ SUBJ)

The notational distinction is preserved when the schemata are instantiated, so that the statements in an f-description are also divided into two classes. Defining equations are interpreted by our solution algorithm in the manner outlined above and thus provide evidence for actually constructing satisfactory structures. Constraining equations are simply not given to the solution algorithm. They are reserved until all defining equations have been processed and all variables have been assigned final f-structure values. At that point, the constraining equations are evaluated, and the string is accepted only if they all turn out to be true. This difference in interpretation accurately reflects the conceptual distinction represented by the two types of equations. It also gives the right result for string (68): since the revised VCOMP requirement in (70) will be false for the f-structure constructed from its defining equations, that string will be rejected without adding the special NONE value to *hands*.

Whether or not a particular cooccurrence restriction should be enforced by consistency among defining equations or the later evaluation of constraining equations depends on the meaning that is most naturally assigned to the absence of a feature specification. A constraining equation is appropriate if, as in the examples above, an unspecified value is intended to be in conflict with all of a feature's real values. On the other hand, a value specification may be omitted for some features as an indication of vagueness, and the restriction is then naturally stated in terms of a defining equation.[21] The case features of English nouns seem to fall into this second category: only pronouns have explicit nominative/accusative markings; all other nouns are intuitively unmarked yet may appear in either subject or object positions. The new subject-NP schema in (71) defines the subject's case to be NOM. The NOM value will thus be included in the f-structure for any sentence with a nominative pronoun or nonpronoun subject. Only strings with accusative pronouns in subject position will have inconsistent f-descriptions and be excluded.

$$(71) \quad S \quad \longrightarrow \quad \begin{array}{cc} NP & VP \\ (\uparrow \text{ SUBJ}) = \downarrow & \uparrow = \downarrow \\ (\downarrow \text{ CASE}) = \text{NOM} & (\uparrow \text{ TENSE}) \end{array}$$

Defining schemata always assert particular values for features and thus always take the form of equations. For constraints, two nonequational specification formats also make sense. The new TENSE schema in (71), for example, is just a designator not embedded in an equality. An instantiation of such a constraint is satisfied just in case the expression has *some* value in the final f-structure; these are called *existential* constraints. The TENSE schema thus expresses the requirement that S-clauses must have tensed verbs and rules out strings like (72):

---

[21]A marking convention account of the defining/constraining distinction would have to provide an alternative lexical entry for each value that the vaguely specified feature could assume. A vague specification would thus be treated as an ambiguity, contrary to intuition.

(72) *A girl handing the baby a toy.

As with equational constraints, it is possible to achieve the effect of an existential schema by introducing ad hoc feature values (e.g., one that discriminates tensed forms from all other verbals), but this special constraint format more directly represents the intuitive content of the requirement.

Finally, constraints may also be formed by adding a negation operator to an equational or existential constraint. The sentence is then acceptable only if the constraint without the negation turns out to be false. Such constraints fall quite naturally within our formal framework and may simplify a variety of grammatical descriptions. The negative existential constraint in (73), for example, is one way of stipulating that the VP after the particle *to* in a VP′ is untensed:

$$(73) \quad \text{VP}' \longrightarrow \quad \begin{pmatrix} to \\ \neg(\uparrow \text{ TENSE}) \end{pmatrix} \quad \begin{matrix} \text{VP} \\ \uparrow = \downarrow \end{matrix}$$

According to these well-formedness conditions, strings are rejected when an f-structure cannot be found that simultaneously satisfies all the explicit defining and constraining statements in the f-description. LFG also includes implicit conventions whose purpose is to make sure that f-structures contain mutually compatible combinations of lexical predicates and grammatical functions. These conventions are defined in terms of a proper subset of all the features and functions that may be represented in an f-structure. That subset consists of all functions whose values can serve as arguments to semantic predicates,[22] such as subject and various objects and complements. We refer to these as the *governable grammatical functions*. A given lexical entry mentions only a few of the governable functions, and we say that that entry *governs* the ones it mentions.[23] Our conditions of functional compatibility simply require that an f-structure contain all of the governable functions that the lexical entry of its predicate actually governs, and that it contain no other governable functions.

This compatibility requirement gives a natural account for many types of ill-formedness. The English c-structure grammar, for example, must permit verbs not followed by NP arguments so that ordinary intransitive sentences can be generated. However, the intransitive VP rule can then be applied with a verb that normally requires objects to yield a c-structure and f-structure for ill-formed strings such as (74):

(74) *The girl handed.

---

[22] In the more refined theory of lexical representation presented in Bresnan (1982b,c), the relevant functions are those that appear in the function-assignment lists of lexical predicates. The two characterizations are essentially equivalent.

[23] For a fuller discussion of government in lexical-functional theory, see Bresnan (1982a).

The unacceptability of this string follows from the fact that the lexical entry for *handed* governs the grammatical functions OBJ and OBJ2 or TO OBJ, which do not appear in its f-structure. On the other hand, there is nothing to stop the c-structure rule that generates objects from applying in strings such as (75), where the verb is intransitive.

(75) *The girl fell the apple the dog.

This string exhibits the opposite kind of incompatibility: the governable functions OBJ and OBJ2 do appear in its f-structure but are not governed by the intransitive verb *fell*.

Stated in more technical terms, string (74) is ungrammatical because its f-structure is not *complete* while (75) fails because its f-structure is not *coherent*. These properties of f-structures are precisely defined as follows:

(76) *Definitions of Completeness and Coherence*
   (a) An f-structure is *locally complete* if and only if it contains all the governable grammatical functions that its predicate governs. An f-structure is *complete* if and only if it and all its subsidiary f-structures are locally complete.
   (b) An f-structure is *locally coherent* if and only if all the governable grammatical functions that it contains are governed by a local predicate. An f-structure is *coherent* if and only if it and all its subsidiary f-structures are locally coherent.

Functional compatibility then enters into our notion of grammaticality by way of the following obvious condition:

(77) *Grammaticality Condition*
   A string is grammatical only if it is assigned a complete and coherent f-structure.

Since coherence and completeness are defined in terms of local configurations of functions, there are straightforward ways of formally verifying that these conditions are satisfied. For example, a set of constraints that encode these requirements can be added to all f-descriptions by a simple redundancy convention. We identify a set of *governable designators* corresponding to the governable grammatical functions and a set of *governed designators* corresponding to the functions governed by a particular lexical entry. The set of governable designators for a language is simply a list of every designator that appears as an argument in a semantic form for at least one entry in the lexicon. Thus the set of governable designators for English includes ($\uparrow$ SUBJ), ($\uparrow$ OBJ), ($\uparrow$ BY OBJ), ($\uparrow$ VCOMP), etc. The set of governed designators for a particular lexical entry then contains only those members of the governable list that appear in that entry. If existential constraints for all the governed designators are instantiated along with the other schemata in the lexical entry, then the f-structure in which the lexical predicate appears will be locally complete if and only if it satisfies all those constraints. The f-structure will be locally coherent if and only if *negative* existential constraints for all the governable but ungoverned designators are also satisfied. Under this interpretation, example (74) above is incomplete because its f-structure does not satisfy the constraining schema (↑ OBJ) and (75) is incoherent because ¬(↑ OBJ) is not satisfied.

It is important to observe that a designator is considered to be governed by an entry if it appears anywhere in the entry, not solely in the semantic form argument-list (though to be governable, it must appear as an argument in *some* lexical entry). In particular, the designator may appear only in a functional control schema or only in a schema defining or constraining some feature. Thus, the lexical entry for *is* in (66) above is considered to govern the designator (↑ SUBJ) because of its appearance in both the number-defining schema and the control schema for the VCOMP's SUBJ. (↑ SUBJ), however, is not assigned to an argument in the semantic form 'prog⟨(↑ VCOMP)⟩'.

A grammatical function is also considered to be governed by an entry even when its value is constrained to be a semantically empty syntactic formative. Among these formatives are the expletives *there* and *it*, plus the components of various idiomatic expressions (e.g., the idiomatic sense of *tabs* in the expression *keep tabs on*). The lexicon marks such items as being in ordinary syntactic categories (pronoun or noun, for example), but their schemata specify a symbol value for a FORM attribute instead of a semantic form value for a PRED attribute:

(78)   *tabs*   N   (↑ FORM) = TABS
                       (↑ NUM) = PL

A *tabs* NP may appear in any c-structure NP position and will be assigned the associated grammatical function. The Coherence Condition ensures that that function is governed by the lexical head of the f-structure; (79) is ruled out for the same reason that (75) is ill-formed:

(79) *The girl fell tabs.

If the f-structure is coherent, then its lexical head makes some specification about the *tabs* function. For the acceptable sentence (80), the lexical entry for the idiomatic *kept* has a constraining schema for the necessary FORM value, as illustrated in (81):

(80)   The girl kept tabs on the baby.

(81) *kept*   V $(\uparrow$ TENSE$) =$ PAST
                     $(\uparrow$ PRED$) =$ 'observe $\langle(\uparrow$ SUBJ$)$, $(\uparrow$ ON OBJ$)\rangle$
                     $(\uparrow$ OBJ FORM$) =_c$ TABS

This constraining schema precludes the OBSERVE reading of *kept* with the nonidiomatic OBJ in (82a) and also rejects OBJ's with the wrong formative feature (82b):

(82) a. *The girl kept the dog on a baby.
      b. *The girl kept there on a baby.

The ill-formedness of (83), however, is not predicted from the functional compatibility conditions we have presented:

(83) *The girl handed there tabs.

In this example a governed function serving as an argument to the predicate 'hand' has a semantically empty value. A separate condition of semantic completeness could easily be added to our grammaticality requirements, but such a restriction would be imposed independently by a semantic translation procedure. A separate syntactic stipulation is therefore unnecessary.

In this section we have described several mechanisms for rejecting as functionally deviant strings that have otherwise valid c-structure derivations. The Uniqueness Condition is the most basic well-formedness requirement, since an f-structure does not even exist if it is not satisfied. If an f-structure does exist, it must satisfy any constraining schemata and the Completeness and Coherence Conditions must hold. The combined effect of these conventions is to impose very strong restrictions among the components of a sentence's f-structure and c-structure, so that semantic forms and grammatical formatives can appear only in the appropriate functional and constituent environments. Because of these functional well-formedness conditions, there is no need for a separate notion of c-structure subcategorization to guarantee that lexical cooccurrence restrictions are satisfied. Indeed, Grimshaw (1982) and Maling (1980) suggest that an account of lexical cooccurrences based on functional compatibility is superior to one based on subcategorization.

These mechanisms ensure that syntactic compatibility holds between a predicate and its arguments. A sentence may have other elements, however, that are syntactically related to the predicate but are not syntactically restricted by it. These are the adverbial and prepositional modifiers that serve as *adjuncts* of a predicate. Although adjuncts and predicates must be associated in an f-structure so that the correct semantic relationship can be determined, adjuncts are not within range of a predicate's syntactic schemata. A predicate imposes neither category nor feature restrictions on its adjuncts, semantic appropriateness being the only requirement that must be satisfied. As the temporal adjuncts in sentence (84) illustrate, adjuncts do not even obey the Uniqueness Condition.

(84)   The girl handed the baby a toy on Tuesday in the morning.

Since adjuncts do not serve as arguments to lexical predicates, they are not governable functions and are thus also immune to the Completeness and Coherence Conditions.

Given the formal devices we have so far presented, there is no f-structure representation of adjuncts that naturally accounts for these properties. If an individual adjunct is assigned as the value of an attribute (e.g., TEMP, LOC, or simply ADJUNCT), the Uniqueness Condition is immediately applicable and syntactic cooccurrence restrictions can in principle be stated. However, the shared properties of adjuncts do follow quite naturally from a simple extension to the notion of what a possible value is. Besides the individual f-structure values for the basic grammatical relations, we allow the value of an attribute to be a *set* of f-structures. Values of this type are specified by a new kind of schema in which the membership symbol $\in$ appears instead of a defining or constraining equal-sign.

The membership schema $\downarrow \in (\uparrow$ ADJUNCTS$)$ in the VP rule (85), for example, indicates that the value of ADJUNCTS is a set containing the PP's f-structure as one of its elements.

(85)   VP $\longrightarrow$ V   NP   NP   PP*

$\qquad\qquad\qquad\qquad$ ($\uparrow$ OBJ)=$\downarrow$ ($\uparrow$ OBJ2)=$\downarrow$ $\downarrow \in$ ($\uparrow$ ADJUNCTS)

The * permits any number of adjuncts to be generated, and the $\downarrow$ metavariable will be instantiated differently for each one. The f-description for sentence (84) will thus have two membership statements, one for the *on Tuesday* PP and one for *in the morning*. These statements will be true only of an f-structure in which ADJUNCTS has a set value containing one element that satisfies all other statements associated with *on Tuesday* and another element satisfying the other statements of *in the morning*. The outline of such an f-structure is shown in (86):

(86)

$$
\begin{bmatrix}
\text{SUBJ} & \begin{bmatrix} \text{SPEC} & \text{A} \\ \text{NUM} & \text{SG} \\ \text{PRED} & \text{`girl'} \end{bmatrix} \\[4pt]
\text{TENSE} & \text{PAST} \\
\text{PRED} & \text{`hand} \langle (\uparrow \text{ SUBJ}), (\uparrow \text{ OBJ}), (\uparrow \text{ OBJ2}) \rangle \text{'} \\[4pt]
\text{OBJ} & \begin{bmatrix} \text{SPEC} & \text{THE} \\ \text{NUM} & \text{SG} \\ \text{PRED} & \text{`baby'} \end{bmatrix} \\[4pt]
\text{OBJ2} & \begin{bmatrix} \text{SPEC} & \text{A} \\ \text{NUM} & \text{SG} \\ \text{PRED} & \text{`toy'} \end{bmatrix} \\[4pt]
\text{ADJUNCTS} & \{ \text{ "ON TUESDAY" "IN THE MORNING" } \}
\end{bmatrix}
$$

The braces in this representation surround the elements of the set value; they are distinct from the braces in c-structure rules that indicate alternative expansions. We have elided the adjuncts' internal functions since they are not immediately relevant to the issue at hand and are the topic of current syntactic and semantic research (e.g., Neidle 1982; Halvorsen 1982).

The peculiar properties of adjuncts now follow from the fact that they are treated syntactically as elements of sets. Membership statements define adjuncts to be elements of a predicate's adjunct "pool", but there is no requirement of mutual syntactic compatibility among the various elements. Hence, the Uniqueness Condition does not apply. Further, since there is no notation for subsequently referring to particular members of that set, there is no way that adjuncts can be restricted by lexical schemata associated with the predicate.[24] Adjuncts are susceptible only to conditions that can be stated on the rule elements that generate them. Their category can be specified, and feature requirements can be imposed by schemata involving the $\downarrow$ metavariable. Since reference to the adjunct via $\downarrow$ is not possible from other places in the string, our formal system makes adjuncts naturally context-free.[25]

Although the PP in (85) appears in the same position as the oblique object PP category in our previous VP rule, the schemata on the two PP rule elements are quite different and apply to alternative lexical entries of the preposition. The oblique object requires the case-marking lexical

---

[24]Unless, of course, the element is also the non-set value of another attribute. The point is that the element is inaccessible in its role as adjunct. An interesting consequence of this representation is that no cooccurrence restrictions between temporal adverbs and tense can be stated in the syntax, a conclusion justified independently by Smith (1978).

[25]Conjoined elements are similar to adjuncts in some of these respects and might also be represented in an f-structure as sets.

entry (with the PCASE feature defined), while semantic translation of the adjunct requires the predicate alternative of the preposition. Adjuncts and oblique objects can both appear in the same sentence and in any order, as illustrated by (87a,b),[26] and sometimes a PP may be interpreted ambiguously as either an adjunct or an oblique object, as in (87c):

(87) a. The baby was handed the toy at five o'clock by the girl.
     b. The baby was handed the toy by the girl at five o'clock.
     c. The baby was handed the toy by the girl by the policeman.

To account for these facts, the adjunct possibility must be added as an alternative to the oblique object PP in our previous VP rule (64a). The star operator outside the braces in (88) means that the choice between the two PP's may be repeated arbitrarily.

(88) VP $\longrightarrow$

$$
V \begin{pmatrix} NP \\ (\uparrow OBJ)=\downarrow \end{pmatrix} \begin{pmatrix} NP \\ (\uparrow OBJ2)=\downarrow \end{pmatrix} \left\{ \begin{matrix} PP \\ (\uparrow(\downarrow PCASE))=\downarrow \\ PP \\ \downarrow\in(\uparrow ADJUNCTS) \end{matrix} \right\}^{*} \begin{pmatrix} VP' \\ (\uparrow VCOMP)=\downarrow \end{pmatrix}
$$

An equivalent but more compact formulation of this rule is given in (89). We have factored the common elements of the two PP alternatives, moving the braces so that they enclose just the alternative schemata.

(89) VP $\longrightarrow$

$$
V \begin{pmatrix} NP \\ (\uparrow OBJ)=\downarrow \end{pmatrix} \begin{pmatrix} NP \\ (\uparrow OBJ2)=\downarrow \end{pmatrix} \begin{matrix} PP^{*} \\ \left\{ \begin{matrix} (\uparrow(\downarrow PCASE))=\downarrow \\ \downarrow\in(\uparrow ADJUNCTS) \end{matrix} \right\} \end{matrix} \begin{pmatrix} VP' \\ (\uparrow VCOMP)=\downarrow \end{pmatrix}
$$

A simple extension to our solution algorithm permits the correct interpretation of membership statements. We use a new operator *Include* for membership statements, just as we use Merge for equalities. If d_1 and d_2 are designators, a statement of the form $d_1 \in d_2$ is processed by performing Include[Locate[d_1], Locate[d_2]]. As formally defined in the Appendix, the Include operator makes the value located for the first designator be an element of the set value located for the second designator; the f-description is marked inconsistent if that second value is known not to be a set. With this extension our algorithm becomes a decision procedure for f-descriptions that contain both membership and equality statements.

---

[26]There is sometimes a preferred ordering of adjuncts and oblique objects. Grammatical descriptions might not be the proper account of these biases; they might result from independent factors operating in the psychological perception and production processes. See Ford, Bresnan, and Kaplan (1982) for further discussion.

6 Levels of representation

We have now covered almost all the major structures and mechanisms of lexical-functional grammar, except for the bounded tree relations that govern long-distance grammatical dependencies. We postpone that discussion for still a few more pages in order to first review and reinforce some earlier claims.

We said at the outset that constituent structures and functional structures are formally quite different, and the descriptions of the preceding pages have amplified that point considerably. However, the mechanisms of our formal system—the immediate domination metavariables and the various grammatical and lexical schemata—presuppose and also help to establish a very close, systematic connection between the two levels of representation. Our claim of formal distinctness would of course be meaningless if this close connection turned out to be an isomorphism, so it is worth describing and motivating some ways in which c-structures and f-structures for English diverge. We show that individual c-structure nodes are not isomorphic to subsidiary f-structures for particular sentences and, more generally, that there is no simple relationship between node configurations and grammatical functions.

We observe first that our instantiation procedure defines only a partial correspondence between c-structure nodes and subsidiary f-structures. There are both c-structure nodes with no corresponding f-structures and also f-structures that do not correspond to c-structure nodes. The former situation is illustrated in our previous examples by every c-structure node which is not assigned a $\downarrow$-variable and therefore has no $\downarrow$ f-structure. The English imperative construction gives a simple illustration of the latter case: the subsidiary f-structure representing 'you' as the "understood" subject is not associated with a c-structure node. Plausible c- and f-structures for the imperative sentence (90a) would be generated by the alternative expansion for S in (90b), assuming that the lexical entry for *hand* has a +-valued INF(initive) feature:[27]

(90) a. Hand the baby a toy.

   b. S $\longrightarrow$ VP
   $$\uparrow = \downarrow$$
   $$(\uparrow \text{ INF})=_c +$$
   $$(\uparrow \text{ SUBJ PRED}) = \text{'you'}$$

With this rule, the c-structure contains no NP dominated by S, yet the $\downarrow$

---

[27] A more realistic example would specify an imperative mood marker and perhaps other features.

f-structure of the S node has as its SUBJ another full-fledged f-structure, defined completely by grammatical schemata:

(91)

$$
\begin{bmatrix}
\text{SUBJ} & \begin{bmatrix} \text{PRED} & \text{'you'} \end{bmatrix} \\
\text{INF} & + \\
\text{PRED} & \text{'hand}\langle(\uparrow \text{ SUBJ}), (\uparrow \text{ OBJ}), (\uparrow \text{ OBJ2})\rangle\text{'} \\
\text{OBJ} & \begin{bmatrix} \text{SPEC} & \text{THE} \\ \text{NUM} & \text{SG} \\ \text{PRED} & \text{'baby'} \end{bmatrix} \\
\text{OBJ2} & \begin{bmatrix} \text{SPEC} & \text{A} \\ \text{NUM} & \text{SG} \\ \text{PRED} & \text{'toy'} \end{bmatrix}
\end{bmatrix}
$$

A standard transformational grammar provides a dummy NP as a deep structure subject so that the correct semantic interpretation can be constructed and the necessary cooccurrence restrictions enforced. Our functional subject is sufficient for these purposes; the dummy NP is without surface justification and therefore does not appear in the c-structure.

Second, when nodes and subsidiary f-structures do correspond, the correspondence is not necessarily one-to-one. An identification schema, for example, usually indicates that two distinct nodes are mapped onto a single f-structure. In (40) a single f-structure is assigned to the ↓-variables for both the S and VP nodes in the c-structure given in (24), in accordance with the identification equation (25b). The two distinct nodes exist in (24) to capture certain generalizations about phrase structure cooccurrences and phonological patterns. The identification has the effect of "promoting" the functional information associated with the VP so that it is at the same hierarchical level as the SUBJ. This brings the SUBJ within range of the PRED semantic form, simplifying the statement of the Completeness and Coherence Conditions and allowing a uniform treatment of subjects and objects. As noted above, this kind of promotion also permits lexical specification of certain contextual restrictions, such as subject-verb number agreements.

Let us now consider the relationship between configurations of c-structure nodes and grammatical functions. The imperative example shows that a single functional role can be filled from distinct node configurations. While it is true for English that an S-dominated NP always yields a SUBJ function, a SUBJ can come from other sources as well. The grammatical schema on the VP for the imperative actually defines the SUBJ's semantic form. For a large class of other examples, the understood subject (that is, not from an S–NP configuration) is supplied through a schema of *functional control*. Control schemata, which identify grammatical relations at two different levels in the f-structure hierarchy, offer a natural account for so-called "equi" and "raising" phenomena.[28]

Sentence (92) contains the equi-type verb *persuaded*. The intuitive interpretation of the *baby* NP in this sentence is as an argument of both PERSUADE and GO. This interpretation will be assigned if *persuaded* has the lexical entry (93), given our previous VP rule (88) and the new schemata in (94) for the VP''s optional *to*.

(92)   The girl persuaded the baby to go.

(93)   *persuaded*   V $(\uparrow \text{TENSE}) = \text{PAST}$
$(\uparrow \text{VCOMP TO}) =_c +$
$(\uparrow \text{VCOMP SUBJ}) = (\uparrow \text{OBJ})$
$(\uparrow \text{PRED}) = \text{'persuade} \langle (\uparrow \text{SUBJ}), (\uparrow \text{OBJ}), (\uparrow \text{VCOMP}) \rangle$

(94) $\text{VP}' \longrightarrow$ $\begin{pmatrix} to \\ (\uparrow \text{TO}) = + \\ (\uparrow \text{INF}) =_c + \end{pmatrix}$ $\begin{array}{c} \text{VP} \\ \uparrow = \downarrow \end{array}$

Our rules generate a c-structure in which *persuaded* is followed by an NP and a VP', where the VP' is expanded as a to-complement. This is shown in (95):

(95)

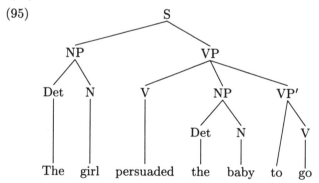

The f-structure for the *baby* NP becomes the OBJ of *persuaded* and the VP' provides the VCOMP. The control schema, the second to last one in (93), identifies the OBJ f-structure as also being the SUBJ of the VCOMP. That f-structure thus appears in two places in the functional hierarchy (96):

---

[28]The term *grammatical control* is sometimes used as a synonym for *functional control*. This kind of identification is distinct from *anaphoric control*, which links pronouns to their antecedents, and *constituent control*, which represents long-distance dependencies. Constituent control is discussed in Section 7. For discussions of functional and anaphoric control, see Andrews (1982b), Bresnan (1982a), Neidle (1982).

(96)

$$
\begin{bmatrix}
\text{SUBJ} & \begin{bmatrix} \text{SPEC} & \text{A} \\ \text{NUM} & \text{SG} \\ \text{PRED} & \text{'girl'} \end{bmatrix} \\[4ex]
\text{TENSE} & \text{PAST} \\
\text{PRED} & \text{'persuade} \langle(\uparrow \text{ SUBJ}), (\uparrow \text{ OBJ}), (\uparrow \text{ VCOMP})\rangle \\[1ex]
\text{OBJ} & \begin{bmatrix} \text{SPEC} & \text{THE} \\ \text{NUM} & \text{SG} \\ \text{PRED} & \text{'baby'} \end{bmatrix} \\[4ex]
\text{VCOMP} & \begin{bmatrix} \text{SUBJ} & \begin{bmatrix} \text{SPEC} & \text{THE} \\ \text{NUM} & \text{SG} \\ \text{PRED} & \text{'baby'} \end{bmatrix} \\[3ex] \text{INF} & + \\ \text{TO} & + \\ \text{PRED} & \text{'go} \langle(\uparrow \text{ SUBJ})\rangle \text{'} \end{bmatrix}
\end{bmatrix}
$$

The complement in this f-structure has essentially the same grammatical relations that would be assigned to the *that*-complement sentence (97), even though the c-structure for the *that*-complement is quite different:

(97)   The girl persuaded the baby that the baby (should) go.

The contrast between oblique objects and adjuncts shows that similar c-structure configurations—a VP dominating a PP—can be mapped into distinct grammatical functions. A comparison of the equi verbs *persuaded* and *promised* provides another illustration of the same point. Sentence (98) is the result of substituting *promised* for *persuaded* in sentence (92):

(98)   The girl promised the baby to go.

This substitution does not change the c-structure configurations, but for (98) the *girl*, not the *baby*, is understood as an argument of both the matrix and complement predicates. This fact is easily accounted for if the control schema in the lexical entry for *promised* identifies the complement SUBJ with the matrix SUBJ instead of the matrix OBJ:

(99)   *promised*   V $(\uparrow \text{ TENSE}) = \text{PAST}$
$(\uparrow \text{ PRED}) = \text{'promise} \langle(\uparrow \text{ SUBJ}), (\uparrow \text{ OBJ}), (\uparrow \text{ VCOMP})\rangle \text{'}$
$(\uparrow \text{ VCOMP TO}) =_c +$
$(\uparrow \text{ VCOMP SUBJ}) = (\uparrow \text{ SUBJ})$

With this lexical entry, the f-structure for (98) correctly defines 'girl' as the argument of 'go':

(100)

$$
\left[
\begin{array}{ll}
\text{SUBJ} & \left[
\begin{array}{ll}
\text{SPEC} & \text{A} \\
\text{NUM} & \text{SG} \\
\text{PRED} & \text{'girl'}
\end{array}
\right] \\
\text{TENSE} & \text{PAST} \\
\text{PRED} & \text{'promise} \langle (\uparrow \text{ SUBJ}), (\uparrow \text{ OBJ}), (\uparrow \text{ VCOMP}) \rangle \\
\text{OBJ} & \left[
\begin{array}{ll}
\text{SPEC} & \text{THE} \\
\text{NUM} & \text{SG} \\
\text{PRED} & \text{'baby'}
\end{array}
\right] \\
\text{VCOMP} & \left[
\begin{array}{ll}
\text{SUBJ} & \left[
\begin{array}{ll}
\text{SPEC} & \text{A} \\
\text{NUM} & \text{SG} \\
\text{PRED} & \text{'girl'}
\end{array}
\right] \\
\text{INF} & + \\
\text{TO} & + \\
\text{PRED} & \text{'go} \langle (\uparrow \text{ SUBJ}) \rangle \text{'}
\end{array}
\right]
\end{array}
\right]
$$

The f-structure difference for the two types of equi verbs thus follows from the differing functional control schemata in their lexical entries, not from any c-structure difference.

From a formal point of view, there is no restriction on which grammatical relations in the matrix and complement may be identified by a schema for functional control. Very strong limitations, however, are imposed by the substantive linguistic theory that is based on our lexical-functional formalism. As discussed by Bresnan (1982a), the functional control schemata of human languages universally identify the SUBJ of a complement with the SUBJ, OBJ, or OBJ2 of the matrix.[29] Control schemata for verb phrase complements different from those above for *promised* and *persuaded* may not appear in the grammar or lexicon of any human language. This universal stipulation explains the familiar contrast in the passivization behavior of *persuade* and *promise*:

(101) a. The baby was persuaded to go by the girl.

  b. *The baby was promised to go by the girl.

Bresnan (1982c) argues that the systematic relationship between actives and their corresponding passives can be expressed by a universal lexical rule. In simple terms, this rule asserts that for any language, if an active lexical entry for a stem mentions the SUBJ and OBJ functions, then there is a passive lexical entry based on the same stem in which SUBJ is replaced by an oblique-object function and OBJ is replaced by SUBJ. For English,

---

[29]The TOPIC function in English relative clauses and in *tough*-movement constructions may also be functionally controlled, as described in Section 7.

the passive oblique object is marked by the preposition *by*, so the English instance of this universal rule is as follows:[30]

(102) ($\uparrow$ SUBJ) $\mapsto$ ($\uparrow$ BY OBJ)
       ($\uparrow$ OBJ) $\mapsto$ ($\uparrow$ SUBJ)
       ($\uparrow$ PARTICIPLE) = PASSIVE

This rule indicates the replacements to be performed and also specifies that a PARTICIPLE schema appears in passive entries in addition to other schemata derived from the stem. Accordingly, the passive lexical entries based on the stems underlying the past tense forms *persuaded* and *promised* are as follows:

(103) a. *persuaded* V ($\uparrow$ PARTICIPLE) = PASSIVE
                            ($\uparrow$ VCOMP TO) $=_c$ +
                            ($\uparrow$ VCOMP SUBJ) = ($\uparrow$ SUBJ)
           ($\uparrow$ PRED) = 'persuade $\langle$($\uparrow$ BY OBJ), ($\uparrow$ SUBJ), ($\uparrow$ VCOMP)$\rangle$'
       b. *promised* V ($\uparrow$ PARTICIPLE) = PASSIVE
                          ($\uparrow$ VCOMP TO) $=_c$ +
                          ($\uparrow$ VCOMP SUBJ) = ($\uparrow$ BY OBJ)
           ($\uparrow$ PRED) = 'promise $\langle$($\uparrow$ BY OBJ), ($\uparrow$ SUBJ), ($\uparrow$ VCOMP)$\rangle$'

Notice that ($\uparrow$ SUBJ) and ($\uparrow$ OBJ), the left-hand designators in the lexical rule, are replaced inside semantic forms as well as in schemata. The control schema in (103a) conforms to the universal restriction on functional control, but the one in (103b) does not. Since (103b) is not a possible lexical entry, *promise* may not be passivized when it takes a verb phrase complement.

We have argued that the *to*-complement and *that*-complement of *persuaded* have essentially the same internal functions. The sentences (92) and (97) in which those complements are embedded are not exact paraphrases, however. The *that*-complement sentence allows a reading in which two separate babies are being discussed, while for sentence (92) there is only one baby who is an argument of both *persuade* and *go*. This difference in interpretation is more obvious when quantifiers are involved: (104a) and (104b) are roughly synonymous, and neither is equivalent to (104c).

(104) a. The girl persuaded every baby to go.
       b. The girl persuaded every baby that he should go.
       c. The girl persuaded every baby that every (other) baby should go.

---

[30]See Bresnan (1982c) for a discussion of the morphological changes that go along with these functional replacements.

Since semantic translation is defined on functional structure, f-structures must mark the difference between occurrences of similar subsidiary f-structures where semantic coreferentiality is implied, as in the *to*-complement, and occurrences where the similarity is only accidental.

The necessary f-structure distinction follows from a simple formal property of semantic forms that we now introduce. The semantic form representations that appear in schemata are treated as "meta" semantic forms, templates for an infinite number of distinct "actual" semantic forms. Just as an actual variable is substituted for a metavariable by the instantiation procedure, so a meta-form is replaced by a unique actual form, identified by attaching an index to the predicate-argument specification. A given schema, say (105a), might be instantiated as (105b) at one node in the tree and (105c) at another:

(105) a. $(\uparrow$ PRED$) = $ 'baby'
       b. $(f_4$ PRED$) = $ 'baby'$_1$
       c. $(f_6$ PRED$) = $ 'baby'$_2$

F-description statements and f-structures thus contain recognizably distinct instances of the semantic forms in the grammar and lexicon. Each indexed actual form enters into predicate-argument relations as indicated by the meta-form, but the different instances are not considered identical for the purposes of semantic translation or functional uniqueness.

Returning to the two complements of *persuaded*, we observe that only one schema with 'baby' is involved in the derivation of the *to*-complement while two such schemata are instantiated for the *that*-complement. The indices of the two occurrences of 'baby' are therefore the same in the indexed version of the *to*-complement's f-structure (106) but different in the f-structure for the *that*-complement (107):[31]

---

[31]F-structure (107) ignores such details as the tense and mood of the *that*-complement.

(106)

$$
\left[
\begin{array}{ll}
\text{SUBJ} & \left[\begin{array}{ll} \text{SPEC} & \text{A} \\ \text{NUM} & \text{SG} \\ \text{PRED} & \text{'girl'}_1 \end{array}\right] \\
\text{TENSE} & \text{PAST} \\
\text{PRED} & \text{'persuade} \langle (\uparrow \text{ SUBJ}), (\uparrow \text{ OBJ}), (\uparrow \text{ VCOMP}) \rangle \text{'}_2 \\
\text{OBJ} & \left[\begin{array}{ll} \text{SPEC} & \text{THE} \\ \text{NUM} & \text{SG} \\ \text{PRED} & \text{'baby'}_3 \end{array}\right] \\
\text{VCOMP} & \left[\begin{array}{ll} \text{SUBJ} & \left[\begin{array}{ll} \text{SPEC} & \text{THE} \\ \text{NUM} & \text{SG} \\ \text{PRED} & \text{'baby'}_3 \end{array}\right] \\ \text{INF} & + \\ \text{TO} & + \\ \text{PRED} & \text{'go} \langle (\uparrow \text{ SUBJ}) \rangle \text{'}_4 \end{array}\right]
\end{array}
\right]
$$

(107)

$$
\left[
\begin{array}{ll}
\text{SUBJ} & \left[\begin{array}{ll} \text{SPEC} & \text{A} \\ \text{NUM} & \text{SG} \\ \text{PRED} & \text{'girl'}_1 \end{array}\right] \\
\text{TENSE} & \text{PAST} \\
\text{PRED} & \text{'persuade} \langle (\uparrow \text{ SUBJ}), (\uparrow \text{ OBJ}), (\uparrow \text{ VCOMP}) \rangle \text{'}_2 \\
\text{OBJ} & \left[\begin{array}{ll} \text{SPEC} & \text{THE} \\ \text{NUM} & \text{SG} \\ \text{PRED} & \text{'baby'}_3 \end{array}\right] \\
\text{SCOMP} & \left[\begin{array}{ll} \text{SUBJ} & \left[\begin{array}{ll} \text{SPEC} & \text{THE} \\ \text{NUM} & \text{SG} \\ \text{PRED} & \text{'baby'}_5 \end{array}\right] \\ \text{INF} & + \\ \text{TO} & + \\ \text{PRED} & \text{'go} \langle (\uparrow \text{ SUBJ}) \rangle \text{'}_4 \end{array}\right]
\end{array}
\right]
$$

The semantic contrast between the two complement types is marked in these f-structures by the differing patterns of semantic form indexing.

It is technically correct to include indices with all semantic forms in f-descriptions and f-structures, but the nonidentity of two forms with dissimilar predicate-argument specifications is clear even without explicit indexing. We adopt the following convention to simplify our representations: two semantic form occurrences are assumed to be distinct unless they have the same predicate-argument specification and the same index. With this convention only the indices on the 'baby' semantic forms are necessary in (106), and none of the indices are needed in (107). Control equations imply that entire substructures to which coindexed semantic forms belong will appear redundantly in several positions in an enclosing f-structure. This suggests a stronger abbreviatory convention which also highlights the cases of f-structure identity. The internal properties of a multiply-appearing subsidiary f-structure are displayed at only one place in an enclosing f-structure. The fact that it is also the value of other attributes is then indicated by drawing lines from the location of those other attributes to the fully expanded value:

(108)
$$
\begin{bmatrix}
\text{SUBJ} & \begin{bmatrix} \text{SPEC} & \text{A} \\ \text{NUM} & \text{SG} \\ \text{PRED} & \text{'girl'} \end{bmatrix} \\
\text{TENSE} & \text{PAST} \\
\text{PRED} & \text{'persuade}\,\langle(\uparrow\,\text{SUBJ}), (\uparrow\,\text{OBJ}), (\uparrow\,\text{VCOMP})\rangle\text{'} \\
\text{OBJ} & \begin{bmatrix} \text{SPEC} & \text{THE} \\ \text{NUM} & \text{SG} \\ \text{PRED} & \text{'baby'} \end{bmatrix} \\
\text{VCOMP} & \begin{bmatrix} \text{SUBJ} & \\ \text{INF} & + \\ \text{TO} & + \\ \text{PRED} & \text{'go}\,\langle(\uparrow\,\text{SUBJ})\rangle\text{'} \end{bmatrix}
\end{bmatrix}
$$

This graphical connection makes it clear even without explicit indices on 'baby' that the object f-structure serves in several functional roles.

While a semantic form instance occurring in several positions indicates semantic coreferentiality, different instances are seen as both semantically and functionally distinct. This means that any attempt to equate different instances will violate the Uniqueness Condition, even if they have the same predicate-argument specification. This is an important consequence of the semantic form instantiation procedure. For example, it rules out an analysis of string (109) in which both prepositional phrases are merged together as the BY OBJ, even though the PP f-structures agree in all other features:

(109) *The baby was given a toy by the girl by the girl.

As another example, the distinctness of semantic form instances permits a natural description of English subject–auxiliary inversion. As shown in (110), the auxiliary can occur either before or after the subject, but it must appear in one and not both of those positions.

(110) a. A girl is handing the baby a toy.
  b. Is a girl handing the baby a toy?
  c. *A girl the baby a toy.
  d. *Is a girl is handing the baby a toy?

In transformational theories, facts of this sort are typically accounted for by a rule that moves a single base-generated item from one position to another. Since no transformational apparatus is included in LFG, we must allow the c-structure grammar to optionally generate the auxiliary in both positions, for example, by means of the following modified S and VP rules:

(111) a.   S $\longrightarrow$ $\begin{pmatrix} V \\ (\downarrow \text{ AUX}) =_c + \end{pmatrix}$ $\begin{matrix} NP \\ (\uparrow \text{ SUBJ}) = \downarrow \\ (\downarrow \text{ CASE}) = \text{NOM} \end{matrix}$ $\begin{matrix} VP \\ \uparrow = \downarrow \\ (\uparrow \text{ TENSE}) \end{matrix}$

       b.   VP $\longrightarrow$

$(V) \begin{pmatrix} NP \\ (\uparrow \text{ OBJ})=\downarrow \end{pmatrix} \begin{pmatrix} NP \\ (\uparrow \text{ OBJ2})=\downarrow \end{pmatrix} \left\{ \begin{matrix} PP^* \\ (\uparrow (\downarrow \text{ PCASE}))=\downarrow \\ \downarrow \in (\uparrow \text{ ADJUNCTS}) \end{matrix} \right\} \begin{pmatrix} VP' \\ (\uparrow \text{ VCOMP})=\downarrow \end{pmatrix}$

These rules provide c-structure derivations for all the strings in (110). However, (110c) is incoherent because there are no PRED's for the NP arguments, and it also fails to satisfy the TENSE existential constraint. The f-description for (110d) is inconsistent because the separately instantiated semantic forms for *is* are both assigned as its PRED. The AUX constraint in (111a) permits only verbs marked with the AUX feature to be fronted.

In Section 5 we treated the auxiliary *is* as a main verb taking an embedded VP complement with a control schema identifying the matrix and embedded subjects (see (70)). *Is* is unlike *persuaded* and *promised* in that the f-structure serving two functional roles is not an argument of two predicates: SUBJ does not appear in the semantic form 'prog⟨(↑ VCOMP)⟩'. The wider class of raising verbs differs from equi verbs in just this respect. Thus, the lexical entry for *persuade* maps the *baby* f-structure in (108) into argument positions of both *persuade* and *go*. The OBJ of the raising verb *expected*, however, is an argument only of the complement's predicate, as stipulated in the lexical entry (112):

(112)   *expected*   V $(\uparrow \text{ TENSE}) = \text{PAST}$
                         $(\uparrow \text{ PRED}) = \text{'expect } \langle (\uparrow \text{ SUBJ}), (\uparrow \text{ VCOMP}) \rangle$
                         $(\uparrow \text{ VCOMP TO}) =_c +$
                         $(\uparrow \text{ VCOMP SUBJ}) = (\uparrow \text{ OBJ})$

Except for the semantic form change, the f-structure for sentence (113a) is identical to (108). This minor change is sufficient to account for the well-known differences in the behavior of these two classes of verbs, as illustrated by (113b) and (113c) (see Bresnan 1982c for a fuller discussion).

(113)   a.   The girl expected the baby to go.
        b.   The girl expected there to be an earthquake.
        c.   *The girl persuaded there to be an earthquake.

The difference between the raising and equi semantic forms shows that the set of grammatical relations in an f-structure cannot be identified with argument positions in a semantic translation. This is evidence for our early claim that the functional level is also distinct from the semantic level of representation. A stronger justification for this distinction comes from considerations of quantifier scope ambiguities. The sentence (114a) has a single f-structure, yet it has two semantic translations or interpretations, corresponding to the readings (114b) and (114c):

(114) a. Every man voted in an election.
      b. 'There was an election such that every man voted in it.'
      c. 'For every man there was an election such that he voted in it.'

The *election* quantifier has narrow scope in (114b) and wide scope in (114c). This ambiguity is not represented at the level of syntactic functions since no syntactic generalizations depend on it. Instead, the alternative readings are generated by the procedure that produces semantic translations or interpretations for f-structures.[32]

The distinctions between c-structure, f-structure, and semantic structure are supported by another scope-related phenomenon. Sentence (115a) also has two readings, as indicated in (115b) and (115c):

(115) a. Everybody has wisely selected their successors.
      b. 'Wisely, everybody has selected their successors (i.e., it is wise of everybody to have selected their successors).'
      c. 'Everybody selected their successors in a wise manner.'

The adverb has sentence scope in (115b) and so-called VP scope in (115c). The single f-structure for this sentence not only fails to represent the ambiguity but also fails even to preserve a VP unit to which the narrow scope might be attached. The f-structure is flattened to facilitate the statement of certain syntactic cooccurrence restrictions, to simplify the Completeness and Coherence Conditions, as mentioned above, and also to permit simple specifications of control relations. Independent motivation for our proposal that the scope of semantic operators is not tied to a VP c-structure node or an f-structure corresponding to it comes from Modern Irish, a VSO language that nonetheless exhibits this kind of ambiguity (McCloskey 1979).

We have shown that functional structure in LFG is an autonomous level of linguistic description. Functional structure contains a mixture of syntactically and semantically motivated information, but it is distinct

---

[32]This line of argumentation was suggested by P. K. Halvorsen (personal communication). Halvorsen (1980, 1983) gives a detailed description of a translation procedure with multiple outputs.

from both constituent structure and semantic representation. Of course, we have not demonstrated the necessity of such an intermediate level for mapping between surface sequences and predicate-argument relations. Indeed, Gazdar (1982) argues that a much more direct mapping is possible. In Gazdar's approach, the semantic connection between a functional controller and controllee, for example, is established by semantic translation rules defined directly on c-structure configurations. The semantic representation for the embedded complement includes a logical variable that is bound to the controller in the semantic representation of the matrix. It seems, however, that there are language-particular and universal generalizations that have no natural expression without an f-structure-like intermediate level. For example, in addition to semantic connections, functional control linkages seem to transmit purely syntactic elements—expletives like *it* and *there*, syntactic case-marking features (Andrews 1982a,b), and semantically empty idiom chunks. Without an f-structure level, either a separate feature propagation mechanism must be introduced to handle this kind of dependency in the c-structure, or otherwise unmotivated semantic entities or types must be introduced so that semantic filtering mechanisms can be applied to the syntactic elements. As another example, Levin (1982) has argued that a natural account of sluicing constructions requires the mixture of information found in f-structures. And finally, Bresnan (1982a,c) and Mohanan (1982a,b) observe that universal characterizations of lexical rules and rules of anaphora are stated more naturally in terms of grammatical functions than in terms of phrase structure configurations or properties of semantic representations. Further investigation should provide even stronger justification for functional structure as an essential and independent level of linguistic description.

7   Long-distance dependencies

We now turn to the formal mechanisms for characterizing the long-distance grammatical dependencies such as those that arise in English questions and relatives. As is well known, in these constructions an element at the front of a clause is understood as filling a particular grammatical role within the clause. Exactly which grammatical function it serves is determined primarily by the arrangement of c-structure nodes inside the clause. The *who* before the indirect question clause is understood as the subject of the question in (116a) but as the object in (116b):

(116) a. The girl wondered who ___ saw the baby.
       b. The girl wondered who the baby saw ___.
       c. *The girl wondered who ___ saw ___.
       d. *The girl wondered who the baby saw the toy.

In both cases, *who* is assigned the clause-internal function appropriate to the c-structure position marked by the blank, a position where an expected element is missing. Examples (116c,d) indicate that there must be one and only one missing element. Sentence (117), in which the *who* is understood as the object of a clause embedded inside the question, shows the long-distance nature of this kind of dependency:

(117)   The girl wondered who John believed that Mary claimed that the baby saw ___.

Sentence (118), however, demonstrates the well-known fact that the regions of the c-structure that such dependencies may cover are limited in some way, although not simply by distance:

(118)   *The girl wondered who John believed that Mary asked who ___ saw ___.

The dependencies illustrated in these sentences are examples of what we call *constituent control*. As with functional control, constituent control establishes a syntactic identity between elements that would otherwise be distinct.[33] In the case of functional control the linkage is between the entities filling particular functional roles and, as described in Section 6, is determined by lexical schemata that are very restricted substantively. Functional control schemata identify particular functions (such as SUBJ or OBJ) at one f-structure level with the SUBJ of a particular complement. Linkages over apparently longer distances, as in (119), are decomposed into several strictly local identifications, each of which links a higher function to the SUBJ one level down.

(119)   John persuaded the girl to be convinced to go.

The f-description for this example contains statements that equate the OBJ of *persuaded* with the SUBJ of *be*, the SUBJ of *be* with the SUBJ of *convinced*, and finally the SUBJ of *convinced* with the SUBJ of *go*. The fact that *girl* is understood as the subject of *go* then follows from the transitivity of the equality relation. However, it is characteristic of functional control that *girl* also bears grammatical relations to all the intermediate verbs, and that the intermediate verbs necessarily carry the required control schemata. A long-distance functional linkage can be made unacceptable by an intermediate lexical change that has no c-structure consequences:

(120)   a.   There was expected to be an earthquake.
        b. *There was persuaded to be an earthquake.

---

[33]The term *syntactic binding* is sometimes used as a synonym for constituent control.

The f-structure becomes semantically incomplete when the equi verb *persuaded* is substituted for the intervening raising verb.

Constituent control differs from functional control in that constituent structure configurations, not functional relations, are the primary conditioning factors. As illustrated in (116–117), at one end of the linkage (called the *constituent controllee*), the clause-internal function may be determined by the position of a c-structure gap. The relative clause in (121) demonstrates that the c-structure environment alone can also define the other end of the linkage (called the *constituent controller*):

(121) The toy the girl handed ___ to the baby was big.

This sentence has no special words to signal that *toy* must enter into a control relationship. Finally, the linked entity bears no grammatical relation to any of the predicates that the constituent dependency covers (e.g., *believed* and *claimed* in (117), and there are no functional requirements on the material that may intervene between the controller and the controllee. Instead, the restrictions on possible linkages involve the configuration of nodes on the controller–controllee c-structure path: for example, the interrogative complement of *asked* on the controller–controllee path in (118) is the source of that string's ungrammaticality.

Decomposing these long-distance constituent dependencies into chains of functional identifications would require introducing otherwise unmotivated functions at intermediate f-structure levels. Such a decomposition therefore cannot be justified. A strategy for avoiding spurious functions is to specify these linkages by sets of alternative direct functional identifications. One alternative would link the *who* to the SUBJ of the clause for (116a), and a second alternative would link to the OBJ for (116b). Question clauses with one embedded sentential complement would require alternatives for the SCOMP SUBJ and SCOMP OBJ; the two embeddings in (117) would require SCOMP SCOMP OBJ; and so on. This strategy has an obvious difficulty: without a bound on the functional distance over which this kind of dependency can operate, the necessary alternative identifications cannot be finitely specified.[34] The functional apparatus of our theory thus does not permit an adequate account of these phenomena.

---

[34] In any event, the schemata in these alternatives violate the substantive restriction on functional control mentioned above. They also run counter to a second substantive restriction, the principle of *functional locality*. This principle states that for human languages, designators in lexical and grammatical schemata may specify no more than two function-applications. This limits the context over which functional properties may be explicitly stipulated. The recursive mechanisms of the c-structure grammar are required to propagate information across wider functional scopes. The locality principle is a functional analogue of the context-free nature of our c-structure grammars.

If a single constituent contains no more than one controllee, it is possible to encode enough information in the c-structure categories to ensure a correspondence between controllers and controllees, as suggested by Gazdar (1982). This encoding obviously captures the fact that these dependencies are sensitive to constituent configurations. Gazdar also shows that appropriate semantic representations can be defined by translations associated with the phrase structure rules. Maling and Zaenen (1980) point out that this approach becomes considerably less attractive if a single constituent can contain more than one controllee, as in the familiar interaction of *tough*-movement and questions in English:

(122)   I wonder which violin the sonatas are easy to play ___ on ___.

Furthermore, no encoding into a finite number of categories is possible for languages such as Swedish and Norwegian, for which, according to Maling and Zaenen (1982) and Engdahl (1980a,b), no natural limit can be set on the number of controllees in a single constituent.

Our problem, then, is to provide a formal mechanism for representing long-distance constituent dependencies that does not require unmotivated grammatical functions or features, allows for an unbounded number of controllees in a single constituent, and permits a succinct statement of the generalizations that govern grammatical phenomena of this sort. The necessary descriptive apparatus is found in the formal interpretation of *bounded domination metavariables*.

The bounded domination metavariables ⇑ and ⇓ are similar to the immediate domination variables ↑ and ↓ in that they appear in grammatical and lexical schemata but are instantiated with actual variables when the f-description is formed. The instantiation procedure for both kinds of variables has the effect of substituting the same actual variable for matched metavariables attached to different nodes in the c-structure. The difference is that for a matched ↓–↑ pair, the schemata must be attached to nodes in a relationship of immediate domination, while matching ⇓ and ⇑ may be attached to nodes separated in the tree by a longer path. These are called "bounded domination metavariables" because that path is limited by the occurrence of certain "bounding" nodes. The ⇓ metavariable is attached to a node at the upper end of the path and represents the controller of a constituent control relationship.[35] The matching ⇑ is lower in the tree and represents the controllee of the relationship. The instantiation procedure for these variables establishes the long-distance

---

[35]Technically, the terms *controller* and *controllee* refer to the bounded domination metavariables and not to the nodes that they are attached to. In this respect, we depart from the way these terms have been used in other theoretical frameworks.

identification of the controller and controllee directly, without reliance on transitive chains of intervening equations.

We illustrate the general properties of our mechanism with a simple example, suppressing for the moment a number of formal and linguistic details. Consider the indirect question sentence (116b), repeated here for convenience:

(116) b.   The girl wondered who the baby saw ___.

We assume that the predicate for *wondered* takes an interrogative complement argument, as indicated in the lexical entry (123):[36]

(123)   *wondered*   V   ($\uparrow$ TENSE) = PAST
$\qquad\qquad\qquad\qquad$ ($\uparrow$ PRED) = 'wonder $\langle$($\uparrow$ SUBJ), ($\uparrow$ SCOMP)$\rangle$ '

According to the rules in (124), SCOMP's are based on constituents in the category S', and S' expands as an NP followed by an S:

(124)   a.   VP $\longrightarrow$ V $\qquad\qquad$ S'
$\qquad\qquad\qquad\qquad\qquad\quad$ ($\uparrow$ SCOMP) = $\downarrow$

$\qquad$ b.   S' $\longrightarrow \qquad\qquad$ NP $\qquad\qquad\qquad$ S
$\qquad\qquad\qquad\qquad$ ($\uparrow$ Q-FOCUS)= $\downarrow$ $\quad$ $\uparrow$ = $\downarrow$
$\qquad\qquad\qquad\qquad\qquad$ $\downarrow$= $\Downarrow$

The schemata in (124b) mark the initial NP as the question's focus (Q-FOCUS) and also identify it with $\Downarrow$, the controller of a gap in the following S. The initial NP for our example is realized as the interrogative pronoun *who*, which has the following lexical entry:

(125)   *who*   N   ($\uparrow$ PRED) = 'who'

The final rule for this example associates the controllee metavariable $\Uparrow$ with a gap position inside the clause. As shown in (126), we allow c-structure rules to expand a nonterminal category as the empty string, symbolized by *e*. This gives a formal representation for the intuition that an element of that category is missing.

(126)   NP $\longrightarrow \qquad e$
$\qquad\qquad\qquad\qquad$ $\uparrow$ = $\Uparrow$

---

[36]Grimshaw (1979) has argued that the sentential complement is restricted to be interrogative by the semantic type of the predicate 'wonder'. A separate functional specification of this restriction is therefore unnecessary.

The schema on the empty expansion introduces the controllee meta-variable.[37] This NP alternative must be utilized for the object of *saw* so that (116b) is assigned the c-structure (127):

(127)

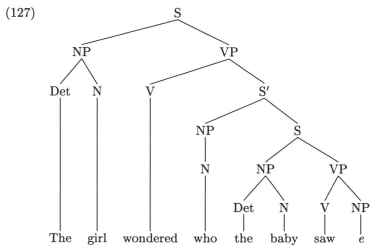

The instantiation procedure for metavariables still has an attachment phase, a variable introduction phase, and a substitution phase, just as it was presented in Section 3. Schemata are attached to appropriate c-structure nodes in the first phase without regard to the kinds of metavariables they contain. The attachments for nodes in the embedded S' subtree are shown in (128):

---

[37]Our controlled *e* is a base-generated analogue of the traces left by Chomsky's (1977) rule of *wh*-movement. However, controlled *e*'s are involved only in the description of constituent control, whereas Chomsky's traces are also used to account for functional control phenomena.

Our controller and controllee metavariables also resemble the hold action and the virtual/retrieve arcs of the ATN formalism. Plausible processing models for both systems require similar computational resources to locate and identify the two ends of the control relationship. Thus, the experimental results showing that ATN resource demands predict human cognitive load (Wanner and Maratsos 1978; Kaplan 1975b) are also compatible with lexical-functional grammar. However, we discuss below certain aspects of our theory for which standard ATN notation has no equivalents: the appearance of controllees in the lexical entries of fully realized items, the root-node specifications, and the bounding node conventions. Moreover, our theory does not have the characteristic left–right asymmetry of the ATN notation and thus applies equally well to languages like Basque, where constituent ordering is reversed.

(128)

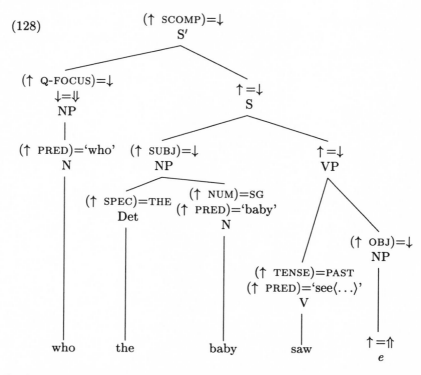

In the second phase, distinct actual variables are introduced for the root node and for every node where a schema contains a ↓ metavariable. This provides the ↓-variables for the nodes, as before. However, an additional variable is introduced for each node with a schema containing the controller metavariable ⇓, providing a ⇓-variable for that node. For this simple example, only the *who* NP node has a controller and receives the extra variable assignment. The annotations ↓:f_5 and ⇓:f_6 on that node in (129) record the association between metavariables and actual variables:

(129)

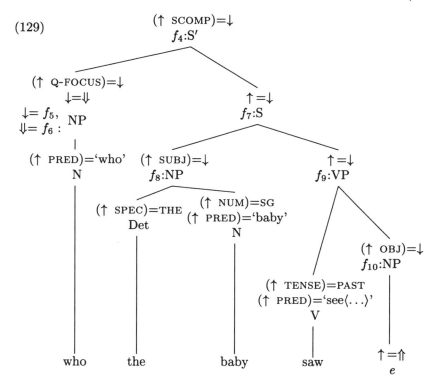

For immediate domination metavariables, the instantiation is completed by substituting a node's ↓-variable for all the ↓'s at that node and for all corresponding ↑'s, those in schemata attached to its daughter nodes. The treatment of bounded domination metavariables is similar in that the ⇓-variable of a node replaces all the ⇓'s at that node and all corresponding ⇑'s. The essential difference is that the nodes to which corresponding ⇑'s are attached may be further away in the c-structure.

The ⇑ corresponding to the ⇓ on the *who* NP in (129) is attached to the empty object of *saw*. The substitution phase of instantiation thus adds the following statements to the f-description:

(130) a. $(f_4 \text{ Q-FOCUS}) = f_5$
       b. $f_5 = f_6$
       c. $(f_5 \text{ PRED}) = \text{'who'}$
       d. $(f_9 \text{ OBJ}) = f_{10}$
       e. $f_{10} = f_6$

Equation (130b) comes from the *who* NP node and (130e) comes from the empty NP expansion. Both equations contain the ⇓-variable f_6 and thereby establish the crucial linkage: the semantic form 'who' serves as the PRED in the object f-structure for *saw* and accounts for the fact that *who* is understood as the second argument of 'see'. This is apparent in f-structure (131), the solution to sentence (116b)'s f-description:

(131)

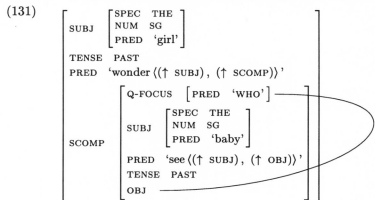

Thus, constituent control dependencies are handled in LFG by extending the instantiation procedure for mapping schemata on c-structure nodes into f-description statements. Because we do not rely on intermediate functional identifications, the statements in (130) are sufficient to establish the same connection over longer c-structure distances, for example, over the intervening *to*-complement in (132):

(132)   The girl wondered who the baby persuaded the boy to see ___.

Except for possibly a different choice of actual variables, the instantiation procedure would again produce the statements (130), correctly representing the constituent control relation. The f-structure for this sentence has both a functional control linkage and a constituent control linkage:

(133)

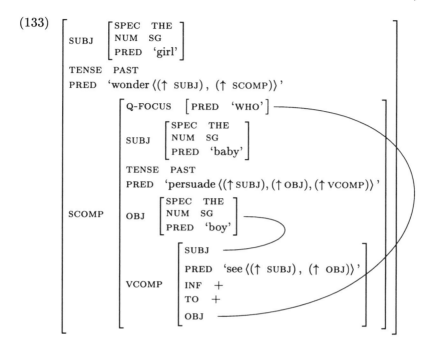

Note that there are no extraneous attributes or values to carry the constituent control linkage through the *persuade* f-structure.

The instantiation procedure as described substitutes the same actual variable for a ⇓ and any "corresponding" ⇑'s. Beneath this vague notion of correspondence lies some additional notation and a rich set of definitions and restrictions that we now make precise. We observe first that corresponding ⇓'s and ⇑'s must meet certain category requirements. As examples (134a,b) indicate, the verb *grow* meaning 'become' may be followed by an adjective phrase but not an NP, while the verb *reach* meaning 'extend to' has just the opposite distribution. Example (134c) shows that a controller may be associated with an AP at the beginning of an indirect question, but its corresponding controllee must then be in an adjectival position. Example (134d) demonstrates that metavariables associated with NP's must also be compatible:

(134) a. She'll grow that tall/*height.
      b. She'll reach that *tall/height.
      c. The girl wondered how tall she would grow/*reach ___.
      d. The girl wondered what height she would *grow/reach ___.

We therefore allow bounded domination metavariables to carry specifications of c-structure categorial features. These specifications are written
as subscripts on the metavariables, and we require that corresponding
controllers and controllees have compatible subscripts. Thus, a $\Downarrow_{NP}$ may
correspond to a $\Uparrow_{NP}$ but not to a $\Uparrow_{AP}$. The contrast in (134d) then follows
from adding the subscript NP to the metavariables in our previous rules:

(135) a. S′ $\longrightarrow$ NP S′

$(\uparrow$ Q-FOCUS$)= \downarrow$ $\uparrow = \downarrow$

$\downarrow= \Downarrow_{NP}$

b. NP $\longrightarrow$ e

$\uparrow = \Uparrow_{NP}$

The rules for handling adjectival and prepositional dependencies have
analogous categorial markings, and cross-categorial correspondences are
thereby excluded.

For these examples, the categorial subscripts are redundant with the
categories of the nodes that the metavariables are associated with, but
this is not always the case. In (136a) the metavariable associated with
the topicalized S′ is matched with a controllee on an e in a c-structure
NP position, a prepositional object. (136b) rules out the possibility that
the S′ is dominated by an NP. The contrast between (136c) and (136d)
shows that a topicalized S′ cannot control an S′ c-structure position.

(136) a. That he might be wrong he didn't think of ___.

b. *He didn't think of that he might be wrong.

c. He didn't think that he might be wrong.

d. *That he might be wrong he didn't think ___.

This pattern follows directly from associating a $\Downarrow_{NP}$ metavariable with
the fronted S′ node.

Another obvious property of acceptable correspondences is that certain tree relations must hold between the nodes to which corresponding
controller and controllee metavariables are attached. The e corresponding to the *who* controller in (129) must be dominated by the adjacent S
node. It cannot be located earlier or later in the main clause, nor inside
a more complicated NP in the *who* position. To put it in more technical
terms, we say that the S node in (129) is the root of a *control domain* for
the *who* $\Downarrow_{NP}$. For a controller attached to a given node in the c-structure,
a control domain consists of the nodes in a subtree that a corresponding
controllee may be attached to. Our notion of corresponding metavariables
thus turns on a rigorous characterization of what nodes can be roots of
control domains and what nodes dominated by the root are contained in
the domain.

A controller metavariable carries still another specification that determines what node may be its domain root. A closer examination of the indirect question construction shows why this is needed. Rule (135a) suggests that any noun phrase may appear at the front of an indirect question, but this is of course not the case. The fronted phrase is restricted to contain an interrogative word of some sort. That word need not be at the top level of the NP as in (116b), but may rather be deeply embedded within it:

(137)   The girl wondered whose playmate's nurse the baby saw ___.

This sentence would be generated by the alternative NP rule (138), which allows for possessors with genitive case in prenominal position:[38]

(138)   NP $\longrightarrow$

$$\begin{array}{cc} \text{NP} & \text{N} \\ (\downarrow \text{ CASE}) =_c \text{GEN} & \\ (\uparrow \text{ POSS}) = \downarrow & \end{array}$$

A very natural way of guaranteeing the presence of a question word in the appropriate contexts is to specify a constituent control relation between the fronted NP of an indirect question and the interrogative embedded underneath it. This is possible because constituent control in our theory may affect not only null elements but also a designated set of lexical items which includes interrogative pronouns, determiners, and adverbs.

Even though interrogative elements differ in their major categorial features, we assume that they are distinguished from other lexical items by the appearance of a morphosyntactic feature [+wh] in their categorial feature matrices, and we use this feature as the metavariable subscript for the interrogative constituent control dependency. However, it is not sufficient to revise our previous S' rule simply by adding a [+wh] controller metavariable to the fronted NP:

(139)   S' $\longrightarrow$

$$\begin{array}{cc} \text{NP} & \text{S} \\ (\uparrow \text{ Q}) = \Downarrow_{[+\text{wh}]} & \uparrow = \downarrow \\ (\uparrow \text{ FOCUS}) = \downarrow & \\ \downarrow = \Downarrow_{\text{NP}} & \end{array}$$

When the schemata from this rule are attached to the nodes in sentence (137)'s c-structure, two different controllers, $\Downarrow_{\text{NP}}$ and $\Downarrow_{[+\text{wh}]}$, are associated with the fronted NP node. While we still intend the S to be the domain root for the $\Downarrow_{\text{NP}}$, we intend the root for $\Downarrow_{[+\text{wh}]}$ to be the fronted NP itself. In order to represent this distinction, we must explicitly mark the individual controllers with category symbols that determine their respective domain roots. The superscript S in the controller $\Downarrow_{\text{NP}}^{\text{S}}$ indicates

---

[38]We assume that morphological rules correlate the genitive case marking with the *'s* suffix, and that *whose* is morphologically composed of *who* + *'s*.

that the corresponding $\Uparrow_{NP}$ must be found in an S-rooted control domain, while the [+wh] controllee for $\Downarrow_{[+wh]}^{NP}$ must be found beneath an NP node. Moreover, the domain roots must be either the nodes to which the controllers are attached or sisters of those nodes, as indicated in the following definition:

(140) *Root node of a constituent control domain*

Suppose $\Downarrow_c^r$ is a controller metavariable attached to a node N. Then a node R is the root node of a control domain for $\Downarrow_c^r$ if and only if

(a) R is a daughter of N's mother, and

(b) R is labeled with category r.

Introducing root-category superscripts into the S' rule, we have:

(141) S' $\longrightarrow$ NP   S

$(\uparrow Q) = \Downarrow_{[+wh]}^{NP}$ $\uparrow = \downarrow$

$(\uparrow FOCUS) = \downarrow$

$\downarrow = \Downarrow_{NP}^{S}$

The [+wh] controllee for the interrogative linkage is associated with a lexically realized N node, not with an empty string expansion, and the schema containing the controllee metavariable does not come from the grammar but rather from the lexical entry for *who*:

(142) *who*   N $(\uparrow PRED) = $ 'who'

$\uparrow = \Uparrow_{[+wh]}$

This lexical entry and our revised question rule yield the following f-structure for sentence (137):[39]

---

[39] Note as an aside that we have changed the Q-FOCUS identification schema from (135a) to (141) because the questioned element is no longer the $\downarrow$ f-structure of the fronted NP. The new schema places the interrogative semantic form in a canonical f-structure location that is independent of its degree of embedding. The complete fronted NP is also recorded in a canonical f-structure location, as the value of the function FOCUS. That NP is accessible as the FOCUS of the question as well as through its clause-internal function OBJ, as indicated by the connecting line in (143). These separate access paths define the scope of different rules for interpreting anaphors. The FOCUS path in the f-structure for sentence (i) permits the ordinary pronoun *she* to be coreferential with *Sally*, even though this is not permitted by its clause-internal object function, as shown by (ii):

i.   Which of the men that Sally dated did she hate ___?

ii.   *She hated one of the men that Sally dated.

iii. I wonder how proud of herself Bill thinks Sally is ___.

The clause-internal function governs the interpretation of reflexive pronouns; (iii) would otherwise be unacceptable because the reflexive is not a clause-mate of the antecedent *Sally*. The problem posed by the contrast between examples (i) and (ii)

(143)

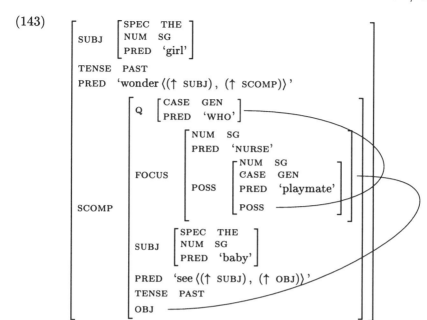

The root-node category specification provides one part of the characterization of what a control domain can be. To complete this characterization, we must define which nodes dominated by the domain root are contained in the domain. The *wh*-island in example (144) demonstrates that at least some nodes in the domain root's subtree do not belong to the domain:

(144) *The girl wondered what the nurse asked who ___ saw ___.

Without some limitation on the extent of a domain, $\Uparrow_{NP}$'s at the gaps would be interpretable as the controllees for *who* and *what*, respectively. Limitations on what nodes may belong to a given control domain come from the fact that nodes in certain c-structure configurations are classified as *bounding nodes*. The path from a node in a domain to the domain root is then restricted as follows:

(145) *Bounding Convention*

A node M belongs to a control domain with root node R if and only if R dominates M and there are no bounding nodes on the path from M up to but not including R.

---

was observed originally by Postal (1971). The solution sketched here is developed in greater detail by Zaenen (1980).

The domain root thus carries a substantial theoretical burden as a c-structure intermediary between the nodes to which a controller metavariable and its corresponding controllees are attached. The categorial superscript on the controller metavariable is a direct and definite selector of its domain roots. However, the path from a root to a corresponding controllee's node, while restricted by the Bounding Convention, is not uniquely determined by the grammar.

It remains to extend our notion of grammaticality to take bounded domination metavariables explicitly into account. Intuitively, we require all controllers to have corresponding controllees and all controllees to have corresponding controllers, so that there are no uninstantiated metavariables in the f-description. We add the following to our previous list of grammaticality conditions:

(146) *Grammaticality Condition*
       A string is grammatical only if its f-description is *properly instantiated*.

The controller/controllee correspondence is one consequence of the formal definition of proper instantiation:

(147) *Definition of Proper Instantiation*
       The f-description from a c-structure with attached schemata is properly instantiated if and only if:
       (a) no node is a domain root for more than one controller,
       (b) every controller metavariable has at least one control domain,
       (c) every controller metavariable corresponds to one and only one controllee in each of its control domains,
       (d) every controllee metavariable corresponds to one and only one controller,
       (e) all metavariable correspondences are *nearly nested*, and
       (f) every domain root has a *lexical signature*.

For a properly instantiated f-description, there is a one-to-one mapping between controllees and domain roots, and each domain root is associated with one and only one controller. This establishes the necessary correspondence between metavariables. The definition of *nearly nested correspondences* and the consequences of the restriction (147e) are presented at the end of this section, where we discuss the possibility of a single constituent containing several controllees.

The lexical signature clause is motivated primarily by formal considerations. It establishes a connection between controlled *e*'s and actual lexical items that plays an important role in the recursiveness proof pre-

sented in Section 8. For each domain root there must be a distinct word
in the terminal string. This word is called the *lexical signature* of the
domain root. The domain root must dominate its lexical signature. The
effect of (147f) is that each domain root, and thus each control domain,
must be reflected in the string in some unique way.[40] One possible interpretation of this formal condition is that a control domain must have
a lexically realized "head". The head can be defined in terms of the X'
category system. It can also be defined purely in functional terms: a
lexical head is the lexical item that contributes the PRED semantic form
to a constituent's $\downarrow$ f-structure.

According to (147), corresponding metavariables of a grammatical sentence must be in a c-structure configuration as outlined in (148):

(148)

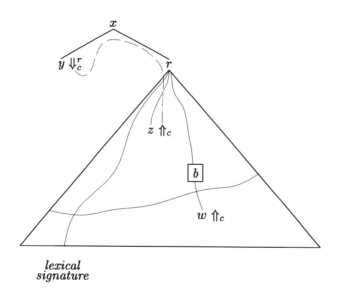

lexical
signature

In this c-structure and in the illustrations below, bounding nodes are
enclosed in boxes. The dashed line passes by the domain root to connect
the corresponding controller and controllee. The lower $\Uparrow_c$ in (148) cannot
correspond to the controller because the bounding node b lies on the path
to the root r.

---

[40]The lexical signature requirement and its formal implications are somewhat reminiscent of Peters' (1973) Survivor property and Wasow's (1978) Subsistence property,
two restrictions that have been proposed to guarantee the recursiveness of transformational grammars. Those conditions are imposed on the input and output trees of a
transformational cycle, whereas (147f) stipulates a property that must hold of a single
c-structure.

Bounding nodes define "islands" of the c-structure that constituent control dependencies may not penetrate. They serve the same descriptive purpose as Ross' (1967) constraints on transformational variables and Chomsky's (1977) notion of cyclic or bounding categories. Those theories, however, have descriptive inadequacies. Ross hypothesized that constraints such as the Complex NP Constraint apply to all human languages, but this has proved not to be the case. All Scandinavian languages, for example, permit long-distance dependencies to cross the boundaries of indirect questions, and all except for Icelandic permit them to cross the boundaries of relative clauses as well (for illustrations, see Erteschik 1973, Allwood 1976, Engdahl 1980a,b, Maling and Zaenen 1982). Moreover, although dependencies into English relative clauses (149a) are unacceptable, Ross himself noted that extractions from phrases within the lexically-filled NP's in examples like (149b,c) are possible even in English:

(149) a. *I wonder who the man that ___ talked to ___ saw Mary.

       b. I wonder who John saw a picture of ___.

       c. Who was it that John denied the claim that he dated ___?

The restrictions on constituent control into English sentential complements and relative clauses seem to be governed by different generalizations; Godard (1980) convincingly argues that a similar pattern holds for complements and relatives in French. In Chomsky's theory, the subjacency convention provides a general limitation on syntactic rules. The domains of rule application are thereby restricted by the occurrence of nodes in specified categories. Chomsky shows that many of the properties of English dependencies follow from the assumption that S' and NP (and possibly S) are bounding categories. One reasonable extension to Chomsky's theory defines bounding categories on a language-by-language basis: stipulating a smaller (or perhaps empty) set of bounding categories in the grammar of Swedish might give an account of the freer dependencies exhibited by that language. However, the English sentences (149b,c) have no natural description in Chomsky's system if *all* NP's in English are bounding nodes.[41]

Bounding node specifications in lexical-functional grammar acknowledge the fact that restrictions on long-distance dependencies may vary between languages and between different nodes of the same category in particular languages. This flexibility does not diminish the explanatory potential of our formal system. We expect that a substantive theory of

---

[41]Chomsky (1977) proposes to derive such examples by restructuring rules that move the *of* prepositional phrase and *that*-complement outside of the *picture* and *claim* NP's before the *wh*-movement rule applies. But such a reanalysis in all the relevant cases cannot be justified, as Godard (1980) shows for French.

human language based on our formalism will stipulate a small, principled set of c-structure configurations in which bounding nodes may appear. The grammars of particular languages must draw from this universal inventory of possible bounding nodes to identify the bounding categories in individual c-structure rules (see Zaenen 1980 for some partial proposals). Further work will of course be needed to formulate and justify a universal bounding node theory. Our goal at present is only to illustrate the notation and formal properties of our constituent control mechanisms. A simple notational device is used to indicate that constituent control is blocked by nodes in particular c-structure configurations: enclosing a category on the right-hand side of a c-structure rule in a box specifies that the nodes derived by that rule element are bounding nodes.

We incorporate this notation into our treatment of indirect questions for the variety of English in which they form islands. The S in these constructions is a bounding node, as shown in the revised rule:

(150)   S′ $\longrightarrow$ NP $\boxed{\text{S}}$
                  $(\uparrow \text{Q}) = \Downarrow^{\text{NP}}_{[+\text{wh}]}$ $\uparrow = \downarrow$
                  $(\uparrow \text{FOCUS}) = \downarrow$
                  $\downarrow = \Downarrow^{\text{S}}_{\text{NP}}$

Notice first that the bounding node introduced by this rule does not block the simple indirect question sentence (116b). As shown in (151), this is because the S is the root node of the controller's control domain. Therefore, in accordance with the bounding convention (145), it does not interfere with the metavariable correspondence.

(151)

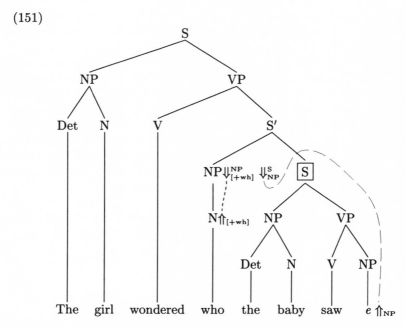

The dashed line in this illustration runs between the corresponding metavariables, not between the nodes they are attached to. The connected metavariables will be instantiated with the same actual variable.

The situation is different for the more complicated string (144). Neither of the gaps inside the *asked* question belongs to the control domain whose root node is the sister of *what*. This is because the *who* domain root is a bounding node on the path from each of the controllees to the root for the *what* $\Downarrow_{\mathrm{NP}}^{\mathrm{S}}$:

(152)

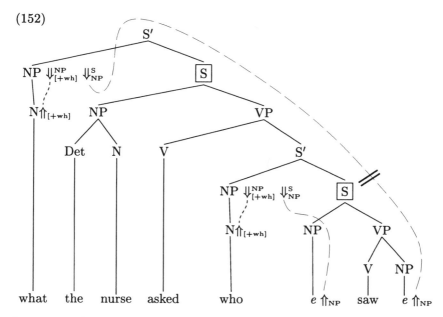

Conditions (147c,d) are not satisfied, and the string is marked ungrammatical.

Our box notation also permits an account of the apparent difference in NP bounding properties illustrated in (149). The S' in the relative clause expansion rule (153) is boxed, thus introducing a bounding node that separates both of the gaps in example (149a) from the *who* controller:

(153)   NP $\longrightarrow$ NP $\boxed{S}$

A proper instantiation for this example is therefore impossible. Constituent control into the other NP constructions in (149) is acceptable because they are derived by alternative rules which do not generate bounding nodes. This distribution of bounding nodes has a further consequence. Together with our hypothesis that the interrogative word inside a fronted NP is subject to constituent control, it explains certain restrictions on the location of the interrogative. Sentence (154a) shows that a fronted NP may contain a relative clause, but example (154b) demonstrates that the interrogative pronoun may not appear *inside* the relative. This is just what we would predict, since the relative clause bounding node that separates the NP metavariables in (154c) also blocks the [+wh] correspondence in (154b):

(154) a. The girl whose pictures of the man that called Mary I saw talked to John.

     b. *The girl the pictures of the man that called whom I saw talked to John.

     c. *The girl who I saw pictures of the man that called talked to John.

Though similar in these examples, there are English constructions in which NP and [+wh] metavariables do not have the same privileges of occurrence. We see in (155) and (156) that a controlled interrogative may, but a controlled e may not, be located in the possessive modifier of an NP:

(155) The girl wondered whose nurse the baby saw ___.

(156) *The girl wondered who the baby saw ___'s nurse.

The ungrammaticality of (156) follows from making the prenominal genitive NP be a bounding node, as in the revised NP rule (157):

(157)   NP $\longrightarrow$ $\boxed{\text{NP}}$ N
$$(\downarrow \text{CASE}) =_c \text{GEN}$$
$$(\uparrow \text{POSS}) = \downarrow$$

The genitive bounding node also blocks a direct correspondence for the [+wh] metavariables in (155), but a simple schema can be added to rule (157) to circumvent the blocking effect just for interrogative dependencies. This schema, $\Uparrow_{[+wh]} = \Downarrow^{NP}_{[+wh]}$, splits what seems to be a single control domain into two separate domains, one embedded inside the other. It equates a [+wh] controllee for the upper domain with a [+wh] controller for a lower domain:

(158)   NP $\longrightarrow$ $\boxed{\text{NP}}$ N
$$(\downarrow \text{CASE}) =_c \text{GEN}$$
$$(\uparrow \text{POSS}) = \downarrow$$
$$\Uparrow_{[+wh]} = \Downarrow^{NP}_{[+wh]}$$

Because this schema links only [+wh] metavariables, constituent control only for interrogatives is possible inside the genitive NP;[42] control for empty NP's is prohibited. The relevant c-structure relations for sentence (155) are illustrated in (159):

---

[42]Constituent control dependencies for relative pronouns also penetrate the genitive NP. This would follow automatically from the hypothesis that relative metavariables share the [+wh] subscript. The well-known distributional differences between relative and interrogative items would be accounted for by additional features in the categorial subscripts for the relative and interrogative dependencies and more selective specifications on the linking schemata associated with other bounding nodes.

(159)

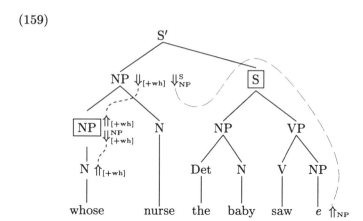

Special constraints have been proposed in transformational theory (e.g., the Left Branch Condition of Ross 1967) to account for the asymmetry in (155) and (156). The lexical-functional description of these facts is stated within the grammar for English, without postulating extragrammatical universal constraints. It thus predicts that this is an area of variation among languages.

In contrast to the nonuniform bounding characteristics of NP's, it can be argued that in languages like English, Icelandic, and French, all S's are bounding nodes (see the discussions of verb inversion in control domains in Bresnan and Grimshaw 1978 and Zaenen 1980). If so, the Bounding Convention would also block the derivation of sentences such as (160), where the controllee is inside a verb phrase *that*-complement:

(160)   The girl wondered who the nurse claimed that the baby saw ___.

The linking schema appearing in the alternative S' rule (161) will let the dependency go through in this case:

(161)   S' $\longrightarrow$ (*that*) $\boxed{\text{S}}$
$\uparrow = \downarrow$
$\Uparrow = \Downarrow^s$

Neither of the metavariables in this linking schema has a categorial subscript. This is an abbreviation for a finite set of alternative schemata of the form $\Uparrow_c = \Downarrow^s_c$, where c is one of the types NP, [+wh], PP, etc. Thus, this schema will link metavariables of any type, passing on to the lower controller the compatibility requirement of the upper one. With this rule, the following c-structure is assigned to the sentential complement in (160):

(162)

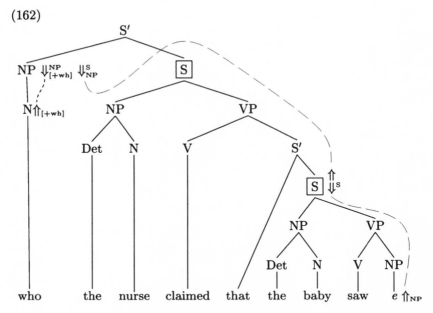

Observe that the *that* node belongs to the control domain of the *who* $\Downarrow_{NP}^{S}$ controller, since there is no bounding node on the path leading down to it. The $\Uparrow$ on the left of the linking schema is thus instantiated with the $\Downarrow_{NP}^{S}$-variable of the *who* node. A separate variable is introduced for the $\Downarrow^{S}$ on the right, and this is substituted for the $\Uparrow_{NP}$ of the empty NP, which belongs to the domain rooted in the complement S. The semantically appropriate connections for (160) are thus established.[43]

The definitions of our theory place controllees in a one-to-one correspondence with domain roots and hence with lexical signatures. Our definitions do not establish such a correspondence between controllees and arbitrary constituents: there is nothing to prevent control domains from overlapping, and any constituent in several domains may contain several

---

[43]Our use of linking schemata has some of the flavor of Chomsky's subjacency condition and COMP to COMP movement (e.g., Chomsky 1977). We mentioned above that our specification of bounding nodes differs from Chomsky's, but there are other significant differences in our approaches. For one, we do not *move* constituents from place to place, we merely assert that a functional equivalence obtains. That equivalence enters into the f-description and is reflected in the ultimate f-structure, but it is never visible in the c-structure. Thus, we have a simple account of cases where *unmoved* constituents are subject to the bounded domination constraints, as in Chinese interrogatives (Huang 1982); in such cases, the theory of Chomsky (1977) fails to provide a uniform explanation.

controllees.[44] Control domains will overlap whenever a domain root belonging to the domain of a higher controller is not marked as a bounding node. The potential for multiple dependencies into a single constituent is greater for languages whose grammars specify fewer bounding nodes. The hypothesis that Swedish has fewer bounding nodes than English would thus account for the less restrictive patterns of Swedish dependencies.

There are examples of multiple dependencies in English, however, which we will use to illustrate the operation of our formal mechanism. The recent literature contains many discussions of the interaction of *tough*-movement and questions (see Chomsky (1977) and Fodor (1978), for example, and the references cited therein):[45]

(163) I wonder which violin the sonata is tough for her to play ___ on
___.

As we will see, the nodes in the VP' in this example lie within two control domains, one rooted in the VP' in the sentential complement of *tough* and the other rooted in the S after *which*. Before exploring the interactions in this sentence, we sketch a grammar for simple *tough*-movement constructions.

A predicate like *tough* is an adjective that can occur as the head of an adjective phrase. Among the alternative expansions for AP is one that allows the adjective to be followed by a sentential complement:

(164) AP $\longrightarrow$ A   S'
$(\uparrow \text{SCOMP}) = \downarrow$

The VP must of course permit AP's as complements to copular verbs, but the details of the VP grammar do not concern us here. *Tough* predicates take infinitival sentential complements, so the category S' must also have an alternative expansion. Rule (165) allows S' to expand as a *for*-complementizer followed by a subject NP and a VP':

---

[44]We also leave open the possibility that a given controller has several domain roots. If several daughters of the controller node's mother are labeled with the controller's categorial superscript, then each such daughter becomes the root of a domain that must contain one corresponding controllee. This distributes the instantiation requirement to each of the domains independently. This suggests a plausible account for the across-the-board properties of coordinate structures, but more intensive investigation of coordination within the lexical-functional framework is needed before a definitive analysis can be given.

[45]Chomsky (1977) has proposed an analysis of these sentences that does not involve a double dependency. He suggests an alternative phrase structure for examples of this type whereby the *on* prepositional phrase belongs somewhere outside the *play* VP. Bach (1977) and Bresnan (1976) point out that this proposal has a number of empirical shortcomings.

(165) S' $\longrightarrow$ *for*   NP   VP'

                              ($\uparrow$ SUBJ) = $\downarrow$ $\uparrow = \downarrow$

                                                              ($\uparrow$ TOPIC) = $\Downarrow^{\text{VP}'}_{\text{NP}}$

The TOPIC schema identifies the TOPIC with an NP controller metavariable whose corresponding controllee must be inside the VP'. Sentences such as (166), where the subject of *tough* has a clause-internal function in an embedded *that*-complement, justify treating this as a constituent control dependency:

(166)   Mary is tough for me to believe that John would ever marry ___.

In some respects the TOPIC function is like the FOCUS function introduced earlier for indirect questions. It raises an entity with a clause-internal function to a canonical position in the f-structure hierarchy, providing an alternative access path for various anaphoric rules (cf. note 39). There are substantive differences between TOPIC and FOCUS, however. The FOCUS relation marks new information in the sentence or discourse and therefore is not identified with any other elements. The TOPIC function is a place-holder for old information; its value *must* be linked, either functionally or anaphorically, to some other element. For *tough* predicates, the TOPIC is functionally controlled by a schema in the adjective's lexical entry:[46]

(167)   *tough*   A   ($\uparrow$ PRED) = 'tough$\langle$($\uparrow$ SCOMP)$\rangle$'

                              ($\uparrow$ SCOMP TOPIC) = ($\uparrow$ SUBJ)

With these specifications, the f-structure for the simple *tough*-movement sentence (168) is as shown in (169), and its c-structure is displayed in (170).

(168)   The sonata is tough for her to play ___ on the violin.

We are now ready to examine the double dependency in (163). In this sentence *violin* has become the FOCUS of an indirect question. The c-structure for the complement of *wonder* is shown in (171). Since the VP' domain is introduced without a bounding node, there is nothing to block the correspondence between the object NP of *on* and the NP controller for *which violin*. The correspondence for the TOPIC metavariables in *tough*'s complement is established just as in the simpler example above. Thus, the metavariables can be properly instantiated, and the intuitively correct f-structure will be assigned to this sentence.

As has frequently been noted, the acceptability of these double dependencies is sensitive to the relative order of controllees and controllers.

---

[46]The preposed item in relative clauses is also a TOPIC. Although the relative TOPIC might be functionally controlled when the clause is embedded next to the NP that it modifies, it must be linked anaphorically when the relative is extraposed.

(169)

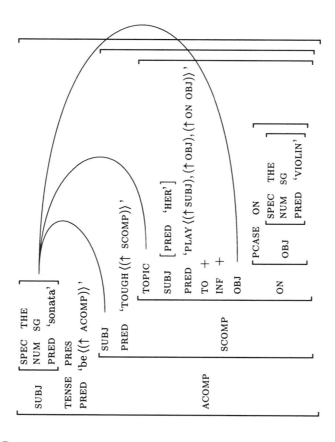

(170)

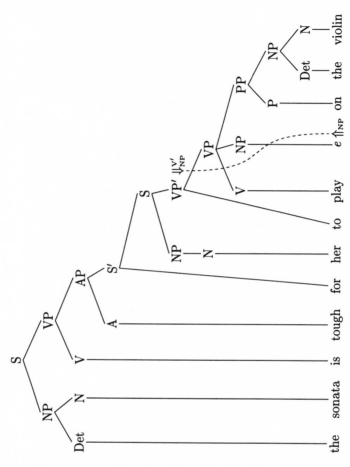

(171)

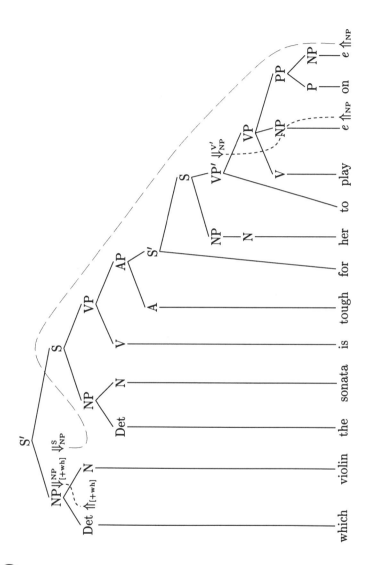

If *sonata* is questioned and *violin* is the *tough* subject, the result is the ungrammatical string (172):

(172) *I wonder which sonata the violin is tough for her to play ___ on ___.

The reading of this sentence in which *which sonata* is the object of *on* and *violin* is the object of *play* is semantically unacceptable, but the semantically well-formed reading of our previous example (163) is not available. Similarly, Bach (1977) observes that potentially ambiguous sentences are rendered unambiguous in these constructions. Sentence (173) can be assigned only the reading in which *doctor* is understood as the object of *to* and *patient* is the object of *about*, even though the alternative interpretation is equally plausible:

(173) Which patient is that doctor easiest to talk to ___ about ___?

As Baker (1977), Fodor (1978), and others have pointed out, there is a simple and intuitive way of characterizing the acceptable dependencies in these examples. If a line is drawn from each gap to the various lexical items that are candidates for filling it, then the permissible dependencies are just those in which the lines for the separate gaps do not cross. Or, to use Fodor's terminology, only nested dependencies seem to be allowed.

The nested pattern of acceptable dependencies is an empirical consequence of the requirement (147e) that corresponding metavariables be nearly nested. However, this restriction in our definition of proper instantiation is strongly motivated by independent theoretical considerations: as we point out in Section 8, this requirement provides a sufficient condition for proving that lexical-functional languages are included within the set of context-sensitive languages. Thus, our restriction offers not only a description of the observed facts but also a formal basis for explaining them.

As the first step in formalizing the notion of a nearly nested correspondence, we establish an ordering on the bounded domination metavariables attached to a c-structure. We order the c-structure nodes so that each node comes before its daughters and right-sister (if any), and all its daughters precede its right-sister. If the node that one metavariable is attached to precedes another metavariable's node, then we say that the first metavariable precedes the second. The ordering of metavariables can be described more perspicuously in terms of a labeled-bracket representation of the c-structure tree. If metavariables are associated with the *open* brackets for the nodes they are attached to, then the left-to-right sequence in the labeled bracketing defines the metavariable ordering. This is illustrated with the (partial) bracketing for sentence (163) shown in Figure 1, sentence (a). We see from this representation that the $\Downarrow_{NP}^{S}$ on the fronted noun phrase is ordered before the $\Downarrow_{NP}^{VP'}$ and that *play*'s direct object $\Uparrow_{NP}$ is ordered before the controllee after *on*.

Drawing lines between corresponding metavariables as ordered in Figure 1, sentence (a) illustrates the intuitive contrast between nested and crossed dependencies. The lines are shown in (b) for the acceptable nested reading of (163) and in (c) for the unacceptable crossed dependency.

A precise formulation of this intuitive distinction can be given in terms of the definition of a crossed correspondence:

(174)   *Definition of Crossed Correspondence*
         The correspondence of two metavariables m_1 and m_2 is *crossed* by
         a controller or controllee m_3 if and only if all three variables have
         compatible categorial subscripts and m_3 but not its corresponding
         controllee or controller is ordered between m_1 and m_2.

Obviously, a correspondence is nested if and only if it is not crossed. All the correspondences in the acceptable readings for the examples above are nested according to this definition, but the correspondences in the unacceptable readings are not.

Metavariable correspondences can be allowed limited departures from strict nesting without undermining the context-sensitivity of lexical- functional languages. We associate with each metavariable correspondence an integer called its *crossing degree*. This is simply the number of controllers and controllees by which that correspondence is crossed. A correspondence is strictly nested if its crossing degree is zero. Further, for each lexical-functional grammar we determine another number, the *crossing limit* of the grammar. A nearly nested correspondence is then defined as follows:

(175)   *Definition of Nearly Nested Correspondence*
         A metavariable correspondence is *nearly nested* if its crossing degree does not exceed the grammar's crossing limit.

The significant formal implication of this definition and the nearly nested restriction on proper instantiation is that for any string the degree of departure from strict nesting is bounded by a constant that is independent of the length of that string.

The examples above suggest that the crossing limit for English is zero. This limit can be maintained even in the face of apparent counterexamples to the nesting proposals of other theories. Since our definition of crossed correspondence (174) only involves metavariables with compatible categorial subscripts, we have no difficulty with acceptable sentences containing crossed dependencies of different categories. Other classes of counterex-

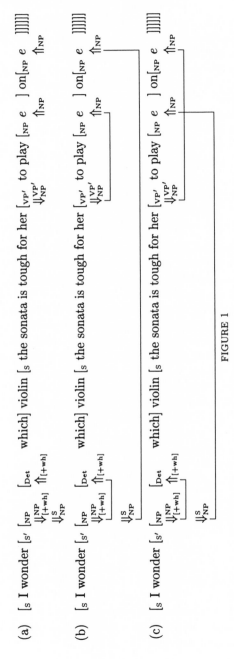

FIGURE 1

amples involve interactions of functional and constituent control, but our restrictions are imposed only for constituent control dependencies. Thus, there is no real cross-over in sentences such as (176):

(176) How nice a man would John be ___ to marry ___?

The *man* NP is linked to the first gap, while *John* is linked to the second. In our theory there is a functional identification between *John*, the SUBJ of the complex predicate *how nice a man*, and the TOPIC of its SCOMP. The controller for the second dependency is thus ordered *after* the first gap. Icelandic stands in contrast to English in having constituent control dependencies that can be described correctly only on the hypothesis that the crossing limit for that language is one (Maling and Zaenen 1982).

We have presented in this section the major formal mechanisms for characterizing the long-distance dependencies of natural language. We have motivated and illustrated our formal apparatus with simple and plausible fragments of English grammar. Constituent control is a syntactic phenomenon of considerable complexity, and there are many empirical and theoretical issues that we have not touched on and some that are still to be resolved. No doubt future research in this area will lead to both substantive and formal refinements of our theory. However, we expect the broad outline of our approach to remain unchanged: lexical-functional grammar treats long-distance dependencies as part of the procedure for producing properly instantiated f-descriptions. These dependencies are governed by c-structure configurations and are not directly sensitive to the f-structures that are ultimately constructed.

8   Generative power

We have seen that lexical-functional grammar offers considerable expressive power for describing linguistic phenomena. In this section we examine the position of LFG in the Chomsky hierarchy of generative capacity. The most important result is that our formal system, with two well-motivated restrictions on c-structure derivations that we discuss below, is *not* as powerful as a general rewriting system or Turing machine. In fact, lexical-functional languages are included within the class of context-sensitive languages. On the lower end of the scale, we show that LFG has greater generative power than the class of context-free grammars.

For a string to be a member of the language generated by a lexical-functional grammar, it must satisfy five requirements:

(177) a. It must be the terminal string of a valid c-structure derivation.

b. There must be a properly instantiated f-description associated with that derivation.

    c.   The f-description must be consistent and determinate, with a unique minimal solution.

    d.   The minimal f-structure solution must satisfy all constraints in the f-description.

    e.   The f-structure must be complete and coherent.

Given a single c-structure derivation for a string of length n (a tree to whose nodes the appropriate functional schemata are attached), there are finite procedures for deciding whether (177b–177e) hold. Determining proper instantiation for immediate domination metavariables is trivial. Since the given tree has only a finite number of finite control domains, it is also computable whether the bounded domination metavariables are properly instantiated. The instantiated f-description has a finite number of statements in it, so the algorithm outlined in Section 4 and in the Appendix produces its unique minimal solution, if it is consistent and determinate. Evaluating a constraining statement requires only a finite traversal of the f-structure,[47] and the Completeness and Coherence Conditions can similarly be checked by a finite computation on the f-structure.

Thus, all that is needed to prove that the grammaticality of any string is decidable is a terminating procedure for enumerating all possible c-structures for the string, so that the functional correctness of each one can then be verified. C-structures are generated by context-free grammars, and there are well-known decision procedures for the membership problem of grammars in this class. That is, there exist algorithms for determining whether there is *at least one* way of deriving the string. Deciding that a string is derivable, however, is not the same as enumerating for inspection all of its derivations. Indeed, there are grammars for which neither the number of derivations that a given string might have nor the number of nodes in a single derivation is bounded. While it may be determined that such a string has one derivation and thus belongs to the language of the c-structure grammar, there is no way of deciding whether or not there exists among all of its derivations one that satisfies the functional requirements of our theory. Suppose that at some point we have examined all derivations with less than m nodes and found them all to be functionally deviant. This does not mean that all derivations with $m + 1$ nodes will also be unsatisfactory. Since this can be true for any m, the grammaticality of that string cannot be decided in a finite number of steps.[48]

---

[47]The evaluation uses operators similar to Locate, Merge, and Include except that they return False whenever the corresponding solution operators would modify the f-structure.

[48]This difficulty arises not just with our formalism but with any system in which the

A context-free grammar can produce an unbounded number of derivations of arbitrary size for a string either because its rules permit a single category to appear twice in a nonbranching chain, or because expansions involving the empty string are not sufficiently restricted. The rules in (178) illustrate the first situation:

(178) X $\longrightarrow$ Y
       Y $\longrightarrow$ Z
       Z $\longrightarrow$ X

Any string which has a derivation including the category X will be infinitely ambiguous. There is a larger derivation with the domination chain X–Y–Z–X replacing the single X, and a still larger one with one of those X's replaced by another chain, and so on. The derivations that result from rules of this sort are in a certain sense peculiar. The nonbranching recursive cycles permit a superstructure of arbitrary size to be constructed over a single terminal or group of terminals (or even over the empty string). The c-structure is thus highly repetitive, and the f-description, which is based on a fixed set of lexical schemata and arbitrary repetitions of a finite set of grammatical schemata, is also. While the c-structure and f-structure can be of unbounded size, they encode only a finite amount of nonredundant information that is relevant to the functional or semantic interpretation of the string.

Such vacuously repetitive structures are without intuitive or empirical motivation. Presumably, neither linguists nor language learners would postulate rules of grammar whose purpose is to produce these derivations. However, linguists and language learners both are likely to propose rules whose purpose is to express certain surface structure generalizations but which have derivations of this sort as unintended consequences. For example, suppose that the grammar that includes (178) also has a large number of alternative rules for expanding Y and Z. Suppose further that except for the undesired cyclic X–Y–Z–X chain, X can dominate everything that Y and Z dominate. Only the intended derivations are permitted if X expands to a new category Y' whose rules are exactly the same as the rules for Y except that another new category Z' appears in place of Z in (178). The rules for Z' are those of Z without the X alternative. This much more complicated grammar does not make explicit the almost complete equivalence of the Y–Y' and Z–Z' categories. Except for the one spurious derivation, the original grammar (178) is a much more revealing description of the linguistic facts.

---

definition of grammaticality involves an evaluation or interpretation of the context-free derivations.

The following rules illustrate how derivations of arbitrary size may also result from unrestricted empty string expansions:

(179) P $\longrightarrow$ P P

     P $\longrightarrow$ e

If a P dominates (either directly or indirectly) a lexical item in one derivation, there will be another derivation in which that P has a mother and sister which are both P, with the sister expanding to the empty string. Without further stipulations, rules of this sort can apply an indefinite number of times. We introduced empty strings in Section 7 to represent the lower end of long-distance dependencies. These e's have controllee metavariables and thus are uniquely associated with the lexical signature of a control domain. The possibility of arbitrary repetitions does not arise because derivations for a string of length n can have no more than n controlled e's. An empty string may appear in a c-structure rule for another reason, however. It can alternate with other rule elements in order to mark them as optional. An *optionality* e is a generalization of the standard parenthesis notation for c-structure optionality; it permits functional schemata to be introduced when the optional constituents are omitted. An optionality e does not have the controllee metavariable that inhibits repetitions of controlled e's and, according to the standard interpretation of context-free rules, may appear in derivations indefinitely many times with no intervening lexical items. These derivations are redundant and unmotivated, just like those with nonbranching dominance cycles. The possibility of repeating rule elements with fixed schema sets and no new lexical information is, again, an unintended consequence of a simple notational device for conflating sets of closely related rules.

Having argued that the vacuous derivations involving nonbranching dominance chains and repeated optionality e's are unmotivated and undesired, we now simply exclude them from functional consideration. We do this by restricting what it means to be a "valid" c-structure derivation in the sense of (177a):

(180) *Definition of Valid Derivation*

    A c-structure derivation is valid if and only if no category appears twice in a nonbranching dominance chain, no nonterminal exhaustively dominates an optionality e, and at least one lexical item or controlled e appears between two optionality e's derived by the same rule element.

This definition, together with the fact that controlled e's are associated with unique lexical signatures, implies that for any string the size and number of c-structure derivations relevant to our notion of grammaticality is bounded as a function of n, even though no such bounds exist according to the standard interpretation for context-free grammars. Note that this restriction on derivations does not affect the language of the c-structure grammar: it is well known that a string has a valid c-structure with no cycles and no e's if and only if it has any c-structure at all (see Hopcroft and Ullman 1969).

With the validity of a derivation defined as in (180), the following theorem can be proved:

(181)   *Decidability Theorem*
For any lexical-functional grammar G and for any string s, it is decidable whether s belongs to the language of G.

We observe that algorithms exist for enumerating just the finite number of valid derivations, if any, that G assigns to s. A conventional context-free parsing algorithm, for example, can easily be modified to notice and avoid nonbranching cycles, to keep track of the source of optionality e's and avoid repetitions, and to postulate no more controlled e's than there are words in the string. With the valid derivations in hand, there are algorithms, as outlined above, for determining whether any of them satisfies the functional conditions (177b–177e). Theorem (181) is thus established.[49]

Theorem (181) sets an upper bound on the generative capacity of lexical-functional grammar: only the recursive as opposed to recursively enumerable languages are generable. It is possible to set a tighter bound on the generative power of our formalism. Because of the nearly nested restriction on proper instantiation, for any lexical-functional grammar G a nondeterministic linear bounded automaton can be constructed that accepts exactly the language of G. Lexical-functional languages are there-

---

[49]Given the functional apparatus of our theory, we can demonstrate that the restrictions in (180) are necessary as well as sufficient for recursiveness. If nonbranching dominance cycles are allowed, there is a straightforward way of simulating the computation of an arbitrary Turing machine. The Turing machine tape is encoded in the f-structure, each level of which corresponds to one cell and has up to three attributes, CONTENTS (whose value is drawn from the TM's tape vocabulary), LEFTCELL (whose value is an encoding of the cell to the left), and RIGHTCELL. Each state of the TM is represented by a nonterminal category, and a transition from state q_i to q_j is represented by a rule rewriting q_i as q_j. A single rule expands the starting category of the grammar to the initial state of the machine, and that rule has schemata that describe the TM's input tape. Starting at the top of the c-structure, each node in the nonbranching tree represents the next transition of the machine, and the f-structure at each node is the tape at that transition. The tape operations of a transition appear as schemata on the corresponding c-structure rule. They inspect the contents of the mother f-structure and produce an appropriate daughter f-structure. The lexical categories correspond to the final states of the machine, and the f-structure for a prelexical node is an encoding of the TM's output tape.

fore included within the context-sensitive languages. The details of this construction are quite complicated and will be presented in a separate paper. In brief, the c-structure with attached schemata for any string of length n can be discovered and represented by an automaton with a working tape whose size is bounded by a linear function of n. This automaton, however, cannot introduce actual variables and substitute them for metavariables as the instantiation procedure specifies, since that would require a nonlinear amount of space (roughly proportional to n log n). Instead, it uses the arrangement of metavariables in the c-structure to determine the implicit synonymy relations that the actual variables would simply make explicit. The nearly nested restriction guarantees that these relations can be computed using a linear amount of working storage.[50] With synonymous metavariables identified, the functional well-formedness conditions (177c–177e) can also be verified in a linear amount of space.

The generative power of lexical-functional grammar is obviously bounded from below by the class of context-free grammars. Any given context-free grammar is a legitimate c-structure grammar with no grammatical schemata. As noted above, the strings with valid c-structure derivations are exactly those that belong to the context-free language. The sets of schemata for those derivations are empty and are vacuously instantiated to produce an empty f-description whose unique minimal solution is the null f-structure. The functional component thus does no filtering, and the c-structure grammar under our interpretation is weakly equivalent to the grammar interpreted in the ordinary context-free way.

In fact, LFG has greater generative power than the class of context-free grammars, for it allows grammars for languages that are known not to be context-free. The language $a^n b^n c^n$ is a classic example of such a language. Its strings consist of a sequence of a's followed by the same number of b's and then c's. A grammar for this language is shown in (182):

$$(182) \quad S \quad \longrightarrow \quad A \qquad B \qquad C$$
$$\uparrow = \downarrow \quad \uparrow = \downarrow \quad \uparrow = \downarrow$$

---

[50]Certain other restrictions on metavariable correspondences will also provide this guarantee. For example, a nearly *crossed* restriction would also suffice, but it would entail more cumbersome models of processing. Formally, what must be excluded is arbitrary degrees of nesting and crossing.

$$A \longrightarrow \left\{ \begin{array}{c} a \\ (\uparrow \text{ COUNT}) = 0 \\ \\ a \qquad A \\ (\uparrow \text{ COUNT}) = \downarrow \end{array} \right\}$$

$$B \longrightarrow \left\{ \begin{array}{c} b \\ (\uparrow \text{ COUNT}) = 0 \\ \\ b \qquad B \\ (\uparrow \text{ COUNT}) = \downarrow \end{array} \right\}$$

$$C \longrightarrow \left\{ \begin{array}{c} c \\ (\uparrow \text{ COUNT}) = 0 \\ \\ c \qquad C \\ (\uparrow \text{ COUNT}) = \downarrow \end{array} \right\}$$

The c-structure rules produce a's, b's, and c's in sequences of arbitrary length, as illustrated by the c-structure for $aaabbc$ in (183):

(183)

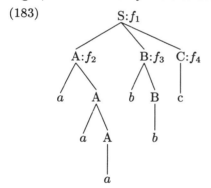

The lengths of those sequences, however, are encoded in the f-structure. For each of the A, B, and C nodes in the tree, the number of COUNT attributes in the $\downarrow$ f-structure of that node is a count of the elements in that node's terminal sequence. Thus, the f-structures shown in (184) for the f_2, f_3, and f_4 nodes have three, two, and one COUNT's, respectively.

(184) f_2[COUNT [COUNT [COUNT 0]]]

f_3[COUNT [COUNT 0]]

f_4[COUNT 0]

The attempt to equate these three f-structures in accordance with the schemata on the S rule leads to a violation of the Uniqueness Condition, and the string is marked ungrammatical. Only if the terminal sequences are all of the same length can the f-structures be combined.

The f-structure in this grammar records the one string property, sequence length, that is crucially needed for this particular context-sensitive test. If instead we let the f-structure be a complete, isomorphic image of the c-structure tree, we can describe a repetition language, another classical example of a non-context-free language. This is a language whose sentences are all of the form $\omega\omega$, where ω stands for an arbitrary string over some vocabulary. We start with a simple context-free grammar for the strings ω, for example, the rule in (185a).

$$(185) \quad \text{a.} \quad W \longrightarrow L \begin{pmatrix} W \\ (\uparrow\ w) = \downarrow \end{pmatrix}$$

$$\text{b.} \quad S \longrightarrow \quad \begin{matrix} W \\ \uparrow = \downarrow \end{matrix} \quad \begin{matrix} W \\ \uparrow = \downarrow \end{matrix}$$

All words in the vocabulary are assumed to belong to the lexical category L, so this rule generates arbitrary strings under right-branching tree structures. If for every word x there is a distinct symbol x, and if x has $(\uparrow\ \text{L}) = \text{X}$ as its only lexical schema, the $\downarrow$ f-structure of a W node will be an exact image of its subtree. For example, (186) shows the c-structure that this grammar would assign to the ungrammatical string $abcdbc$, and (187) gives the f-structures for the two topmost W nodes:

(186)

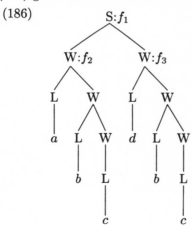

(187)

$$f_2: \begin{bmatrix} \text{L} & \text{A} \\ \text{W} & \begin{bmatrix} \text{L} & \text{B} \\ \text{W} & [\text{L} \quad \text{C}] \end{bmatrix} \end{bmatrix}$$

$$f_3: \begin{bmatrix} \text{L} & \text{D} \\ \text{W} & \begin{bmatrix} \text{L} & \text{B} \\ \text{W} & [\text{L} \quad \text{C}] \end{bmatrix} \end{bmatrix}$$

These f-structures contradict the schemata on the S rule, which assert that they are identical. The f-structures for the two W's in sequence will be the same only if their subtrees and hence their terminal strings are also the same.

We can thus characterize within our formalism at least some of the non-context-free context-sensitive languages. There is nothing devious or obscure about the grammars for these languages: they use ordinary functional mechanisms in perfectly straightforward ways. The additional generative power comes from two features of LFG, function composition and the equality predicate. Function composition permits f-structures to encode a wide range of tree properties, while the equality predicate can enforce a match between the properties encoded from different nodes. We can be even more specific about the source of our context-sensitive power. If all schemata in a grammar equate attribute values only to constants (e.g., schemata of the form $d_1 = d_2$, where d_2 designates a symbol or semantic form), then a weakly equivalent context-free grammar can be constructed. In this grammar the information contained in the f-structure is encoded in an enlarged set of context-free categories. The additional power of lexical-functional grammar stems from schemata that equate two f-structures, for example, the identification schemata in the examples above.

We have shown that lexical-functional languages properly include the context-free languages and are included within the context-sensitive languages. LFG's generative capacity is both a strong point of our theory and also something of an embarrassment. Huybregts (1976) has argued that dependencies of the sort illustrated by (185) are quite productive in Dutch,[51] and such phenomena have been claimed to exist in other languages as well (e.g., Mohawk (Postal 1964) and the English *respectively* construction). Mechanisms of this power must therefore be a part of any adequate theory of human language.

On the other hand, the problem of recognizing languages with context sensitivities can be computationally much more complex than the

---

[51]Bresnan et al. (1982) discuss the formal consequences of the Dutch dependencies and provide a simple lexical-functional description of them.

recognition problem for context-free languages. If our system turns out to have full context-sensitive power, then there are no known solutions to the recognition problem that require less than exponential computational resources in the worst case. It might therefore seem that, contrary to the Competence Hypothesis, lexical-functional grammars cannot be naturally incorporated into performance models that simulate the apparent ease of human comprehension.

There are several reasons why this conclusion does not necessarily follow. First, an explanatory linguistic theory undoubtedly will impose a variety of substantive constraints on how our formal devices may be employed in grammars of human languages. Some candidate constraints have been mentioned in passing (e.g., the constraints on functional control schemata and the principle of functional locality), and others are under current investigation. It is quite possible that the worst case computational complexity for the subset of lexical-functional grammars that conform to such constraints will be plausibly sub-exponential. Second, while the Competence Hypothesis asserts that a grammar will be a significant component of a performance model, the grammar is not identified with the processor that interprets it. An adequate theory of performance might impose certain space and time limitations on the processor's capabilities or specify certain non-grammatical heuristic strategies to guide the processor's computations (see for example the scheduling heuristics described by Ford, Bresnan, and Kaplan (1982)). Given these further assumptions, the performance model might actually exhibit the worst case behavior very rarely and then only under special circumstances. Finally, it is quite possible that the exponential explosion is in fact psychologically realistic. For our formal system, this processing complexity is not the result of a lengthy search along erroneous paths of computation. Rather, it comes about only when the c-structure grammar assigns an exponential number of c-structure ambiguities to a string. To the extent that c-structure is a psychologically real level of representation, it seems plausible that ambiguities at that level will be associated with increased cognitive load.

We conjecture, then, that the generative power of our system is not only necessary for adequate linguistic descriptions but is also compatible with realistic models of psycholinguistic performance. In keeping with the Competence Hypothesis, we believe that performance models that incorporate linguistically justified lexical-functional grammars will ultimately provide an explanatory account of the mental operations that underlie human linguistic abilities.

Appendix: F-description solution operators

An intuitive description of our f-description solution algorithm was presented in Section 4. The algorithm involves three basic operators: Locate, Merge, and Include. If d_1 and d_2 are designators, then an f-description equality of the form $d_1 = d_2$ is processed by performing:

$$\text{Merge}[\text{Locate}[d_1], \text{Locate}[d_2]]$$

and a membership statement of the form $d_1 \in d_2$ is processed by performing:

$$\text{Include}[\text{Locate}[d_1], \text{Locate}[d_2]]$$

We now give the formal definitions of these operators.

Locate, Merge, and Include all cause modifications to a collection of entities and variable assignments C, either by modifying an already existing entity or by substituting one entity for every occurrence of another. We specify substitution as a separate suboperator, since it is common to all three operators:

(188)   *Definition of Substitute*

For two entities *old* and *new*, Substitute[*new*, *old*] replaces all occurrences of *old* in C with *new*, assigns *new* as the value of variables that previously had *old* as their assignment (in addition to any variables that had *new* as their value previously), and removes *old* from C.

Applying the Substitute operator makes all previous designators of *old* and *new* be designators of *new*.

The Locate operator takes a designator d as input. If successful, it finds a value for d in a possibly modified entity collection,

(189) *Definition of Locate*

   (a) If d is an entity in C, then Locate[d] is simply d.

   (b) If d is a symbol or semantic form character string, Locate[d] is the symbol or semantic form with that representation.

   (c) If d is a variable,

        If d is already assigned a value in C, Locate[d] is that value.

        Otherwise, a new place-holder is added to C and assigned as the value of d. Locate[d] is that new place-holder.

   (d) Otherwise, d is a function-application expression of the form $(f\ s)$. Let F and S be the entities Locate[f] and Locate[s] respectively.

        If S is not a symbol or place-holder, or if F is not an f-structure or place-holder, the f-description has no solution.

        If F is an f-structure:

           If S is a symbol or place-holder with a value defined in F, then Locate[d] is that value.

           Otherwise, S is a place-holder or a symbol for which F has no value. F is modified to define a new place-holder as the value of S. Locate[d] is that place-holder.

        Otherwise, F is a place-holder. A new f-structure F' is constructed with a single pair that assigns a new place-holder value to S, and Substitute[F', F] is performed. Locate[d] is then the new place-holder value.

(189a) provides closure by allowing an entity to serve as a designator of itself. The recursive invocations of Locate that yield F and S in (189d) enable the values of all functional compositions to be obtained. The consistency check is specified in the first clause of (189d). A Locate attempt fails if it requires an entity already known not to be an f-structure to be applied as a function, or an entity known not to be a symbol to be used as an argument. The Merge operator is also defined recursively. It takes two entities e_1 and e_2 as input. Its result is an entity e, which might be newly constructed. The new entity is substituted for both e_1 and e_2 in C so that all designators of e_1 and e_2 become designators of e instead.

(190)   *Definition of Merge*

  a. If e_1 and e_2 are the same entity, then Merge[e_1, e_2] is that entity and C is not modified.

  b. If e_1 and e_2 are both symbols or both semantic forms, the f-description has no solution.

  c. If e_1 and e_2 are both f-structures, let A_1 and A_2 be the sets of attributes of e_1 and e_2, respectively. Then a new f-structure e is constructed with

$$e = \{\langle a, v\rangle | a \in A_1 \cup A_2 \text{ and } v = \text{Merge}[\text{Locate}[(e_1\ a)],\\ \text{Locate}[(e_2\ a)]]\}$$

  Substitute[e, e_1] and Substitute[e, e_2] are both performed, and the result of Merge[e_1, e_2] is then e.

  d. If e_1 and e_2 are both sets, then a new set $e = e_1 \cup e_2$ is constructed. Substitute[e, e_1] and Substitute[e, e_2] are both performed, and the result of Merge[e_1, e_2] is then e.

  e. If e_1 is a place-holder, then Substitute[e_2, e_1] is performed and the result of Merge[e_1, e_2] is e_2.

  f. If e_2 is a place-holder, then Substitute[e_1, e_2] is performed and the result of Merge[e_1, e_2] is e_1.

  g. Otherwise, e_1 and e_2 are entities of different types, and the f-description has no solution.

The consistency check in (190b) ensures that nonidentical symbols and semantic forms are not combined, and the checks in (190c,d) guarantee that entities of different known types (i.e., excluding place-holders) cannot be merged. The recursion in (190c) propagates these checks to all the substructures of two f-structures, building compatible values for common function names as it proceeds down level by level until it reaches non-f-structure values.[52]

---

[52]The recursive specification in (190c) must be slightly complicated if f-structures are allowed to be cyclic, that is, to contain themselves as one of their attribute values, either directly or indirectly through some intervening f-structure levels. Structures of this kind would be induced by equations of the form $(f\ \alpha) = f$. If a Merge of two such structures is attempted, the recursive sequence might never reach a non-f-structure and terminate. However, any infinitely recursive sequence must repeat the merger of the same two f-structures within a finite number of steps. Merges after the first will have no effect, so the sequence can be truncated before attempting step (190c) for the second time. The Merge operator must simply keep a record of which pairs of f-structures it is still in the process of merging. The Locate operator is immune to this problem, since the number of its recursions is determined by the number of function-applications in the designator, which, being derived from the grammar or lexicon, is finite. While presenting no major formal difficulties, cyclic structures seem to be linguistically unmotivated.

The Include operator has a particularly simple specification in terms of the Merge operator. It takes two entities e and s as input and is defined as follows:

(191)   *Definition of Include*
       Perform Merge[$\{e\}, s$].

The first entity given to Merge is a new set with e as its only member. The set-relevant clauses of the Merge definition are thus applicable: if s is also a set, for example, (190d) indicates how its other elements will be combined with e.

With these operator definitions, the fundamental theorem that our algorithm produces solutions for all and only consistent f-descriptions can easily be proved by induction on the number of statements in the f-description. Suppose an entity collection C is a solution for an f-description of $n - 1$ statements. Then the collection after successfully performing Merge[Locate[d_1], Locate[d_2]] is a solution for the description formed by adding $d_1 = d_2$ as an nth statement, and the collection after successfully performing Include[Locate[d_1], Locate[d_2]] is a solution for the description formed by adding $d_1 \in d_2$ as an nth statement. If the Locate, Merge, or Include operators fail, the larger f-description is inconsistent and has no solution at all.

Acknowledgments

We are indebted to Martin Kay, Beau Sheil, and Tom Wasow for valuable suggestions and fruitful discussions over a period of several years. We also wish to thank Ken Church, Elisabet Engdahl, Kris Halvorsen, and Annie Zaenen for commenting on earlier drafts of this paper. This work was supported in part by a grant from the Alfred P. Sloan Foundation for research in cognitive science at the Massachusetts Institute of Technology.

References

Ackermann, Wilhelm. 1954. *Solvable Cases of the Decision Problem.* Amsterdam: North-Holland.

Akmajian, Adrian, Susan M. Steele, and Thomas Wasow. 1979. The Category AUX in Universal Grammar. *Linguistic Inquiry* 10(1):1–64.

Allwood, J. 1976. The Complex NP Constraint as a non-universal rule and some semantic factors influencing the acceptability of Swedish sentences which violate the CNPC Construction. In *University of Massachusetts Occasional Papers in Linguistics*, ed. J. Stillings. Amherst, MA: University of Massachusetts at Amherst.

Andrews, III, Avery. 1982a. Long Distance Agreement in Modern Icelandic. In *The Nature of Syntactic Representation*, ed. Pauline Jacobson and Geoffrey K. Pullum. 1–33. Dordrecht: D. Reidel.

Andrews, III, Avery. 1982b. The Representation of Case in Modern Icelandic. In *The Mental Representation of Grammatical Relations*, ed. Joan Bresnan. 427–503. Cambridge, MA: The MIT Press.

Bach, Emmon. 1977. Comments on the Paper by Chomsky. In *Formal Syntax*, ed. Peter W. Culicover, Thomas Wasow, and Adrian Akmajian. 133–155. New York: Academic Press.

Baker, C. L. 1977. Comments on the Paper by Culicover and Wexler. In *Formal Syntax*, ed. Peter W. Culicover, Thomas Wasow, and Adrian Akmajian. 61–70. New York: Academic Press.

Bell, Sara. 1980. Comparative restrictiveness of relational grammar and lexical syntax. Unpublished MS, University of British Columbia.

Bresnan, Joan. 1976. Evidence for a Theory of Unbounded Transformations. *Linguistic Analysis* 2:353–393.

Bresnan, Joan. 1978. A realistic transformational grammar. In *Linguistic theory and psychological reality*, ed. Morris Halle, Joan Bresnan, and George A. Miller. Cambridge, MA: The MIT Press.

Bresnan, Joan, and Jane Grimshaw. 1978. The Syntax of Free Relatives in English. *Linguistic Inquiry* 9(3):331–391.

Bresnan, Joan. 1982a. Control and Complementation. In *The Mental Representation of Grammatical Relations*, ed. Joan Bresnan. 282–390. Cambridge, MA: The MIT Press.

Bresnan, Joan. 1982b. Polyadicity. In *The Mental Representation of Grammatical Relations*, ed. Joan Bresnan. 149–172. Cambridge, MA: The MIT Press.

Bresnan, Joan. 1982c. The Passive in Lexical Theory. In *The Mental Representation of Grammatical Relations*, ed. Joan Bresnan. 3–86. Cambridge, MA: The MIT Press.

Bresnan, Joan, Ronald M. Kaplan, Stanley Peters, and Annie Zaenen. 1982. Cross-serial Dependencies in Dutch. *Linguistic Inquiry* 13:613–635.

Chomsky, Noam. 1965. *Aspects of the theory of syntax*. Cambridge MA: The MIT Press.

Chomsky, Noam. 1977. On WH-Movement. In *Formal Syntax*, ed. Peter W. Culicover, Thomas Wasow, and Adrian Akmajian. 71–132. New York: Academic Press.

Chomsky, Noam, and Howard Lasnik. 1977. Filters and Control. *Linguistic Inquiry* 8(3):425–504.

Engdahl, Elisabet. 1980a. *The syntax and semantics of questions in Swedish*. Doctoral dissertation, University of Massachusetts at Amherst.

Engdahl, Elisabet. 1980b. Wh-constructions in Swedish and the relevance of subjacency. In *Proceedings of the Tenth Annual Meeting of the North Eastern Linguistic Society*. University of Massachusetts at Amherst.

Erteschik, Nomi. 1973. *On the Nature of Island Constraints*. Doctoral dissertation, MIT.

Fodor, Janet Dean. 1978. Parsing strategies and constraints on transformations. *Linguistic Inquiry* 9:427–473.

Ford, Marilyn, Joan Bresnan, and Ronald M. Kaplan. 1982. A Competence-Based Theory of Syntactic Closure. In *The Mental Representation of Grammatical Relations*, ed. Joan Bresnan. 727–796. Cambridge, MA: The MIT Press.

Gazdar, Gerald. 1982. Phrase Structure Grammar. In *The Nature of Syntactic Representation*, ed. Pauline Jacobson and Geoffrey K. Pullum. 131–186. Dordrecht: D. Reidel.

Godard, Danièle. 1980. *Les relatives complexes en français: une évaluation des conditions sur les règles de mouvement*. Doctoral dissertation, Université de Paris X.

Grimshaw, Jane. 1979. Complement selection and the lexicon. *Linguistic Inquiry* 10:279–326.

Grimshaw, Jane. 1982. Subcategorization and grammatical relations. In *Subjects and other subjects*, ed. Annie Zaenen. 35–56. Bloomington, IN: Indiana University Linguistics Club.

Halvorsen, Per-Kristian. 1980. Modelling linguistic behavior: Notes on the computational modelling of theories of syntactic and semantic processing. Paper presented at the Symposium on Models in Linguistics, Oslo and Telemarch, Norway.

Halvorsen, Per-Kristian. 1982. Formal and functional explanations in semantics: The theory of adverbs. Unpublished MS, MIT.

Halvorsen, Per-Kristian. 1983. Semantics for Lexical-Functional Grammar. *Linguistic Inquiry* 14(4):567–615.

Hopcroft, John E., and Jeffrey D. Ullman. 1969. *Formal Languages and Their Relation to Automata*. Reading, MA: Addison-Wesley.

Huang, C.-T. James. 1982. *Logical Relations in Chinese and the Theory of Grammar*. Doctoral dissertation, MIT.

Huybregts, M. 1976. Overlapping dependencies in Dutch. In *Utrecht working papers in linguistics*, ed. G. de Haan and W. Zonneveld. Utrecht: Instituut A. W. de Groot voor Algemene Taalwetenshap.

Kaplan, Ronald M. 1972. Augmented transition networks as psychological models of sentence comprehension. *Artificial Intelligence* 3:77–100.

Kaplan, Ronald M. 1973. A multi-processing approach to natural language. In *Proceedings of the 1973 National Computer Conference*, 435–440. Montvale, N. J. AFIPS Press.

Kaplan, Ronald M. 1975a. On Process Models for Sentence Analysis. In *Explorations in cognition*, ed. Donald A. Norman and David E. Rumelhart. San Francisco: W. H. Freeman.

Kaplan, Ronald M. 1975b. *Transient Processing Load in Relative Clauses*. Doctoral dissertation, Harvard University.

Kay, Martin. 1979. Functional Grammar. In *Proceedings of the Fifth Annual Meeting of the Berkeley Linguistic Society*, ed. Christine Chiarello, John Kingston, Eve E. Sweetser, James Collins, Haruko Kawasaki, John Manley-Buser, Dorothy W. Marschak, Catherine O'Connor, David Shaul, Marta Tobey, Henry Thompson, and Katherine Turner, 142–158. The University of California at Berkeley. Berkeley Linguistics Society.

Levin, Lori S. 1982. Sluicing. In *The Mental Representation of Grammatical Relations*, ed. Joan W. Bresnan. 590–654. Cambridge, MA: The MIT Press.

Maling, Joan. 1980. Adjective complements: A case of categorial reanalysis. Paper presented at the Fourth Groningen Round Table: Problems in the Identification of Natural Categories, July 4-8.

Maling, Joan and Annie Zaenen. 1980. Notes on base-generation and unbounded dependencies. Paper presented to the Sloan Workshop on Alternatives to Transformational Grammar, Stanford University.

Maling, Joan, and Annie Zaenen. 1982. A Phrase Structure Account of Scandinavian Extraction Phenomena. In *The Nature of Syntactic Representation*, ed. Pauline Jacobson and Geoffrey K. Pullum. 229–282. Dordrecht: D. Reidel.

McCloskey, James. 1979. *Transformational syntax and model theoretic semantics : a case study in modern Irish*. Dordrecht: D. Reidel.

Mohanan, K. P. 1982a. Grammatical Relations and Clause Structure in Malayalam. In *The Mental Representation of Grammatical Relations*, ed. Joan W. Bresnan. 504–589. Cambridge, MA: The MIT Press.

Mohanan, K. P. 1982b. Grammatical Relations and Anaphora in Malayalam. In *MIT Working Papers in Linguistics*, vol. 4, ed. Alec Marantz and Tim Stowell. Cambridge, MA: Dept. of Linguistics and Philosophy, MIT.

Neidle, Carol. 1982. Case Agreement in Russian. In *The Mental Representation of Grammatical Relations*, ed. Joan Bresnan. 391–426. Cambridge, MA: The MIT Press.

Nelson, Greg, and Derek C. Oppen. 1980. Fast Decision Procedures Based on Congruence Closure. *Journal of the ACM* 27(2):356–364.

Perlmutter, David. 1983. *Studies in Relational Grammar 1*. Chicago: The University of Chicago Press.

Peters, Stanley. 1973. On Restricting Deletion Transformations. In *The Formal Analysis of Natural Language*, ed. Maurice Gross, Morris Halle, and Marcel-Paul Schützenberger. 171–188. The Hague: Mouton.

Pinker, Steven. 1982. A Theory of the Acquisition of Lexical-Interpretive Grammars. In *The Mental Representation of Grammatical Relations*, ed. Joan Bresnan. 655–726. Cambridge, MA: The MIT Press.

Postal, Paul M. 1964. *Constituent Structure*. Bloomington, IN: Indiana University Press.

Postal, Paul M. 1971. *Crossover Phenomena*. New York: Holt, Rinehart, and Winston.

Ross, John Robert. 1967. *Constraints on variables in syntax.* Doctoral dissertation, MIT.

Smith, Carlota. 1978. The syntax and interpretation of temporal expressions in English. *Linguistics and Philosophy* 2:43–100.

Wanner, E., and M. Maratsos. 1978. An ATN Approach to Comprehension. In *Linguistic Theory and Psychological Reality*, ed. Morris Halle, Joan Bresnan, and George A. Miller. Cambridge, MA: The MIT Press.

Wasow, Thomas. 1978. On constraining the class of transformational languages. *Synthese* 39:81–104.

Woods, William A. 1970. Transition Network Grammars for Natural Language Analysis. *Communications of the ACM* 13(10):591–606.

Zaenen, Annie. 1980. *Extraction rules in Icelandic.* Doctoral dissertation, Harvard University. Reprinted by Garland Press, New York, 1985.

Part II

Nonlocal Dependencies

Early work within LFG on the characterization of long-distance dependencies was based on the then-standard assumption that the relationship between a 'filler' and a 'gap' was properly characterized in c-structural terms. On analogy with the up arrow ↑, relating a c-structure node to its corresponding f-structure, Kaplan and Bresnan (1982) introduced the double arrows ⇑ and ⇓ to relate a local f-structure to the f-structure of a more distant, displaced constituent. This was done for two reasons: first, the c-structure was thought to provide the proper vocabulary for the statement of constraints on the relation of a filler to a gap. Second, there was thought to be no way to finitely encode a potentially infinite long-distance dependency in f-structure terms. Kaplan and Bresnan outlined the initial justification for this approach, and subsequent work provided further supporting evidence (Zaenen 1980, 1983).

However, LFG theory has evolved away from this initial c-structure encoding of long-distance dependencies. Long-distance dependencies interact strongly with subcategorization restrictions, and a c-structure approach therefore meshes well with theories in which subcategorization is expressed in terms of constituent structure frames. But subcategorization in LFG is defined on the functional structure, by means of the Completeness and Coherence conditions on the appearance of governable grammatical functions. Thus, the interactions of subcategorization and long-distance dependencies would be easier to account for if long-distance dependencies were also characterized in f-structure terms.

A second motivation emerged from the early work on coordination within LFG. Bresnan, Kaplan, and Peterson (1985) showed that many coordinate reduction facts follow from a simple extension to the interpretation of f-structure constraints. Bresnan, Kaplan, and Peterson proposed to represent a coordination construction in f-structure as a set containing the f-structures of the individual conjuncts. They then interpreted the assignment of an attribute-value to a *set* of f-structures as the assignment of that attribute-value separately to all the elements of that set. They showed that this had the desired effect of distributing information from outside the coordination to the representations of each of the conjuncts. But there are well-known interactions between coordination and long-distance dependencies, as characterized for example by the Across the Board Convention of transformational grammar (Williams 1977). These interactions would again be difficult to formalize if coordination is described in f-structure terms but long-distance dependencies are not.

These two motivations for moving long-distance dependencies to the f-structure component led to a deeper consideration of the formal difficulty presented by the need to encode potentially infinitely many possibilities in constraints that must be embedded in a finite grammar. In the CSLI Monthly Newsletter, Kaplan, Maxwell, and Zaenen (1987) first described a method for solving this mathematical problem. They provided a finite encoding of an infinite set of possible f-structural relations by permitting expressions denoting regular languages to appear in place of simple attributes in f-structure constraints. They called this new descriptive mechanism *functional uncertainty*, since it can be used to indicate that one of a set of alternative grammatical function assignments is acceptable even though a particular function cannot be uniquely determined from locally available information.

Given this new formal device, it became possible to characterize the relation between a filler and a gap in purely f-structural terms. The first paper in this section, "Long-Distance Dependencies, Constituent Structure, and Functional Uncertainty" by Kaplan and Zaenen, presents an analysis of long-distance dependencies along these lines. It argues that generalizations on the relation between a filler and a gap are best stated in terms of configurations of grammatical functions rather than configurations of c-structure nodes. Thus they provide linguistic justification for the functional account that goes beyond the original considerations involving subcategorization and coordination.

The third paper, "An Algorithm for Functional Uncertainty" by Kaplan and Maxwell, discusses the mathematical and computational properties of functional uncertainty. This paper shows that the satisfiability problem remains decidable when a system of LFG functional constraints is augmented with expressions of functional uncertainty. Kaplan and Maxwell establish this fact by presenting an algorithm for determining whether such an augmented system has a solution, and if so, for constructing a minimal set of satisfying f-structures. This is an incremental, constructive algorithm and thus can be incorporated into LFG-based computational implementations or psycholinguistic models.

This original formal analysis has stimulated other researchers to investigate mathematical issues that Kaplan and Maxwell did not address. Using only formal language techniques, Kaplan and Maxwell were unable to prove that the satisfiability of uncertainty constraints is decidable over a domain that includes cyclic f-structures. Bakhofen (1993) used algebraic and logical methods to resolve the question, showing that satisfiability is in fact decidable over these more complicated domains. On the other hand, it has now also been shown that constraint systems that combine (constructive) negation with uncertainty are *not* decidable. This was demonstrated directly by Baader et al. (1991) and Keller (1991, 1993), and it follows indirectly from the work of Blackburn and Spaan (1993). Blackburn and Spaan observe that systems containing a 'universal modality' are undecidable, and it is easy to create such a modal operator by combining negation and uncertainty. However, if functional uncertainties are limited in their use to nonconstructive constraining equations instead of defining equations, to use the original Kaplan and Bresnan (1982) distinction, then the satisfiability problem reduces to the verification problem and these undecidability results no longer apply. Keller (1993) has also shown how LFG's notion of functional uncertainty can be ported to grammatical systems that have Rounds-Kasper logic as their mathematical underpinning, and he has translated the Kaplan/Maxwell solution algorithm to that framework.

The interaction of long-distance and local dependencies with coordination is a prime focus of the fourth paper in this section, "Constituent Coordination in Lexical-Functional Grammar" by Kaplan and Maxwell. The paper is an outgrowth of the earlier work by Bresnan, Kaplan, and Peterson (1985), which first presented and argued for the approach to coordination that Kaplan and Maxwell develop.

Seen as a means for stating the relation between two f-structures, functional uncertainty was further extended with the introduction of 'inside-out functional uncertainty' (Kaplan 1988). While (standard) functional uncertainty is used to state the relation between a less embedded f-structure and a more embedded one (as in the case of the relation between a less embedded filler and a more deeply embedded gap), 'inside-out' functional uncertainty was used in the opposite way: to state a relation between a more embedded f-structure and a less-embedded one.

This additional way of specifying f-structural relationships has been applied to linguistic phenomena other than traditional filler-gap dependencies. Halvorsen and Kaplan (1988) used it in conjunction with constraints on the semantic projection to characterize the scope of quantifiers in certain configurations. Huang (1993) proposed a treatment of Mandarin questions which used inside-out functional uncertainty to specify the scope of in-situ wh-words. Inside-out uncertainty has also been used to state the relation between an anaphor and its antecedent, and that application is the subject of the second paper in this section, "Modeling Syntactic Constraints on Anaphoric Binding" by Dalrymple, Maxwell, and Zaenen. This work was further developed by Dalrymple (1990, 1993) and by Dalrymple and Zaenen (1991).

The question of the status of the 'gap' in a filler-gap dependency remains an open one in LFG. The first paper in this section includes a set of arguments by Kaplan and Zaenen that there are no 'gaps' or empty categories at c-structure; on their approach, the 'gap' is present only at f-structure. However, in Part III of this book, Bresnan argues in her paper 'Bound Anaphora on Functional Structures' that gaps must be represented in the c-structure as well as the f-structure. The resolution of this issue awaits further research.

References

Baader, F., H.-J. Bürckert, B. Nebel, W. Nutt, and G. Smolka. 1991. On the expressivity of feature logics with negation, functional uncertainty and sort equations. Technical Report RR-91-01. Saarbrücken: DFKI.

Bakhofen, Rolf. 1993. On the Decidability of Functional Uncertainty. In *Proceedings of the Thirty-First Annual Meeting of the ACL*, 201–208. Columbus, Ohio. Association for Computational Linguistics.

Blackburn, Patrick, and Edith Spaan. 1993. A Modal Perspective on the Computational Complexity of Attribute Value Grammar. *Journal of Logic, Language and Information* 2:129–169.

Bresnan, Joan, Ronald M. Kaplan, and Peter Peterson. 1985. Coordination and the Flow of Information through Phrase Structure. MS, Xerox PARC.

Dalrymple, Mary. 1990. *Syntactic Constraints on Anaphoric Binding*. Doctoral dissertation, Stanford University.

Dalrymple, Mary. 1993. *The Syntax of Anaphoric Binding*. CSLI Lecture Notes, No. 36. Stanford University: Center for the Study of Language and Information.

Dalrymple, Mary, and Annie Zaenen. 1991. Modeling Anaphoric Superiority. In *Proceedings of the International Conference on Current Issues in Computational Linguistics*, 235–247. Penang, Malaysia.

Halvorsen, Per-Kristian, and Ronald M. Kaplan. 1988. Projections and Semantic Description in Lexical-Functional Grammar. In *Proceedings of the International Conference on Fifth Generation Computer Systems*, 1116–1122. Tokyo, Japan. Institute for New Generation Systems.

Kaplan, Ronald M. 1988. Correspondences and their inverses. Paper presented at the Titisee Workshop on Unification Formalisms: Syntax, Semantics and Implementation, Titisee, Germany.

Kaplan, Ronald M., and Joan Bresnan. 1982. Lexical-Functional Grammar: A Formal System for Grammatical Representation. In *The Mental Representation of Grammatical Relations*, ed. Joan Bresnan. 173–281. Cambridge, MA: The MIT Press.

Kaplan, Ronald M., John T. Maxwell, and Annie Zaenen. 1987. Functional Uncertainty. *CSLI Monthly Newsletter*. January.

Keller, Bill. 1991. Feature Logics, Infinitary Descriptions, and the Logical Treatment of Grammar. Technical report. University of Sussex. Cognitive Science Research Report 205.

Keller, Bill. 1993. *Feature Logics, Infinitary Descriptions, and Grammar*. Stanford University: Center for the Study of Language and Information.

Williams, Edwin S. 1977. Across-the-Board Application of Rules. *Linguistic Inquiry* 8(2):419–423.

Zaenen, Annie. 1980. *Extraction rules in Icelandic*. Doctoral dissertation, Harvard University. Reprinted by Garland Press, New York, 1985.

Zaenen, Annie. 1983. On syntactic binding. *Linguistic Inquiry* 14:469–504.

3

Long-distance Dependencies, Constituent Structure, and Functional Uncertainty

RONALD M. KAPLAN AND ANNIE ZAENEN

1 Introduction

Tree representations are used in generative grammar to represent very different types of information. Whereas in structuralist practice (at least as reconstructed by early transformationalists), Phrase Structure Markers were used to represent surface cooccurrence patterns, transformational grammar extended their use to more abstract underlying structures where they represent, for example, 'grammatical relations'. The claim embodied in this extension is that the primitives of a tree representation, namely, linear order, dominance (but not multi-dominance) relations and syntactic category labels, are adequate to represent several types of information that seem quite dissimilar in nature. They have been used, for example, to represent the dependencies between predicates and arguments needed for semantic interpretation and also the organization of phrases that supports phonological interpretation.

Lexical-Functional Grammar (like Relational Grammar) rejects this claim[1] and proposes to represent information about predicate argument

---

This paper originally appeared in *Alternative Conceptions of Phrase Structure*, ed. Mark Baltin and Anthony Kroch (Chicago: Chicago University Press, 1989), 17–42. © 1989 by The University of Chicago Press. All rights reserved.

[1]In recent work in phrase-structure-based frameworks there has been some weakening of this claim. For example, almost all proposals now separate out linear order from dominance relations and represent grammatical functions mainly in terms of the latter and not the former. See Pullum (1982) for an early proposal separating these two aspects.

Formal Issues in Lexical-Functional Grammar
edited by
Mary Dalrymple
Ronald M. Kaplan
John T. Maxwell III
Annie Zaenen
Copyright © 1995, Stanford University

dependencies in structures that allow multi-dominance and ignore linear order. Moreover these frameworks claim that the primitives in these representations are not categories like noun or sentence. Rather they are of a different nature that approximates the more traditional functional notions of subject, object, etc. In a certain sense LFG formalizes a more traditional approach than the one found in transformational grammar. The use of tree representations (called constituent structures or c-structures in LFG) is restricted to the surface structure, which is assumed to be the input to the phonological component; information about predicate argument dependencies and the like is represented in the functional structure (f-structure).

Given this view on the use of phrase structure representations, it is a bit of an anomaly that the original formulation of LFG (Kaplan and Bresnan 1982) used c-structures to state generalizations about so-called long-distance dependencies of the type illustrated in (1):

(1)   Who did Bill claim that Mary had seen?

Most previous accounts of long-distance phenomena, done in generative frameworks where no other explanatory devices are available, were stated in phrase structure terms. Early LFG proposals (Kaplan and Bresnan 1982, Zaenen 1980, 1983) in effect incorporated and developed such c-structural notions without seriously examining the assumptions underlying them. But given that LFG makes a clear distinction between the functional and phrasal properties of an utterance and encodes predicate-argument relations specifically in functional structure (f-structure), this approach embodies the claim that these relations are not directly relevant to long-distance dependencies. This is a surprising consequence of this approach, given that so many other syntactic phenomena are more sensitive to properties and relations of f-structure than to those of c-structure. Indeed, a deeper investigation of long distance dependencies reveals that they too obey functional rather than phrase structure constraints. This motivates the revision to the LFG treatment of long distance dependencies that we propose in this paper. This treatment depends on a new formal device for characterizing systematic uncertainties in functional assignments.

The organization of the paper is as follows: in the first section we give an argument based on data from Icelandic that functional notions are necessary to account for generalizations about islands in that language. In the second section we sketch the mechanism of functional uncertainty that is needed to formalize these generalizations (for a more extensive discussion of the mathematical and computational aspects of this mechanism, see Kaplan and Maxwell 1988). In the third section we show how the system handles some rather recalcitrant data from English, and in the last section we discuss a case in which multi-dominance (or a similar many-to-one mechanism) is needed to get the right result.

2   The Relevance of Functional Information: Icelandic Island Constraints

It is well known that long distance dependencies involving adjuncts are more restricted than those involving arguments. To give an example from English, we can contrast example (1), where the initial *Who* is interpreted as an argument of the predicate *see* within the sentential complement of *claim*, with the following:

(2)   *Which picture did they all blush when they saw?

In (1) the embedded *see*-clause is an argument of the matrix verb *claim*, whereas in (2) the embedded clause is an adjunct to the main proposition. This contrast cannot be accounted for simply in terms of node labels, because in both (1) and (2) S and/or S' appear in the 'syntactic binding domain' (as defined, for example, in Zaenen 1983). In English, it can be plausibly claimed that these sentences differ in the configurations in which the nodes appear, so that a c-structure account of the contrast is not implausible. A similar contrast in acceptability is found in Icelandic. In the Icelandic case, however, it can be shown that no difference in surface phrase structure configuration can plausibly support an account of this kind of contrast.

To show this we will first quickly summarize the arguments given for surface structure in Thráinsson (1986) and then consider how they bear on the issue of extraction out of sentences dominated by PP's. Thráinsson (1986)[2] shows that sentences with an auxiliary or a modal have a surface structure that is different from those that have no auxiliary or modal. Both types are illustrated in (3a) and (3b) respectively:

(3)   a.   Hann mun stinga smjörinu í vasann.
           He will put butter-the in pocket-the.
           'He will put the butter in his pocket.'
      b.   Hann stingur smjörinu í vasann.
           He puts butter-the in pocket-the.
           'He puts the butter in his pocket.'

---

[2]Thráinsson's paper is written in a transformational framework but his generalizations translate in an obvious way into the framework used here. We use his analysis because it gives a very intuitive account of the data, but of course our remarks apply to all phrase structure accounts that hypothesize that the two types of PP's discussed below have the same attachment at some moment of the derivation.

A first place where the difference shows up is when a so-called wandering adverb is added to either of these sentences: whereas for (3a) there are only two possible positions for such an adverb as illustrated in (4), for (3b) there are the additional possibilities illustrated in (5):

(4) a. Hann mun **sjaldan** stinga smjörinu í vasann.
           He will seldom put butter-the in pocket-the.
           'He will seldom put the butter in his pocket.'

      b. *Hann mun stinga **sjaldan** smjörinu í vasann.
           He will put seldom butter-the in pocket-the.

      c. *Hann mun stinga smjörinu **sjaldan** í vasann.
           He will put butter-the seldom in pocket-the.

      d. Hann mun stinga smjörinu í vasann **sjaldan**.
           He will put butter-the in pocket-the seldom.

(5) a. Hann stingur **sjaldan** smjörinu í vasann.
           He puts seldom butter-the in pocket-the.
           'He seldom puts the butter in his pocket.'

      b. Hann stingur smjörinu **sjaldan** í vasann.
           He puts butter-the seldom in pocket-the.

      c. Hann stingur smjörinu í vasann **sjaldan**.
           He puts butter-the in pocket-the seldom.

This is not the only contrast between the two types of sentences; indefinite subjects and 'floating' quantifiers show the same placement contrasts. We refer to Thráinsson (1986) for examples of these two latter phenomena.

Rather than proposing that these three types of elements are introduced by different rules in sentences with and without auxiliaries, Thráinsson proposes that it is the constituent structure of the clause that differs while the constraints on the distribution of the adverbs, indefinite subjects and quantifiers remain the same. The generalization is that the adverbs, indefinite subjects and quantifiers are daughters of S but can appear in any linear position. Thus they can be placed between each pair of their sister constituents (modulo the verb second constraint, which prohibits them from coming between the first constituent of the S and the tensed verb). This will give the right results if we assume that the c-structure for sentences with an auxiliary is as in (6) whereas sentences without an auxiliary have the structure in (7):

(6)

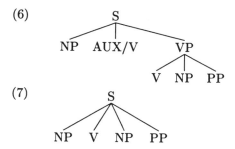

(7)

To be a bit more concrete, we propose to capture this insight in the following partial dominance and order constraints; these account for word order and adverb distribution in the sentences above:

(8)   Dominance Constraints:

  • S can immediately dominate {V, VP, NP, PP, ADV}
  • VP can immediately dominate {V, VP, NP, PP}
  • V is obligatory both in S and in VP.

(9)   Ordering Constraints:

  • for both S and VP: V<NP<PP<VP
  • for S: XP immediately precedes V[+tense]
    (verb-second constraint)

These constraints (given here in a partial and informal formulation), together with LFG's coherence, completeness, and consistency requirements, provide the surface structures embodying the generalization proposed by Thráinsson.

Given this independently motivated difference in c-structure, let us now return to the difference between arguments and adjuncts. Icelandic differs from English in allowing Ss in PPs, as shown in (10) to (13):[3]

(10)   Hann fór eftir að ég lauk verkinu.
       He went after that I finished work-the.
       'He left after I finished the work.'

---

[3]These constructions are analyzed as PP's in Icelandic because in all these cases the S′ alternates with a simple NP:

(i)   Jón kom eftir kvöldmatinn.
      'Jon came after dinner.'
(ii) Jón var að hugsa um Maríu.
      'Jon was thinking about Maria.'

In general, the simplest hypothesis about Icelandic phrase structure rules is that an S′ is permitted wherever an NP can appear (if the meaning allows it).

(11) Jón var að þvo golfið eftir að María hafði skrifað bréfið.
John was at wash floor-the after that Mary had written letter-the.
'John was washing the floor after Mary had written the letter.'

(12) þú vonaðist til að hann fengi bíl.
You hoped for that he will-get car.
'You hope that he will get a car.'

(13) Jón var að hugsa um að María hefði líklega skrifað bréfið.
John was at think about that Mary had probably written letter-the.
'John was thinking that Mary had probably written the letter.'

(10) and (11) illustrate cases in which the PP clause is an adjunct, whereas (12) and (13) are examples in which the PP clause is an argument. We will use these complex embedded structures because they allow a straightforward illustration of the patterns of long-distance dependencies: we find cases that exhibit the same local categorial configurations (PP over S'), but differ in their long-distance possibilities:

(14) *Hvaða verki fór hann eftir að ég lauk?
Which job went he after that I finished?
'Which job did he go after I finished?'

(15) *þessi bréf var Jón að þvo golfið eftir að María hafði skrifað.
This letter was John at wash floor-the after that Mary had written.
'This letter John was washing the floor after Mary had written.'

(16) Hvaða bíl vonaðist þú til að hann fengi?
Which car hoped you for that he will-get?
'Which car did you hope that he would get?'

(17) þessi bréf var Jón að hugsa um að María hefði líklega skrifað.
This letter was John at think about that Mary had probably written.
'This letter John was thinking that Mary had probably written.'

What these examples illustrate is that extractions are allowed from the PP-S' configuration only when it is an argument; it forms a wh-island when it functions as an adjunct.[4]

In defining the original c-structure formalization for long-distance dependencies, Kaplan and Bresnan (1982) noted that the correlation of ex-

---

[4]This is true for tensed clauses, but we have not yet investigated infinitives. It is well known that they tend to be less strong as islands, but further studies are needed to understand fully the influence of tense on island constraints.

traction constraints with categorial configurations is far less than perfect. They allowed bounding-node specifications in individual phrase-structure rules to characterize the variations of long-distance dependency restrictions across languages and across different nodes of the same category in a particular language. Indeed, the formal devices they introduced are sufficient to accurately describe these Icelandic facts: The argument and adjunct PP's can be introduced in separate phrase-structure expansions, with only the PP receiving the ADJunct function assignment boxed as a bounding node. But it is clear that the boxing device is used to import functional distinctions into the c-structure. Looking back at the discussion in Kaplan and Bresnan (1982) one realizes that it is always the case that when one instance of a given category is boxed as a bounding node and another is not, those instances also have different functional schemata attached (ADJ vs. one of the oblique argument functions in the Icelandic example, or the COMP vs. RELMOD functions that distinguish English *that*-complement S's from relative clauses.). Kaplan and Bresnan, while realizing that extraction domains cannot be defined in terms of obvious natural classes of c-structure categories or configurations, did not then recognize that natural classes do exist at the functional level.

They actually considered but quickly rejected the possibility of defining long-distance dependencies in terms of f-structure configurations partly because no rigorous functional formalization was at hand and partly because examples like (18) (Kaplan and Bresnan 1982, 134) seemed to indicate the long-distance relevance of at least some categorial information that would not be available in f-structure:

(18) a. She'll grow that tall/*height.
      b. She'll reach that *tall/height.
      c. The girl wondered how tall she would grow/*reach.
      d. The girl wondered what height she would *grow/reach.

These examples suggest that adjective phrases can only be extracted from AP positions and noun phrases only from NP positions, and, more generally, that fillers and gaps must have matching categories. Thus, they ignored the apparently functional constraints on long-distance extractions and defined special formal mechanisms for encoding those constraints in c-structure terms. In this they remained similar to other structure-oriented theories of the day.

The Icelandic data given above, however, suggest that a more functional approach would capture the facts more directly. In section 3, we will show that the data in (18) can also be naturally analyzed in functional terms. In fact constraints on extraction that in LFG terms are functional in nature have also been proposed by syntacticians working in a completely structure-oriented theory. The Icelandic data discussed above can be seen as a case of the Condition on Extraction Domain proposed in Huang (1982), which can be interpreted as an emerging functional perspective formulated in structural terms. It states that

(19)   No element can be extracted from a domain that is not properly governed.

Intuitively the distinction between governed and nongoverned corresponds to the difference between argument and nonargument. But it is clear from Thráinsson's arguments for the difference in structure between sentences with and without an auxiliary that the correct notion of government cannot be simply defined over c-structures. To represent the difference between the two types of PP's as in (20) would go against Thráinsson's generalization.

(20) a.

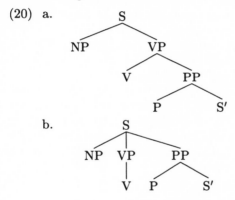

        b.

Indeed, adverb placement shows that both adjunct and argument PP's are sisters of S when there is no auxiliary but are both in the VP when an auxiliary is present:[5]

(21) a.   Ég vonaðist **alltaf** til að hann fengi bíl.
           I hoped always for that he will-get car.
           'I always hoped that he would get a car.'
      b.   Ég hef **alltaf** vonast til að hann fengi bíl.
           I have always hoped for that he will-get car.
           'I have always hoped that he would get a car.'

---

[5]Zaenen (1980) proposes that the extractability from an S is determined by a lexical property of the complementizer that introduces it. Under that hypothesis the adjunct/argument contrast discussed here would be unstatable, since the same complementizer appears in both constructions.

  c. *Ég hef vonast **alltaf** til að hann fengi bíl.
   I have hoped always for that he will-get car.

(22) a. Hann fór **alltaf** eftir að ég lauk verkinu.
    He went always after that I finished work-the.
    'He always went after I finished the work.'

  b. Hann hefur **alltaf** farið eftir að ég lyk verkinu.
    He has always gone after that I finished work-the.
    'He has always gone after I finished the work.'

  c. *Hann hefur farid **alltaf** eftir að ég lyk verkinu.
    He has gone always after that I finished work-the.

This pattern does not change when in the context of a long-distance dependency, as the following contrast illustrates:

(23) a. *Hvaða verki fór hann **alltaf** eftir að ég lauk?
    Which job went he always after that I finished?
    'Which job did he always go after I finished?'

  b. Hvaða bíl vonaðist bú **alltaf** til að hann fengi?
    Which car hoped you always for that he will-get?
    'Which car did you always hope he would get?'

Thus in Icelandic the same c-structure configuration allows for extraction when the PP is an argument but not when the PP is an adjunct. Netter (1987) draws a similar conclusion from data concerning extraposition of relative clauses in German. Given these facts, an adequate structurally-based account will have to appeal to stages in a derivation[6] and assume different tree structures for these sentences at the moment the relevant movement takes place. Whether this is feasible or not will depend on one's view on principles like cyclicity and the like and we leave it to practitioners of structural approaches to elaborate these accounts. From our nonderivational perspective the most straightforward approach seems also the most reasonable one: we will assume that long distance dependencies are sensitive to functional information and investigate further how such constraints can be formulated in functional terms.[7]

---

[6] A reanalysis of the verb and the prepositions as one unit would not obviously account for this contrast, and in any event, such an analysis has no independent motivation. Maling and Zaenen (1980) argue explicitly that there is no such reanalysis in Icelandic, and the fact that an adverb cannot be placed between the preposition and the following clause is further evidence against such a proposal:

 (i) *Ég vonaðist til **alltaf** að hann fengi bíl.
   I hoped for always that he will-get car.

[7] As far as we can see, the Icelandic data also do not allow for a syntactic account in frameworks like GPSG which define 'government' solely on the surface structure.

3   The Formal Account: Functional uncertainty

Standing back from the details of particular constructions or particular languages, long-distance dependencies seem difficult to characterize because they involve rather loose and uncertain connections between the superficial properties of local regions of a string and its more abstract functional and predicate-argument relations. For many sentences this connection is very direct and unambiguous. If, for example, the first few words of an English sentence have the internal organization of an NP, it is often the case that those words also function as the subject of the sentence. Of course, there are uncertainties and ambiguities even in simple sentences: in a garden-path sentence such as (24), it is not clear only from the local evidence which words make up the initial NP, and those words thus are compatible with two different functional configurations. This local ambiguity is resolved only when information about the later words is also taken into account.

(24)   The cherry blossoms in the spring.

Local uncertainties of this sort have never seemed difficult to describe, since all grammatical theories admit alternative rules and lexical entries to account for all the local possibilities and provide some method of composition that may reject some of them on the basis of more global contextual information. What distinguishes the uncertainties in long-distance dependencies is that the superficial string properties local to, say, a fronted English topic are compatible with an unbounded number of within-clause functional or predicate-argument relations. The infinite set of possibilities cannot be specified in any finite number of alternatives in basic rules or lexical entries, and which of these possibilities is admissible depends on information that may be available arbitrarily far away in the string.

Structural approaches typically handle this kind of unbounded uncertainty through conspiracies of transformations that introduce empty nodes and prune other nodes and thereby destroy the simple connection between the surface and underlying tree structures. Our solution to the uncertainty problem is much more direct: we utilize a formal device that permits an infinite set of functionally constrained possibilities to be finitely specified in individual rules and lexical entries.

Kaplan and Bresnan (1982) observed that each of the possible underlying positions of an initial phrase could be specified in a simple equation locally associated with that phrase. In the topicalized sentence (25):

(25)   Mary John telephoned yesterday.

the equation (in LFG notation) ($\uparrow$ TOPIC) = ($\uparrow$ OBJ) specifies that *Mary* is to be interpreted as the object of the predicate *telephoned*. In (26):

(26)   Mary John claimed that Bill telephoned yesterday.

the appropriate equation is ($\uparrow$ TOPIC) = ($\uparrow$ COMP OBJ), indicating that *Mary* is still the object of *telephoned*, which because of subsequent words in the string is itself the complement (indicated by the function name COMP) of the top-level predicate *claim*. The sentence can obviously be extended by introducing additional complement predicates (*Mary John claimed that Bill said that .... that Henry telephoned yesterday*), for each of which some equation of the general form

$$(\uparrow \text{ TOPIC}) = (\uparrow \text{ COMP COMP} \ldots \text{ OBJ})$$

would be appropriate. The problem, of course, is that this is an infinite family of equations, and hence impossible to enumerate in a finite disjunction appearing on a particular rule of grammar. For this technical reason, Kaplan and Bresnan abandoned the possibility of specifying unbounded uncertainty directly in functional terms.

   Instead of formulating uncertainty by an explicit disjunctive enumeration, however, a formal specification can be provided that characterizes the family of equations as a whole. A characterization of a family of equations may be finitely represented in a grammar even though the family itself has an infinite number of members. This can be accomplished by a simple extension of the elementary descriptive device in LFG, the functional-application expression. In the original formalism function-application expressions were given the following interpretation:

(27) $(f\, s) = v$ holds if and only if f is an f-structure, s is a symbol, and the pair $<s,\, v> \in f$.

This notation was straightforwardly extended to allow for strings of symbols, as illustrated in expressions such as ($\uparrow$ COMP OBJ) above. If $x = sy$ is a string composed of an initial symbol s followed by a (possibly empty) suffix string y, then

(28) $(f\, x) \equiv ((f\, s)\, y)$
       $(f\, \epsilon) \equiv f$, where ϵ is the empty string.

The crucial extension to handle unbounded uncertainty is to allow the argument position in these expressions to denote a set of strings. The interpretation of expressions involving sets of strings is derived in the following way from the interpretation (28) for individual strings. Suppose α is a (possibly infinite) set of strings. Then we say

(29) $(f\, \alpha) = v$ holds if and only if
       $((f\, s)\, \text{Suff}(s,\, \alpha)) = v$ for some symbol s,
       where $\text{Suff}(s,\, \alpha)$ is the set of suffix strings y such that $sy \in \alpha$.

In effect, an equation with a string-set argument holds if it would hold for a string in the set that results from a sequence of left-to-right symbol choices. For the case in which α is a finite set this formulation is equivalent to a finite disjunction of equations over the strings in α. Passing from finite disjunction to existential quantification captures the intuition that unbounded uncertainties involve an underspecification of exactly which choice of strings in α will be compatible with the functional information carried by the surrounding surface environment.

We of course impose the requirement that the membership of α be characterized in finite specifications. More particularly, it seems linguistically, mathematically, and computationally advantageous to require that α in fact be drawn from the class of *regular languages*. The characterization of uncertainty in a particular grammatical equation can then be stated as a regular expression over the vocabulary of grammatical function names. The infinite uncertainty for the topicalization example above can now be specified by the equation given in (30):

(30) $(\uparrow \text{TOPIC}) = (\uparrow \text{COMP}^* \text{ OBJ})$

involving the Kleene closure operator. One remarkable consequence of our functional approach is that appropriate predicate-argument relations can be defined without relying on empty nodes or traces in phrase-structure trees. This allows us to make the phrase-structure representations much more faithful to the sentence's superficial organization. Note that a particular within-clause grammatical function can be assigned by a long-distance dependency only if the phrase-structure rules optionally introduce the nodes that would normally carry that function in simple clauses.[8] This formulation is possible only because subcategorization in LFG is defined on f-structure via the Completeness and Coherence conditions and is independent of phrase-structure configurations.

The mathematical and computational properties of functional uncertainty are discussed further in Kaplan and Maxwell (1988). Here we summarize the mathematical characteristics briefly: it is clearly decidable whether a given f-structure satisfies a functional description that includes uncertainty specifications. Since a given f-structure contains only a finite number of function-application sequences, it contains only a finite number of strings that might satisfy an uncertainty equation. The membership problem for the regular sets is decidable and each of those strings can therefore be tested to see if it makes the equation hold.

---

[8]Thus a constraint like the one proposed by Perlmutter (1971) that (tensed) clauses must have local surface subjects (and hence that question movement of the subject is not allowed) would follow in a straightforward way from making the NP constituent bearing the subject equation obligatory in the phrase structure rule.

It is less obvious that the satisfiability problem is decidable. Given a set of equations describing a functional structure for a sentence, can it be determined that a structure satisfying all the equations does in fact exist? For a trivial description with a single equation, the question is easy to answer. If the equation has an empty uncertainty language, containing no strings whatsoever, the description is unsatisfiable. Otherwise, it is satisfied by the f-structure that meets the requirements of any string in the language, say the shortest one. The difficult case arises when the functional description has two uncertainty equations, say $(f\,\alpha) = v_\alpha$ and $(f\,\beta) = v_\beta$. If α contains (perhaps infinitely many) strings that are initial prefixes of strings in β, then the strings that will be mutually satisfiable cannot be chosen independently from the two languages. For example, the choice of x from α and xy from β implies a further constraint on the values v_α and v_β: for this particular choice we have $(f\,x) = v_\alpha$ and $(f\,xy) = ((f\,x)\,y) = v_\beta$, which can hold only if $(v_\alpha\,y) = v_\beta$. Kaplan and Maxwell (1988) show, based on a state-decomposition of the finite-state machines that represent the regular languages, that there are only a finite number of ways in which the choice of strings from two uncertainty expressions can interact. The original equations can therefore be transformed into an equivalent finite disjunction of derived equations whose remaining uncertainty expressions are guaranteed to be independent. The original functional description is thus reducible to a description without uncertainty when each of the remaining regular languages is replaced by a freely chosen member string. The satisfiability of descriptions of this sort is well-established. A similar proof of satisfiability has been developed by Mark Johnson (p. c.).

If the residual uncertainties include an infinite number of strings, then an infinite number of possible f-structures will satisfy the original description and are thus candidates for the f-structure that the grammar assigns to the sentence. This situation closely resembles the general case that arises for descriptions without uncertainties. As Kaplan and Bresnan (1982) noted, if a description is consistent then an infinite number of f-structures will satisfy it. These f-structures are ordered by a subsumption relation and Kaplan and Bresnan defined the subsumption-minimal satisfying structure to be the grammatically relevant one. The family of f-structures that satisfy the residual uncertainties is also ordered, not just according to subsumption but also according to the lengths of the strings that are chosen from the regular set. We extend the minimality condition of LFG by requiring that the f-structure assigned to a sentence include only the shortest strings realizing a particular uncertainty. In this way we follow the general LFG strategy of excluding from consideration structures that involve arbitrarily redundant information. See Kaplan and Maxwell (1988) for further discussion.

This is a general formalism that may apply to phenomena that are traditionally not thought of as falling into the same class as long-distance dependencies but that nevertheless seem to involve some degree of uncertainty. Johnson (1986) and Netter (1986) have used it in the analysis of Germanic infinitival complements and Karttunen (1989) discusses how similar extensions to Categorial Unification Grammar can account for related facts in Finnish that would otherwise require type-raising. Halvorsen (1988) has extended its use to the semantic domain, where it offers a simple characterization of various kinds of quantifier scope ambiguities. In this paper we illustrate the formalism by showing how it can be used to represent different conditions on long-distance dependencies. Consider the multi-complement sentence (31) whose c-structure and f-structure are given in (32) and (33):

(31)   Mary John claimed that Bill said that Henry telephoned.

(32)

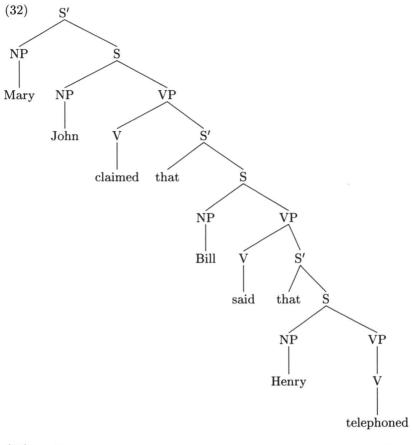

(33)

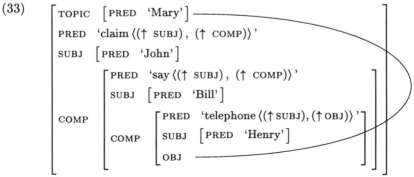

Notice that the tree in (32) has no empty NP node in the embedded clause. The link in the functional structure (33) indicates that the relation between the topic and the object of the most deeply embedded complement is one of functional identity, just like the relation between a functional controller in a raising or equi construction and its controllee (see the discussion of functional control in Kaplan and Bresnan 1982). Thus the same subsidiary f-structure serves as the value of both the TOPIC function and the OBJ function in the complement. The linguistic conditions on the linkages in functional control and long-distance dependencies are quite different, however. The conditions on functional uncertainty in long-distance dependencies can be subdivided into conditions on the potential functions at the end of the uncertainty path (the *bottom*, OBJ in this example) and conditions on the functions in the middle of the path (the *body*, here COMP*).

In the example above, the bottom is the function OBJ. Of course, there are a variety of other within-clause functions that the topic can have, and the equation might be generalized to

(34) $(\uparrow \text{TOPIC}) = (\uparrow \text{COMP}^* \text{ GF})$

where GF denotes the set of primitive grammatical functions. As we discuss in Section 3, this is too general for English since the topic cannot serve as a within-clause complement. A more accurate specification is

(35) $(\uparrow \text{TOPIC}) = (\uparrow \text{COMP}^* (\text{GF}-\text{COMP}))$

where GF−COMP denotes the set of grammatical functions other than COMP. This might appear to be still much too general, in that it permits a great number of possible bottom functions most of which would be unacceptable in any particular sentence. But whatever bottom function is chosen will have to be compatible with all other requirements that are imposed on it, not only case-marking and agreement etc. but also the general principles of consistency, completeness, and coherence. Although phrase-structure rules no longer play a role in insuring that the topicalized constituent will be linked to the 'right' place within the sentence, these functional conditions will rule out unacceptable sentences like (35):

(36)   *Mary, he said that John claimed that Bill saw Peter.

(This sentence does have an interpretation with *Mary* as a vocative but we ignore that possibility here.) If OBJ is chosen as the bottom function and the body reaches down to the lowest clause, the features of *Mary* will be inconsistent with the features of the local object *Peter*. An inconsistency would arise even if *Peter* were replaced by a repetition of the word *Mary* because of the instantiation property of LFG's semantic forms (Kaplan and Bresnan 1982, 225). If the body does not reach down to the lowest

clause, then one of the intermediate f-structures will be incoherent: neither of the predicates *claim* nor *say* take objects. The f-structure would
also be incoherent if some other function, say OBJ2, were chosen as the
bottom or if the body were extended below the lowest clause.

The following sentence has the same c-structure as (36) but is grammatical and even ambiguous, because the function ADJ can be chosen as
the bottom:

(37)   Yesterday, he said that Mary claimed that Bill telephoned Peter.

This is acceptable because ADJ is in GF but is not one of the *governable*
grammatical functions, one that can serve as an argument to a lexical
predicate, and thus is not subject to the coherence condition as defined
by Kaplan and Bresnan (1982).

Similarly, restrictions on the sequence of functions forming the body
can be stated in terms of regular predicates. The restriction for Icelandic
that adjunct clauses are islands might be expressed with the equation:

(38) $(\uparrow \text{TOPIC}) = (\uparrow (\text{GF}-\text{ADJ})^* \text{GF})$

This asserts that the body of the path to the clause-internal function
can be any sequence of non-adjunct grammatical functions, with the bottom being any grammatical function that may or may not be ADJ. For
English the body restriction is even more severe, allowing only closed and
open complements (COMP and XCOMP in LFG terms) on the path, as
indicated in (39):

(39) $(\uparrow \text{TOPIC}) = (\uparrow \{\text{COMP}, \text{XCOMP}\}^* (\text{GF}-\text{COMP}))$

Given this formalism, the theory of island constraints becomes a theory of the generalizations about the body of possible functional paths,
expressible as regular predicates on the set of uncertainty strings. For
example, if RELMOD is the function assigned to relative-clause modifiers
of noun-phrases, that function would be excluded from the body in languages that obey the complex-NP constraint.

Other conditions can be stated in the phrase-structure rules that introduce the uncertainty expression. These rules are of the general form
indicated in (39):

(40)   S′ $\longrightarrow$ Ω Σ
                        $(\uparrow \text{DF}) = \downarrow$
                $(\uparrow \text{DF}) = (\uparrow \text{ body bottom})$

where Ω is to be realized as a maximal phrasal category, Σ is some sentential category, and DF is taken from the set of discourse functions (TOPIC,
FOCUS, etc.). This schema expresses the common observation that constituents introducing long-distance dependencies are maximal projections

and are sisters of sentential nodes. Restricting the introduction of discourse functions to rules of this sort also accounts for the observation that discourse functions need to be linked to within-clause functions (see Fassi-Fehri 1988 for further discussion). The rule in (41) for English topicalization is an instance of this general schema:

(41)   S′   →   XP or S′   S
                                ($\uparrow$ TOPIC) = $\downarrow$
              ($\uparrow$ TOPIC) = ($\uparrow$ {COMP, XCOMP}* (GF−COMP))

In English, S′ and any XP can occur in topic position. Spanish, on the other hand, seems to be a language in which some topic constructions allow NP's but not PP's (Grimshaw 1982).

4   Illustrations from English

As mentioned above, Kaplan and Bresnan (1982) noticed an apparent category-matching requirement in sentences like (42)–(43) (Kaplan and Bresnan 1982, example 134):

(42)   a.   The girl wondered how tall she would grow.
       b.   *The girl wondered how tall she would reach.

(43)   a.   The girl wondered what height she would reach.
       b.   *The girl wondered what height she would grow.

Grow seems to subcategorize for an AP and *reach* for an NP. But subcategorization in LFG is done in functional terms, and it turns out that independently motivated functional constraints also provide an account of these facts. First observe that *reach* but not *grow* governs the OBJ function, as indicated by the contrast in (44):

(44)   a.   *That tall has been grown.
       b.   That height has been reached.

Grimshaw (1982) shows that passivization is not dependent on syntactic category but on whether the verb takes an OBJ.[9] The verb *grow*, on the other hand, establishes a predicational relationship between its subject and its adjectival complement and thus governs the XCOMP function. The relevant lexical entries for *reach* and *grow* are as follows:

(45)   a.   reach: ($\uparrow$ PRED) = 'reach<($\uparrow$ SUBJ)($\uparrow$ OBJ)>'
       b.   grow: ($\uparrow$ PRED) = 'grow<($\uparrow$ SUBJ)($\uparrow$ XCOMP)>'
                    ($\uparrow$ SUBJ) = ($\uparrow$ XCOMP SUBJ)

---

[9]Jacobson (1982) points out that the verbs *ask* and *hope* are not susceptible to this analysis.

Sentence (42a) is acceptable if XCOMP is chosen as the bottom function: XCOMP makes the local f-structure for *grow* complete. *Tall*, being a predicative adjective, also requires a local subject, and that requirement is satisfied by virtue of the control equation ($\uparrow$ SUBJ) = ($\uparrow$ XCOMP SUBJ). The choice of XCOMP in (42b) is unacceptable because it makes the local f-structure for *reach* be incoherent. Choosing OBJ satisfies the requirements of *reach*, but the sentence is still ungrammatical because the f-structure for *tall*, in the absence of a control equation, does not satisfy the completeness condition. In (43a) the choice of OBJ at the bottom satisfies all grammaticality conditions. If OBJ is chosen for (43b), however, the f-structure for *grow* is incoherent. If XCOMP is chosen the f-structure for *grow* is complete and coherent, and the sentence would be acceptable if *what height* could take the controlled subject. Although some noun-phrases can be used as predicate nominals (*She became a doctor*, *She seems a fool*), others, in particular *what height*, cannot (**She became that/a height*, **She seems that height*, **I wonder what height she became/seemed*). Whether or not the restrictions ultimately turn out to be functional or semantic in nature, it is clear from the contrasts with *become* and *seem* that they have nothing to do with syntactic categories.

Not only is category-matching unnecessary, it does not always yield the correct results. Kaplan and Bresnan (1982) discussed the examples in (46) (their 136) where a simple category-matching approach fails:

(46) a. That he might be wrong he didn't think of.

　　 b. *That he might be wrong he didn't think.

　　 c. *He didn't think of that he might be wrong.

　　 d. He didn't think that he might be wrong.

In these examples the category of a fronted S' can only be linked to a within-clause position that is normally associated with an NP. Kaplan and Bresnan complicated the treatment of constituent control to account for these cases by allowing the categories of the controller and controllee both to be specified in the topicalization rule. A closer look at the lexical requirements of the verbs involved, however, gives a more insightful account. Bresnan (1982) proposes association principles between syntactic categories and grammatical functions. These principles lead to the following VP rule for English:

(47)　VP　$\rightarrow$

$$\begin{array}{cccccc} \text{V} & \text{(NP)} & \text{(NP)} & \text{PP*} & \cdots & \text{(S')} \\ & (\uparrow \text{OBJ}) = \downarrow & (\uparrow \text{OBJ2}) = \downarrow & (\uparrow (\downarrow \text{PCASE})) = \downarrow & & (\uparrow \text{COMP}) = \downarrow \end{array}$$

This rule embodies the claim that in English the OBJ function is only associated with NP's and the COMP function only with S'. Adopting these principles, we propose the following partial lexical entries for *think* and *think-of*:[10]

(48) a.   think: $(\uparrow \text{PRED}) = \text{'think}<(\uparrow \text{SUBJ}) (\uparrow \text{COMP})>\text{'}$
     b.   think: $(\uparrow \text{PRED}) = \text{'think}<(\uparrow \text{SUBJ}) (\uparrow \text{OBL}_{\text{OF}})>\text{'}$

The difference between the grammatical and ungrammatical sentences in (46) follows if COMPs cannot be the bottom of an uncertainty in English (whereas OBJ, OBJ2, and obliques such as OBL_{OF} can). For (46a) the choice of OBL_{OF} for the bottom is compatible with the semantic form in (48b), so the sentence is acceptable. Since COMP cannot be the bottom, OBL_{OF} and (48b) are also the only possible choices for (46b), but with this string the requirement that the preposition *of* be present is violated (this requirement is similar to the conditions on idiosyncratic case-marking, the details of which do not concern us here).[11]

It is true that the OBL_{OF} slot in (46a) is filled in a way that would be impossible in sentence internal position (46c), but this follows simply from the phrase-structure rules of English. There is no rule that expands PP as a preposition followed by an S', no matter what functional annotations might be provided; as we have seen in Section 1, this is a very language-specific restriction. But as far as the functional requirements of *think-of* go, nothing in the f-structure corresponding to an S' prevents it from serving as the OBL_{OF}.

Under this account of long-distance dependencies, then, there is no need to parameterize them in terms of particular phrase-structure categories. This proposal also easily handles the following contrasts, discussed in Stowell (1981):

(49)   Kevin persuaded Roger that these hamburgers were worth buying.

(50)   *That these hamburgers were worth buying, Kevin persuaded Roger.

(51)   Louise told me that Denny was mean to her.

---

[10]This analysis assumes an unlayered f-structure representation of oblique objects related to the proposal of Bresnan (1982) and slightly different from the two-level approach discussed by Kaplan and Bresnan (1982) and Levin (1986). The only change necessary to accommodate the two-level representation would be to allow the bottom to be a two-element sequence such as OBL_{OF} OBJ, the same sequence that *think-of* would subcategorize for under that approach.

[11]One kind of sentence that is not ruled out on syntactic grounds is:

That John saw Mary Bill kissed.

We assume that this is out for semantic reasons: that-clauses, regardless of their grammatical function, correspond to semantic propositions and propositions are not kissable.

(52)   That Denny was mean to her Louise told me (already).

They can be compared to

(53)   *Kevin persuaded Roger the news.

(54)   Louise told me the story.

(53) shows that *persuade* does not subcategorize for an OBJ2, while (54) shows that *tell* does take an OBJ2 as an alternative to the COMP assignment for (51). The relevant lexical information is given in (55).[12]

(55)   tell: $(\uparrow$ PRED$) = $ 'tell$<(\uparrow$ SUBJ$)$ $(\uparrow$ OBJ$)$ $(\uparrow$ OBJ2$)$ $>$'

or

$(\uparrow$ PRED$) = $ 'tell$<(\uparrow$ SUBJ$)$ $(\uparrow$ OBJ$)$ $(\uparrow$ COMP$)>$'

persuade: $(\uparrow$ PRED$) = $ 'persuade$<($ $\uparrow$ SUBJ$)$ $(\uparrow$ OBJ$)$ $(\uparrow$ COMP$)>$'

The ungrammaticality of (50) follows again from the fact that the bottom cannot be a COMP, whereas (52) is acceptable because an OBJ2 is permitted.

Our proposal is different from the one made in Stowell (1981) in that adjacency plays no role for us, so we do not need incorporation rules to account for (51–52). This is in keeping with our view that phrase-structure rules and functional structure are in a much looser relation to each other than in the theory that Stowell assumes. The fact that the incorporation analysis of (51) is not independently motivated is in turn a confirmation for this view.

Both the present proposal and the one elaborated in Stowell (1981) can be seen as accounts of a generalization made in phrase-structure terms by Higgins (1973), namely, that S′ topicalization is only possible from an NP position. Indeed, the present functional approach covers the cases

---

[12]Notice that according to our proposal the grammaticality of (i) does not license (ii):

(i)   John persuaded Roger.

(ii)   *That these hamburgers were worth buying, John persuaded.

Arguments slots in LFG are reserved for certain semantically restricted types, as the following unacceptable string illustrates:

(iii)   *John persuaded the fact.

One way to achieve this is to assume that each GF is associated with a thematic role and that lexical rules do not change these associations. For instance, a verb like *give* takes a goal and a theme, and in the OBJ, OBL$_{GOAL}$ realization the theme is linked to the OBJ and the goal to the OBL$_{GOAL}$. In the OBJ, OBJ2 construction, however, it is the goal that is linked to the OBJ and the theme to the OBJ2. For different ways to formulate this correspondence that preserve thematic role assignments, see Bresnan (1982) and Levin (1986). With *persuade*, the goal argument is obligatory and the prepositional argument is optional, as is shown by (iv):

(iv)   *John persuaded that Bill had left.

Higgins himself discusses. These include contrasts involving extraposition like those in (56):

(56) a. That Susan would be late John didn't think was very likely.

   b. *That Susan would be late John didn't think it was very likely.

Extraposition is a lexical rule that for each extraposable entry of the form in (57a) adds a lexical entry of the form shown in (57b):

(57) a. $(\uparrow \text{PRED}) = \text{'R}\langle(\uparrow \text{SUBJ}) \ldots \rangle\text{'}$

   b. $(\uparrow \text{PRED}) = \text{'R}\langle(\uparrow \text{COMP}) \ldots\rangle(\uparrow \text{SUBJ})\text{'}$
      $(\uparrow \text{SUBJ PERS}) = 3$
      $(\uparrow \text{SUBJ NUM}) = \text{SG}$
      $(\uparrow \text{SUBJ GEND}) = \text{NEUT}$

This rule applied to the lexical entry for *likely* yields (58) and accounts for the alternation in (59):

(58) likely: $(\uparrow \text{PRED}) = \text{'likely}\langle(\uparrow \text{COMP})\rangle(\uparrow \text{SUBJ})\text{'}$
      $(\uparrow \text{SUBJ PERS}) = 3$
      $(\uparrow \text{SUBJ NUM}) = \text{SG}$
      $(\uparrow \text{SUBJ GEND}) = \text{NEUT}$

(59) a. That Susan will be late is likely

   b. It is likely that Susan will be late.

Since a PRED value must be linked to a thematic function, either directly or by a chain of functional control, expletive *it* as in (59) is the only possible realization of the nonthematic SUBJ in (59b):

(60) it: $(\uparrow \text{PERS}) = 3$
      $(\uparrow \text{NUM}) = \text{SG}$
      $(\uparrow \text{GEND}) = \text{NEUT}$
      $\neg(\uparrow \text{PRED})$

With the extraposition entry in (58) the ungrammaticality of (56b) easily follows. The function COMP is not a legal uncertainty bottom, so that with this entry a complete functional structure cannot be assigned. Choosing SUBJ as the uncertainty bottom would be compatible with the entry corresponding to (57a), but this choice would result in the subject having a sentential PRED value, which the features for expletive *it* do not allow.

   The lexical extraposition rule also interacts with the phrase structure rule that introduces sentential subjects to exclude (60):

(61) *John didn't think (that) that Susan would be late was very likely.

Whereas the phrase-structure rule for embedded clauses is as given in (62a), main clauses also allow the one given in (62b):

(62) a. S $\longrightarrow$ (NP)   VP
         ($\uparrow$ SUBJ) = $\downarrow$

      b. E $\longrightarrow$ (XP)   VP
         ($\uparrow$ SUBJ) = $\downarrow$

E is the category for a root-node expression and XP can be any phrase that can bear the subject function, namely S', PP (as in *Into the room jumped a rabbit*; see Levin 1986 for discussion) and NP. In embedded position, however, we only find NP.[13]

Our discussion ignores embedded questions but it is clear that some contrasts like the one exemplified in (62) can be treated along the same lines:

(63) a. *Whether John would come early she didn't wonder.

      b. Whether John would come early she didn't know.

Translating the observations of Grimshaw (1979) into our framework, we would hypothesize that *wonder* takes a COMP only whereas *know* allows for a COMP and an OBJ. But the general problem of embedded questions needs further study: it is well known that in some cases they are more OBJ-like than *that*-clauses. We have not studied their behavior in enough detail to propose a general treatment.

We have shown in this section that a functional approach can account for the basic correspondences that characterize long-distance dependencies as well as previous category-matching approaches do, and also for a variety of additional facts that have seemed rather puzzling under a categorial analysis.

5 Interactions with Functional Control: Japanese Relatives

There are no multiply dominated substructures in phrase-structure trees, and, hence, any two nodes are connected by just one path. This is not the case with paths in functional structure. The following example shows such a multiple-path configuration:

(64) Mary John expected to walk.

---

[13]These rules also allow us to account for the ungrammaticality of (i) and (ii):

 (i) *That John will be late seems.

 (ii) *That John will be late Bill doesn't think seems.

We simply assume that *seem* has only the 'derived' lexical entry in (57b) and not the one in (57a). Thus the thematic argument with *seem* is always a COMP and never a SUBJ, and indeed there are no sentences like (iii) that might lead to (ii):

 (iii) *John/The fact seems.

(65)

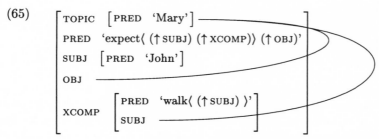

The matrix OBJ and the XCOMP SUBJ in this example are identified by an equation of functional control. This means that there are two equivalent ways of resolving the topic uncertainty in this construction, if XCOMP is allowed in the body and OBJ and SUBJ are both allowed at the bottom. Although there appears to be no need for both of these uncertainty paths in English, this formal possibility offers a simple account for certain interactions between coordination and long-distance dependencies in Japanese.

Saiki (1985) observes that some relative clauses in Japanese are constrained so that in a coordinate structure, when a SUBJ is bound in one conjunct, a SUBJ must also be bound in the other.[14] When there is a nonsubject in the one there has to be a nonsubject in the other conjunct too. The pattern is illustrated by the following examples:

(66) Takashi ga kat-te Reiko ga tabeta ringo.
      Takashi SUBJ bought Reiko SUBJ ate apple.
      'the apple which Takashi bought and Reiko ate.'

(67) Hon o yon-de rekoodo o kiita gakusei.
      Book OBJ read record OBJ listened-to student.
      'the student who read a book and listened to a record.'

(68) *Ookiku-te Reiko ga katta suika.
      Big Reiko SUBJ buy watermelon.
      'the watermelon which was big and which Reiko bought.'

(69) *Takashi ga nagut-te Reiko o ketobashita otoko.
      Takashi SUBJ hit Reiko OBJ kicked man.
      'the man whom Takashi hit and who kicked Reiko.'

Bresnan, Kaplan, and Peterson (1985) present a functionally-based theory of coordination within the LFG framework. According to this theory, coordinate structures are represented formally as a set in f-structure,

---

[14]Native speakers of Japanese seem to differ about the exact generalizations here. Our analysis is meant to illustrate the interaction between different components of the grammar, but as we are not experts in Japanese grammar, we remain agnostic about the exact analysis of Japanese.

with the elements of the set being the f-structures corresponding to the individual conjuncts. LFG's function-application primitive is extended in a natural way to apply to sets of f-structures: a set is treated as if it were a function with the properties that are common to all its f-structure elements. As Bresnan, Kaplan, and Peterson show, this simple extension, which is orthogonal to the extension (27) that we are proposing here, is sufficient to provide elegant accounts for the wide variety of facts that coordinate reduction rules and across-the-board conventions attempt to handle. The theory of coordination also interacts properly with the present theory of long-distance dependencies: a path of functional uncertainty that passes into a set will be resolved independently for each of the set's elements. Thus, for sentence (70a) the topic uncertainty will be resolved as XCOMP OBJ for the first conjunct and as XCOMP OBL$_{TO}$ for the second.

(70) a. Mary John expected to see and give the book to.
    b. *Mary John expected to see Bill and give the book to.

But even though the paths are allowed to differ from one conjunct to the other, it must be the case that if an uncertainty is resolved inside one of the functions it must also be resolved inside the other, as illustrated by (70b).

The fact that uncertainties are resolved independently for each conjunct, as required for the English example (70a), may seem incompatible with the Japanese pattern in (66–69). Indeed, if the within-clause role of the relative clause head is specified by a single uncertainty expression whose bottom allows either SUBJ or non-SUBJ functions, the constraint against mixing functions would not be satisfied. There is an obvious way of describing these facts, however, by specifying the within-clause function as a choice between two uncertainties, one with a SUBJ bottom and one with GF−SUBJ, as in the following rule for Japanese relative modifiers, adapted from Saiki (1985):

(71) NP →   S'   NP
        (↑ RELMOD) = ↓   (↑ RELMOD $\left\{ \begin{matrix} \text{XCOMP} \\ \text{COMP} \end{matrix} \right\}$* SUBJ) = ↓
                              or
                    (↑ RELMOD $\left\{ \begin{matrix} \text{XCOMP} \\ \text{COMP} \end{matrix} \right\}$* (GF−SUBJ)) = ↓

The analysis of these examples does not depend on the fact that f-structures can contain separate but equivalent paths. But there are other Japanese examples that contain two equivalent paths, one of which ends in a SUBJ and the other in a non-SUBJ. This situation arises in causatives, which, following Ishikawa (1985), are assumed to have the following lexical schemata:

(72) ($\uparrow$ PRED) = 'cause<($\uparrow$ SUBJ)($\uparrow$ OBJ2)($\uparrow$ XCOMP)>'
      ($\uparrow$ XCOMP SUBJ) = ($\uparrow$ OBJ2)

The functional control equation identifies the XCOMP's SUBJ with the OBJ2 of the matrix. Saiki (1985) noticed that in this situation our formalization predicts that either of the uncertainties in (71) can lead to the common element, so that causative phrases ought to be conjoinable with other clauses in which either a SUBJ or non-SUBJ is relativized. That this prediction is correct is shown by the acceptability of the following phrases (Saiki 1985):

(73) Takashi o nagutte, Reiko ga Satoru o ketobas-ase-ta otoko
      Takashi OBJ hit, Reiko SUBJ Satoru OBJ kick CAUS man
      'the man who hit Takashi and who Reiko caused to kick Satoru.'

(74) Takashi ga nagutte, Reiko ga Satoru o ketobas-ase-ta otoko
      Takashi SUBJ hit, Reiko SUBJ Satoru OBJ kick CAUS man
      'the man who Takashi hit and who Reiko caused to kick Satoru.'

Within a classical transformational framework, the causative could be analyzed as a raising or equi construction, but at the moment of wh-movement, the information about the 'deep structure' subjecthood of the noun phrase would be unavailable. It would thus be expected to behave only as an object. With trace theory and other enrichments of phrase structure approaches, one can imagine stating the right conditions on the long distance dependency. Again, however, there is no convergence of surface structure configuration and the configuration that must be postulated to account for these cases.

6   Conclusion

LFG proposes a distinction between functionally conditioned and c-structure dependent phenomena. We have argued that long-distance wh-constructions are in fact functionally conditioned, contrary to what was previously assumed, and hence should be accounted for in the f-structure. The Icelandic facts show that c-structure dominance relations are not always relevant, the English facts show that node labels alone do not allow the proper distinctions to be made, and the Japanese causative illustrates a case in which multi-dominance is necessary. In short, the primitives of phrase-structure representation are much less adequate than those of functional structure.

Of course phrase-structure accounts of these phenomena are possible if several (successive) tree structures are admitted to encode different types of information and if traces and/or reconstruction are introduced to give the effect of multi-dominance. It is clear, though, that these accounts are not more economical than the LFG approach: besides the succession of tree structures and abstract traces, further principles must be defined to govern the mapping from one tree representation to another (such as the pruning convention proposed in Thráinsson (1986) and distinctions between casemarked and non-casemarked positions as in Stowell (1981)). We are not suggesting that such representations and principles are incapable of yielding the right empirical results. But for the claim that functional generalizations can be stated in terms of structural primitives to be interesting, it has to be shown that the postulated phrase structures are independently motivated. As the Icelandic case illustrates, there are clear cases where they are not. Given this lack of convergence, we conclude that phrase-structure accounts obscure the basically functional nature of long-distance dependencies. In part this is because they do not formally distinguish them from purely distributional generalizations such as those concerning the ordering of adverbs in Icelandic.

Acknowledgments

Joan Bresnan, Per-Kristian Halvorsen, Lauri Karttunen, John Maxwell and an anonymous reviewer are thanked for comments on earlier versions of this paper, Joan Maling and Höskuldur Thráinsson for help with the Icelandic data and the students of the LFG course (Stanford, winter 1987) and the audience of the conference on Alternative Conceptions of Phrase Structure (NYU, July 1986) for reactions to oral presentations.

References

Bresnan, Joan. 1982. Control and Complementation. In *The Mental Representation of Grammatical Relations*, ed. Joan Bresnan, 282–390. Cambridge, MA: The MIT Press.

Bresnan, Joan, Ronald M. Kaplan, and Peter Peterson. 1985. Coordination and the Flow of Information through Phrase Structure. Unpublished MS.

Fassi-Fehri, Abdulkader. 1988. Agreement in Arabic, Binding, and Coherence. In *Agreement in natural language: Approaches, theories, descriptions*, ed. Michael Barlow and Charles A. Ferguson. Stanford University: CSLI/The University of Chicago Press.

Grimshaw, Jane. 1979. Complement selection and the lexicon. *Linguistic Inquiry* 10:279–326.

Grimshaw, Jane. 1982. Subcategorization and grammatical relations. In *Subjects and other subjects*, ed. Annie Zaenen. 35–56. Bloomington: Indiana University Linguistics Club.

Halvorsen, Per-Kristian. 1988. Situation Semantics and Semantic Interpretation in Constraint–Based Grammars. In *Proceedings of the International Conference on Fifth Generation Computer Systems, FGCS-88*, 471–478. Tokyo, Japan, November. Also published as CSLI Technical Report CSLI-TR-101, Stanford University, 1987. Reprinted in Part IV of this volume.

Higgins, F. R. 1973. On J. Emonds's analysis of extraposition. In *Syntax and Semantics*, ed. John P. Kimball, Vol. 2, 149–195. New York: Academic Press.

Huang, C.-T. James. 1982. *Logical Relations in Chinese and the Theory of Grammar*. Doctoral dissertation, MIT.

Ishikawa, Akira. 1985. *Complex predicates and lexical operations in Japanese*. Doctoral dissertation, Stanford University.

Jacobson, Pauline. 1982. Comments on 'Subcategorization and Grammatical Relations'. In *Subjects and other subjects*, ed. Annie Zaenen. 57–70. Bloomington: Indiana University Linguistics Club.

Johnson, Mark. 1986. The LFG treatment of discontinuity and the double infinitive construction in Dutch. In *Proceedings of the Fifth West Coast Conference on Formal Linguistics*, ed. Mary Dalrymple, Jeffrey Goldberg, Kristin Hanson, Michael Inman, Chris Piñon, and Stephen Wechsler, 102–118. Stanford University. Stanford Linguistics Association.

Kaplan, Ronald M., and Joan Bresnan. 1982. Lexical-Functional Grammar: A Formal System for Grammatical Representation. In *The Mental Representation of Grammatical Relations*, ed. Joan Bresnan, 173–281. Cambridge, MA: The MIT Press. Reprinted in Part I of this volume.

Kaplan, Ronald M., and John T. Maxwell. 1988. An Algorithm for Functional Uncertainty. In *Proceedings of COLING-88*, Vol. 1, 297–302. Budapest. Reprinted in Part II of this volume.

Karttunen, Lauri. 1989. Radical Lexicalism. In *Alternative Conceptions of Phrase Structure*, ed. Mark Baltin and Anthony Kroch. 43–65. Chicago University Press.

Levin, Lori S. 1986. *Operations on lexical forms: Unaccusative rules in Germanic languages*. Doctoral dissertation, MIT.

Maling, Joan, and Annie Zaenen. 1985. Preposition stranding and passive. *Nordic Journal of Linguistics* 8.

Netter, Klaus. 1986. Getting things out of order. In *Proceedings of COLING-86*, 494–496. Bonn.

Netter, Klaus. 1987. Nonlocal dependencies and infinitival constructions in German. Unpublished MS, University of Stuttgart.

Perlmutter, David. 1971. *Deep and Surface Structure Constraints in Syntax*. New York: Holt, Reinhart, and Winston.

Pullum, Geoffrey K. 1982. Free Word Order and Phrase Structure Rules. In *Proceedings of the Twelfth Annual Meeting of the North Eastern Linguistic Society*, ed. James Pustejovsky and Peter Sells, 209–220. University of Massachusetts at Amherst.

Saiki, Mariko. 1985. On the coordination of gapped constituents in Japanese. In *Papers from the Twenty-First Regional Meeting of the Chicago Linguistic Society*, ed. William H. Eilfort, Paul D. Kroeber, and Karen L. Peterson, 371–387. University of Chicago. Chicago Linguistic Society.

Stowell, Timothy. 1981. *The Origins of Phrase Structure*. Doctoral dissertation, MIT.

Thráinsson, Höskuldur. 1986. On auxiliaries, AUX and VP's in Icelandic. In *Topics in Scandinavian Syntax*, ed. Kirsti Koch Christiansen and Lars Hellan. Dordrecht: D. Reidel.

Zaenen, Annie. 1980. *Extraction rules in Icelandic*. Doctoral dissertation, Harvard University. Reprinted by Garland Press, New York, 1985.

Zaenen, Annie. 1983. On syntactic binding. *Linguistic Inquiry* 14:469–504.

4

Modeling Syntactic Constraints on Anaphoric Binding

MARY DALRYMPLE, JOHN T. MAXWELL III, AND ANNIE ZAENEN

Abstract. Syntactic constraints on antecedent-anaphor relations can be stated within the theory of Lexical Functional Grammar (henceforth LFG) through the use of functional uncertainty (Kaplan and Maxwell 1988; Halvorsen and Kaplan 1988; Kaplan and Zaenen 1989). In the following, we summarize the general characteristics of syntactic constraints on anaphoric binding. Next, we describe a variation of functional uncertainty called *inside-out* functional uncertainty and show how it can be used to model anaphoric binding. Finally, we discuss some binding constraints claimed to hold in natural language to exemplify the mechanism. We limit our attention throughout to coreference possibilities between definite antecedents and anaphoric elements and ignore interactions with quantifiers. We also limit our discussion to intrasentential relations.

1 General characteristics of syntactic constraints on anaphoric binding

The relation between an anaphor and its antecedent is semantic in nature. In the simple cases that we limit our attention to here, the two are coreferent.[1] This semantic relation is subject to syntactic constraints, however, and it is the statement of these constraints that we focus on. In the LFG

This paper originally appeared in *Proceedings of COLING-90*, vol. 2 (Helsinki, 1990), 72–76.

[1] This is of course not always the case. Reciprocals and binding by quantified NP's are two well-known cases in which the semantic relation is more complicated.

Formal Issues in Lexical-Functional Grammar
edited by
Mary Dalrymple
Ronald M. Kaplan
John T. Maxwell III
Annie Zaenen

approach to these constraints proposed in Bresnan et al. (1985),[2] binding conditions are stated as conditions on f-structure configurations rather than conditions on c-structures. Two kinds of syntactic factors are shown to influence anaphoric binding possibilities: the grammatical function of the potential antecedent (in particular whether or not it is a subject) and the characteristics of the syntactic domain in which the potential antecedent and the anaphor are found (for example, whether that domain is tensed or whether it has a subject). In Bresnan et al. (1985), anaphors are consequently annotated for both domain and antecedent constraints. Some constraints are stated in positive terms: the antecedent must be found within a particular domain or have a particular function. In other cases the constraints are negative: the antecedent and the anaphor cannot both be part of a particular domain, or the antecedent cannot bear a particular grammatical function. Under such negative conditions, the anaphor is *disjoint* in reference from its antecedent.

2 Modeling binding constraints with functional uncertainty

In some cases, f-structure relations are not characterizable as a finite disjunction over paths: for example, dependencies between 'fillers' and 'gaps' in relative clauses and wh-questions. Functional uncertainty was developed for the analysis of such dependencies. Kaplan and Maxwell (1988) and Kaplan and Zaenen (1989) develop a formal specification of relations involving disjunction over paths by allowing the argument position of functional equations to denote a set of strings. Suppose α is a (possibly infinite) set of symbol strings; then

(1) $(f\ \alpha)\ =\ v$ holds if and only if

     a. $f\ =\ v$ and $\epsilon \in \alpha$, or

     b. $((f\ s)\ \mathrm{Suff}(s,\alpha))\ =\ v$ for some symbol s, where $\mathrm{Suff}(s,\alpha)$ is the set of suffix strings y such that $sy \in \alpha$.

An equation with a string-set argument holds if and only if it holds for some string in that set. This kind of equation is trivially unsatisfiable if α denotes the empty set. If α is a finite set, this formula is equivalent to a finite disjunction of equations over the strings in α. Passing from finite disjunction to existential quantification enables us to capture the intuition of unbounded uncertainty as an underspecification of exactly which choice of strings in α will be compatible with the functional information carried by the surrounding surface environment.

[2]For a summary of the views in Bresnan et al. (1985), see Sells (1985).

Kaplan and Zaenen (1989) require that α be drawn from the class of *regular languages*. The characterization of uncertainty in a particular grammatical equation can then be stated as a regular expression over the vocabulary of grammatical function names. Functional uncertainty can also be used in the case of negative constraining equations. In that situation, the requirement is that there be *no* path picked out by the regular expression that makes the equation true. That is, the negation of an expression involving functional uncertainty has the effect of negating an existentially quantified expression.

Kaplan and Zaenen (1989) consider only expressions of the form

$$(f\ \alpha)$$

where α is a regular expression. In expressions such as these, α represents a path through the f-structure f. We refer to paths of this type as *PathIn*, and to functional uncertainty of this type as *outside-in* functional uncertainty.

In Halvorsen and Kaplan (1988), expressions of the form

$$(\alpha f)$$

are introduced. We will refer to the path in expressions of this form as *PathOut*, and to functional uncertainty of this type as *inside-out* functional uncertainty. Expressions involving inside-out functional uncertainty are interpreted as denoting f-structures from which f is reachable over some path in α.

More formally:

(2) $(\alpha f) = g \in \{h \mid \exists s \in \alpha[(hs) =_c f]\}$

(αf) denotes some f-structure g through which there is a path in the set of strings α leading to f. The equation $=_c$ is a constraining equation checking for the existence of such an f-structure.

Similarly, relations between anaphors and their antecedents are not always characterizable as a finite disjunction of paths within f-structures; for this reason, the use of functional uncertainty in characterizing the anaphor-antecedent relation seems appropriate. In our view, modeling anaphoric binding constraints consists of specifying a set of f-structure paths relating anaphors with elements that are either possible or disallowed antecedents. We use inside-out functional uncertainty to characterize the relation between an anaphor and these elements.

To illustrate, the antecedent of the Norwegian anaphor *seg* must be a subject outside of the minimal complete clause nucleus[3] in which *seg*

---

[3] A *clause nucleus* is formed by any predicate (regardless of its syntactic category) and its dependents. A *complete clause nucleus* is a clause nucleus with a subject dependent.

appears; this antecedent can be at an indefinite distance away from the anaphor, as long as no nucleus other than the highest one in the domain contains a tense marker (Hellan 1988; p. 73):

(3) Jon bad   oss forsøke å få deg til å snakke pent om   seg
     Jon$_i$ asked us to try to get you to talk   nicely about him$_i$

Under an LFG analysis, the path between the antecedent and the anaphor in (3) contains three XCOMPs, as diagrammed in (4):

(4)
$$
1:\begin{bmatrix} \text{SUBJ} & 5:[\ ] \\ \text{XCOMP} & 2:\begin{bmatrix} \text{SUBJ} & 6:[\ ] \\ \text{XCOMP} & 3:\begin{bmatrix} \text{SUBJ} & 7:[\ ] \\ \text{XCOMP} & 4:\begin{bmatrix} \text{SUBJ} & 8:[\ ] \\ \text{OBJ} & 9:[(\text{anaphor})] \end{bmatrix} \end{bmatrix} \end{bmatrix} \end{bmatrix}
$$

Assume that $\uparrow_A$ denotes the f-structure for *seg*, the structure labeled 9 in example (4). The set of nested f-structures containing 9 is characterized by the regular expression

(5) (XCOMP* OBJ $\uparrow_A$)

In example (4), this set consists of the structures labeled 1, 2, 3, and 4. The expression in (6) designates the subjects of these four f-structures, those labeled 5, 6, 7 and 8:

(6) ((XCOMP* OBJ $\uparrow_A$) SUBJ)

F-structures 5, 6, and 7 are the f-structures of the possible antecedents of *seg*: the subjects outside of the minimal clause nucleus in which *seg* appears. F-structure 8 is not a possible antecedent for *seg*, since it appears in the same minimal clause nucleus as *seg*; f-structure 8 will be excluded from the set of possible antecedents for *seg* by a negative constraint.

More schematically, the set of possible antecedents of an anaphoric phrase can be characterized by an expression of the form in (7):

(7) ((PathOut $\uparrow_A$) PathIn)

(PathOut $\uparrow_A$) picks out the set of f-structures which contain the anaphor and within which the antecedent must be located. PathIn characterizes the functional role of the antecedent. It is a general constraint on antecedent-anaphor relations that the antecedent must *f-command* [4] the anaphor; for this reason, the PathIn is always of length one. The PathIn,

---

[4]Bresnan (1982) defines f-command as follows: for any functions GF1, GF2 in an f-structure, GF1 f-commands GF2 iff GF1 does not contain GF2 and every f-structure that contains GF1 contains GF2.

then, consists of (and constrains) the grammatical function borne by the antecedent.

Conditions on the binding domain are formalizable as conditions on the PathOut, since the PathOut characterizes the domain in which both the anaphor and its antecedent are found. We will look in detail at one such constraint; before doing so, however, we make a simplifying assumption about the semantics of the anaphor-antecedent relation.

In the simple cases we are considering here, the relation is represented as identity between the semantic content of the anaphor and its antecedent. Elaboration of this representation would require us to introduce the LFG mechanism of *projections* (Halvorsen and Kaplan 1988), which is beyond the scope of this paper.

Here we will use the notation in (8):

(8) $\sigma((\text{PathOut } \uparrow_A) \text{ PathIn}) = \sigma \uparrow_A$

to indicate that the semantics of the anaphor, $\sigma \uparrow_A$, is to be identified with the semantics of its antecedent. The σ stands for the mapping (not further specified) between the syntax and the semantics.

To prevent the anaphoric element from being contained in its antecedent, we formulate the constraint in (9), where $\uparrow_{ANT}$ stands for the f-structure of the antecedent:

(9) $\neg \, [(\uparrow_{ANT} \text{ GF}^+) = \uparrow_A]$

The effect of this constraint is very similar to the i-within-i condition in Government-Binding Theory (Chomsky 1981). It has been argued that this constraint should be relaxed (see e.g. Hellan 1988) but the correct analysis of putative counterexamples is not clear. We will assume here that the constraint can be maintained. We now describe how to model a domain constraint that holds of some anaphors: some anaphors must be bound within the minimal complete nucleus, the minimal nucleus containing a subject.

Let F_1 designate an f-structure containing the anaphor. We can characterize F_1 in the following way:

(10) $F_1 = (\text{GF}^+ \uparrow_A)$

where GF denotes the set of grammatical function labels.

For F_1 to be a valid binding domain for anaphors subject to this constraint, it must not contain any smaller f-structure that properly contains the anaphor and a subject. That is, F_1 must be the *smallest* complete nucleus. We will define DPF ('domain path f-structure') as any of the f-structures that contain the anaphor and are properly contained in F_1:

(11) $(\text{DPF}_1 \text{ GF}^+) =_c \uparrow_A$

$$\text{DPF}_1 =_c (\text{F}_1 \text{ GF}^+)$$

It is these intermediate f-structures that must not contain a subject:

(12) $\neg(\text{DPF}_1 \text{ SUBJ})$

The constraint that an anaphor must be bound within the minimal complete nucleus can, then, be stated as follows:

(13)   a. $\sigma(\text{F}_1 \text{ GF}) = \sigma\uparrow_A$
       b. $\neg(\text{DPF}_1 \text{ SUBJ})$

These two equations ensure identity between the semantic content of the anaphor and its antecedent, where the antecedent is the value of some GF of an f-structure F_1 that contains the anaphor. There may not be a f-structure DPF_1 that is properly contained in F_1 and which has a subject.

3   Examples of anaphoric binding

We now illustrate the use of these binding constraints with some of the conditions that have been proposed for English, Marathi, and Scandinavian pronouns and reflexives.[5]   The English reflexive pronoun was described in Bresnan et al. (1985) as having to be bound in the minimal complete nucleus, as illustrated by the following contrast:

(14)   a.   He$_i$ told us about himself$_i$.
       b.   We told him$_i$ about himself$_i$.
       c.   *He$_i$ asked us to tell Mary about himself$_i$.

As discussed in Section 2, this pattern of grammaticality judgments can be modeled by the constraints given in (10) through (13).

The antecedent of the Marathi reflexive *swataah* must be a subject, but may be at an indefinite distance from the anaphor, so long as the antecedent and the anaphor appear in the same minimal tensed domain. This requirement can be translated into the following path specification.

(15)   a. $\sigma(\text{F}_1 \text{ SUBJ}) = \sigma\uparrow_A$
       b. $\neg(\text{DPF}_1 \text{ TENSE}) = +$
            where F_1 and DPF_1 are as defined above

According to these equations, the antecedent of the anaphor must be contained in an f-structure F_1; further, there must not be an f-structure DPF_1 properly contained in F_1 that has a TENSE attribute with value +.

A more interesting case arises when a binding relation is subject to both a negative and a positive constraint. An example is the Swedish anaphor *honom själv*. Its antecedent must appear in its minimal complete

---

[5]Data are from Bresnan et al. (1985), Hellan (1988), and Dalrymple (1990).

clause nucleus, but it must be disjoint from subjects. This anaphor occurs felicitously within the following sentence:

(16) Martin bad   oss berätta för honom om   honom själv
      Martin$_i$ asked us to talk to him$_i$ about himself$_i$

Conditions on *honom själv* do not prohibit *Martin* and *honom själv* from being interpreted as coreferent, though *Martin* bears the grammatical function SUBJ. This is because *Martin* appears outside the binding domain of *honom själv* and is thus not considered when either positive or negative binding constraints are applied.

In our framework, two constraints are required for *honom själv*. One, (17a), states the positive constraint: the domain in which the antecedent of *honom själv* must be found. The other, (17b), states the negative constraint: *honom själv* must be disjoint from the subject in that domain.

(17) a. $[F_1 = (\text{GF}^+ \uparrow_A) \wedge$
          $\sigma(F_1 \text{ GF}) = \sigma\uparrow_A \wedge$
          $\neg(\text{DPF}_1 \text{ SUBJ})]$
      b. $\neg \, [F_2 = (\text{GF}^+ \uparrow_A) \wedge$
          $\sigma(F_2 \text{ SUBJ}) = \sigma\uparrow_A \wedge$
          $\neg(\text{DPF}_2 \text{ SUBJ})]$

The negative constraint rules out coreference only between the anaphor and the subject of the minimal complete clause nucleus; it does not prevent coreference between the anaphor *honom själv* and a subject *Martin* outside the binding domain. In general, negative binding constraints do not hold in a larger domain than is specified by the positive equation.

For the Norwegian anaphoric form *hans*, the only specifications are negative (Hellan 1988, Bresnan et al. 1985); it must be disjoint from the immediately higher subject. We can encode this requirement as:

(18) $\neg \, [F_1 = (\text{GF}^+ \uparrow_A) \wedge$
      $\sigma(F_1 \text{ SUBJ}) = \sigma\uparrow_A \wedge$
      $\neg(\text{DPF}_1 \text{ SUBJ})]$

This is the same negative requirement as was illustrated above, in example (17). As no positive requirement is given, no antecedent relation is imposed. It is assumed that another module, presumably the discourse component, will supply a referent for the pronoun.

4   Conclusion

We have sketched a way to use inside-out functional uncertainty to constrain the relation between an anaphor and an antecedent. A formal theory of anaphoric binding will involve a specification of a universal inventory of anaphoric binding possibilities and possible dependencies between them. A general discussion of such a theory is beyond the scope of this paper, but we conclude by indicating how our approach captures a few of the cross-linguistic properties of anaphoric binding.

If the domain and antecedent binding requirements for an anaphor are both positive or both negative, the requirements must be satisfied by the same element. This is enforced by requiring that only one positive and one negative equation can be associated with each anaphor.

Additionally, only elements that are *superior* to the element should be considered in applying the constraints. GF1 is *superior* to GF2 if:

1. GF1 asymmetrically f-commands GF2, or
2. GF1 and GF2 f-command each other, and GF1 is higher on the following hierarchy of grammatical functions:

$$\text{SUBJ} > \text{OBJ} > \text{OBJ2} > \text{OBL} > \text{ADJ}$$

As noted above, the f-command requirement is enforced by the requirement that the PathOut be non-null and the PathIn be of length one. The modelling of the functional hierarchy within our framework is, however, a task that remains to be done.

A final observation is that inside-out functional uncertainty can interact with outside-in functional uncertainty as used in the analysis of dependencies between 'fillers' and 'gaps', as in the following:

(19) a. *Bill_i said that Sue likes himself_i.
     b. Himself_i, Bill_i said that Sue likes.

Preliminary research indicates that no special machinery is needed to model the right interactions in these cases.

References

Bresnan, Joan. 1982. Control and Complementation. In *The Mental Representation of Grammatical Relations*, ed. Joan Bresnan, 282–390. Cambridge, MA: The MIT Press.

Bresnan, Joan, Per-Kristian Halvorsen, and Joan Maling. 1985. Logophoricity and Bound Anaphors. Unpublished MS, Stanford University.

Chomsky, Noam. 1981. *Lectures on Government and Binding*. Dordrecht: Foris Publications.

Dalrymple, Mary. 1990. *Syntactic Constraints on Anaphoric Binding*. Doctoral dissertation, Stanford University.

Halvorsen, Per-Kristian, and Ronald M. Kaplan. 1988. Projections and Semantic Description in Lexical-Functional Grammar. In *Proceedings of the International Conference on Fifth Generation Computer Systems*, 1116–1122. Tokyo, Japan. Institute for New Generation Systems. Reprinted in Part IV of this volume.

Hellan, Lars. 1988. *Anaphora in Norwegian and the Theory of Grammar*. Dordrecht: Foris Publications.

Kaplan, Ronald M., and John T. Maxwell. 1988. An Algorithm for Functional Uncertainty. In *Proceedings of COLING-88*, Vol. 1, 297–302. Budapest. Reprinted in Part II of this volume.

Kaplan, Ronald M., and Annie Zaenen. 1989. Long-distance Dependencies, Constituent Structure, and Functional Uncertainty. In *Alternative Conceptions of Phrase Structure*, ed. Mark Baltin and Anthony Kroch. Chicago University Press. Reprinted in Part II of this volume.

Sells, Peter. 1985. *Lectures on Contemporary Syntactic Theories*. No. 3 CSLI Lecture Notes. Stanford University: CSLI/The University of Chicago Press.

5

An Algorithm for Functional Uncertainty

RONALD M. KAPLAN AND JOHN T. MAXWELL III

Abstract. The formal device of functional uncertainty has been introduced into linguistic theory as a means of characterizing long-distance dependencies alternative to conventional phrase-structure-based approaches. In this paper we briefly outline the uncertainty concept, and then present an algorithm for determining the satisfiability of acyclic grammatical descriptions containing uncertainty expressions and for synthesizing the grammatically relevant solutions to those descriptions.

1 Long-Distance Dependencies and Functional Uncertainty

In most linguistic theories long-distance dependencies such as are found in topicalization and relative clause constructions are characterized in terms of categories and configurations of phrase structure nodes. Kaplan and Zaenen (1989) have compared this kind of analysis with one based on the functional organization of sentences, and suggest that the relevant generalizations are instead best stated in functional or predicate-argument terms. They defined and investigated a new formal device called "functional uncertainty" that permits a functional statement of constraints on unbounded dependencies. In this paper, after reviewing their formal specification of functional uncertainty, we present an algorithm for determining the satisfiability of grammatical descriptions that incorporate uncertainty specifications and for synthesizing the smallest solutions to such descriptions.

This paper originally appeared in *Proceedings of COLING-88*, vol. 1 (Budapest, 1988), 297–302.

Kaplan and Zaenen (1989) started from an idea that Kaplan and Bresnan (1982) briefly considered but quickly rejected on mathematical and (Kaplan and Zaenen suggest, mistaken) linguistic grounds. They observed that each of the possible underlying positions of an initial phrase could be specified in a simple equation locally associated with that phrase. In the topicalized sentence *Mary John telephoned yesterday*, the equation (in LFG notation) (↑ TOPIC) = (↑ OBJ) specifies that *Mary* is to be interpreted as the object of the predicate *telephoned*. In *Mary John claimed that Bill telephoned yesterday*, the appropriate equation is (↑ TOPIC) = (↑ COMP OBJ), indicating that *Mary* is still the object of *telephoned*, which because of subsequent words in the string is itself the complement (indicated by the function name COMP) of the top-level predicate *claim*. The sentence can obviously be extended by introducing additional complement predicates (*Mary John claimed that Bill said that ... that Henry telephoned yesterday*), for each of which some equation of the general form (↑ TOPIC) = (↑ COMP COMP ... OBJ) would be appropriate. The problem, of course, is that this is an infinite family of equations, and hence impossible to enumerate in a finite disjunction appearing on a particular rule of grammar. For this technical reason, Kaplan and Bresnan (1982) abandoned the possibility of specifying unbounded uncertainty directly in functional terms.

Kaplan and Zaenen (1989) reconsidered the general strategy that Kaplan and Bresnan (1982) began to explore. Instead of formulating uncertainty by an explicit disjunctive enumeration, however, they provided a formal specification, repeated here, that characterizes the family of equations as a whole. A characterization of a family of equations may be finitely represented in a grammar even though the family itself has an infinite number of members. They developed this notion from the elementary descriptive device in LFG, the functional-application expression. Using square-brackets to denote the interpretation of an expression in a model F, this has the following interpretation:

$$F \models (f\ s) = v \text{ iff } [\![f]\!] \text{ is an f-structure, } [\![s]\!] \text{ is a symbol, and}$$
$$[\![v]\!] = [\![f]\!]([\![s]\!]) \ (= [\![(f\ s)]\!]).$$

An f-structure is a hierarchical finite function from symbols to either symbols, semantic forms, f-structures, or sets of f-structures, and a parenthetic expression thus denotes the value that a function takes for a particular symbol. This notation is straightforwardly extended to allow for strings of symbols, as illustrated in expressions such as (↑ COMP OBJ) above. If x is a string sy composed of an initial symbol s followed by a (possibly empty) suffix string y, then

(1) $(f\ x) \equiv ((f\ s)\ y)$,
     $(f\ \epsilon) \equiv f$, where ϵ is the empty string.

The crucial extension to handle unbounded uncertainty is to allow the argument position in these expressions to denote a set of strings. Suppose α is a (possibly infinite) set of symbol strings. Then, following Kaplan and Zaenen (1989), we say that

$F \models (f\ \alpha) = v$ iff (i) $F \models f = v$ and $\epsilon \in \alpha$, or

(ii) $F \models ((f\ s)\ \mathit{Suff}(s, \alpha)) = v$, for some symbol s, where $\mathit{Suff}(s, \alpha)$ is the set of suffix strings y such that $sy \in \alpha$.

Thus, an equation with a string-set argument is satisfied if it would be satisfied for a string in the set that results from a sequence of left-to-right symbol choices. This kind of equation is trivially unsatisfiable if α is the empty set. If α is a finite set, this formulation is equivalent to a finite disjunction of equations over the strings in α. Passing from finite disjunction to existential quantification enables us to capture the intuition that unbounded uncertainty is an underspecification of exactly which choice of strings in α will be compatible with the functional information carried by the surrounding surface environment.

Kaplan and Zaenen (1989) of course imposed the further requirement that the membership of α be characterized in finite specifications. Specifically, for linguistic, mathematical, and computational reasons they required that α in fact be drawn from the class of *regular languages*. The characterization of uncertainty in a particular grammatical equation can then be stated as a regular expression over the vocabulary of grammatical function names. The infinite uncertainty for the topicalization example above, for example, can be specified by the equation ($\uparrow$ TOPIC) = ($\uparrow$ COMP* OBJ), involving the Kleene closure operator. A specification for a broader class of topicalization sentences might be ($\uparrow$ TOPIC) = ($\uparrow$ COMP* GF), where GF stands for the set of primitive grammatical functions {SUBJ, OBJ, OBJ2, XCOMP, ...}. Various restrictions on the domain over which these dependencies can operate—the equivalent of the so-called island constraints—can be easily formulated by constraining the uncertainty language in different ways. For example, the restriction for English and Icelandic that adjunct clauses are islands (Kaplan and Zaenen 1989) might be expressed with the equation ($\uparrow$ TOPIC) = ($\uparrow$ (GF − ADJ)* GF). One noteworthy consequence of this functional approach is that appropriate predicate-argument relations can be defined without relying on empty nodes or traces in constituent structure.

In the present paper we study the mathematical and computational properties of regular uncertainty. Specifically, we show that two important problems are decidable and present algorithms for computing their solutions. In LFG the f-structures assigned to a string are characterized by a *functional description* ('f-description'), a Boolean combination of equalities and set-membership assertions that acceptable f-structures must satisfy. We show first that the verification problem is decidable for any functional description that contains regular uncertainties. We then prove that the satisfiability problem is decidable for a linguistically interesting subset of descriptions, namely, those that characterize acyclic structures.

2 Verification

The verification problem is the problem of determining whether or not a given model F satisfies a particular functional description for some assignment to the variables in the description. This question is important in lexical-functional theory because the proper evaluation of LFG's non-defining constraint equations (involving negation or '$=_c$') depends on it. It is easy to show that the verification problem for an f-description including an uncertainty such as $(f\ \alpha) = v$ is decidable if $[\![f]\!]$ is a noncyclic f-structure. If $[\![f]\!]$ is noncyclic, it contains only a finite number of function-application sequences and thus only a finite number of strings that might satisfy the uncertainty equation. The membership problem for the regular sets is decidable and each of those strings can therefore be tested to see whether it belongs to the uncertainty language, and if so, whether the uncertainty equation holds when the uncertainty is instantiated to that string. Alternatively, the set of application strings can be treated as a (finite) regular language that can be intersected with the uncertainty language to determine the set of strings (if any) for which the equation must be evaluated.

This alternative approach easily generalizes to the more complex situation in which the given f-structure contains cycles of applications. A cyclic $[\![f]\!]$ contains at least one element $[\![g]\!]$ that satisfies an equation of the form $(g\ y) = g$ for some nonempty string y. It thus involves an infinite number of function-application sequences and hence an infinite number of strings any of which might satisfy an uncertainty. But a finite state machine can easily be constructed that accepts exactly the strings of attributes in these application sequences: the states of this machine correspond to $[\![f]\!]$ and all its values and the transitions correspond to the attribute-value pairs of $[\![f]\!]$ and the f-structures it includes. These strings thus form a regular language whose intersection with the uncertainty language is a regular set I containing all the strings for which the equation must be evaluated. If I is empty, the uncertainty is unsatisfiable. Otherwise, the set may be infinite, but if F satisfies the uncertainty equation for any string at all, we can show the equation will be satisfied when the uncertainty is instantiated to one of a finite number of short strings in I. Let n be the number of states in a minimum-state deterministic finite-state acceptor for I and suppose that the uncertainty equation holds for a string w in I whose length $|w|$ is greater than n. From the pumping lemma for regular sets we know there are strings x, y, and z such that $w = xyz$, $|y| \geq 1$, and for all $m \geq 0$ the string $xy^m z$ is in I. But these latter strings can be application-sequences in $[\![f]\!]$ only if y picks out a cyclic path, so that $F \models ((f\ x)\ y) = (f\ x)$. Thus we have

$$F \models (f\ w) = v \text{ iff}$$
$$F \models (f\ xyz) = v \text{ iff}$$
$$F \models (((f\ x)\ y)\ z) = v \text{ iff}$$
$$F \models ((f\ x)\ z) = v \text{ iff}$$
$$F \models (f\ xz) = v$$

with xz shorter than w but still in I and hence in the uncertainty language α. If $|xz|$ is greater then n, this argument can be reapplied to find yet a shorter string that satisfies the uncertainty. Since w was a finite string to begin with, this process will eventually terminate with a satisfying string whose length is less than or equal to n. We can therefore determine whether or not the uncertainty holds by examining only a finite number of strings, namely, the strings in I whose length is bounded by n.

This argument can be translated to an efficient, practical solution to the verification problem by interleaving the intersection and testing steps. We enumerate common paths from the start state of a minimum-state acceptor for α and from the f-structure denoted by f in F. In this traversal we keep track of the pairs of states and subsidiary f-structures we have encountered and avoid retraversing paths from a state/f-structure pair we have already visited. We then test the uncertainty condition against the f-structure values we reach along with final states in the α acceptor.

3 Satisfiability

It is more difficult to show that the satisfiability problem is decidable. Given a functional description, can it be determined that a structure satisfying all its conditions does in fact exist? For trivial descriptions consisting of a single uncertainty equation, the question is easy to answer. If the equation has an empty uncertainty language, containing no strings whatsoever, the description is unsatisfiable. Otherwise, it is satisfied by the model whose f-structure meets the requirements of any string freely chosen from the language, for instance, one of the shortest ones. For example, the description containing only $(f$ TOPIC$) = (f$ COMP* GF$)$ is obviously satisfiable because $(f$ TOPIC$) = (f$ SUBJ$)$ clearly has a model.

There is a large class of nontrivial descriptions where satisfiability is easy to determine for essentially the same reason. If we know that the satisfiability of the description is the same no matter which strings we choose from the (nonempty) uncertainty languages, we can instantiate the uncertainties with freely chosen strings and evaluate the resulting description with any of the well-known satisfiability procedures that work on descriptions without uncertainties (for example, ordinary attribute-value unification). The important point is that for descriptions in this class we only need to look at a single string from each uncertainty language, not all the strings it contains, to determine the satisfiability of the whole system. Particular models that satisfy the description will depend on the strings that instantiate the uncertainties, of course, but whether or not such models exist is independent of the strings we choose.

Not all descriptions have this desirable free-choice characteristic. If the description includes a conjunction of an uncertainty equation with another equation that defines a property of the same variable, the description may be satisfiable for some instantiations of the uncertainty but not for others.

Suppose that the equation $(f$ TOPIC$) = (f$ COMP* GF$)$ is conjoined with the equations $(f$ COMP SUBJ NUM$) =$ SG and $(f$ TOPIC NUM$) =$ PL. This description is satisfiable on the string COMP COMP SUBJ but not on the shorter string COMP SUBJ because of the SG/PL inconsistency that arises. More generally, if two equations $(f\ \alpha) = v_\alpha$ and $(f\ \beta) = v_\beta$ are conjoined in a description and there are strings in α that share a common prefix with strings in β, then the description as a whole may be satisfiable for some strings but not for others. The choice of x from α and xy from β, for example, implies a further constraint on the values v_α and v_β: $(f\ x) = v_\alpha$ and $(f\ xy) = ((f\ x)\ y) = v_\beta$ can hold only if $(v_\alpha\ y) = v_\beta$, and this may or may not be consistent with other equations for v_α.

In what follows, we give an algorithm that converts an arbitrary description with acyclic models into an equi-satisfiable one that has the free-choice characteristic. We thus show that the satisfiability of all such descriptions is decidable.

We can formulate more precisely the conditions under which the uncertainties in a description may be freely instantiated without affecting satisfiability. For simplicity, in the analysis below we consider a particular string of one or more symbols in a non-uncertain application expression to be the trivial uncertainty language containing just that string. Also, although our satisfiability procedure is actually implemented within the general framework of a directed graph unification algorithm (the congruence closure method outlined by Kaplan and Bresnan (1982)), we present it here as a formula rewriting system in the style of Johnson (1987). This enables us to abstract away from specific details of data and control structure which are irrelevant to the general line of argument. We begin with a few definitions.

(2)   DEFINITION. We say that a description is in *canonical form* if and only if

    (i)   it is in disjunctive normal form,

    (ii) application expressions appear only as the left-sides of equations,

    (iii) none of its uncertainty languages is the empty string ϵ, and

    (iv) for any equation $f = g$ between two distinct variables, one of the variables appears in no other conjoined equation.

(3)   LEMMA. There is an algorithm for converting any description to a logically equivalent canonical form.

PROOF. First, every statement containing an application expression $(g\ \beta)$ not to the left of an equality is replaced by the conjunction of an equation $(g\ \beta) = h$, for h a new variable, with the statement formed by substituting h for $(g\ \beta)$ in the original statement. This step is iterated until no offending application expressions remain. The equation $(f\ \alpha) = (g\ \beta)$, for example, is replaced by the conjunction of equations $(f\ \alpha) = h\ \wedge\ (g\ \beta) = h$, and the membership statement $(g\ \beta) \in f$ becomes $h \in f\ \wedge\ (g\ \beta) = h$. Next, every equation of the form $(f\ \epsilon) = v$ is replaced by the equation $f = v$ in accordance with the identity in (1) above. The description is then transformed to disjunctive normal form. Finally, for every equation of the form $f = g$ between two distinct variables both of which appear in other conjoined equations, all occurrences of g in those other equations are replaced by f. Each of these transformations preserves logical equivalence and the algorithm terminates after introducing only a finite number of new equations and variables and performing a finite number of substitutions.   □

Now let Σ be the alphabet of attributes in a description and define the set of first attributes in a language α as follows:

(4)   DEFINITION.
    $First(\alpha) \equiv \{s \in \Sigma \mid sz \in \alpha \text{ for some string } z \in \Sigma^*\}$

(5) DEFINITION. We say that

    (i)   two application expressions $(f\ \alpha)$ and $(g\ \beta)$ are *free* if and only if

        (a) f and g are distinct, or

        (b) $First(\alpha) \cap First(\beta) = \emptyset$ and ϵ is in neither α nor β,

    (ii)   two equations are *free* if and only if their application expressions are pairwise free,

    (iii)   a functional description is *free* if and only if it is in canonical form and all its conjoined equations are pairwise free.

If all the attribute strings on the same variable in a canonical description differ on their first element, there can be no shared prefixes. The free descriptions are thus exactly those whose satisfiability is not affected by different uncertainty instantiations.

3.1 Removing Interactions

We attack the satisfiability problem by providing a procedure for transforming a functional description D to a logically equivalent but free description D' any of whose instantiations can be tested for satisfiability by traditional algorithms. We show that this procedure terminates for the descriptions that usually appear in linguistic grammars, namely, the descriptions whose minimal models are all acyclic. Although the procedure can detect that a description may have a cyclic minimal model, we cannot yet show that the procedure will always terminate with a correct answer if a cyclic specification interacts with an infinite uncertainty language.

The key ingredient of this procedure is a transformation that converts a conjunction of two equations that are not free into an equivalent finite disjunction of conjoined equations that are pairwise free. Consider the conjoined equations $(f\ \alpha) = v_\alpha$ and $(f\ \beta) = v_\beta$ for some value expressions v_α and v_β, where $(f\ \alpha)$ and $(f\ \beta)$ are not free. Strings x and y arbitrarily chosen from α and β, respectively, might be related in any of three significant ways: Either

    (a) x is a prefix of y (y is xy' for some string y'),

    (b) y is a prefix of x (x is yx'), or

    (c) x and y are identical up to some point and then diverge (x is $zs_x x'$ and y is $zs_y y'$ with symbol s_x distinct from s_y).

Note that the possibility that x and y are identical strings is covered by both (a) and (b) with either y' or x' being empty, and that noninteracting strings fall into case (c) with z being empty. In each of these cases there is a logically equivalent reformulation involving either distinct variables or strings that share no first symbols:

(6) a. x is a prefix of y:

$(f\ x) = v_\alpha \wedge (f\ xy') = v_\beta$ iff

$(f\ x) = v_\alpha \wedge (f\ x)\ y') = v_\beta$ iff

$(f\ x) = v_\alpha \wedge (v_\alpha\ y') = v_\beta$ (by substituting v_α for $(f\ x)$),

b. y is a prefix of x:

$(f\ y) = v_\beta \wedge (f\ yx') = v_\alpha$ iff

$(f\ y) = v_\beta \wedge (v_\beta\ x') = v_\alpha$,

c. x and y have a (possibly empty) common prefix and then diverge:

$(f\ zs_x x') = v_\alpha \wedge (f\ zs_y y') = v_\beta$ iff

$(f\ z) = g \wedge (g\ s_x x') = v_\alpha \wedge (g\ s_y y') = v_\beta$

for g a new variable and symbols $s_x \neq s_y$.

All ways in which the chosen strings can interact are covered by the disjunction of these reformulations. We observe that if these specific attribute strings are considered as trivial uncertainties and if v_α and v_β are distinct from f, the resulting equations in each case are pairwise free.

In this analysis we transfer the dependencies among chosen strings into different branches of a disjunction. Although we have reasoned so far only about specific strings, an analogous line of argument can be provided for families of strings in infinite uncertainty languages. The strings in these languages fall into a finite set of classes to which a similar case analysis applies. Let $\langle Q_\alpha, \Sigma, \delta_\alpha, q_\alpha, F_\alpha \rangle$ be the states, alphabet, transition function, start state and final states of a finite state machine that accepts α and let $\langle Q_\beta, \Sigma, \delta_\beta, q_\beta, F_\beta \rangle$ be an acceptor for β. For convenience and without loss of generality, we restrict ourselves to finite state acceptors that are deterministic.

(7) DEFINITION. Let δ^* be the usual extension of δ to strings in Σ^* and define

(i) $Pre(\alpha, q) \equiv \{x \mid \delta_\alpha^*(q_\alpha, x) = q\}$ (the prefix strings that lead from the start state to state q),

(ii) $Suf(\alpha, q) \equiv \{x \mid \delta_\alpha^*(q, x) \in F_\alpha\}$ (the suffix strings that lead from state q to a final state).

Note that $Pre(\alpha, q)$ and $Suf(\alpha, q)$ are regular sets for all q in Q_α (since finite state acceptors for them can easily be constructed from the acceptor for α). Further, every string in α belongs to the concatenation of $Pre(\alpha, q)$ and $Suf(\alpha, q)$ for some state q in Q_α. The prefixes of all strings in α thus belong to a finite number of languages $Pre(\alpha, q)$, and every prefix that is shared between a string in α and a string in β also belongs to a finite number of classes formed by intersecting two regular sets of this type. The common prefix languages fill the role of the prefix strings in the three-way analysis above. All interactions of the strings in α and β that lead through states q and r, respectively, are covered by the following possibilities:

(8) a. strings from α are prefixes of strings from β:
$$(f\ \alpha \cap Pre(\beta, r)) = v_\alpha \wedge (v_\alpha\ Suf(\beta, r)) = v_\beta,$$

b. strings from β are prefixes of strings from α:
$$(f\ \beta \cap Pre(\alpha, q)) = v_\beta \wedge (v_\beta\ Suf(\alpha, q)) = v_\alpha,$$

c. strings have a common prefix and then diverge on some s_α and s_β in Σ:
$$(f\ Pre(\alpha, q) \cap Pre(\beta, r)) = g_{q,r} \wedge$$
$$\left[\begin{array}{l} (g_{q,r}\ s_\alpha Suf(\alpha, \delta_\alpha(q, s_\alpha))) = v_\alpha\ \wedge \\ (g_{q,r}\ s_\beta Suf(\beta, \delta_\beta(r, s_\beta))) = v_\beta \end{array} \right],$$
where the $g_{q,r}$ is a new variable and $s_\alpha \neq s_\beta$.

(9) DEFINITION. Taking the disjunction of these cases over the cross-product of states in Q_α and Q_β and pairs of distinct symbols in Σ, we define the following operator:

$$Free((f\ \alpha) = v_\alpha, (f\ \beta) = v_\beta) \equiv$$

$$\bigvee_{\substack{q \in Q_\alpha \\ r \in Q_\beta}} \left[\begin{array}{l} [(f\ \alpha \cap Pre(\beta, r)) = v_\alpha \wedge (v_\alpha\ Suf(\beta, r)) = v_\beta] \qquad \text{(i)} \\ \vee\ [(f\ \beta \cap Pre(\alpha, q)) = v_\beta \wedge (v_\beta\ Suf(\alpha, q)) = v_\alpha] \qquad \text{(ii)} \\ \vee \left[\begin{array}{l} (f\ Pre(\alpha, q) \cap Pre(\beta, r)) = g_{q,r}\ \wedge \\ \bigvee_{\substack{s_\alpha, s_\beta \in \Sigma \\ s_\alpha \neq s_\beta}} \left[\begin{array}{l} (g_{q,r}\ s_\alpha Suf(\alpha, \delta_\alpha(q, s_\alpha))) = v_\alpha\ \wedge \\ (g_{q,r}\ s_\beta Suf(\beta, \delta_\beta(r, s_\beta))) = v_\beta \end{array} \right] \end{array} \right] \qquad \text{(iii)} \end{array} \right]$$

This operator is the central component of our satisfiability procedure. We show that *Free* preserves satisfiability by showing:

(10) LEMMA. $Free((f\ \alpha) = v_\alpha, (f\ \beta) = v_\beta)$ is logically equivalent to the conjunction $(f\ \alpha) = v_\alpha \wedge (f\ \beta) = v_\beta$.

PROOF. Any strings x and y that satisfy the uncertainties in the conjunction must fall into one of the cases in (6). If $y = xy'$ applies (case 6a), we have $(f\ x) = v_\alpha \wedge (v_\alpha\ y') = v_\beta$. But x leads to some state r_x in Q_β and therefore belongs to $Pre(\beta, r_x)$ while y' belongs to $Suf(\beta, r_x)$. Thus, x satisfies $(f\ \alpha \cap Pre(\beta, r_x)) = v_\alpha$ and y' satisfies $(v_\alpha\ Suf(\beta, r_x)) = v_\beta$, and (9i) is satisfied for one of the r_x disjunctions. A symmetric argument goes through if case (6b) obtains.

Now suppose the strings diverge to $s_x x'$ and $s_y y'$ for distinct s_x and s_y after a common prefix z (case (6c)) and that z leads to

q in Q_α and r in Q_β. Then z belongs to $Pre(\alpha, q) \cap Pre(\beta, r)$ and satisfies the uncertainty $(f\ Pre(\alpha, q) \cap Pre(\beta, r)) = g_{q,r}$. Since x' belongs to $Suf(\alpha, \delta_\alpha(q, s_x))$ and y' belongs to $Suf(\beta, \delta_\beta(r, s_y))$, the $g_{q,r}$ equations in the s_α, s_β disjunction also hold. Thus, if both original equations are satisfied, one of the disjunctions in definition (9) will also be satisfied.

Conversely, if one of the disjunctions in definition (9) holds for some particular strings, then we can find other strings that satisfy both original equations. If $(f\ \alpha \cap Pre(\beta, r)) = v_\alpha$ holds for some string x in α leading to state r in β's acceptor and $(v_\alpha\ Suf(\beta, r)) = v_\beta$ holds for some string y' in $Suf(\beta, r)$, then $(f\ \alpha) = v_\alpha$ holds because x is in α and $(f\ \beta) = v_\beta$ holds because $((f\ x)\ y') = v_\beta = (f\ xy')$ and xy' is in β. The arguments for the other cases in definition (9) are similarly easy to construct.

Thus, logical equivalence is established by reasoning back and forth between strings and languages and between strings and their prefixes and suffixes. □

If the operands to *Free* are from a description in canonical form, then the canonical form of the result is a free description—all its conjoined equations are pairwise free. This is true whether or not the original equations were free, provided that the value expressions v_α and v_β are distinct from f (if either value was f, the original equations would have only cyclic models, a point we will return to below).

(11)   LEMMA. *Free*$((f\ \alpha) = v_\alpha, (f\ \beta) = v_\beta)$ yields a free description if $(f\ \alpha) = v_\alpha \wedge (f\ \beta) = v_\beta$ has acyclic models.

PROOF. In the first two cases in definition (9), the resulting equations are free because they have distinct variables (if neither v_α nor v_β is f). In the third case, the f equation is free of the other two because $g_{q,r}$ is a new variable, and the two $g_{q,r}$ equations are free because the first symbols of their uncertainties are distinct. □

In sum, the *Free* operator transforms a conjunction of two non-free equations into a logically equivalent formula whose canonical form is free.

The procedure for converting a description D to free form is now straightforward. The procedure has four steps.

(12)   a.   Place D in canonical form.
   b.   If all conjoined equations in D are pairwise free, stop. D is free.
   c.   Pick a conjunction C in D with a pair of non-free equations $(f\ \alpha) = v_\alpha$ and $(f\ \beta) = v_\beta$, and replace C in D with the

canonical form of its other equations conjoined with
$Free((f\ \alpha) = v_\alpha, (f\ \beta) = v_\beta)$.

d. Go to step (a).

Thus, we can determine the satisfiability of any description D by converting it to free form, instantiating the residual uncertainties with freely chosen strings, and applying any familiar satisfiability procedure to the instantiated description.

EXAMPLE. Consider the constraints

$$(f\ (\text{A}|\text{B})^*) = v_\alpha \text{ and } (f\ (\text{A}|\text{B})^*) = v_\beta.$$

These constraints are not free because

$$First((\text{A}|\text{B})^*) \cap First((\text{A}|\text{B})^*) \neq \emptyset.$$

We can represent the languages of these constraints with finite state machines with a single state. Let q be the state of the first machine and r the state of the second machine. Then

$$Pre((\text{A}|\text{B})^*, q) = (\text{A}|\text{B})^*$$

and

$$Suf((\text{A}|\text{B})^*, q) = (\text{A}|\text{B})^*.$$

Similarly for r. From (9i) we get:

$$(f\ (\text{A}|\text{B})^* \cap Pre((\text{A}|\text{B})^*, r)) = v_\alpha \wedge (v_\alpha\ Suf((\text{A}|\text{B})^*, r)) = v_\beta$$
$$\rightarrow (f\ (\text{A}|\text{B})^* \cap (\text{A}|\text{B})^*) = v_\alpha \wedge (v_\alpha\ (\text{A}|\text{B})^*) = v_\beta$$
$$\rightarrow (f\ (\text{A}|\text{B})^*) = v_\alpha \wedge (v_\alpha\ (\text{A}|\text{B})^*) = v_\beta.$$

From (9ii) we get:

$$(f\ (\text{A}|\text{B})^* \cap Pre((\text{A}|\text{B})^*, q)) = v_\beta \wedge (v_\beta\ Suf((\text{A}|\text{B})^*, q)) = v_\alpha$$
$$\rightarrow (f\ (\text{A}|\text{B})^* \cap (\text{A}|\text{B})^*) = v_\beta \wedge (v_\beta\ (\text{A}|\text{B})^*) = v_\alpha$$
$$\rightarrow (f\ (\text{A}|\text{B})^*) = v_\beta \wedge (v_\beta\ (\text{A}|\text{B})^*) = v_\alpha.$$

From (9iii) with $s_\alpha = \text{B}$ and $s_\beta = \text{A}$ we get:

$$(f\ Pre((\text{A}|\text{B})^*, q) \cap Pre((\text{A}|\text{B})^*, r)) = g$$
$$\wedge (g\ \text{B}\ Suf((\text{A}|\text{B})^*, \delta(q, \text{B}))) = v_\alpha$$
$$\wedge (g\ \text{A}\ Suf((\text{A}|\text{B})^*, \delta(r, \text{A}))) = v_\beta$$
$$\rightarrow (f\ (\text{A}|\text{B})^* \cap (\text{A}|\text{B})^*) = g \wedge (g\ \text{B}\ (\text{A}|\text{B})^*) = v_\alpha \wedge (g\ \text{A}\ (\text{A}|\text{B})^*) = v_\beta$$
$$\rightarrow (f\ (\text{A}|\text{B})^*) = g \wedge (g\ \text{B}\ (\text{A}|\text{B})^*) = v_\alpha \wedge (g\ \text{A}\ (\text{A}|\text{B})^*) = v_\beta.$$

Finally, from (9iii) with $s_\alpha = A$ and $s_\beta = B$ we get:

$$(f \; Pre((A|B)^*, q) \cap Pre((A|B)^*, r)) = g$$
$$\wedge \, (g \; A \; Suf((A|B)^*, \delta(q, A))) = v_\alpha$$
$$\wedge \, (g \; B \; Suf((A|B)^*, \delta(r, B))) = v_\beta)$$
$$\rightarrow (f \; (A|B)^* \cap (A|B)^*) = g \wedge (g \; A \; (A|B)^*) = v_\alpha \wedge (g \; B \; (A|B)^*) = v_\beta$$
$$\rightarrow (f \; (A|B)^*) = g \wedge (g \; A \; (A|B)^*) = v_\alpha \wedge (g \; B \; (A|B)^*) = v_\beta.$$

Thus the result is a four way disjunction of cases that are each free.

3.2 Termination

If D has only acyclic minimal models, the procedure in (12) will terminate after a finite number of iterations. We argue that there are a certain number of ways in which the equations in each conjunction in D's canonical form can interact. Initially, for a conjunction C of n equations, the maximal number of non-free pairs is $n(n-1)/2$, on the worst-case assumption that every equation may potentially interact with every other equation. Suppose step (12c) is applied to two interacting equations in C. The result will be a disjunction of conjunctions each of which includes the remaining equations from C and new equations introduced by one of the cases in definition (9). In cases (9i) and (9ii) the interaction is removed from the common variable of the two equations (f) and transferred to a new variable (either v_α or v_β). In case (9iii), the interaction is actually removed from the system as a new variable is introduced. Since new variables are introduced only when an interaction is removed, the number of new variables is bounded. Thus each interaction is processed only a bounded number of times before it is either removed (9iii) or transferred to a variable that it was previously associated with (9i,ii). However, it can only transfer to a previous variable if the description has cyclic minimal models. Suppose that f is reached again through a series of (9i,ii) steps. Then there is a conjoined sequence of equations $(f \; \alpha) = v_\alpha, (v_\alpha \; \alpha_1) = v_{\alpha_1}, .., (v_{\alpha_n} \; \alpha_{n+1}) = f$. But these can only be satisfied if there is some string x in $\alpha\alpha_1...\alpha_{n+1}$ such that $(f \; x) = f$ and this holds only of cyclic models. Since the number of variables introduced is bounded by the original number of possible interactions, all actual interactions in the system must eventually disappear either through the application of (9iii) or by being transferred to a variable whose other equations it does not interact with.

As we noted above, the satisfiability of a free description can be determined by arbitrarily instantiating the residual uncertainties to particular strings and then applying any traditional satisfiability algorithm to the result. Given the *Free* operator and the procedure in (12), the satisfiability of any description with acyclic models is thus decidable.

(13) THEOREM. The satisfiability of acyclic descriptions containing uncertainty expressions is decidable.

The possibility of nontermination with cyclic descriptions may or may not be a problem in linguistic practice. Although the formal system makes it easy to write descriptions of this sort, very few linguistic analyses have made use of them. The only example we are aware of involves modification structures (such as relative clauses) that both belong to the element they modify (the head) and also contain that element internally as an attribute value. But our procedure will in fact terminate in these sorts of cases. The difficulty with cycles comes from their interaction with infinite uncertainties. That is, the description may have cyclic models, but the cyclic specifications will not always lead to repeating variable transfers and nontermination. For example, if the cycle is required by an uncertainty that interacts with no other *infinite* uncertainty, the procedure will eventually terminate with a free description. This is what happens in the modification case, because the cycle involves a grammatical function (say RELCLAUSE or MOD) which belongs to no infinite uncertainty.

For cycles that are not of this type, there is a straightforward modification to the procedure in (12) that at least enables them to be detected. We maintain with each uncertainty a record of all the variables that it or any of its ancestors have been associated with, and recognize a potentially nonterminating cycle when a transfer to a variable already in the set is attempted. If we terminate the procedure when this happens, assuming in effect that all subsequent disjunctions are unsatisfiable, we cannot be sure that all possible solutions will be accounted for and thus cannot guarantee the completeness of our procedure in the cyclic case. We can refine this strategy by recording and avoiding iteration over combinations of variables and uncertainty languages. We thus safely explore more of the solution possibilities but perhaps still not all of them. It is an open question whether or not there is a satisfiability procedure different from the one we have presented that terminates correctly in all cases. On the other hand, it is also not clear that potential solutions that might be lost through early termination are linguistically significant. Perhaps they should be excluded by definition, much as Kaplan and Bresnan (1982) excluded c-structure derivations with nonbranching dominance chains because of their linguistically uninteresting redundancies.

4 The Smallest Models

The satisfiability of a description in free form is independent of the choice of strings from its uncertainty languages, but of course different string choices result in different satisfying models for the description. An infinite number of strings can be chosen from even a very simple functional uncertainty such as $(f \text{ COMP}^* \text{ SUBJ}) = v$, and thus there are an infinite number of distinct possible models. This is reminiscent of the infinite number of models for descriptions with no uncertainties at all (just $(f \text{ SUBJ}) = v$), but in this case the models are systematically related in the natural subsumption ordering on the f-structure lattice. There is one smallest structure; the others include the information it contains and thus satisfy the description. But they also include arbitrary amounts of additional information that the description does not call for. This is discussed by Kaplan and Bresnan (1982), where the subsumption-minimal structure is defined to be the grammatically relevant one.

The models corresponding to the choice of different strings from an infinite uncertainty are also systematically related to each other but on a metric that is orthogonal to the subsumption ordering. Again appealing to the pumping lemma for regular sets, strings that are longer than the number of states in an uncertainty's minimal-state finite-state acceptor include a substring that is accepted by some repeating sequence of transitions. Replicating this substring arbitrarily still yields a string in the uncertainty, so in a certain sense these replications contribute no new grammatically interesting information. Since all the information is essentially contained in the shorter string that has no occurrence of this particular substring, we define this to be the grammatically relevant representative for the whole class. Thus a description with uncertainties has only a finite number of linguistically significant models, those that result from the finite disjunctions that are introduced in converting the description to free form and from choosing among the finite number of short strings in the residual uncertainties.

5 Performance Considerations

We have outlined a general, abstract procedure for solving uncertainty descriptions, making the smallest number of assumptions about the details of its operation. The efficiency of any implementation will depend in large measure in just how details of data structure and explicit computational control are fixed.

There are a number of obvious optimizations that can be made. First, the cases in the *Free* operator are not mutually distinct: if identical strings belong to the two uncertainty languages, those would fall into both cases

(i) and (ii) and hence be processed twice with exactly equivalent results. The solution to this redundancy is to restrict one of the cases (say (i)) so that it only handles proper prefixes, consigning the identical strings to the other case. Second, when pairs of symbols are enumerated in the (iii) case, there is obviously no point in even considering symbols that are in the alphabet but are not *First* symbols of the suffix uncertainties. This optimization is applied automatically if only the transitions leaving the start states are enumerated and the finite state machines are represented with partial transition functions pruned of transitions to failure states.

Third, a derivative uncertainty produced by the *Free* operator will sometimes be empty. Since equations with empty uncertainties are unsatisfiable by definition, this case should be detected and that disjunctive branch immediately discarded. Fourth, the same derivative suffix and prefix languages of a particular state may appear in pursuing different branches of the disjunction or processing different combinations of equations. Some computational advantage may be gained by saving the derivative finite state machines in a cache associated with the states they are based on. Finally, successive iterations of the *Free* procedure may lead to transparent inconsistencies (an assertion of equality between two distinct symbols or equating a symbol to a variable that is also used as a function). It is important to detect these inconsistencies when they first appear and again discard the corresponding disjunctive branch. In fact, if this is done systematically, iterated application of the *Free* operator by itself simulates the effect of traditional unification algorithms, with variables corresponding to f-structures or nodes of a directed graph.

There are also some less obvious but also quite important performance considerations. What we have described is an equational rewriting system that is quite different from the usual recursive unification algorithm that operates on directed graph representations. Directed graph data structures index the information in the equations so that related structures are quickly accessible through the recursive control structure. Since our procedure does not depend for its correctness on the order in which interacting equations are chosen for processing, it ought to be easy to embed *Free* as a simple extension of a traditional algorithm. However, traditional unification algorithms do not deal with disjunction gracefully. In particular, they typically do not expect new disjunctive branches to arise during the course of a recursive invocation; this would require inserting a fork in the recursive control structure or saving a complete copy of the current computational context for each new disjunction. We avoid this awkwardness by postponing the processing of the functional uncertainty until all simple unifications are complete. Before performing a simple unification step, we remove from the data structures all uncertainties that need to be resolved and store them with a pointer to their containing structures on a queue or agenda of pending unifications. Uncertainty processing can be resumed at a later, more convenient time, after the simpler unifications have been completed. (Indeed, if one of the simpler unifications fails, the uncertainty may never be processed at all.) Waiting until simpler unifications are done means that no computational state has to be preserved; only data structures have to be copied to insure the independence of the various disjunctive paths.

We also note that as long as the machinery for postponing functional uncertainty for some amount of time is needed, it is often advantageous to postpone it even longer than is absolutely necessary. In particular, we found that if uncertainties are postponed until predicates (semantic form values for PRED attributes) are assigned to the f-structures they belong to, the number of cases that must be explored is dramatically reduced. This is because of the coherence condition that LFG imposes on f-structures with predicates: an f-structure with a predicate can only contain those governable functions that are explicitly mentioned by the predicate. Any other governable functions are considered unacceptable. Thus, if we wait until the predicate is identified, we need only consider the small number of governable attributes that any particular predicate allows, even though the initial attributes in an uncertainty may include the entire set of governable functions (SUBJ, OBJ, and various kinds of obliques and complements), and this may be quite large. The effect is to make the processing of long-distance dependencies sensitive to the subcategorization frame of the predicate; we have observed enormous overall performance improvements from applying this delay strategy. Note that in a left-to-right parsing model, the processing load therefore increases in relative clauses just after the predicate is seen, and this might have a variety of interesting psycholinguistic implications.

Finally, we observe that there is a specialization of the *Free* operator that applies when an uncertainty interacts with several non-uncertainty equations (equations whose attribute expressions have singleton *First* sets). Instead of separating one interaction from the uncertainty with each application of *Free*, the uncertainty is divided in a single step into a minimum number of disjunctive possibilities each of which interacts with just one of the other equations. The disjunction contains one branch for each symbol in the uncertainty's *First* set that is an initial attribute in one of the other equations, plus a single branch for all of the residual initial symbols:

$$(f\ \alpha) = v \text{ iff } (f\ s_1 Suf(\alpha, \delta(q_\alpha, s_1))) = v \lor ... \lor$$
$$(f\ s_n Suf(\alpha, \delta(q_\alpha, s_n))) = v \lor$$
$$(f\ \alpha - \{s_1, .., s_n\}\Sigma^*) = v.$$

The statement of the generic *Free* algorithm (definition 9) is simplified by considering specific attributes as trivial regular languages, but this suggests that complex finite state machinery would be required to process them. This alternative works in the opposite direction: it reduces leading terms in an uncertainty to simple attributes before pursuing their interactions, so that efficient attribute matching routines of a normal unification procedure can be applied. This alternative has a second computational advantage. The generic algorithm unwinds the uncertainty one attribute at a time, constructing a residual regular set at each step, which is then processed against the other non-uncertain equations. The alternative processes them all at once, avoiding the construction of these intermediate residual languages. This is a very important optimization, since we found it to be the most common case when we embedded uncertainty resolution in our recursive unification algorithm.

Uncertainty specifications are a compact way of expressing a large number of disjunctive possibilities that are uncovered one by one as our procedure operates. It might seem that this is an extremely expensive descriptive device, one which should be avoided in favor of apparently simpler mechanisms. But the disjunctions that emerge from processing uncertainties are real: they represent independent grammatical possibilities that would require additional computational resources no matter how they were expressed. In theories in which long-distance dependencies are based on empty phrase structure nodes and implemented, for example, by gap-threading machinery, ATN HOLD lists, and the like, the exact location of these empty nodes is not signaled by any information directly visible in the sentence. This increases the number of phrase structure rules that can be applied. What we see as the computational cost of functional uncertainty shows up in these systems as additional resources needed for phrase structure analysis and for functional evaluation of the larger number of trees that the phrase structure component produces. Unlike phrasally-based specifications, functional uncertainties in LFG are defined on the same level of representation as the subcategorization restrictions that constrain how they can be resolved, which our coherence-delay strategy easily takes advantage of. But the fact remains that functional uncertainties do generate disjunctions, and can benefit from the recent advances in efficient disjunction-processing techniques for LFG and related grammatical formalisms (Kasper 1987, Eisele and Dörre 1988, Maxwell and Kaplan 1989, Dörre and Eisele 1990).

6 Conclusion

The notion of regular functional uncertainty thus has very nice mathematical properties. Our state-decomposition algorithm provides a very attractive method for resolving functional uncertainties as other phrasal and functional constraints are computed during the parse of a sentence. This algorithm expands the uncertainties incrementally, introducing at each point only as much disjunction as is necessary to avoid interactions with other functional information that has already been taken into account. We have recently added this algorithm and the functional uncertainty notation to our LFG Grammar Writer's Workbench, and we can now rigorously but easily test a wide range of linguistic hypotheses. We have also begun to investigate a number of other computational heuristics for the efficient, controlled expansion of uncertainty.

Kaplan and Zaenen (1989) first proposed the idea of functional uncertainty as sketched in this paper to account for the properties of long-distance dependencies within the LFG framework. In this framework, it has already shed new light on long-standing problems like island constraints (see, e.g., Saiki (1985) for an application to Japanese). But the notion is potentially of much wider use: first, it can be adapted to other unification grammar formalisms to handle facts of a similar nature; and second, it can be used to handle phenomena that are traditionally not thought of as falling into the same class as long-distance dependencies but that nevertheless seem to involve nonlocal uncertainty. A discussion of its application in the LFG framework to infinitival complements can be found in Johnson (1986a) for Dutch and Netter (1986) for German; Karttunen (1989) discusses how similar extensions to Categorial Unification Grammar (CUG) can account in a simple way for related facts in Finnish that would otherwise require type-raising. Halvorsen and Kaplan (1988) have suggested that scope ambiguities in semantic structures might also be characterized by this device.

Acknowledgments

Our understanding of the linguistic applications of functional uncertainty developed over a long period of time in discussions with Joan Bresnan, Kris Halvorsen and Annie Zaenen. We also benefitted from early discussions with Mark Johnson, who was also investigating the mathematical properties of regular uncertainty (see Johnson 1986b). Finally, Bill

Rounds assisted us in understanding the difficulties of the cyclic case. We are grateful for the invaluable assistance these colleagues have provided.

References

Dörre, Jochen, and Andreas Eisele. 1990. Feature Logic with Disjunctive Unification. In *Proceedings of COLING-90*. Helsinki.

Eisele, Andreas, and Jochen Dörre. 1988. Unification of Disjunctive Feature Descriptions. In *Proceedings of the Twenty-Sixth Annual Meeting of the ACL*, 286–294. Buffalo, NY. Association for Computational Linguistics.

Halvorsen, Per-Kristian, and Ronald M. Kaplan. 1988. Projections and Semantic Description in Lexical-Functional Grammar. In *Proceedings of the International Conference on Fifth Generation Computer Systems*, 1116–1122. Tokyo, Japan. Institute for New Generation Systems. Reprinted in Part IV of this volume.

Johnson, Mark. 1986a. The LFG Treatment of Discontinuity and the Double Infinitive Construction in Dutch. In *Proceedings of the Fifth West Coast Conference on Formal Linguistics*, ed. Mary Dalrymple, Jeffrey Goldberg, Kristin Hanson, Michael Inman, Chris Piñon, and Stephen Wechsler, 102–118. Stanford University. Stanford Linguistics Association.

Johnson, Mark. 1986b. Computing with Regular Path Formulas. Unpublished MS, Stanford University.

Johnson, Mark. 1987. *Attribute-Value Logic and the Theory of Grammar*. Doctoral dissertation, Stanford University. Also published as CSLI Lecture Notes, No. 16. Stanford University: CSLI/The University of Chicago Press. 1988.

Kaplan, Ronald M., and Joan Bresnan. 1982. Lexical-Functional Grammar: A Formal System for Grammatical Representation. In *The Mental Representation of Grammatical Relations*, ed. Joan Bresnan, 173–281. Cambridge, MA: The MIT Press. Reprinted in Part I of this volume.

Kaplan, Ronald M., and Annie Zaenen. 1989. Long-distance Dependencies, Constituent Structure, and Functional Uncertainty. In *Alternative Conceptions of Phrase Structure*, ed. Mark Baltin and Anthony Kroch. Chicago University Press. Reprinted in Part II of this volume.

Karttunen, Lauri. 1989. Radical Lexicalism. In *Alternative Conceptions of Phrase Structure*, ed. Mark Baltin and Anthony Kroch. Chicago University Press.

Kasper, Robert T. 1987. A Unification Method for Disjunctive Feature Descriptions. In *Proceedings of the Twenty-Fifth Annual Meeting of the ACL*, 235–242. Stanford, CA. Association for Computational Linguistics.

Maxwell, John T., and Ronald Kaplan. 1989. An Overview of Disjunctive Constraint Satisfaction. In *Proceedings of the International Workshop on Parsing Technologies*, 18–27. Also published as 'A Method for Disjunctive Constraint Satisfaction', M. Tomita, editor, *Current Issues in Parsing*

Technology, Kluwer Academic Publishers, 1991. Reprinted in Part V of this volume.

Netter, Klaus. 1986. Getting things out of order. In *Proceedings of COLING-86*, 494–496. Bonn.

Saiki, Mariko. 1985. On the coordination of gapped constituents in Japanese. In *Papers from the Twenty-First Regional Meeting of the Chicago Linguistic Society*, ed. William H. Eilfort, Paul D. Kroeber, and Karen L. Peterson, 371–387. University of Chicago. Chicago Linguistic Society.

6

Constituent Coordination in Lexical-Functional Grammar

RONALD M. KAPLAN AND JOHN T. MAXWELL III

Abstract. This paper outlines a theory of constituent coordination for Lexical-Functional Grammar. On this theory LFG's flat, unstructured sets are used as the functional representation of coordinate constructions. Function-application is extended to sets by treating a set formally as the generalization of its functional elements. This causes properties attributed externally to a coordinate structure to be uniformly distributed across its elements, without requiring additional grammatical specifications.

1 Introduction

A proper treatment of coordination has long been an elusive goal of both theoretical and computational approaches to language. The original transformational formulation in terms of the Coordinate Reduction rule (e.g. Dougherty 1970) was quickly shown to have many theoretical and empirical inadequacies, and only recently have linguistic theories (e.g. GPSG, Gazdar et al. 1985; Categorial grammar, Steedman 1985) made substantial progress on characterizing the complex restrictions on coordinate constructions and also on their semantic interpretations. Coordination has also presented descriptive problems for computational approaches. Typically these have been solved by special devices that are added to the parsing algorithms to analyze coordinate constructions that cannot easily be characterized in explicit rules of grammar. The best known examples of this kind of approach are SYSCONJ (Woods 1973), LSP (Sager 1981), and MSG (Dahl and McCord 1983).

This paper originally appeared in *Proceedings of COLING-88*, vol. 1 (Budapest, 1988), 303–305.

Formal Issues in Lexical-Functional Grammar
edited by
Mary Dalrymple
Ronald M. Kaplan
John T. Maxwell III
Annie Zaenen

199

Coordination phenomena are usually divided into two classes, the so-called constituent coordinations where the coordinated elements look like otherwise well-motivated phrasal constituents (1), and nonconstituent coordination where the coordinated elements look like fragments of phrasal constituents (2).

(1) a.   A girl saw Mary and ran to Bill. (Coordinated verb phrases)

    b.   A girl saw and heard Mary. (Coordinated verbs)

(2)   Bill went to Chicago on Wednesday and New York on Thursday.

Of course, what is or is not a well-motivated constituent depends on the details of the particular grammatical theory. Constituents in transformationally oriented theories, for example, are units that simplify the feeding relations of transformational rules, whereas "constituents" in categorial grammars merely reflect the order of binary combinations and have no other special motivation. In Lexical-Functional Grammar, surface constituents are taken to be the units of phonological interpretation. These may differ markedly from the units of functional or semantic interpretation, as shown in the analysis of Dutch cross serial dependencies given by Bresnan et al. (1982).

Nonconstituent coordination, of course, presents a wide variety of complex and difficult descriptive problems, but constituent coordination also raises important linguistic issues. It is the latter that we focus on in this brief paper.

To a first approximation, constituent coordinations can be analyzed as the result of taking two independent clauses and factoring out their common subparts. The verb coordination in (1b) is thus related to the fuller sentence coordination in (3). This intuition, which was the basis of the Coordinate Reduction Transformation, accounts for more complex patterns of acceptability such as (4) illustrates. The coordination in (4c) is acceptable because both (4a) and (4b) are, while (4e) is bad because of the independent subcategorization violation in (4d).

(3)   A girl saw Mary and a girl heard Mary.

(4) a.   A girl dedicated a pie to Bill.

    b.   A girl gave a pie to Bill.

    c.   A girl dedicated and gave a pie to Bill.

    d.   *A girl ate a pie to Bill.

    e.   *A girl dedicated and ate a pie to Bill.

This first approximation is fraught with difficulties. It ensures that constituents of like categories can be conjoined only if they share some finer details of specification, but there are more subtle conditions that it does not cover. For example, even though (5a) and (5b) are both independently grammatical, the coordination in (5c) is unacceptable:

(5) a. The girl promised John to go.
  b. The girl persuaded John to go.
  c. *The girl promised and persuaded John to go.
    (Hint: Who is going?)

Another well-known difficulty with this approach is that it does not obviously allow for the necessary semantic distinctions to be made, on the assumption that the semantic properties of reduced coordinations are to be explicated in terms of the semantic representations of the propositional coordinations that they are related to. This is illustrated by the contrasting semantic entailments in (6): Sentence (6a) allows for the possibility that two different girls are involved while (6b) implies that a single (but indefinite) girl performed both actions.

(6) a. A girl saw Mary and a girl talked to Bill.
  b. A girl saw Mary and talked to Bill.

Despite its deficiencies, it has not been easy to find a satisfactory alternative to this first approximation. The theoretical challenge is to embed coordination in a grammatical system in a way that is independent of the other generalizations that are being expressed (e.g. actives correspond to passives, NP's in English can be followed by relative clauses, English relative clauses look like S's with a missing NP) but which interacts with those specifications in just the right ways. That is, a possible but unacceptable solution to this descriptive dilemma would be to add to the grammar new versions of all the basic rules designed specifically to account for the vagaries of coordination.

Coordination was not discussed in the original formulation of Lexical-Functional Grammar (Kaplan and Bresnan 1982), although mathematical objects (finite sets of f-structures) were introduced to provide an underlying representation for grammatical constructions which, like the parts of a coordination, do not seem to obey the uniqueness condition that normally applies to grammatical functions and features. Adjuncts and other modifying constructions are the major example of this that Kaplan and Bresnan discussed, but they also suggested that the same mathematical representations might also be used in the analysis of coordination phenomena. In the present paper we extend the LFG formalism to provide a simple account of coordination that follows along the general lines of the Kaplan/Bresnan suggestion and does not involve detailed specifications of the coordination properties of particular constituents. We illustrate the consequences of this extension by discussing a small number of grammatical constructions; Bresnan, Kaplan, and Peterson (1985) discuss a much wider range of phenomena and provide more general linguistic motivation for this approach.

2   Simple Coordination

A Lexical-Functional Grammar assigns two syntactic levels of representation to each grammatical string in a language. The constituent structure, or c-structure, is a conventional tree that indicates the organization of surface words and phrases, while the functional structure (f-structure) is a hierarchy of attributes and values that represents the grammatical functions and features of the sentence. LFG assumes as a basic axiom that there is a piecewise function, called a structural correspondence or "projection", that maps from the nodes in the c-structure to the units in an abstract f-structure (see Kaplan and Bresnan 1982 and Kaplan 1987 for details). This means that the properties of the f-structure can be specified in terms of the mother-daughter and precedence relations in the c-structure, even though the f-structure is formally not at all a tree-like structure.

Now let us consider a simple example of coordination wherein two sentences are conjoined together (7). A plausible c-structure for this sentence is given in (8), and we propose (9) to represent the functional properties of this sentence.

(7)   John bought apples and John ate apples.

(8)

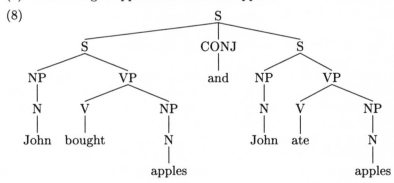

(9)

$$\left\{ \begin{array}{l} \begin{bmatrix} \text{PRED} & \text{'buy} \langle (\uparrow \text{ SUBJ}), (\uparrow \text{ OBJ}) \rangle\,' \\ \text{TENSE} & \text{PAST} \\ \text{SUBJ} & \begin{bmatrix} \text{PRED} & \text{'John'} \\ \text{NUM} & \text{SG} \end{bmatrix} \\ \text{OBJ} & \begin{bmatrix} \text{PRED} & \text{'apple'} \\ \text{NUM} & \text{PL} \end{bmatrix} \end{bmatrix} \\[3em] \begin{bmatrix} \text{PRED} & \text{'eat} \langle (\uparrow \text{ SUBJ}), (\uparrow \text{ OBJ}) \rangle\,' \\ \text{TENSE} & \text{PAST} \\ \text{SUBJ} & \begin{bmatrix} \text{PRED} & \text{'John'} \\ \text{NUM} & \text{SG} \end{bmatrix} \\ \text{OBJ} & \begin{bmatrix} \text{PRED} & \text{'apple'} \\ \text{NUM} & \text{PL} \end{bmatrix} \end{bmatrix} \end{array} \right\}$$

The structure in (9) is a set containing the f-structures that correspond to the component sentences of the coordination. As Bresnan, Kaplan, and Peterson (1985) observe, sets constitute a plausible formal representation for coordination since an unlimited number of items can be conjoined in a single construction and none of those items dominates or has scope over the others. Neither particular functional attributes nor recursive embeddings of attributes can provide the appropriate representation that flat, unstructured sets allow.

To obtain the representation of coordination shown in (8) and (9), all we need is the following alternative way of expanding S:

(10)   S $\longrightarrow$ S   CONJ   S
                $\downarrow \in \uparrow$ $\downarrow \in \uparrow$

This rule says that a conjoined sentence consists of a sentence followed by a conjunction followed by another sentence, where the f-structure of each sub-sentence is an element of the f-structure that represents their coordination.

3   Coordination with Distribution

The next step is to consider constituent coordinations where some parts of the sentence are shared by the coordinated constituents. Consider the following sentence:

(11)   John bought and ate apples.

(12)

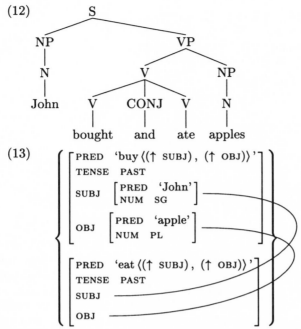

(13)

The desired c-structure and f-structure for (11) are shown in (12) and (13) respectively. Notice that the subjects and objects of *buy* and *eat* are linked, so that the f-structure is different from the one in (9) for *John bought apples and John ate apples*. The identity links in this structure account for the different semantic entailments of sentences (7) and (11) as well as for the differences in (6a) and (6b).

This is an example of verb coordination, so the following alternative is added to the grammar:

(14) V $\longrightarrow$ V CONJ V
                          $\downarrow \in \uparrow$ $\downarrow \in \uparrow$

This rule permits the appropriate c-structure configuration but its functional specifications are no different than the ones for simple sentential coordination. How then do the links in (13) arise? The basic descriptive device of the LFG formalism is the function application expression:

(15) $(f\ a) = v$

As originally formulated by Kaplan and Bresnan (1982), this equation (15) holds if and only if f denotes an f-structure which yields the value v when applied to the attribute a. According to the original definition, the value of an application expression is undefined when f denotes a set of f-structures instead of a single function and an equation such as (15) would therefore be false. Following Bresnan, Kaplan, and Peterson (1985), we propose extending the function-application device so that it is defined for sets of functions. If s denotes a set of functions, we say that $(s\ a) = v$ holds if and only if v is the *generalization* of all the elements of s applied to a:

(16) $(s\ a) = \prod(f\ a)$ if $(f\ a)$ is defined for all $f \in s$.

The generalization $f_1 \prod f_2$ of two functions or f-structures f_1 and f_2 is defined recursively as follows:

(17) a. If $f_1 = f_2$ then $f_1 \prod f_2 = f_1$
      b. If f_1 and f_2 are f-structures, then
          $f_1 \prod f_2 = \{<a, (f_1\ a)\prod(f_2\ a)>|\ a \in \text{DOM}(f_1) \cap \text{DOM}(f_2)\}$.
      c. Otherwise, $f_1 \prod f_2 = \bot$.

The generalization is the greatest lower bound in the subsumption ordering on the f-structure lattice. The symbol $\bot$ denotes the bottom-most element in this lattice, the element that subsumes all other elements and about which no information is known. With this element explicitly represented, we simplify the determinacy and completeness conditions of Kaplan and Bresnan (1982) by defining minimal solutions containing $\bot$ to be invalid.

These definitions have two consequences. The first is that v subsumes $(f\ a)$ for all $f \in s$. Thus the properties asserted on a set as a whole must be distributed across the elements of the set. This explains why the subject and object of (11) are distributed across both verbs without having to change the VP rule in (18) below. The equation on the object NP of (18) is $(\uparrow \text{OBJ}) = \downarrow$. The meta-variable $\uparrow$ denotes a set because the f-structure of the VP node is the same as the f-structure of the conjoined V node, which by (14) is a set. Therefore the effect of rule (18) is that each of the elements of the $\uparrow$ set will have an OBJ attribute whose value is subsumed by the f-structure corresponding to *apples*.

(18)   VP $\longrightarrow$ V   NP
                      $\uparrow = \downarrow$ $(\uparrow$ OBJ$) = \downarrow$

The second consequence of (16) is that v takes on the attributes and values that all of the $(f\ a)$ have in common. This is useful in explaining the ungrammaticality of the *promise and persuade* sentence in (5c). (We are indebted to Andreas Eisele and Stefan Momma for calling our attention to this example.) The analysis for this sentence is in (20) and (21):

(19) *The girl promised and persuaded John to go.

(20)

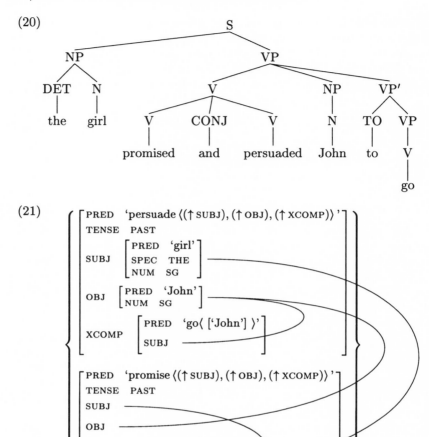

(21)

At first glance, (21) seems to provide a perfectly reasonable analysis of (19). *Promise* and *persuade* share an object, a subject, and a verb complement. The verb complements have different subjects as a result of the different control equations for *promise* and *persuade* (The lexical entry for *promise* specifies subject control (↑ XCOMP SUBJ) = (↑ SUBJ), while *persuade* specifies object control (↑ XCOMP SUBJ) = (↑ OBJ)). There is no inconsistency, incompleteness or incoherence in this structure.

However, in LFG the completeness conditions apply to the f-structures mapped from all the c-structure nodes, whether or not they are part of the structure corresponding to the root node. And if we look at the f-structure that corresponds to the verb-complement node, we discover that it contains ⊥ and thus is incomplete:

(22)
$$\begin{bmatrix} \text{PRED} & \text{`go}\langle\,[\,]\,\rangle\text{'} \\ \text{SUBJ} & \begin{bmatrix} \text{PRED} & \bot \\ \text{NUM} & \text{SG} \end{bmatrix} \end{bmatrix}$$

This f-structure is the generalization of (s XCOMP) for the set given in (21). Everything that the two XCOMPs have in common is given by this f-structure. However, the subject of the f-structure has ⊥ for its predicate. It thus violates the "semantic completeness" condition of LFG, which in essence requires that something must be known about the predicate of every thematic function. If the XCOMPs had had a subject in common (as in the sentence *The girl urged and persuaded John to go*) then the sentence would have been perfectly legal.

4 Interactions with Long-distance Dependencies

Under certain circumstances a shared constituent plays different roles in the conjoined constituents. For instance, in (23) *The robot* is the object for *Bill gave Mary*, and it is the oblique object for *John gave a ball to*.

(23)   The robot that Bill gave Mary and John gave a ball to

This variation reflects a more general uncertainty about what role the head of a relative clause can play in the relative clause, as illustrated in (24):

(24)   The robot that Bill gave Mary
       The robot that gave Bill Mary
       The robot that John said Bill gave Mary
       The robot that Tom claimed John said Bill gave Mary, etc.

In fact, the number of roles that the head of a relative clause can play is theoretically unbounded.

To deal with these possibilities, the notion of *functional uncertainty* has been introduced into LFG theory (Kaplan and Maxwell 1988; Kaplan and Zaenen 1989). With functional uncertainty the attribute of a functional equation is allowed to consist of a (possibly infinite) regular set of attribute strings. For instance, normally the role that a constituent plays in the f-structure is given by a simple equation such as (25):

(25) $(f_1 \text{ OBJ}) = f_2$

A functionally uncertain equation that could be used to express the relationship between the head of a relative clause and the role that it plays in the clause might look like (26):

(26) $(f_1 \text{ COMP}^* \text{ GF}) = f_2$

Equation (26) says that the functional relationship between f_1 and f_2 could consist of any number of COMPs followed by a grammatical function, such as SUBJ or OBJ.

The definition of functional uncertainty given by Kaplan and Zaenen (1989) is essentially as follows:

(27) If α is a regular expression, then $(f\,\alpha) = v$ holds if and only $((f\,a)\,\text{Suff}(a, \alpha)) = v$ for some symbol a, where Suff(a, α) is the set of suffix strings y such that ay $\in \alpha$.

We will not discuss functional uncertainty further in this paper, except to show how it fits into our model for sets. To achieve the proper interaction between sets and regular expressions, we merge (27) with (16):

(28) $(s\,\alpha) = v = \prod (f_i\,\alpha)$, for all $f_i \in s$
      $= \prod ((f_i\,a_i)\,\text{Suff}(a_i\,\alpha))$, for all $f_i \in s$

Allowing different a_i to be chosen for each f_i provides the variation needed for (23). The uncertainty can be realized by a different functional path in each of the coordinated elements, but the uncertainty must be resolved somehow in each element and this accounts for the familiar Across the Board and Coordinate Structure Constraints.

5   Representing the Conjunction

We have not yet indicated how the identity of the particular conjunction is represented. If we look at rule (14) again, we notice that it is missing any equation to tell us how the f-structure for CONJ is related to ↑:

(29) V $\longrightarrow$ V   CONJ   V
           ↓∈↑   ?   ↓∈↑

If we replace the ? with ↑=↓, then the f-structure for CONJ will be identified with the set corresponding to ↑, which will have the effect of distributing all of its information across the f-structures corresponding to the conjoined verbs. As was pointed out to us by researchers at the University of Manchester (UMIST), this arrangement leads to inconsistencies when coordinations of different types (*and* vs. *or*) are mutually embedded. On the other hand, if we replace the ? with ↓∈↑, then the f-structure for CONJ will be another element of the set, on a par with the f-structures corresponding to the conjoined verbs. This is clearly counterintuitive and also erroneously implies that the shared elements will be distributed across the conjunction as well as the elements of the set.

We observe, however, that the identity of the particular conjunction does not seem to enter into any syntactic or functional generalizations, and therefore, that there is no motivation for including it in the functional structure at all. Instead, it is necessary to encode this information only on the semantic level of representation, as defined by a semantic structural correspondence or *projection* (Kaplan 1987). A projection is a piecewise function mapping from the units of one kind of structure to the units of another. The projection that is most central to LFG theory is the ϕ projection, the one that maps from constituent structure nodes into functional structures. But other projections are being introduced into LFG theory so that generalizations about various other subsystems of linguistic information can be formalized. In particular, Halvorsen and Kaplan (1988) have discussed the σ projection that maps from f-structures into a range of semantic structures. Given the projection concept, the various linguistic levels can be related to one another through *codescription*, that is, the equations that describe the mapping between f-structures and s-structures (semantic structures) are generated in terms of the same c-structure node configurations as the equations that map between c-structures and f-structures. This means that even though the s-structure is mapped from the f-structure, it may contain information that is not computable from the f-structure but is strongly correlated with it via codescription. We exploit this possibility to encode the identity of the conjunction only in semantic structure.

Consider a modified version of (29) that has equations describing the semantic structures corresponding to the f-structure units:

$$(30) \quad V \;\rightarrow\; \begin{array}{ccc} V & \text{CONJ} & V \\ \downarrow \in \uparrow & \sigma(\uparrow \text{ REL}) = \sigma\downarrow & \downarrow \in \uparrow \\ \sigma\downarrow = (\sigma\uparrow \text{ ARG1}) & & \sigma\downarrow = (\sigma\uparrow \text{ ARG2}) \end{array}$$

Rule (30) says that the unit of semantic structure corresponding to the f-structure of the conjoined verb contains the conjunction as its main relation (REL), plus two ARGs consisting of the semantic structures corresponding to the f-structures that correspond to the individual V's. The semantic structure generated by (30) is something like this:

$$(31) \quad \begin{bmatrix} \text{REL} & \text{AND} \\ \text{ARG1} & \begin{bmatrix} \text{REL} & \text{BUY} \\ \cdots & \cdots \end{bmatrix} \\ \text{ARG2} & \begin{bmatrix} \text{REL} & \text{EAT} \\ \cdots & \cdots \end{bmatrix} \end{bmatrix}$$

It describes the conjoined verb as a relation, AND, which is applied to the arguments consisting of the relation BUY and the relation EAT. Each of these relations also has arguments, the semantic structures corresponding to the shared subject and object of the sentence. Notice how this structure differs from the one that we find at the functional level (e.g. (13)). Rule (30) does not assign any functional role to the conjunction, yet all the necessary syntactic and semantic information is available in the complex of corresponding structures assigned to the sentence.

References

Bresnan, Joan, Ronald M. Kaplan, and Peter Peterson. 1985. Coordination and the Flow of Information through Phrase Structure. Unpublished MS.

Dahl, Veronica, and Michael McCord. 1983. Treating coordination in logic grammars. *Computational Linguistics* 9:69–91.

Dougherty, Ray C. 1970. A Grammar of Coordinate Conjoined Structures, I. *Language* 46(4):850–898.

Gazdar, Gerald, Ewan Klein, Geoffrey K. Pullum, and Ivan A. Sag. 1985. *Generalized Phrase Structure Grammar*. Cambridge, MA: Harvard University Press.

Halvorsen, Per-Kristian, and Ronald M. Kaplan. 1988. Projections and Semantic Description in Lexical-Functional Grammar. In *Proceedings of the International Conference on Fifth Generation Computer Systems*, 1116–1122. Tokyo, Japan. Institute for New Generation Systems. Reprinted in Part IV of this volume.

Kaplan, Ronald M., and Joan Bresnan. 1982. Lexical-Functional Grammar: A Formal System for Grammatical Representation. In *The Mental Representation of Grammatical Relations*, ed. Joan Bresnan, 173–281. Cambridge, MA: The MIT Press. Reprinted in Part I of this volume.

Kaplan, Ronald M. 1987. Three Seductions of Computational Psycholinguistics. In *Linguistic Theory and Computer Applications*, ed. Peter Whitelock, Harold Somers, Paul Bennett, Rod Johnson, and Mary McGee Wood, 149–188. London: Academic Press. Reprinted in Part V of this volume.

Kaplan, Ronald M., and John T. Maxwell. 1988. An Algorithm for Functional Uncertainty. In *Proceedings of COLING-88*, Vol. 1, 297–302. Reprinted in Part II of this volume.

Kaplan, Ronald M., and Annie Zaenen. 1989. Long-distance Dependencies, Constituent Structure, and Functional Uncertainty. In *Alternative Conceptions of Phrase Structure*, ed. Mark Baltin and Anthony Kroch. Chicago University Press. Reprinted in Part II of this volume.

Sager, N. 1981. *Natural language information processing*. Reading, MA: Addison-Wesley.

Steedman, Mark J. 1985. Dependency and coordination in the grammar of Dutch and English. *Language* 61:523–568.

Woods, William A. 1973. An Experimental Parsing System for Transition Network Grammars. In *Natural Language Processing*, ed. R. Rustin, 111–154. New York: Algorithmics Press.

Part III

Word Order

A central feature of LFG is its separation of syntactic information into two separate modules, the *constituent structure* or c-structure and the *functional structure* or f-structure. The f-structure encodes information about agreement, grammatical functions, and syntactic subcategorization, while the c-structure tree encodes information about category, precedence, and dominance. The two levels are related to each other by a structural correspondence, a piece-wise function that maps c-structure nodes into units of f-structure. A fundamental claim of LFG is that generalizations at the different levels of representation are relatively independent and that the modular separation of constituent structure from functional structure thus encourages a natural characterization of many syntactic phenomena.

According to this division of explanatory labor, constraints on the order of words and phrases are specified primarily in c-structure terms, using an extended regular expression notation for the right-hand sides of c-structure rules; for discussions of such notations, see Kaplan (1989) or Kaplan and Maxwell (1994). Simple regular-equivalent notations, for example, allow for the statement of separate constraints on immediate dominance and linear precedence without changing the formal power of the grammatical machinery. However, as LFG analyses have been developed for a wider variety of linguistic phenomena, it has become apparent that there are some dependencies that involve a stronger interaction between linear precedence and grammatical function assignments than would be permitted by the arrangement of strict modularity. Even though precedence is not defined as a native relation on f-structures, it is sometimes simpler and more intuitive to state precedence constraints in functional terms—to say, for example, that the subject of a clause comes before the object of a complement—than to specify the order of particular noun phrases in the c-structure. The papers in this section provide a formal characterization of this intuition by means of the *functional precedence* relation.

Functional precedence, or f-precedence, is a relation between functional structures that is derived from the c-structural linear precedence relation. It was first introduced by Bresnan in her 1984 BLS paper "Bound anaphora on functional structures" to specify linear ordering constraints between an anaphor and its antecedent; the second paper in this section, Bresnan's "Linear Order, Syntactic Rank, and Empty Categories: On Weak Crossover", evolved from this earlier work.

Subsequently, functional precedence was used by other researchers in their work on encoding constraints on word order in functional terms, in particular by Kameyama (1989) in her analysis of Japanese anaphora. Work on the formal properties of functional precedence was carried out by Kaplan (1987, originally presented in 1985) in the paper "Three Seductions of Computational Psycholinguistics", reprinted in Part V of this volume. This paper provided a formalization in terms of the inverse of the correspondence between c-structure nodes and f-structure units. Additionally, Kaplan (1988) considered other ways in which correspondence inverses could allow for minor and controlled but still systematic deviations from the hypothesis of strict modularity.

The first paper in this section, Zaenen and Kaplan's "Formal Devices for Linguistic Generalizations: West Germanic Word Order in LFG", presents an analysis of word order and constituency in Germanic infinitivals, continuing work on Germanic word order which began with the 1982 paper "Cross-serial Dependencies in Dutch", by Bresnan, Kaplan, Peters, and Zaenen. The paper builds directly on proposals described in Kaplan and Zaenen's 1988 paper "Functional uncertainty and functional precedence in continental West Germanic" and in their 1989 paper "Functional precedence and constituent structure". The paper included in this volume deals with a broader set of grammatical constructions than do the earlier papers, and also takes into account certain formal problems with the 1982 approach to Dutch, first noted by Johnson (1986). The Zaenen and Kaplan solution relies heavily on f-structural properties to constrain the relation between a verb and its arguments in Germanic. Their work also makes use of *functional uncertainty*, a formal device that is explored more fully in Part II of this book, Nonlocal Dependencies, to encode long-distance relations between a verb and its arguments.

Whereas Zaenen and Kaplan are concerned primarily with interactions between word order and other syntactic properties, the second paper in this section, Bresnan's "Linear Order, Syntactic Rank, and Empty Categories: On Weak Crossover", focuses on the effect of word order on the determination of pronoun reference. It is often assumed that constraints on pronoun reference possibilities are statable in terms of constituent structure configurations, but Bresnan shows that this assumption cannot be maintained. Considering evidence from Malayalam, Palauan, and Hindi in addition to English, she makes use of f-precedence to give a comprehensive account of a complex pattern of acceptable coreference: the correct results follow from a definition of syntactic rank in functional terms, together with constraints on f-precedence relations between pronouns and their antecedents.

There is still some controversy about the proper definition of functional precedence. Bresnan's account in this paper uses a slightly different definition from the one that she proposed in 1984 and that Kameyama, Zaenen, and Kaplan have adopted. Both the original definition and Bresnan's new definition are stated in terms of precedence relations among nodes of the c-structure tree that are picked out by the inverse of the c-structure to f-structure correspondence; in both cases, the relation of f-precedence between two f-structures is defined in terms of the precedence relation on c-structure nodes with which they are in correspondence. The two definitions differ in that the original formulation took all of the c-structure nodes that map to a particular f-structure into account, whereas Bresnan's more recent proposal counts only the rightmost nodes in the inverse image of that f-structure. Preliminary results indicate that accounts based on the original definition can be reformulated so as to be compatible with the new proposal, but it is not yet clear whether the nature of the linguistic generalizations will change or whether the basic intuitions of the original work will be preserved under these reformulations.

Bresnan's weak crossover account also relies on the assignment of phrase-structure positions to functional elements that are related by long-distance dependencies. In introducing functional uncertainty as a means of characterizing long-distance dependencies, Kaplan and Zaenen (1989b) note that much of the traditional motivation for traces and other empty c-structure elements is undermined by the introduction of functional uncertainty (see the preface to Section II for further discussion). However, Bresnan's arguments in the present paper suggest new LFG-internal support for those notions. We expect these formal differences to be resolved by continuing lines of research.

References

Bresnan, Joan. 1984. Bound anaphora on functional structures. Presented at the Tenth Annual Meeting of the Berkeley Linguistics Society, February 17, 1984.

Bresnan, Joan, Ronald M. Kaplan, Stanley Peters, and Annie Zaenen. 1982. Cross-serial dependencies in Dutch. *Linguistic Inquiry*, 13:613–635.

Johnson, Mark. 1986. The LFG treatment of discontinuity and the double infinitive construction in Dutch. In Mary Dalrymple, Jeffrey Goldberg, Kristin Hanson, Michael Inman, Chris Piñon, and Stephen Wechsler, editors, *Proceedings of the Fifth West Coast Conference on Formal Linguistics*, pages 102–118, Stanford University. Stanford Linguistics Association.

Kameyama, Megumi. 1989. Functional precedence conditions on overt and zero pronominals. MS, Stanford University.

Kaplan, Ronald M. 1987. Three seductions of computational psycholinguistics. In Peter Whitelock, Mary McGee Wood, Harold L. Somers, Rod Johnson, and Paul Bennett, editors, *Linguistic Theory and Computer Applications*. Academic Press, London, pages 149–188. Reprinted in Part V of this volume.

Kaplan, Ronald M. 1988. Correspondences and their inverses. Paper presented at the Titisee Workshop on Unification Formalisms: Syntax, Semantics and Implementation, Titisee, Germany.

Kaplan, Ronald M. 1989. The formal architecture of Lexical-Functional Grammar. In Chu-Ren Huang and Keh-Jiann Chen, editors, *Proceedings of ROCLING II*, pages 1–18. Reprinted in Part I of this volume.

Kaplan, Ronald M. and John T. Maxwell. 1994. LFG Grammar Writer's Workbench. Technical report, Xerox Palo Alto Research Center.

Kaplan, Ronald M. and Annie Zaenen. 1988. Functional uncertainty and functional precedence in continental West Germanic. In Harald Trost, editor, *Österreichische Artificial-Intelligence-Tagung, Proceedings*, pages 114–123, Berlin. Springer-Verlag.

Kaplan, Ronald M. and Annie Zaenen. 1989a. Functional precedence and constituent structure. In Chu-Ren Huang and Keh-Jiann Chen, editors, *Proceedings of ROCLING II*, pages 19–40, Taipei, Republic of China.

Kaplan, Ronald M., and Annie Zaenen. 1989b. Long-distance Dependencies, Constituent Structure, and Functional Uncertainty. In *Alternative Conceptions of Phrase Structure*, ed. Mark Baltin and Anthony Kroch. Chicago University Press. Reprinted in Part II of this volume.

7

Formal Devices for Linguistic Generalizations: West Germanic Word Order in LFG

ANNIE ZAENEN AND RONALD M. KAPLAN

1 Introduction

In LFG the phrase structure representation of a sentence is used to divide linguistic strings into a hierarchy of ordered phrasal constituents. It is well known that this kind of representation does not capture all the syntactically significant dependencies that exist in sentences. In this paper we look at some dependencies that cannot be captured in this superficial representation but seem nevertheless to be affected by the order of elements of the string. These dependencies are illustrated by word order constraints in Germanic infinitivals. German infinitivals exhibit a syntactic dependency that is not local in the sense that elements that are syntactically closely dependent on each other are in string positions separated by 'extraneous' material. This case is different from that of the wh-constructions discussed in Kaplan and Zaenen (1989) in that there are no clearly fixed positions for the separated elements of the infinitivals. We show that existing mechanisms, specifically functional uncertainty and functional precedence, that were developed to account for other phenomena can be exploited to model the new data in an insightful way.

This paper also appears in *Linguistics and Computation*, ed. Jennifer S. Cole, Georgia M. Green, and Jerry L. Morgan (Stanford, CA: CSLI, to appear), 3–27.

Formal Issues in Lexical-Functional Grammar
edited by
Mary Dalrymple
Ronald M. Kaplan
John T. Maxwell III
Annie Zaenen
Copyright © 1995, Stanford University

2 A case study: Dutch cross serial dependencies

2.1 Basic facts.

Since Evers (1975) several syntactic models have been proposed to account for sentences of the type illustrated in the Dutch example in (1):

(1) ... dat Jan zijn zoon geneeskunde wil laten studeren.
     ... that John his son medicine wants let study.

What is interesting about this sentence pattern is that the verbs and the nominal or prepositional elements that they govern are not adjacent in the surface string or in the phrase structure representation. In Dutch all the dependent elements have to precede all the verbs, but there is no requirement that the verb and its dependents be adjacent either in the string or in the surface tree representation one would naturally assign to such a sentence. In other variants of West-Germanic the verbs and their dependents can be interleaved, as we discuss in Section 4. As an illustration we show in (2) the surface structure proposed in Evers (1975) with the f-structure showing the dependencies that hold in the sentence, assuming some plausible lexical entries consistent with this f-structure. They are given in (3).

(2)

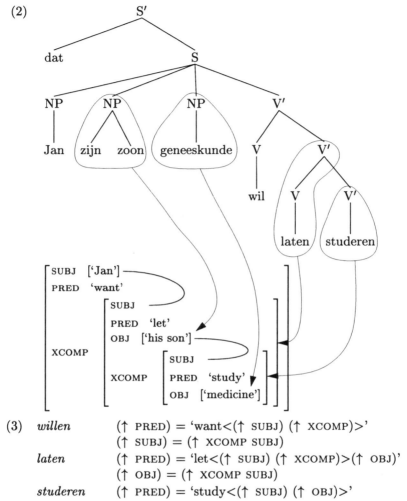

(3) *willen*   ($\uparrow$ PRED) = 'want<($\uparrow$ SUBJ) ($\uparrow$ XCOMP)>'
            ($\uparrow$ SUBJ) = ($\uparrow$ XCOMP SUBJ)

   laten   ($\uparrow$ PRED) = 'let<($\uparrow$ SUBJ) ($\uparrow$ XCOMP)>($\uparrow$ OBJ)'
            ($\uparrow$ OBJ) = ($\uparrow$ XCOMP SUBJ)

   studeren ($\uparrow$ PRED) = 'study<($\uparrow$ SUBJ) ($\uparrow$ OBJ)>'

Of course, if we allowed crossing branches in the c-structure, we could express the dependencies in the c-structure itself, but the c-structures in LFG are assumed to be of the traditional noncrossing type. Given that they are supposed to have a rather direct relation to the phonological representation, it seems reasonable to keep this constraint.

Our problem then is to find a grammar that expresses the correspondences illustrated in (2).

2.2 An early LFG approach

LFG has no movement rules, but discontinuous government dependencies present no problem because of the way the mapping from c-structure to f-structure is defined. As some of the notions we want to use later crucially depend on particular characteristics of this mapping, we summarize here its relevant properties. LFG assumes there is a correspondence function ϕ from c-structure nodes to f-structure units, but this correspondence is not assumed to be one-to-one nor is it required to be onto (Kaplan and Bresnan 1982; Kaplan 1987). Both of these properties are illustrated by the following example of an English gerund construction:

(4)

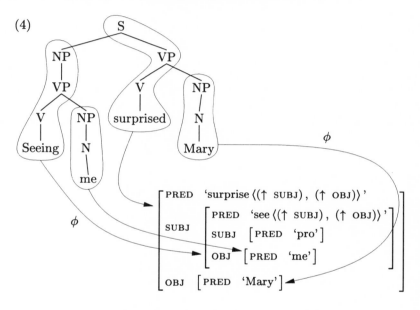

The functional annotations on the English phrase-structure rules would make all the nodes in a circled collection map to the same f-structure unit, demonstrating the many-to-one property of ϕ. There is no node in the c-structure that maps to the pronoun subject of the predicate *see*, so that ϕ is not onto. In English, nodes that map onto the same f-structure tend to stand in simple mother-daughter relations, but this is not the only possible configuration for many-to-one mappings. Bresnan et al. (1982) account for the Dutch discontinuous constituents by mapping two noncontiguous c-structure components into one f-structure. This is specified by the following two simple rules:

(5) a. VP $\longrightarrow$ $\begin{pmatrix} \text{NP} \\ (\uparrow \text{OBJ})=\downarrow \end{pmatrix}$ $\begin{pmatrix} \text{VP} \\ (\uparrow \text{XCOMP})=\downarrow \end{pmatrix}$ (V′)

b. V′ $\longrightarrow$ V $\begin{pmatrix} \text{V}' \\ (\uparrow \text{XCOMP})=\downarrow \end{pmatrix}$

and the (simplified) verbal lexical entries given in (3). These rules make use of the standard LFG convention that unannotated categories are assumed to carry the $\uparrow=\downarrow$ head-marking schema.

The annotation on the VP preceding the V′ in (5a) and the annotation on the V′ expanding the V′ in (5b) are the same, and hence they both provide information about the shared corresponding f-structure. The main constraint on dependencies of this kind in Dutch is that all the arguments of a higher verb precede those of a lower verb; the arguments of each verb are ordered as in simple clauses. The c-structure rules in (5) insure this ordering because the VP expands to an (optional) NP object followed by an open complement VP (XCOMP). The phrase structure rules thus impose the right ordering: less embedded OBJs always precede more embedded ones. The different parts of the more and more embedded XCOMPs link up in the right way because the XCOMPs are associated with successive expansions on both the VP and V′ spines of the tree, as illustrated in (6):

(6)

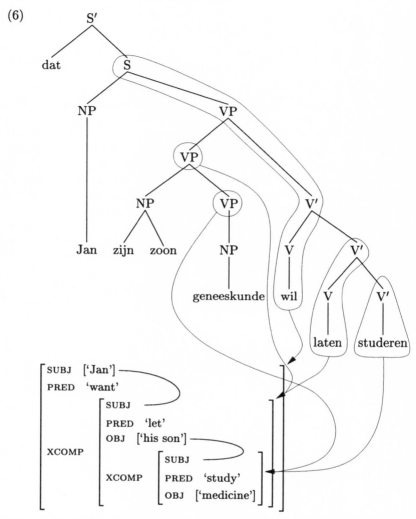

In this approach the context free part of the phrase structure rules encodes the surface linear order and the assumed surface hierarchical order but not the government relations. These are encoded in the functional annotations added to this context free skeleton.

2.3 Inadequacies of this solution

This system gives a correct description of the data considered in Bresnan et al. (1982) and can be extended in a straightforward way to cover further infinitival constructions as shown in Johnson (1986, 1988). However, three drawbacks of this approach have been pointed out, one theoretical, one technical, and one linguistic.

We will not discuss the theoretical problem in great detail. Schuurman (1987) points out that, according to X-bar theory, the VP node should dominate a verb. But, even if one thinks that X-bar principles have some value, it is not clear how they should be adapted to a nontransformational functionally oriented framework like LFG. X-bar theory was mainly developed to allow for the notion head in a representation in which this notion was not native (Lyons 1968). In transformation-based theories the head relation is expressed in deep or underlying tree structures by means of the X-bar schemata (of course, in the surface structure these schemata are only respected by virtue of abstract linking devices such as traces). The head notion itself is functional in nature, however, and LFG provides more explicit and flexible ways of expressing functional relations. For example, LFG identifies the head of a constituent by means of the ↑=↓ annotation, and it marks the non-head dependents with annotations of the form (↑ GF)=↓, where GF stands for any governable grammatical function. Still, it may be worthwhile to establish some invariant connections between functions and the phrase structures they correspond to, and Bresnan (1982) offers one proposal along these lines. As a more natural alternative to X-bar theory for characterizing the relation between lexical heads and phrasal categories, we suggest the principle in (7a). This characterizes configurations of the sort illustrated in (7b) in addition to the usual endocentric arrangement in (7c).

(7) a. A maximal (non lexical) category is of type XP if it corresponds to an f-structure that also corresponds to a lexical category of type X.

  b.

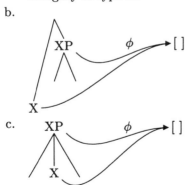

  c.

In formal terms, a maximal node n is of category XP if the set of nodes

$\phi^{-1}(\phi(n))$ contains a node of category X. This principle for determining category labels justifies the VP label in (6) even though the VP does not dominate the V.

The technical problem was pointed out in Johnson (1986) and in Netter (1988). They observed that the obvious extensions to the Bresnan et al. solution needed to account for a new class of data lead to phrase structure trees that violate the LFG constraint against nonbranching dominance chains (Kaplan and Bresnan 1982). According to this condition on valid c-structures, derivations of the form A →* A, which permit an indefinite number of A nodes dominating another node of the same category, are prohibited. This restriction against nonbranching dominance chains disallows c-structure nodes that provide no information and insures that the parsing problem for LFG grammars is decidable. An example adapted from Johnson (1986) that violates this constraint is given in (8):

(8) ... dat Jan een liedje heeft willen zingen.
    ... that John a song has wanted to sing.

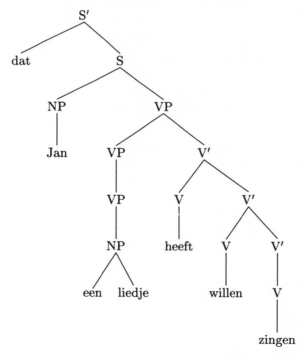

Een liedje is the direct object of the most embedded verb *zingen* and the intermediate VPs are needed to provide the right number of XCOMP levels. In the absence of further difficulties with this approach, we might be tempted to reconsider the value of this formal restriction. But relaxing this condition would not be enough to protect the Bresnan et al. solution from empirical inadequacies.

The linguistic problem is that this analysis does not account for sentences like (9), which are considered perfectly grammatical by most speakers (M. Moortgat, p.c.):

(9) ...dat Jan een liedje schreef en trachtte te verkopen.
     ...that John a song wrote and tried to sell.

Here *een liedje* 'a song' is the OBJ of *schreef* 'wrote' and of *verkopen* 'sell', but these verbs are at different levels of embedding. To be interpreted as the argument of *schreef*, *een liedje* has to be the object, but to be interpreted as an argument of *verkopen*, it has to be the object of the XCOMP. According to the LFG theory of coordination, a coordinate structure is represented formally as a set in f-structure, with the elements of the set being the f-structures corresponding to the individual conjuncts. LFG's function-application primitive is extended in a natural way to apply to sets of f-structures: a set is treated as if it were a function with the properties that are common to all its f-structure elements (see Kaplan and Maxwell 1988b for formal details). As Bresnan, Kaplan, and Peterson (1985) show, this simple extension is sufficient to provide elegant accounts for the wide variety of facts that coordinate reduction rules and across-the-board conventions attempt to handle. Given the rules in (5) and this theory of coordination, *een liedje* will not be properly distributed across the two conjuncts in (9), since it has to have a different function in each. The problem is illustrated by the disjunctive function assignments in diagram (10):

(10)

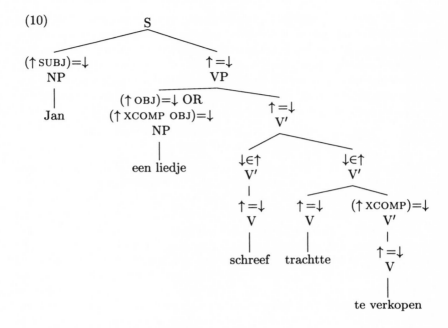

3   A Functional Approach

We now propose a revision that takes care of these problems and then examine some of its other consequences. Some of the elements of this new account can also be found in Johnson (1986) and, for a different set of data, in Netter (1988).

To solve the nonbranching dominance problem, Johnson (1986) proposes to replace the phrase-structure rule (5a) by the one given in (11) (see also Netter 1988):

$$(11) \quad \text{VP} \longrightarrow \begin{pmatrix} \text{NP} \\ (\uparrow\text{OBJ})=\downarrow \end{pmatrix} \begin{pmatrix} \text{VP} \\ (\uparrow\text{XCOMP}^+)=\downarrow \end{pmatrix} (\text{V}')$$

The only difference is in the schema attached to the optional VP. This schema now uses the device of functional uncertainty that was introduced in Kaplan and Zaenen (1989) and developed further in Kaplan and Maxwell (1988a). The f-structure associated with this VP is not asserted to be the XCOMP of the V′ at the corresponding level of c-structure embedding. Rather, it is asserted only that it is the value at the end of a chain of one or more XCOMPs, as denoted by the regular expression XCOMP⁺. This possibility obviates the need for VP expansions in which a VP exhaustively dominates another VP. Predicates and arguments will still be linked up properly because of the completeness and coherence conditions that are independently imposed on f-structure. The right word order is also maintained because the material contained in the VP following an OBJ NP is always at least one level further embedded than the OBJ itself: the annotation is XCOMP⁺, not XCOMP*. The revised rule associates the correct f-structure for sentence (8) with the more compact tree in (8'):

(8')

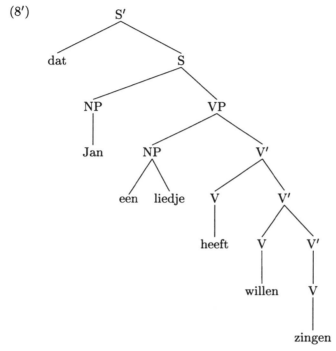

Notice, however, that the rule in (11) does not account for example (9). If the NP is generated as the OBJ of the highest VP under S, then its only function is OBJ, and it cannot be distributed into the second conjunct as an XCOMP OBJ. On the other hand, if it is generated under an embedded VP so that it has the proper function for the second conjunct, it cannot be a simple OBJ for the first conjunct. If we change the annotation on the VP from XCOMP⁺ to XCOMP*, so that the NP is properly distributed to both conjuncts, then we lose all possibility of imposing the cross-serial ordering constraints by phrase-structure encoding. There are more complicated functional annotations for these rules that will give the desired result in Dutch, but in what follows we explore a different type of solution. This solution exploits functional uncertainty together with functional precedence to assign simpler phrase-structure trees. It accounts for all the data that we have discussed above, including example (9), and has the additional advantage of generalizing in a straightforward way to account for word-order facts in other languages, as is shown in Section 4.

Functional uncertainty was originally developed to characterize wh-movement constructions and to insure their proper interaction with co-ordination. A second formal device that was introduced into LFG theory after Bresnan et al. (1982) was published is functional precedence. This was applied to anaphoric dependencies by Bresnan (1984) and formally defined in Kaplan (1987). Precedence is a defining relation among the constituents in a c-structure, in the sense that trees with different node-orderings are interpreted as formally different trees. There is no native precedence relation among the parts of an f-structure, but the image of c-structure precedence under the ϕ mapping from c-structure to f-structure naturally induces a relation on f-structure, which we have called f-precedence:

(12) For two f-structure elements f_1 and f_2, f_1 *f-precedes* f_2 if and only if all the nodes that map onto f_1 c-precede all the nodes that map onto f_2:

$$f_1 <_f f_2 \text{ iff for all } n_1 \in \phi^{-1}(f_1) \text{ and for all } n_2 \in \phi^{-1}(f_2), n_1 <_c n_2$$

Even though this relation is defined in terms of conventional c-structure precedence, it has some surprising properties because, as we noted, the mapping from c-structure to f-structure may be neither one-to-one nor onto. For example, if the mapping is many-to-one and f_1 and f_2 correspond to interleaved sets of c-structure nodes, then neither f_1 f-precedes f_2 nor f_2 f-precedes f_1. If the mapping is not onto so that f_1 corresponds to no node at all, then vacuously both f_1 f-precedes f_2 and f_2 f-precedes f_1 for all f_2. This characteristic is exploited in the analysis of null anaphors by Bresnan (1984) and Kameyama (1989) (summarized in Kaplan and Zaenen 1989). Because of this characteristic, f-precedence is neither transitive nor anti-symmetric and hence is technically not a true ordering relation. Its name is meant to indicate only that it is a functional image of c-precedence, not that it is a precedence relation on f-structure. F-precedence also differs from c-precedence in its linguistic implications: while c-precedence restrictions can only directly order sister constituents, f-precedence constraints can implicitly restrict ordering relations among non-sister nodes by virtue of the common f-structure units they correspond to.

We use the f-precedence relation to provide alternatives to the rules in (5) and (11). We dispense with the VP-dominated subtree altogether and assume a simple succession of NP nodes each of which assigns an OBJ at some indefinite level of XCOMP embedding. Then we add the requirement that the predicate's XCOMP$^+$ OBJ does not precede its immediate OBJ. The revised rules are given in (13):

(13) VP $\longrightarrow$ $\qquad$ NP* $\qquad$ V'
$$(\uparrow \text{XCOMP}^*\text{OBJ})=\downarrow$$

$$V' \longrightarrow V \left(\begin{array}{c} V' \\ (\uparrow \text{XCOMP})=\downarrow \\ (\uparrow \text{XCOMP}^+ \text{OBJ}) \not<_f (\uparrow \text{OBJ}) \end{array}\right)$$

The f-precedence condition is stated negatively because the existential interpretation of a positive relation over uncertainty (namely, that there be *some* string in the uncertainty language for which the relation holds) does not provide the desired effect that the relation must hold for *all* strings chosen from the uncertainty language. The negative statement implicitly transforms the existential into a universal. Moreover, we also assume a non-constructive interpretation of functional uncertainty in which the uncertainty strings range only over paths that are independently instantiated in the f-structure. Under these conventions, the rules above can be easily generalized, for example, by replacing OBJ by a disjunction of OBJ and OBJ2. In this way, the f-precedence constraint on order allows us to propose maximally simple c-structure expansions for Dutch infinitival constructions while still accounting for the ordering dependencies and functional assignments.

A similar flat structure was rejected in Bresnan et al. (1982) for two reasons, one based on word order constraints and the other on the low acceptability of certain coordination constructions. It was thought that the VP node was necessary to account for the fact that the oblique PP arguments of an XCOMP cannot precede an OBJ on a higher level of embedding whereas in a simple clause a PP can precede its OBJ. This argument depends on the assumption that the word order condition can only be stated in c-precedence terms, an assumption which we now reject in favor of the f-precedence relation. The observed pattern of acceptability easily follows when we extend the flat c-structure rules in (13) to include PPs as well.

The unacceptable coordination is exemplified in (14) (example (20) from Bresnan et al.):

(14)??...dat Jan de meisjes een treintje aan Piet en de jongens een pop
  ...that John the girls a toy train to Pete and the boys a doll

  aan Henk zag geven voor Marie.
  to Hank saw give for Marie

... 'that John saw the boys give a toy train to Pete and the girls give a doll to Hank for Marie.'

This is not considered ungrammatical by all speakers,[1] but even if it were completely out, it would justify the proposed hierarchical c-structure only on the assumption that nothing but a single constituent can be right-node raised in Dutch. This assumption is clearly incorrect since sentences like the following are completely acceptable:

(15) ... dat Annie witte en Marie bruine suiker op haar boterham wil
    ... that Annie white and Marie brown sugar on her bread wants.
    ... 'that Annie wants brown sugar on her bread and Marie white sugar.'

(16) ... dat drugmisbruik veel bij tennis- en bij voetbalspelers onder
    ... that drug abuse often in tennis- and in soccer-players under

de dertig voorkomt.
thirty occurs.

... that drug abuse occurs often in tennis players and in soccer players under thirty.

Here the material shared across the conjuncts is not a constituent. While this observation does not explain the contrast noted in Bresnan et al. (1982), it does undermine their second argument in favor of the hierarchical structure of the NP sequence.

We conclude, then, that the use of functional uncertainty and f-precedence allows a treatment of the Dutch infinitival constructions that avoids the technical and linguistic problems of the Bresnan et al. account. In particular, the NP functional uncertainty in the VP rule (13) interacts with LFG's formal account of constituent coordination (Kaplan and Maxwell 1988b) to provide the appropriate analysis of the Dutch coordination in example (9): the uncertainty on *een liedje* is realized as OBJ in one conjunct and as XCOMP OBJ in the other. It would be surprising, however, if the Dutch facts alone would require f-precedence and functional uncertainty as desirable ingredients in an account of the syntactic

---

[1]Some speakers (W. de Geest, p.c.) consider this sentence to be grammatical as well as the one in (i) which we assume to be a case of right node raising:

(i) ... dat Jan de meisjes een treintje aan Piet en de jongens een pop aan Henk
    ... that John the girls a toy train to Pete and the boys a doll to Hank

zag geven.
saw give.

... 'that John saw the boys give a toy train to Pete and the girls give a doll to Hank.

Other speakers seem to consider both versions to be ungrammatical (Schuurman 1987).

properties of infinitival constructions. In what follows we examine some facts of Zurich German that are also naturally handled in these functional terms.

4 Extending the solution to Swiss German

The infinitival constructions of Zurich German are similar to the Dutch ones discussed above in that the verbs generally come in the same order (the least embedded ones precede the more embedded ones). Sentences that are grammatical in Dutch will also be acceptable in Zurich German as the sentence in (17) illustrates:

(17)   ...das er sini chind mediziin wil la schtudiere.
       (transcription as given in Cooper 1988)
       ...'that he wants to let his children study medicine.'

The language allows a broader range of possibilities, however. The verbs have to cluster together in Standard Dutch, whereas NPs and PPs can be interleaved with the verbs in Zurich German, as illustrated in (18):

(18)   a.   ...das er wil sini chind la mediziin schtudiere.
       b.   ...das er sini chind wil la mediziin schtudiere.
       c.   ...das er mediziin sini chind wil la schtudiere.
       d.   ...das er sini chind wil mediziin la schtudiere.

But not all orders are allowed:

(19)   *...das er wil la sini chind mediziin schtudiere.

The main constraint on the word order in infinitival constructions in Zurich German seems to be:

(20)   All the nominal arguments of a particular verb precede it.

There is some disagreement about whether this is the only syntactic constraint on order. Haegeman and van Riemsdijk (1986) add the requirement that the arguments of a higher verb have to precede those of a lower one. Lötscher (1978) does not imply such a constraint, and Cooper (1988) explicitly rejects it. We will follow Cooper here, although Kaplan and Zaenen (1988) modeled the account given by Haegeman and van Riemsdijk. It seems to us that the disagreement might be less about the data per se than about what counts as marked and unmarked word order, but a further study of the conditions influencing the different orders would be necessary to establish this.

The constraint in (20) also holds in Standard Dutch, as we saw in Section 2, but for Zurich German it cannot be formulated in the same way as was done in Bresnan et al. (1982) for Dutch. This is because in Zurich German the NPs and the Vs whose relative order has to be maintained do not have to be adjacent.

The use of functional uncertainty in conjunction with f-precedence allows us to account for these data again without violating the nonbranching dominance constraint. The appropriate rules are given in (21). The VP rule uses an immediate dominance notation to express the free categorial ordering; this adds nothing to the formal power of LFG (Kaplan 1989). The symbol NGF ranges over the grammatical functions SUBJ, OBJ, ... that are usually associated with nominals.

(21)   VP $\longrightarrow$ [NP*   ,   V'*   ]
                 ($\uparrow$ XCOMP*NGF)=$\downarrow$ ($\uparrow$ XCOMP)=$\downarrow$

     V' $\longrightarrow$ V
                 $\downarrow \not\prec_f (\uparrow$ NGF)

In this section we have deployed LFG's descriptive devices to account for dependencies and order without relying on nested tree structure configurations to provide the necessary f-structure embeddings.[2] We have illustrated this by developing a flat structure for the NP dependents in infinitival constructions. A moment's reflection will show, however, that

---

[2]We could flatten the structure further. If we include the ordering statements in the lexical entries of the verbs themselves, we can dispense with the V'. Instead of (21), we then get:

(i)   VP $\longrightarrow$ [NP*   ,   V*   ]
              ($\uparrow$ XCOMP*NGF)=$\downarrow$ ($\uparrow$ XCOMP)=$\downarrow$

Relevant lexical entries would be the following:

(ii)   *wil*   V   ($\uparrow$ PRED)=$\downarrow$
                 $\downarrow$ = 'want<($\uparrow$ SUBJ)($\uparrow$ XCOMP)>'
                 ($\uparrow$ SUBJ) = ($\uparrow$XCOMP SUBJ)
                 $\downarrow \not\prec_f (\uparrow$ NGF)
                 ($\uparrow$ XCOMP) $\not\prec_f \downarrow$

(iii)   *schtudiere*   V   ($\uparrow$ PRED)=$\downarrow$
                 $\downarrow$ = 'study<($\uparrow$ SUBJ)($\uparrow$ OBJ)>'
                 $\downarrow \not\prec_f (\uparrow$ NGF)

(iv)   *laa*   V   ($\uparrow$ PRED)=$\downarrow$
                 $\downarrow$ = 'let<($\uparrow$ SUBJ)($\uparrow$ XCOMP)>($\uparrow$ OBJ)'
                 ($\uparrow$ OBJ) = ($\uparrow$ XCOMP SUBJ)
                 $\downarrow \not\prec_f (\uparrow$ NGF)
                 ($\uparrow$ XCOMP) $\not\prec_f \downarrow$

The annotations in these entries associate the semantic form predicate of each verb explicitly with its lexical node, so that it can take a position in the f-precedence relation distinct from that of the larger f-structure that it heads. The schema $\downarrow \not\prec_f (\uparrow$ NGF) specifies that the nominal arguments of every verb must not follow it. For the predicates *laa* and *wil*, the additional schema ($\uparrow$ XCOMP) $\not\prec_f \downarrow$ indicates that the open complement must come after the verb. The tree representations that these entries and rules allow us to generate are completely flat, as exemplified in (v):

we could also use these formal devices to obtain the same f-structures from c-structures that exhibit more hierarchy, e.g. binary right branching trees. We see then that the availability of richer formal devices to capture linguistic dependencies leaves the c-structure underdetermined. In the conclusion we discuss briefly the general problem of motivating c-structure in LFG.

5 Other infinitival patterns in Dutch

5.1 Extraposition.

It is well known that the verb-raising patterns discussed above are not the only patterns for verbs taking infinitival complements in West Germanic. Another pattern is so-called extraposition, in which the whole infinitival clause follows the matrix verb. This is illustrated for Dutch in (22):

(22) omdat [Jan Marie verbood [Piet toe te laten [het boek te lezen]]]
      because John Marie prohibited Pete to allow the book to read.
      'because John prohibited Marie to allow Pete to read the book.'
      (relevant internal clause boundaries are indicated by [ ])

Following Schuurman (1991) we hypothesize that extraposed and non-extraposed infinitival complements differ in that extraposed complements are COMPs and non-extraposed ones are XCOMPs. Evidence for the distinction comes from the fact that impersonal passives are possible only with extraposed complements. This is illustrated in the contrasts in (23) and (24). The (a) sentences illustrate that *trachten* 'try' can take both verb-raising and extraposition; the (b) sentences show that the imper-

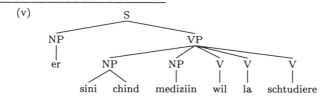

Having proposed a completely flat structure for Zurich German, we could propose a comparable account for Dutch. There are two differences between Dutch and Zurich German: (1) the nominal arguments of higher predicates must precede those of lower ones, and (2) all the NP constituents must precede all the verbs. A lexical entry like *laten* (corresponding to the Zurich German *laa*) will have the additional ordering constraint given in (vi) and the phrase structure grammar will include the c-structure linear-precedence constraint in (vii):

(vi) $(\uparrow \text{XCOMP}^+ \text{NGF}) \not<_f (\uparrow \text{NGF})$

(vii) $\text{NP} <_c \text{V}$

In section 5, we discuss some facts that argue against this flattening of the verbal complex.

232 / Annie Zaenen and Ronald M. Kaplan

sonal passive is possible with the extraposed variant but not with the verb-raising variant.

(23) a. omdat Jan heeft getracht Marie te helpen.
      because John has tried Marie to help.
   b. omdat er (door iedereen) werd getracht Marie te helpen.
      because there (by everybody) was tried Marie to help.

(24) a. omdat Jan Marie heeft trachten te helpen.
      because John Marie has tried to help.
      'because John has tried to help Marie.'
   b. *omdat er (door iedereen) Marie werd trachten te helpen.
      because there (by everybody) Marie has tried to help.

In LFG the subject of an XCOMP is identified with a function of the higher clause by an equation of functional control. According to Bresnan (1982), such an equation can only specify the subject or object of the higher predicate. The rule of impersonal passive formation, however, would produce a control equation that does not satisfy this condition because it identifies the XCOMP SUBJ with an oblique agent function. This accounts for the ungrammaticality of (24b). In the extraposed version the COMP function does not require a functional control equation. Thus, the impersonal passive is permitted, and the appropriate referential dependency is then established by an identity of semantic structure. In functional control all the syntactic features of the controller and the controllee are identical. In a relation of semantic identity, only the referential properties of the two are identified; the syntactic features are allowed to diverge.[3]

There is another distinction between the extraposition and verb-raising constructions, as pointed out in den Besten et al. (1988): in verb-raising constructions the complement of the auxiliary is in the infinitive (24a) while for extraposition it is a participle (23a). This can be regulated with a simple feature that we will not spell out here.

We allow for the possibility of extraposed complements by replacing the Dutch VP rule in (13) with the one in (25):

$$(25) \quad \text{VP} \longrightarrow \quad \begin{matrix} \text{NP}^* \\ (\uparrow \text{XCOMP}^*\text{NGF}) = \downarrow \end{matrix} \quad \text{V}' \quad \left(\begin{matrix} \text{VP} \\ (\uparrow \text{XCOMP}^*\text{COMP}) = \downarrow \end{matrix} \right)$$

The position of the COMP is unambiguously fixed by the phrase structure rules, so it will always show up in sentence-final position.

_____

[3]In Icelandic and German (Netter, p.c.) adjuncts that agree with the understood subject show up in the nominative, providing further evidence against a functional control solution (see Andrews, 1982, for discussion).

5.2 The 'derde constructie'

In some dialects of Dutch, there are sentences that look like a mix of the two constructions discussed above. This is studied in detail in den Besten et al. (1988) under the name *de derde constructie*, the third construction. An example is given in (26):

(26) omdat Jan Marie getracht heeft te helpen.
because John Marie tried has to help.
'because John has tried to help Marie.'

As we noted above, verb-raising and extraposition are distinguished by the fact that the complement of the auxiliary is in the infinitive with verb-raising and in the participle form with extraposition. Here, however, we see a sentence that looks like a verb-raising structure but has the complement of the auxiliary in the participle form. Under our account, it is simple to model this dialect: the only difference with the standard language is that now the COMP can also be introduced by functional uncertainty. The annotated phrase structure rule is given in (27):

$$(27) \quad \text{VP} \longrightarrow \qquad \text{NP}^* \qquad\qquad \text{V}' \qquad \left(\begin{array}{c} \text{VP} \\ (\uparrow \text{COMP})=\downarrow \end{array} \right)$$
$$(\uparrow \left\{ \begin{array}{c} \text{XCOMP} \\ \text{COMP} \end{array} \right\}^* \text{NGF})=\downarrow$$

We presume that the NP ordering constraints will be similar to those for XCOMP elements. In the absence of any data on this, we leave it as an open question here.

6 Ordering constraints with topicalizations: Relativized f-precedence

In the preceding section we have shown that our account gracefully models some of the differences in the West Germanic infinitival constructions, but there are some interactions that we have ignored. A rather crucial one is the interaction between topicalization and word order in what is traditionally called the middle field (the part of the sentence between the subject and the verb in final position, thus excluding topicalized or extraposed elements).

6.1 Basic facts

In (28) we illustrate the basic topicalization patterns found in Dutch.

(28) a. Het boek heeft Jan zeker gelezen.
The book has John certainly read.
'The book John has certainly read.'

    b. Gelezen heeft Jan het boek zeker.
        Read has John the book certainly.
        'John has certainly read the book.'

    c. Het boek gelezen heeft Jan zeker.
        The book read has John certainly.
        'Read the book, John certainly has.'

    d. Jan het boek gegeven heeft Piet zeker.
        John the book given has Pete certainly.
        'Pete has certainly given the book to John.'

    e. Het boek heeft Piet Jan zeker gegeven.
        The book has Pete John certainly given.
        'Pete has certainly given the book to John.'

  f.%Het boek gegeven heeft Piet Jan zeker.
        The book given has Pete John certainly.
        'Pete has certainly given the book to John.'

    g. Het boek heeft Jan de kinderen laten lezen.
        The book has John the children let read.
        'John let the children read this book'.

NP dependents can be topicalized regardless of their level of embedding in an XCOMP. This is illustrated in (a), (c), (e) and (g). Complete XCOMPs can also be topicalized when embedded under auxiliaries or modals, as illustrated in (d). Participles (or infinitives) can also be topicalized as shown in (b). The topicalization of partial XCOMPs is not acceptable in the dialect of the native speaker co-author of this paper, but its equivalent is acceptable in German. We have the impression that speakers vary in their acceptance of several of these patterns and are here describing a rather lax dialect.

6.2 Interactions

The word order constraints that we have discussed above apply properly to arguments and complements when they appear in the middle field, but when we take ordering in topicalized position into account, those constraints are no longer adequate. This is illustrated in (28g), where *het boek* 'the book' precedes *de kinderen* 'the children' although it is a dependent of a lower XCOMP. This topicalized word-order would be generated by the phrase-structure rule (29a),[4] but it would violate the f-precedence condition stated in the rules in (13), generalized here as (29b):

(29) a. $S' \longrightarrow XP \quad S$, where

$$XP = \{ \quad \underset{(\uparrow \left\{ \begin{matrix} XCOMP \\ COMP \end{matrix} \right\}^{*} NGF)=\downarrow}{NP} \quad | \quad \underset{(\uparrow XCOMP^{+})=\downarrow}{VP} \quad | \dots \}$$

b. $VP \longrightarrow \underset{(\uparrow XCOMP^{*}NGF)=\downarrow}{NP^{*}} \quad V'$

$$V' \longrightarrow V \quad \begin{pmatrix} V' \\ (\uparrow XCOMP)=\downarrow \\ (\uparrow XCOMP^{+} NGF) \not\prec_{f} (\uparrow NGF) \end{pmatrix}$$

Intuitively, it seems that the restrictions on word-order that apply to dependents in their middle-field positions do not operate when those elements appear in topic position. However, the word order constraints imposed by the f-precedence condition in (29b) apply globally across the whole sentence; they are not limited to operate just within the middle field. Given our phrase structure rules, we must be able to restrict our ordering conditions to operate just within the VP domain. In essence, the f-precedence predicate used in (29b), which is not sensitive to domains of constituent structure, must be replaced by a more specific one that takes certain dominance relations into account. This new predicate, f-precedence relative to a category X, defines a relation on f-structure el-

---

[4]According to this phrase structure rule COMPs cannot be topicalized in Dutch. In Dutch there are apparent exceptions:

(i) ??Dit boek te lezen zal ik niet vergeten.
This book read will I not forget.

Naar school gaan verzuimt ze nooit.
To school go failed she never.

?* Naar school gaan tracht ze nooit.
To school go tries she never.

As in English they only seem to occur with verbs that also take NP objects (cf. examples in (ii)), so an account along the lines of the one given in Kaplan and Zaenen (1989) should be possible.

(ii) Haar plicht verzuimt ze nooit.
Her duty failed she never.

* De taak tracht ze nooit.
The task tries she never.

Whether this would generalize to German is not clear. Reis (p.c.) gives German *sich verweigern* as a verb that does not take an NP but allows topicalization. We have not investigated the situation in enough detail to propose an account of the COMP topicalization facts.

ements according to the c-structure order of only some of the nodes they correspond to. In particular, the c-structure order of two nodes is taken into account only when the lowest node of type X that dominates one is also the lowest node of type X that dominates the other. Formally, we say that two nodes that appear in such a configuration are *X codominated*; the nodes n_1 and n_2 in trees in (30a) and (30b) are VP codominated whereas those nodes in (30c) are not:

(30) a.

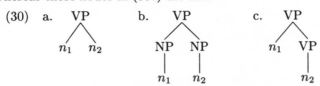

The condition of X codomination enters into a relativized version of f-precedence according to the following definition:

(31)   For two f-structure elements f_1 and f_2 and a category X,
f_1 *f-precedes* f_2 *relative to* X iff for all n_1 in $\phi^{-1}(f_1)$ and for all n_2 in $\phi^{-1}(f_2)$, n_1 and n_2 are X co-dominated and $n_1 <_c n_2$.

We write $f_1 <_f^X f_2$ to indicate that f_1 f-precedes f_2 relative to X, and use this predicate in the modified version of the V' rule:

(32) $V' \longrightarrow V \begin{pmatrix} V' \\ (\uparrow \text{XCOMP})=\downarrow \\ (\uparrow \text{XCOMP}^+ \text{ NGF}) \not<_f^{VP} (\uparrow \text{NGF}) \end{pmatrix}$

This rule imposes ordering constraints only on the nodes that are codominated by VP (in this case the VP under S), and thus ignores topicalized constituents that are outside of this ordering domain. Note that when a VP itself is topicalized as allowed by (29a), the relativized f-precedence condition must also hold of constituents within that VP.

In section 3 and 4 we proposed a flat structure for the NP dependents of XCOMPs regardless of the level of embedding, but we did not flatten the V' verbal complex. The formal techniques that we have developed could be further exploited to eliminate the intermediate V' constituents. But there are other conditions on what can be topicalized that argue against such a phrase structure simplification. Consider example (33):

(33)   ... dat ze het boek heeft willen kopen.
       ... that she the book has wanted to buy.

It is possible to topicalize either of the infinitival complements, as shown in (34), but it is not possible to topicalize the object of a more embedded verb along with a higher verb, leaving the more embedded verb in its middle-field position. This is shown in (35):[5]

(34)   Het boek willen kopen heeft ze.
      The book wanted to buy has she.

  ? Het boek kopen heeft ze gewild.
     The book buy has she wanted.

(35) *Het boek willen heeft ze kopen.
     The book wanted has she buy.

If we allow for a completely flat VP in which all the verbs are sisters of each other and daughters of the VP, it would be difficult to state this constraint. If we keep the right branching V′ chain as in rule (32), the proper ordering directly emerges. The equation attached to the VP in the topicalization rule (29a) insures that the topicalized material as a whole is part of an XCOMP. The organization of the V′ both in topicalized position and in the middle field guarantees that there are no 'holes' in either verbal complex.

7 Conclusion

In this paper we have treated some of the word order variation in infinitival complements in West Germanic. We have shown that our approach allows us to account for the differences and similarities between Dutch and Zurich German in a straightforward way. Within the confines of this paper it is not possible to discuss the corresponding data for all variants of West Germanic, but we think that our approach extends easily to these other dialects. We have also not dealt with certain other issues in full detail: for instance, the constraints on partial VP topicalization are not exactly known and we have probably modeled them incompletely.

At a more fundamental level, our account raises questions about the status of c-structure and of ordering constraints. LFG is different from other frameworks in that it makes a clear division between a level of representation that directly encodes order, the c-structure, and other levels that do not, e.g. the f-structure. This allows us to isolate ordering constraints as either conditions on the c-structure itself or on the interaction between the c-structure and other levels. The study of the constraints in West Germanic show a rather intricate pattern of interactions: on the one hand, ordering constraints have to be sensitive to f-structure information without relying on a c-structure encoding of the f-structure hierarchy; on the other hand, they are sensitive to some basic hierarchical organization of the c-structure that divides the sentence into domains that have

---

[5]For a discussion of the participle/infinitive alternation see den Besten et al. (1988).

traditionally been recognized (e.g. the middle field and the Vorfeld, corresponding here to the topicalization domain) but that are not recognized as major subdivisions of the sentence in the generative tradition. Further study should give us more insight into what motivates these domains.

References

Andrews, III, Avery. 1982. The Representation of Case in Modern Icelandic. In *The Mental Representation of Grammatical Relations*, ed. Joan Bresnan. 427–503. Cambridge, MA: The MIT Press.

den Besten, Hans, Jean Rutten, Tonjes Veenstra and Jacques Veld. 1988. Verb raising, extrapostie en de derde Constructie. Unpublished MS, University of Amsterdam.

Bresnan, Joan. 1982. Control and Complementation. In *The Mental Representation of Grammatical Relations*, ed. Joan Bresnan. 282–390. Cambridge, MA: The MIT Press.

Bresnan, Joan, Ronald M. Kaplan, Stanley Peters, and Annie Zaenen. 1982. Cross-serial Dependencies in Dutch. *Linguistic Inquiry* 13:613–635.

Bresnan, Joan. 1984. Bound anaphora on functional structures. Presented at the annual meeting of the Berkeley Linguistic Society, Berkeley, California.

Bresnan, Joan, Ronald M. Kaplan, and Peter Peterson. 1985. Coordination and the Flow of Information through Phrase Structure. Unpublished MS.

Cooper, Katrin. 1988. Word order in bare infinitival complement constructions in Swiss German. Master's thesis, University of Edinburgh.

Evers, A. 1975. *The transformational cycle in Dutch*. Doctoral dissertation, University of Utrecht.

Haegeman, Liliane, and Henk van Riemsdijk. 1986. Verb Projection Raising, Scope, and the Typology of Rules Affecting Verbs. *Linguistic Inquiry* 17(3):417–466.

Johnson, Mark. 1986. The LFG treatment of discontinuity and the double infinitive construction in Dutch. In *Proceedings of the Fifth West Coast Conference on Formal Linguistics*, ed. Mary Dalrymple, Jeffrey Goldberg, Kristin Hanson, Michael Inman, Chris Piñon, and Stephen Wechsler, 102–118. Stanford University. Stanford Linguistics Association.

Johnson, Mark. 1988. *Attribute-Value Logic and the Theory of Grammar*. CSLI Lecture Notes, No. 16. Stanford University: CSLI/The University of Chicago Press.

Kaplan, Ronald M., and Joan Bresnan. 1982. Lexical-Functional Grammar: A Formal System for Grammatical Representation. In *The Mental Representation of Grammatical Relations*, ed. Joan Bresnan. 173–281. Cambridge, MA: The MIT Press. Reprinted in Part I of this volume.

Kaplan, Ronald M. 1987. Three Seductions of Computational Psycholinguistics. In *Linguistic Theory and Computer Applications*, ed. Peter Whitelock, Harold Somers, Paul Bennett, Rod Johnson, and Mary McGee Wood. 149–188. London: Academic Press. Reprinted in Part V of this volume.

Kaplan, Ronald M., and John T. Maxwell. 1988a. An Algorithm for Functional Uncertainty. In *Proceedings of COLING-88*, 297–302. Budapest. Reprinted in Part II of this volume.

Kaplan, Ronald M., and John T. Maxwell. 1988b. Constituent Coordination in Lexical-Functional Grammar. In *Proceedings of COLING-88*, 303–305. Budapest. Reprinted in Part II of this volume.

Kaplan, Ronald and Annie Zaenen. 1988. Functional Uncertainty and Functional Precedence in Continental West Germanic. In H. Trost (ed.)*4*. *Österreichische Artifical-Intelligence-Tagung, Proceedings*. Berlin. Springer-Verlag, 114-23.

Kaplan, Ronald M. 1989. The Formal Architecture of Lexical-Functional Grammar. In *Proceedings of ROCLING II*, ed. Chu-Ren Huang and Keh-Jiann Chen, 1–18. Also published in *Journal of Information Science and Engineering 5*, 305-322. Reprinted in Part I of this volume.

Kaplan, Ronald M., and Annie Zaenen. 1989. Long-distance Dependencies, Constituent Structure, and Functional Uncertainty. In *Alternative Conceptions of Phrase Structure*, ed. Mark Baltin and Anthony Kroch. Chicago University Press. Reprinted in Part II of this volume.

Kameyama, Megumi. 1989. Functional Precedence Conditions on Overt and Zero Pronominals. Unpublished MS, MCC, Austin, Texas.

Lötscher, Andreas. 1978. Zur Verbstellung im Zürichdeutschen und in andren Varianten des Deutschen. *Zeitschrift fuer Dialektologie und Linguistik* 45:1–29.

Lyons, John. 1968. *Introduction to theoretical linguistics*. London: Cambridge University Press.

Netter, Klaus. 1988. Non-local dependencies and infinitival constructions in German. In *Natural language parsing and linguistic theories*, ed. Uwe Reyle and Christian Rohrer. Dordrecht: D. Reidel.

Schuurman, Ineke. 1987. A lexical-functional treatment of cross-serial dependencies. Paper presented at The XIVth International Congress of Linguists.

Schuurman, Ineke. 1991. Functional uncertainty and verb-raising dependencies. In *Trends in Germanic Syntax*, ed. W. Kosmeijer W. Abraham and E. Reuland. 223–249. Berlin: Mouton de Gruyter.

8

Linear Order, Syntactic Rank, and Empty Categories: On Weak Crossover

JOAN BRESNAN

Weak crossover has long been used as a diagnostic for syntactic phrase structure configurations (e.g. Reinhart 1983a,b, Farmer, Hale and Tsujimura 1986, Saito and Hoji 1983, Hoji 1985, Speas 1990, Mahajan 1990, among many others). Languages that have English-like weak crossover effects, such as Japanese according to Hoji (1985), are assumed to have an underlying configurational structure resembling that of English. Languages that do not have English-like weak crossover effects, such as Hungarian according to Kiss (1987) and Hindi according to Mahajan (1990), have been claimed either to have a nonconfigurational structure lacking a VP altogether or to have scrambling out of VP into A-positions, a mechanism which preserves configurational structure but effectively destroys the unique configuration for subject-object asymmetries provided by the VP. The common assumption of such proposals is that the principles governing weak crossover reduce to c-command relations on syntactic phrase structure configurations.

It is my purpose to challenge this common assumption by showing that it is neither necessary nor sufficient to explain weak crossover effects. It is not necessary because all of the evidence for subject-object asymmetries

This paper is a revision of "Linear Order vs. Syntactic Rank: Evidence from Weak Crossover", *CLS 30-I: Papers from the Thirtieth Regional Meeting of the Chicago Linguistic Society*, ed. Katie Beals, Jeannette Denton, Bob Knippen, Lynette Melnar, Hisami Suzuki and Erika Zeinfeld (Chicago, 1994). Portions are reprinted with permission of the Chicago Linguistics Society. The work originates in ideas first presented in Bresnan (1984).

Formal Issues in Lexical-Functional Grammar
edited by
Mary Dalrymple
Ronald M. Kaplan
John T. Maxwell III
Annie Zaenen
Copyright © 1995, Stanford University

in weak crossover can be explained in terms of the **syntactic rank** of pronoun and operator without any reference to c-command configurations. It is not sufficient because there is an orthogonal condition on the **linear order** of lexically represented constituents that constrains weak crossover independently of syntactic rank.

I will begin by explaining the theoretical assumptions behind my use of the concepts of syntactic rank and linear order. Then I will turn to evidence that supports the need for linear order and shows the existence of two types of null elements in both "pro-drop" and "movement" phenomena: those which are represented in c-structure and those which are represented only in f-structure.

1 Theoretical Assumptions

1.1 Correspondences between Parallel Structures

Lexical-functional grammar (LFG) factors the syntactic representation of a sentence into parallel structures, including the c-structure and the f-structure, as illustrated in (1).[1] Each grammar defines a mapping μ[2] from c-structure nodes to f-structures, illustrated by the connecting arrows in (1) (Kaplan and Bresnan 1982, Kaplan 1987):

---

[1] Formally related architectures include Kac (1978), Sadock (1991), Jackendoff (1994), and Andrews and Manning (1993), which connects some of these ideas to HPSG (Pollard and Sag 1994).

On the inclusion of a level of argument structure distinct from c- and f-structure, see Bresnan (1994a) and the references cited there.

[2] In Kaplan (1987) and elsewhere in this volume, the correspondence mapping between c-structure and f-structure is designated by ϕ instead of μ.

(1) Mapping μ between c- and f-structure:

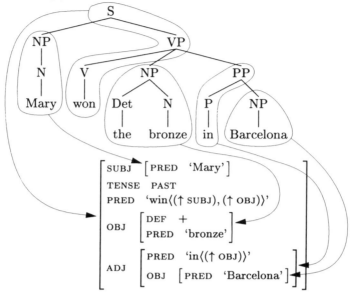

μ is mathematically a function, mapping each c-structure node onto a unique f-structure. Among its functional properties are first, that it is *many-to-one*, allowing different c-structure nodes to be mapped into the same f-structure. An example is the initial focused constituent and the gap node in (2). (In (1) and (2) nodes functionally connected by the "head of" relation are also mapped into the same f-structures, although this is not so in some recent work (Andrews and Manning 1993, Alsina 1993).)

(2)   Many-to-one:

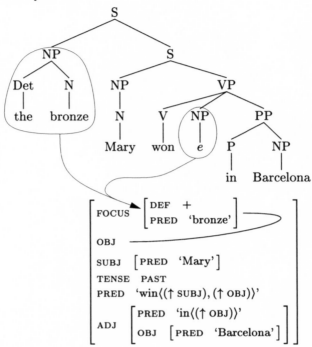

Second, μ is *not onto*: there are f-structures which do not correspond
to any c-structure node. An example is the null pronominal f-structure
circled in (3).

(3) Not onto:

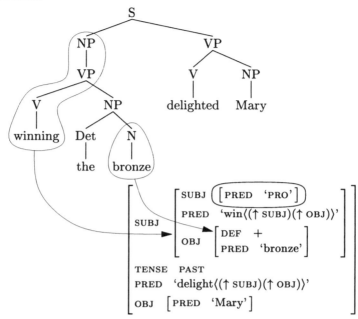

The null subject of the gerund is represented in the f-structure of (3), but not in the c-structure. This null pronominal is a functional property of nonfinite verbs in English. Because the verb is the head of its f-structure clause, it can specify properties of that f-structure, such as the presence of a null pronominal SUBJ (Bresnan 1982) and OBJ (Mohanan 1983, Simpson 1991, Hale 1983, Austin and Bresnan 1994). This manner of representation reflects a basic intuition underlying the design of the theory. F-structure represents the abstract function-argument organization of syntax. C-structure represents the surface order and constituency of forms of expression. According to this view, the proliferation of empty categories in phrase structure is an unnecessary projection of functional information onto the level of expression.

We can impose a condition on c-structure nodes to limit the use of empty categories. According to this condition, every c-structure node must be identified with a lexical element under the correspondence mapping μ:

(4) **Principle of Lexical Expression:**
     The mapping μ from c-structure to f-structure must satisfy this

condition: for every c-structure node N there is a lexical element w such that $\mu(N) = \mu(w)$.

(4) constrains the distribution of null c-structure categories: for every node N in c-structure, either (i) N dominates a lexical element with which it is identified through μ (namely, the head), or else (ii) N has the same image under the mapping μ as another node N' that satisfies condition (i). Suppose we had a null subject NP in c-structure as in (5):

(5)

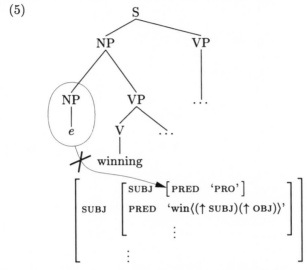

Such a null NP is excluded by (4) because there is no lexical element w such that $\mu(w) = \mu([_{\text{NP}} \ e \ ])$. In contrast, the empty category in (2) representing the gap is allowed because it is mapped by μ onto the same f-structure as the initial focused constituent.

1.2   Syntactic Rank on F-structure

Only at f-structure are all grammatical pronominals, including null pronominals, represented. In this framework, therefore, syntactic conditions on pronominal binding must be defined on f-structures, not c-structures. In place of the c-command relation which is assumed to constrain pronominal binding (Reinhart 1983a,b), there is a ranking of f-structure elements according to the functional hierarchy:[3]

---

[3]This formulation draws on unpublished proposals of K. P. Mohanan dating from 1980–1982 and J. Bresnan dated January 1987. Pollard and Sag's (1992) conception of 'o(bliqueness)-command' is essentially equivalent. All of these conceptions draw on the functional hierarchy of Keenan and Comrie (1977) and others. Reinhart (1983b: 101–6) proposes a similar formulation in terms of the relational hierarchy. Her arguments

(6) **Syntactic Rank:**
For all f-structure elements A, B: A outranks B if A and B belong to the same f-structure and A is more prominent than B on the functional hierarchy (SUBJ > OBJ > OBL > COMPL > ...), or A outranks some C which contains B.

In terms of this ranking relation we can formulate an analogue of the well known 'noncoreference' condition, which applies to null and overt pronominals alike (Langacker 1969):

(7) **Syntactic rank and noncoreference:**
A pronominal P cannot outrank a constituent on which P is referentially dependent.

This condition can be illustrated by the following pattern of facts (Ross 1967):

(8) a. Mary$_i$'s firing her$_i$ friends
      b. *her$_i$ firing Mary$_i$'s friends

In (a) and (b), the subject of the gerund is superior to the possessor of its object. Hence, the latter can be referentially dependent on the former (a), but the former cannot be dependent on the latter (b). In (9a) the overt pronominal object *her* controls the implicit subject of the gerund, and again the subject of the gerund—along with its controller—cannot be referentially dependent on the gerund object's possessor. In (9b) the controller is now *her mother*, so (7) no longer applies.

(9) a. *Visiting Mary$_i$'s friends delighted her$_i$.
      b. Visiting Mary$_i$'s friends delighted her$_i$ mother.

In English the rank of phrases on the functional hierarchy (SUBJ > OBJ > OBL > COMPL > ...) roughly corresponds to their depth of embedding

against such a formulation (pp. 103–6) either do not apply to the relational hierarchy given here (which includes predicate and sentential complements below other argument functions, and excludes adjuncts not included within arguments) or else fail to control for independent differences in stress prominence between subjects and objects (Sells 1987). Thus, the apparent coreference asymmetry in (i) and (ii) disappears when the subject is destressed as in (iii) or the object is given focus stress as in (iv):

(i)   *He$_i$ was fired before John$_i$ could get his pension.
(ii)   They fired him$_i$ before John$_i$ could get his pension.
(iii) It would be WRONG for him$_i$ to be fired before John$_i$ could get his pension.
(iv) *HIM$_i$ they fired before John$_i$ could get his pension.

Subtypes of objects and oblique functions can be distinguished and ranked according to their semantic case or thematic role (the O$_\theta$ and OBL$_\theta$ of Bresnan and Kanerva 1989, Bresnan and Zaenen 1990, and elsewhere). See Dalrymple and Zaenen (1991) and Dalrymple (1993: 168–77) for one formalization. COMPL designates other complements, such as predicate complements and sentential complements (the XCOMPs and COMPs of Bresnan 1982).

in c-structure. Nevertheless, there are differences, which show that f-structure rank offers some advantages over c-command. For example, syntactic rank correctly captures the coreference patterns in examples (10a,b), because the sentential complement is lower on the functional hierarchy than the object NP in (a) and the oblique PP in (b):[4]

(10) a. *I convinced her$_i$ that Mary$_i$ should be my domestic partner.
   b. *I proposed to her$_i$ that Mary$_i$ should be my domestic partner.

In (b) *her* fails to c-command *Mary*, but the noncoreference effect is the same as in (a). The preposition in (b) functions to mark an oblique complement of the verb, and in this case, the extra structural embedding created by the PP over the NP is irrelevant to the noncoreference condition, which looks only at the functional relation.

1.3 Linear Order on C-structure

While syntactic rank determines noncoreference relations in languages like English, linear order is clearly implicated in other languages. Mohanan (1983: 664–5) observes that in Malayalam, a Dravidian language of southern India, pronouns cannot precede their antecedents, but null pronominals are exempt from this restriction. Mohanan attributes this exemption to the absence of null pronominals from c-structure. The linear order condition is illustrated in (11a,b) from Mohanan. Example (11a) contains an overt pronoun which precedes the antecedent, and hence cannot be coreferential with it; in example (11b) the null pronoun replaces the overt pronoun, and coreference is possible.[5]

(11) a. [**awan** aanaye   ṇuḷḷiyaṭinə śeesam] **kuṭṭi**   uraṇṇi
       he.N   elephant.A pinched.it after   child.N slept
       'The child slept, after someone else/*the child pinched the elephant.'

   b. [aanaye   ṇuḷḷiyaṭinə śeesam] **kuṭṭi**   uraṇṇi
      elephant.A pinched.it after   child.N slept
      'The child slept, after the child/someone else pinched the elephant.'

If we reverse the order of the clause containing the pronominals and the antecedent, coreference becomes possible in both cases.[6]

---

[4]The problem posed by such examples is observed by Reinhart (1983b: 179) and Bach and Partee (1980: 13).

[5]The glosses of Mohanan (1981, 1983) are followed here; N and A abbreviate 'nominative' and 'accusative' case, respectively.

[6]These particular examples resemble English participle constructions, which exhibit subject control. However, as Mohanan (1983) shows, null pronominals in Malayalam differ from English controlled 'PRO' constructions in that they can occur in all of

Linear order is a relation on c-structure; hence, elements that are not represented in c-structure cannot enter into linear ordering relations.[7] Although f-structures are unordered, we can take into account some of the c-structure properties of pronominals, such as their linear order, through the correspondence mapping μ. μ induces an inverse image function μ^{-1} from f-structure to c-structure, defined by assigning to each f-structure the set of c-structure nodes mapped onto that f-structure by μ, and assigning the empty set $\emptyset$ to an f-structure element that has no corresponding c-structure node under μ. Referring to (2), one can see that the inverse image of the FOCUS f-structure consists of the two NP nodes dominating *the bronze* and the gap e; in (3), the inverse image of the circled f-structure is the empty set.

Using the inverse mapping μ^{-1}, we can define a relation of *f-precedence* as follows.[8] An f-structure f_1 will f-precede another f-structure f_2 if all of the nodes in f_1's inverse image under μ precede some node in f_2's inverse image. In other words, all of the c-structures nodes that correspond to f_1 must precede at least some of the c-structure nodes that correspond to f_2.

(12) **F-precedence:**
f_1 f-precedes f_2 if and only if $\mu^{-1}(f_1)$ and $\mu^{-1}(f_2)$ are nonempty and all c_1 in $\mu^{-1}(f_1)$ precede some c_2 in $\mu^{-1}(f_2)$.

This formulation takes account of the fact that f-structures may correspond to sets of discontinuous or 'scattered' constituents in c-structure, because of the many-to-one property of μ. From this definition it follows that a scattered constituent cannot f-precede itself. If it did, all of its nodes would precede at least one of its nodes, but that one node could not precede itself. It also follows that a scattered constituent f-precedes another constituent when all of its scattered parts precede the other (13), but a constituent f-precedes a scattered constituent when (all of) it precedes any scattered part (14). $\mathcal{A}_1$ and $\mathcal{A}_2$ represent a scattered constituent $\mathcal{A}$ in (13) and (14).

(13) ... $\mathcal{A}_1$ ... $\mathcal{A}_2$ ... $\mathcal{C}$ ... [$\mathcal{A}$ f-precedes $\mathcal{C}$]

---

the nonoblique functions (subject, object, secondary object) and they can occur with tensed verb forms.

[7]A similar proposal is made in Kameyama (1985), following Bresnan (1984).

[8]The original definition of f-precedence given in Bresnan (1984) is adopted in Kameyama (1985) and Kaplan and Zaenen (1988, 1989). It differs from the present definition (12) in allowing the empty set of c-structure nodes to satisfy the f-precedence relation vacuously, with the result that f-precedence is not an ordering relation on f-structures. The present formulation yields an ordering relation, as sketched below. Previous studies employing the original definition can readily be adapted to incorporate the present definition. See Kaplan and Zaenen (this volume).

(14)   ... $\mathcal{A}_1$ ... $\mathcal{C}$ ... $\mathcal{A}_2$ ...   [$\mathcal{C}$ f-precedes $\mathcal{A}$]

Hence, of two scattered constituents which are interleaved, only one can f-precede the other—the one whose rightmost part precedes the rightmost part of the other, as in (15):

(15)   ... $\mathcal{A}_1 \, \mathcal{B}_1$ ... $\mathcal{A}_2 \, \mathcal{B}_2$ ...   [$\mathcal{A}$ f-precedes $\mathcal{B}$; $\mathcal{B}$ does not f-precede $\mathcal{A}$]

This last observation suggests an alternative definition of f-precedence: that f_1 f-precedes f_2 if and only if the rightmost element of $\mu^{-1}(f_1)$ precedes the rightmost element of $\mu^{-1}(f_2)$. This alternative definition is broader in scope than the definition in (12), as we can see by considering the diagram in (16):

(16)

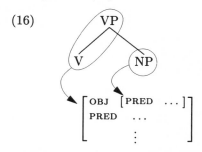

$$\begin{bmatrix} \text{OBJ} & [\text{PRED} \ \dots\,] \\ \text{PRED} & \dots \\ & \vdots \end{bmatrix}$$

According to (12), $\mu(\text{V})$ does not f-precede $\mu(\text{NP})$ in (16), because VP is mapped onto the same f-structure as V, yet VP cannot precede the NP it dominates. If we could pick out V and disregard the dominating node VP in determining the c-structure order relations, then f-precedence would hold. That is the effect of the revised definition of f-precedence given in (17):[9]

(17)   **F-precedence (revised):**
  f_1 f-precedes f_2 if and only if there are c_1 and c_2 such that c_1 is a rightmost element in $\mu^{-1}(f_1)$, c_2 is a rightmost element in $\mu^{-1}(f_2)$, and c_1 precedes c_2.

How does f-precedence compare to c-structure precedence? Both c-structure precedence and f-precedence are ordering relations, but f-precedence is not equivalent to c-structure precedence, because of the mismatches between f-structure and c-structure. For example, it is possible that c_1 precedes c_2 but $\mu(c_1)$ does not f-precede $\mu(c_2)$. Consider (2). In that example *the bronze* precedes *Mary* in c-structure, but $\mu(\textit{the bronze})$

---

[9]The revised definition gives symmetrical results whether the VP in the c-structure of (16) is head-initial or head-final; the earlier formulation (12) allows f-precedence to hold only in the head-final case because of the asymmetry in quantification.

does not f-precede $\mu(Mary)$ in f-structure. The reason is that *the bronze* and its gap are both mapped onto the same f-structure, and the gap fails to precede *Mary*, which would be required for f-precedence to hold (cf. (14) and (15)). However, $\mu(the\ bronze)$ does f-precede the ADJ(unct) *in Barcelona*.

It is also possible that f_1 f-precedes f_2, while c_1 in $\mu^{-1}(f_1)$ does not precede c_2 in $\mu^{-1}(f_2)$. Consider (18):

(18)

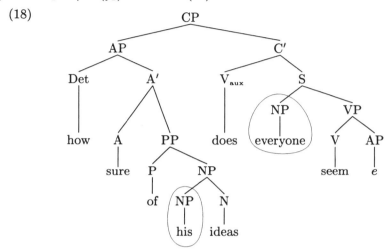

Here $\mu(his)$ f-precedes $\mu(e) = \mu(how\ sure\ of\ his\ ideas)$ because *his* precedes the gap e, but *his* does not precede the AP *how sure of his ideas* because the latter dominates it.

We can now formulate the condition on Malayalam noncoreference given by Mohanan (1983: 664) in terms of the relation of f-precedence:

(19) **Linear order and noncoreference:**
A pronominal P cannot f-precede a constituent on which P is referentially dependent.

Essentially, f-precedence allows f-structure elements to inherit a linear order relation from the c-structure elements they correspond to under the mapping μ. In the case of pronominals, f-precedence will distinguish those which are represented by a lexical element in c-structure from those which are not. Only the former will bear precedence relations to other constituents. Thus the null pronominal in (11) does not f-precede $\mu(kutti)$, the f-structure corresponding to the antecedent 'the child', because the inverse image of the null pronominal under μ is empty and the condition for f-precedence is not met. In other words, a null pronoun in f-structure has no linear ordering relations in c-structure to inherit.

1.4 Weak Crossover

Both syntactic rank and linear order potentially restrict the binding of pronominals by operators, producing so-called 'weak crossover' effects. We can formulate these conditions as in (20) and (21):

(20) **Syntactic rank and operator binding:**
The pronominal binding domain of an operator O is restricted to the set of f-structure elements that O outranks.

(21) **Linear order and operator binding:**
The pronominal binding domain of an operator O excludes all f-structure elements that f-precede O.

Let us take the term 'operator' for the moment to include quantifier phrases such as *everyone, no woman,* and *wh*-interrogative phrases such as *who, which suspect.* What counts as an operator is discussed in more detail subsequently (section 4.1).

Observe that the syntactic rank of the quantifier and pronoun differ in (22b) and (23b).

(22) a. His$_i$ mother visited John$_i$ on the night of the murder.
b. *His$_i$ mother visited everyone$_i$ on the night of the murder.

(23) a. John$_i$ was visited by his$_i$ mother on the night of the murder.
b. Everyone$_i$ was visited by his$_i$ mother on the night of the murder.

In the bad example of operator binding (22b), the quantifier is the object of a verb, while the pronoun is contained in the subject of the same verb; the object does not outrank the subject or the subject's constituents. In the good example of operator binding (23b), the operator is now the subject of the passivized verb, and the pronoun is contained in the prepositional object immediately following the verb; the subject outranks the prepositional object and its constituents.[10] The relative rank of the operator and pronoun correlates with their linear order: in the bad example, the pronoun f-precedes the operator; in the good example, it does not.

The domain conditions (20) and (21) also explain similar contrasts involving a *wh*- phrase operator extracted from the object or subject position, as in (24):

---

[10]The insight that an operator can bind only those pronominals that it outranks is due in essence to Reinhart (1976, 1983a), who originally formulates it in terms of c-command. As we have already observed, c-command correlates fairly closely with syntactic rank in English.

(24) a. ?*Which suspect$_i$ did his$_i$ mother visit ___ on the night of the murder?

b. Which suspect$_i$ ___ was visited by his$_i$ mother on the night of the murder?

In (24a), just as in the preceding ungrammatical case, the operator does not outrank the pronoun that it binds, because *which suspect* is the object of *visit*, while *his* is contained in the subject. Although the fronted *wh*-word actually c-commands the pronoun, only the extraction site of the *wh*- phrase (___) counts for purposes of syntactic rank. This fact follows from our formulation in terms of the functional hierarchy in (6). Most accounts based on c-command stipulate that only 'argument positions' in phrase structure—that is, the clause-internal positions of subjects, objects, and other complements—count for calculations of relative syntactic rank for binding purposes; the nonargument ('$\overline{\text{A}}$') positions of extracted constituents are excluded. In (24b), the operator is the subject and so outranks the pronominal contained in the prepositional object. In both (24a) and (24b) there is again a correlation between syntactic rank and linear order: the pronoun precedes the extraction gap in the (a) example, but not in the (b) example; hence the pronoun f-precedes the *wh*- phrase in the (a) example, but not in the (b) example.

Reinhart (1976, 1983a) argues that a syntactic rank condition is needed independently of linear order in cases such as (25):

(25) *Your eating everyone$_i$'s food annoyed him$_i$.

Here the pronoun is not in the domain of the operator and the variable binding interpretation, "For every person x, your eating x's food annoyed x" is not possible.[11]

In summary, in the predominantly right-branching syntax of English, the syntactic rank of the major clausal phrases corresponds not only to their depth of embedding, but also fairly closely to their linear order in the clause, a phrase on the left outranking a phrase to its right. Thus, the subject of a verb precedes the more deeply embedded object, and the object precedes the more deeply embedded prepositional object. Linear order relations are therefore roughly parallel to relations of syntactic rank. In each of the bad weak crossover cases discussed above, the pronoun in fact f-precedes the operator that binds it, but because the operator is also lower in rank than the pronoun, syntactic rank alone can explain the effect.

---

[11] Note that coreference with a plural pronoun is possible, giving a group interpretation of *everyone* which, following Reinhart, we can assume is not an operator: *Your eating everyone$_i$'s food annoyed them$_i$*. See section 4.1 for analysis of violations of syntactic rank similar to (25) but acceptable.

2 Linear Order vs. Syntactic Rank

A number of researchers have argued for an effect of linear order on weak crossover, including Mohanan (1981), Bresnan (1984), Sells (1984) (cf. Shlonsky 1992), Haider (1989), Georgopoulos (1991a,b), and Williams (1994). In fact, early generative work recognized a leftness effect on pronoun antecedent relations (Langacker 1969) and the binding of pronouns by quantifiers and other operators (Postal 1972, Jacobson 1977, Chomsky 1976). But following the lead of Reinhart (1976, 1983a,b), subsequent work has attempted to reduce all leftness effects to c-command and other order-free conditions on operator binding relations, such as bi-uniqueness (Koopman and Sportiche 1983) or parallelism (Safir 1984). More recently, the proposal that linear order affects the pronominal binding domain of operators in English has been revived from data on double objects by Barss and Lasnik (1986), only to be demolished by Larson's (1988) reanalysis of the verb phrase, which is expressly designed to build up a direct correspondence between the linear order of objects in the VP and their depth of embedding, a correspondence further extended in Pesetsky (1992). The idea that scrambling can consist of movement to an A-position (Mahajan 1990) further reduces many leftness effects on pronominal binding found in scrambling languages to c-command. Such work has led to what is now the consensus view among many theorists that precedence plays no role in binding theory or conditions on operator binding. Indeed, in very recent work by Kayne (1993) it is proposed that precedence relations between constituents are simply a homomorphic projection of their asymmetric c-command relations.

Despite the difficulties of disentangling precedence effects from those of rank in English and typologically similar languages, there is evidence that the linear order of constituents can independently influence binding. In what follows, I will first show that a leftness effect on operator binding of pronominals is present even in English, although it is largely masked by the coincidence of syntactic rank, linear order, and depth of embedding in the overall syntax of the language. Next, I will consider weak crossover in Palauan, a Western Austronesian language spoken in the Western Carolines of the Pacific (Georgopoulos 1991a,b). In this VOS language the linear order of object and subject are opposite to their syntactic rank. Finally, I will consider weak crossover in Malayalam, which allows extensive free order or scrambling (Mohanan 1981, 1983). In the Malayalam data I present, linear order and NOT syntactic rank determines the pronominal binding domain of operators.

2.1 English

There are several sources of evidence for linear order effects on weak crossover in English. First, oblique arguments can often be fairly freely reordered, and in such cases we find a contrast in possible binding, as in (26a,b) and (27a,b):[12]

(26) a. *Who$_i$ did you talk about her$_i$ parents with?

   b. Who$_i$ did you talk with about her$_i$ parents?

(27) a. *Who$_i$ did you talk with her$_i$ parents about?

   b. Who$_i$ did you talk about with her$_i$ parents?

Second, in (28a) pronominal binding by an operator is excluded from the PP into the AP. Yet the noncoreference effect in (28b) shows that the PP complement to *seems* outranks the predicate complement AP. In (28c) the linear order of PP and the predicate complement is reversed, eliminating the weak crossover effect:

(28) a. *Clinton seems proud of her$_i$ to every woman appointee$_i$.

   b. *Clinton seems proud of Mary$_i$ to her$_i$.

   c. Clinton seems to every woman appointee$_i$ to be proud of her$_i$.

Third, some verbs allow reordering of their PP and CP complements. Again, a precedence effect is observable, as in (29):

(29) a. ?*They explained how he$_i$ should dress to every male applicant$_i$.

   b. They explained to every male applicant$_i$ how he$_i$ should dress.

---

[12]Examples like these have been much discussed in the literature. Jackendoff (1990: 432–4) provides a number of examples parallel to (26) in his critique of Larson's (1988) analysis of the VP. In his reply to Jackendoff, Larson (1990: 607–9) proposes that while the first PP c-commands the second PP in examples like (26b), examples like (26a) are derived by "light predicate raising", which creates a structure in which neither PP c-commands the other. However, Larson's proposal wrongly predicts that both of (26a) and (27b) are ungrammatical as weak crossover violations. (Larson's example (31e) is *Which man$_i$ did you talk about to his$_i$ son? Yet this example is quite awkward independently of weak crossover: cf. ??Which man did you talk about to us? Larson's example is grammatical with *with* replacing *to*, as in (27b)). While the two PP complements of *talk* are asymmetrical in some other respects, as Larson notes, these may well be attributable to differing internal functions of the prepositions: the *to, with* preposition may serve to grammatically mark an NP argument of the verb (thus lacking a PRED attribute in f-structure), while the *about* preposition may semantically head the PP (thus having a PRED attribute in f-structure). This difference would interact with reflexive binding, on the theory of Dalrymple (1993). However, it would not affect weak crossover, given the definition of operator complex in section 4.1 below.

Fourth, fronting of an AP complement containing a bound pronominal to a position preceding the operator destroys the binding relation:

(30) a. How sure of his$_i$ ideas does John$_i$ seem?

     b. *How sure of his$_i$ ideas does everyone$_i$ seem?

     (Cf. How sure does everyone seem?)

Observe that the subject in (30a,b) outranks the AP complement and its constituents, including the pronominal *his*, just as in the unmoved versions.[13] This is shown in (31):

(31) a. John$_i$ seems sure of his$_i$ ideas.

     b. Everyone$_i$ seems sure of his$_i$ ideas.

Thus it must be the linear order of the pronoun and quantifier and not their f-structure relations that are affecting the pronominal binding.

These facts of English suggest that there is indeed a leftness effect on operator binding independent of syntactic rank, though it is largely masked by the coincidence of order and syntactic rank in the overall syntax of the language. English has both the linear order and syntactic rank conditions on pronominal binding by operators, given in (20) and (21).

2.2 Palauan

In languages in which left-to-right linear order does not correspond to descending syntactic rank, linear order effects can be seen clearly. In a VOS language, for example, the subject outranks the object, but the object precedes the subject, reversing the linear order we find in English. All things being equal, if rank alone determines the domain of operators, we would expect exactly the same pronominal binding effects that we have in English. If linear order restricts the domain, however, then the binding effects should diverge. Palauan, a Western Austronesian language of Micronesia with VOS order, provides an excellent test case, because its pronominal binding properties have been thoroughly studied by Georgopoulos (1991a,b).

Georgopoulos (1991a: 210–11) observes that weak crossover phenomena in Palauan "exhibited practically the mirror-image of what is predicted of these constructions" under various order-free formulations of the constraints on operator binding. That c-command alone (or syntactic rank in our terms) is not sufficient is shown by examples like (32). Here the quantifier subject outranks the pronominal contained in the object, but the VOS order means that the pronominal f-precedes the quantifier:[14]

---

[13]In fact, because the f-structures of extracted constituents are shared by two functions (the FOC or TOP function of the displaced constituent and the within-clause function of the gap), the f-structures of (31a,b) are actually substructures of those of (30a,b).

[14]The possessive pronominal represented by the possessive inflection on the head noun

(32) *toltoir   er [a rederir] a   **rebek el 'ad**
      R.3p.*love* P   *mother*.3p$_i$.(pro$_i$) [*every* L   *person*]$_i$
      'Everyone$_i$ loves their$_i$ mother.'
      (Georgopoulos 1991a: ex. (57c), p. 211)

That linear order alone is not sufficient for binding is shown by examples like (33). Here the quantifier object f-precedes but does not outrank the pronominal contained in the subject:

(33) *toltoir   er a **rebek el 'ad**   [a rederir]
      R.3p.*love* P   [*every* L   *person*]$_i$ *mother*.3p$_i$.(pro$_i$)
      'Their$_i$ mother loves everyone$_i$.'
      (Georgopoulos 1991a: ex. (56c), p. 211)

Thus, Georgopoulos (1991a: 211) suggests that Palauan requires both c-command and linear precedence of the binder at s-structure. This corresponds exactly to our generalization about weak crossover in English given above. English and Palauan have the same linear order and syntactic rank conditions on operator binding given in (20) and (21).

There is one respect in which Palauan weak crossover effects seem NOT to match those of English. When the subject of the preceding Palauan example is topicalized or questioned, the result has "unblemished grammaticality" (Georgopoulos 1991a: 212):

(34) a **rebek el 'ad**   a oltoir er [a rederir]
      [*every* L   *person*]$_i$ R.*love* P   *mother*.3p$_i$.(pro$_i$)
      'Everyone$_i$ loves their$_i$ mother.'
      (Georgopoulos 1991a: ex. (58c), p. 212)

English operator extractions, in contrast, preserve the binding violations:

(35) a. *His$_i$ mother loves everyone$_i$ in that room.
      b. *Everyone$_i$ in that room, his$_i$ mother loves.

However, there is a straightforward explanation for this difference between the two languages. Georgopoulos (1991a) shows that unlike English, Palauan extractions always involve an *in situ* resumptive pronominal and are not subject to the 'island' or 'subjacency' constraints on extractions found in English. Weak crossover effects disappear when such a pronominal replaces the operator:

(36) Everyone$_i$ in that room is such that his$_i$ mother loves him$_i$.

In general, constructions in which resumptive pronouns are bound by operators lack weak crossover effects; this has been observed for Swedish

---

is glossed as *pro* by Georgopoulos. Georgopoulos' glossing abbreviations used here include L for 'linker', P for 'preposition', R for 'realis mood', and 3p for 'third person'.

and Hebrew (Sells 1984, Shlonsky 1992), Irish (McCloskey 1990), and Tuki (Biloa 1993), for example. In such cases there is no extraction and there is no gap; within the clause the resumptive pronoun occupies the argument position and bears the subject or object function. The clause-internal pronouns are anaphorically bound to the clause-external phrase by a separate mechanism that is not specific to operators (Bresnan and Mchombo 1987).

In sum, our comparison reveals common principles underlying the superficially differing weak crossover constraints on operator-pronominal binding in English and Palauan. In both languages, the domain of variable-binding operators is restricted by linear order AND syntactic rank ((20) and (21)). In the core cases of English, precedence coincides with syntactic rank. In the core cases of Palauan, precedence and syntactic rank are opposed.

2.3 Malayalam

Another language type in which linear order does not necessarily correspond to syntactic rank is a scrambling or so-called free word order language, such as the Dravidian language Malayalam of southern India. We have already seen an illustration of Mohanan's (1983: 664-5) observation that in Malayalam pronouns cannot precede their antecedents. In the following Malayalam examples, the antecedent is an operator, in this case a quantifier phrase (QP), and the same generalization holds.[15] Example (37) shows that a quantifier phrase (QP) subject may bind both null and overt pronominals embedded in a following object:

> (37) innə   **ooṟoo kuṭṭiyum** sahaayiccu
>   *today each   child.*N   *helped*
>   [iṇṇale   (**awaṟe**) ṣakaaṟicca   ṣtriikaḷe]
>   *yesterday (they.*A) *scolded.*REL *woman.*A
>   'Today each child$_i$ helped the women who scolded them$_i$
>   yesterday.'

Example (38) differs only in the ordering of the main constituents of the sentence, the object containing the embedded pronouns now preceding the subject QP antecedent. A difference emerges in the binding possibilities of this example:

---

[15]These data on operator binding of pronominals in Malayalam were obtained by questionnaire from Tara Mohanan and K. P. Mohanan (personal communication, November 16, 1993). The glossing abbreviations are N, A, and REL for 'nominative', 'accusative', and 'relative'. The data given here reflect the judgments of K. P. Mohanan, except where otherwise noted.

(38) [iṇṇale   (*awaṟe) ṣakaaṟicca s̱riikaḻe]
       *yesterday (they.*A)   *scolded.*REL *woman.*A
       iṇṇə ooṟoo kuṭṭiyum sahaayiccu
       *today each   child.*N   *helped*
       'Today each child$_i$ helped the women who scolded them$_i$ yesterday.'

Here the overt pronoun cannot precede its QP binder, and the null pronominal is exempt from this condition. (The overt pronoun is ungrammatical only for the interpretation indicated, in which it is bound by the operator. It may grammatically be used for other reference.)

An even more striking contrast emerges in examples (39) and (40), where the quantifier phrase is an object binding an overt or null pronominal embedded in the subject. The possibility of binding again depends on the relative linear order of pronominal and QP, exactly as in the preceding examples:

(39) ooṟoo kuṭṭiyeeyum iṇṇə   sahaayiccu
       *each   child.*A   *today helped*
       [iṇṇale   (awaṟə) ṣakaaṟicca s̱rii]
       *yesterday (they.*N) *scolded.*REL *woman.*N
       'The woman who they$_i$ scolded yesterday helped each child$_i$ today.'

(40) [iṇṇale   (*awaṟə) ṣakaaṟicca s̱rii]
       *yesterday (they.*N) *scolded.*REL *woman.*N
       iṇṇə ooṟoo kuṭṭiyeeyum sahaayiccu
       *today each   child.*A   *helped*
       'The woman who they$_i$ scolded yesterday helped each child$_i$ today.'

Observe that in these examples, the operator does not outrank the pronominal. Thus operator binding is constrained by linear order and NOT by syntactic rank, as originally observed by Mohanan (1981, 1983).[16] (Again, the overt pronoun is ungrammatical only for the interpretation indicated, in which it is bound by the operator. It may grammatically be used for other reference.)

One might suspect that these examples do not involve true operator binding: in view of the use of the plural forms of the pronoun *awaṟe*

---

[16]Here the judgments of Tara Mohanan differ from those of K. P. Mohanan: she disallows example (39) with a null pronoun and finds example (40) questionable with a null pronoun. These judgments suggest the tentative generalization that in her speech the operator must either outrank or f-precede the pronominal. Tara Mohanan also differs from K. P. Mohanan in being a bilingual speaker of Hindi.

'they' used in these examples, the pattern might simply reflect ordinary coreference of a plural pronoun with a group-denoting phrase (cf. n. 11). A referential NP of this type would be subject to the same noncoreference condition previously observed in (19) for nonoperator NPs, and that would explain the data without any implications for operator binding and weak crossover. However, Mohanan (1981: pp. 50e,f) shows that both interrogative and quantifier phrase operators in Malayalam differ in their binding conditions from simple referential NPs such as proper nouns: unlike simple NPs, the operators must f-command the pronoun they bind.[17] In other words, the minimal clause or predication structure that contains the operator must also contain the pronoun. This difference is illustrated in (41a–c):

> (41) a. [meeři **joonine** umma weccu enno]
>   *Mary.*N *John.*A *kiss placed that*
>   **awan** parañňu.
>   *he.*N *said*
>   Lit.: 'He$_i$ said that Mary kissed John$_i$.'
>
> b. *[meeři **aaře** umma weccu enno]
>   *Mary.*N *who.*A *kiss placed that*
>   **awan** parañňu.
>   *he.*N *said*
>   Lit.: 'Who$_i$ did he$_i$ say that Mary kissed?'
>
> c. *[meeři **ellaawařeyum** umma weccu enno]
>   *Mary.*N *all.*A *kiss placed that*
>   **awar** parañňu.
>   *they.*N *said*
>   Lit.: 'They$_i$ said that Mary kissed everyone$_i$.'

Observe that in (41c) a plural pronoun is used with the quantifier, which is subject to the same f-command condition on operator binding as the other operators. We can therefore conclude that these Malayalam examples involve true operator binding.

How do we know that the left-to-right linear order of constituents in Malayalam does not necessarily correspond to their asymmetric c-command relations? After all, Mahajan's (1990) analysis of Hindi (an Indic language with many areal similarities to Dravidian) builds exactly this correspondence into the theory of scrambling. For Mahajan (1990:

---

[17]Mohanan (1981) refers to this relation as c-command, assuming a VP-less c-structure for Malayalam; f-command (Bresnan 1982) provides an equivalent constraint here, irrespective of the presence of a VP. However, the f-command formulation also encompasses null pronominals not represented in c-structure.

p. 42), "clause internal leftward scrambling is to an A position"—such as the Specifier of a higher functional projection; clause external scrambling is leftward to an A' position. Thus scrambling produces binary right-branching structures in which a phrase c-commands everything to its right and is c-commanded by everything to its left. Now weak crossover for Mahajan requires that "to be construed as a bound variable, a pronoun must be c-commanded by a binder and its variable (if there is one) at s-structure" (p. 23). The innovation of requiring the binder itself and not just its variable to c-command the bound pronoun means in the context of the scrambling theory that a binder must precede any pronoun it binds.

These assumptions can account for Malayalam examples like (37) and (39), where the binder is to the left of the bound pronoun. (Note in (39) in particular the assumption that the clause-initial position of the object is an A-position prevents its trace in the pre-scrambling position from counting as a variable and thereby triggering a weak crossover violation.) But they cannot explain the binding of the null pronouns in the phrases which precede the binder in (38) and (40). Nor would it help to invoke reconstruction (the replacement of moved material back into its pre-movement position in Logical Form) to explain the binding of the null pronominals: in (40) the operator object never c-commands the null pronominal contained in the subject, even after reconstruction. Nor can these assumptions explain noncoreference effects in (11) with nonoperator antecedents.

In contrast, these binding differences between the null and overt pronouns follow from the linear order condition on c-structure (which is Mohanan's original insight formalized here in terms of f-precedence). Moreover, the f-precedence condition can account not only for the Malayalam generalizations but for Mahajan's Hindi data on weak crossover as well. We need only assume for Hindi, following Mohanan (1990), Butt (1993) for Urdu, and Mohanan (1982) for Malayalam, that the clause-internal ordering of nominal constituents is syntactically free, so that alternative orders are base-generated without extraction gaps. Mahajan's data on weak crossover in Hindi then follow from the same linear order condition given for Malayalam: a pronoun cannot f-precede its binder. Hence, linear order can provide a more general account of pronominal binding than c-command for some scrambling or free word order languages.[18]

---

[18]This claim appears to be true as well for Hungarian (Kiss 1987). For German (Haider 1989) and Korean (Lee 1993), linear order overrides syntactic rank under certain circumstances (Choi 1994).

In sum, these generalizations from Malayalam, Palauan, and English show us that quite independently of syntactic rank, linear order can restrict the pronominal binding domain of operators.

3 Probing for Empty Categories

The existence of an irreducible linear order condition on binding has interesting consequences. Linear order can be used as a probe for empty categories: if empty categories exist in phrase structure, then they bear precedence relations for binding, as originally observed by Mohanan (1983) (also Bresnan 1984, Kameyama 1985). It turns out that some kinds of hypothesized empty categories do bear predecence relations, and some do not.

In Malayalam or Hindi, if the clause-internal scrambling of an operator over a pronoun left an extraction gap, the pronoun would f-precede the operator, causing a weak crossover violation as illustrated in (42):

(42) * $[\text{Op}_i]_{\text{OBJ}}$ ... $[$... pron_i ...$]_{\text{SUBJ}}$ ... $[e_i]$ ...

But this kind of violation does not occur in Malayalam according to Mohanan (1981) or Hindi according to Mahajan (1990). A Hindi example is shown in (43):[19]

(43) [kis-ko$_i$ uskii$_i$ bahin   pyaar kartii   thii?]
      who-(DO) his   sister.(SUB) love do.IMP.F be.PST.F
      'Who$_i$ was loved by his$_i$ sister?' Lit.: *'Who$_i$ did his$_i$ sister
      love?'   (Mahajan 1990: p. 26)

We can infer that there is no gap in (43) and the clause internal order is simply syntactically free constituent order.[20] In contrast, extraction of the operator from a clause-internal to a clause-external position in Hindi does produce a weak crossover violation, as illustrated in (44):

(44) *[kis-ko$_i$ uskii$_i$ bahin-ne   socaa   [ki
      who.(DO) his   sister-(SUB) thought that

---

[19]Mahajan's (1990) glosses are used here. They include DO, SUB, EDO and ESUB for 'direct object', 'subject', 'embedded direct object' and 'embedded subject'; IMP, F, and PST stand for 'imperfect', 'feminine', and 'past'.

[20]Free order of this type could be represented either by a flat c-structure in which subject and object are unordered sister constituents, as in Mohanan (1982), T. Mohanan (1990), Simpson (1991), and Butt (1993a,b), or by a hierarchical c-structure in which subject and object can be generated *in situ* in TOPIC and FOCUS positions, as in King (1993). The latter analysis requires no extraction gaps as long as all arguments occur within the local region of c-structure projections that are co-mapped into the same f-structure (approximately corresponding to Grimshaw's (1991) 'extended projection'). The choice among representations must depend upon constituency considerations instead of binding behavior.

raam-ne $[e]_i$ dekhaa thaa]?]
Ram-(ESUB)   *seen*   be.PST
'Who$_i$ was it that his$_i$ sister thought that Ram had seen him$_i$?' Lit.: *'Who$_i$ did his$_i$ sister think that Ram had seen?   (Mahajan 1990: p. 39)

In (44) the pronoun lies in the matrix clause, where it must precede any gap within the following embedded clause. If the pronoun instead occurred in the embedded clause, then by clause-internal free order, it could follow the gap and there should be no weak crossover violation. This prediction is true, as shown in (45):

(45)   [**kis-ko**$_i$ raam-ne   socaa   [ki $[e]_i$
          who.(EDO)   *Ram.*(SUB)   *thought that*
          uskii$_i$ bahin-ne   dekhaa thaa]?]
          his   *sister.*(SUB)   *seen*   be.PST
          'Who$_i$ did Ram think was seen by his$_i$ sister?' Lit.: 'Who$_i$ did Ram think that his$_i$ sister had seen?' (Mahajan 1990: p. 42)

Thus we can infer that clause-internal reorderings in Hindi as in Malayalam are free constituent order (under one of the interpretations in footnote 20), while nonlocal reorderings involve extraction gaps.

We can also see that English interrogative and topicalization extractions also leave gaps, even when local to the clause:

(46)   a.   ?*To whom$_i$ did Mary seem proud of him$_i$ ___?

      b.   ??Who(m) did they explain how he$_i$ should dress to ___?

      c.   ?*Everyone$_i$ in the room, I talked about his$_i$ coursework with

         ___.

The problem in each of the examples can be attributed to the pronominal binding, as control examples in (47) indicate:

(47)   a.   To whom did Mary seem proud of herself ___?

      b.   Who(m) did they explain how we should dress to ___?

      c.   Everyone$_i$ in the room, I talked about coursework with

         ___.

If we assume that the gaps in (46) are represented by empty categories in c-structure, then the failure of binding is explained. In (46a), for example, the pronoun then f-precedes *to whom*, because the gap following the pronoun is mapped by μ onto the same f-structure as the *wh*-phrase.[21] If there were no gap in this example, then the interrogative

---

[21]This example is an instance of (14), with the pronoun as C preceding the gap as A_2.

would f-precede the pronoun and the similarity to (28a) *Clinton seems proud of her$_i$ to every woman appointee$_i$ could not be captured. Syntactic rank cannot explain these examples, because as we observed above, the operator outranks the pronoun in each case.

The further contrast between (46b) and (48) also follows at once, because the controlled null subject of the infinitive in (48), lacking a c-structure category, does not precede the wh- gap, and so fails to f-precede the wh- operator:

(48)   Who(m) did they explain how to dress to ___?

Similarly, as we have seen, the null pronominals of Malayalam have no linear order effects on binding.

We see that extraction gaps crucially determine the precedence relations that restrict operator binding domains, while free ordering and null pronominals do not. These results are consistent with our hypothesis that only the former are represented in c-structure, by the Principle of Lexical Expression (4). Null pronominals are completely unexpressed in c-structure.

At first sight, the precedence effect in the Palauan example cited above (32) seems to show that null pronominals pattern with overt pronouns.[22] Here, however, the noun *rederir* 'mother.3p' is inflected for a third person possessor. When an overt NP possessor is not present, a third person pronominal possessor is implied by the possessive inflection. This inflection is thus analogous to the Chicheŵa verbal subject prefix, which is shown by Bresnan and Mchombo (1986, 1987) to be functionally ambiguous between a marker of grammatical agreement and a morphologically bound pronoun.[23] To speak of "null pro(noun)s" or "pro drop" in such cases is inaccurate because, as noted by Bresnan and Mchombo (1987:

---

[22]Jaeggli and Safir (1989: p. 18) also note that Spanish null pronouns pattern like overt pronouns rather than PRO with respect to weak crossover.

[23]Georgopoulos (1991a: pp. 48-51) argues against the interpretation of the Palauan agreement inflections as bound pronouns, appealing to the noncomplementary distribution of the inflections and lexically filled NPs, whether as simple arguments or conjuncts, and their parallel role in binding phenomena. She then observes (p. 50), "As an alternative to the foregoing arguments for *pro*, we could assume that an NP node is present only when it contains lexical material, even though an argument selected by a head is not always lexical." (This is, in effect, the analysis advocated by Bresnan and Mchombo 1987.) After pointing out that on this alternative, transitivity could not be defined uniformly on the phrase structure representation (it is defined on the f-structure for Bresnan and Mchombo 1987), she concludes: "Such a consequence is not only incompatible with X′ theory, theta theory, and theories of the lexicon, but it requires parallel principles of structure where one (that the argument position is always present [in phrase structure—JWB]) will do. The alternative approach is therefore rejected." This reasoning, of course, begs the question: the arguments in favor of the theoretical architecture she assumes simply reduce to a restatement of the

765), the affix itself is the pronoun: the mapping μ from c-structure to f-structure associates an f-structure pronominal with the affix of the inflected verb or noun, as illustrated schematically in (49).[24]

(49)

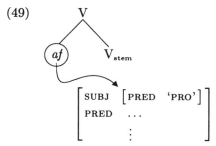

Pronominals expressed by such affixes therefore inherit linear order relations from the affix. Malayalam, in contrast, lacks agreement affixes. Hence, the null pronominals of Malayalam cannot inherit linear order relations from their morphological expression.[25] The same is true of the null controlled pronominal in English.

The evidence from Malayalam thus supports the hypothesis that true null pronominals are exempt from the precedence restriction on binding domains, while extraction gaps are not. These results conflict both with the proposal that there are no empty categories (Kaplan and Zaenen 1988, Zaenen 1989, Pollard and Sag 1994: ch. 9, Sag and Fodor 1994) and with the assumption that all lexical arguments are syntactically represented by phrase structure categories via the Projection Principle (Chomsky 1981). Instead, it appears that empty categories exist for extraction gaps, but not for (true) null pronominals, and the principle which distinguishes the two types is something like the Principle of Lexical Expression (4). In other words, null elements can exhibit precedence effects only if they are represented by some lexical element (such as a displaced *wh-* constituent or an agreement inflection) in c-structure.

4   Other Factors

A number of known factors not specific to the proposal advanced here affect weak crossover.

---

basic assumptions of that theoretical architecture. In fact, no duplication of principles of binding is required if they are defined over f-structures rather than c-structures.

[24]For more on the relation between inflections and f-structure, see Andrews (1990).

[25]The verb in Malayalam optionally specifies the pronominal content of its direct verbal arguments as properties of the f-structure of the entire clause headed by the verb.

4.1 Operator Complexes

The class of variable binding operators subject to the domain conditions discussed here is generally held to include not only QPs headed by *every*, *no*, and the like, but also interrogative phrases *who*, *what*, *which X*, *whose X*, and focused or topicalized constituents.[26] It is necessary to extend this class to a larger set of constituents that I will call *operator complexes*.

A simple characterization of operator complex is that it is a phrase that "Pied Pipes" (Ross 1967) with an operator, as illustrated in the following example:

(50)

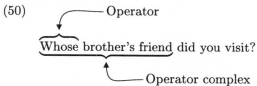

What counts as an operator complex varies across languages and may be somewhat variable across speakers of the same language.[27] Common English operator complexes include phrases whose specifiers are (true) variable-binding quantifiers (e.g. *every woman*, *no man*, *which book*), possessors (e.g. *no man's children*, *whose sister's friend*), and prepositional phrases dominating operator-complex objects (e.g. *to every woman*, etc.). In the case of simple NP (or DP) operators such as *who*, *whom*, *everyone*, *no one*, which are not dominated by Pied Piping material, we can take the phrase itself to be its own operator complex.

The crucial property of operator complexes is this: an operator O which by itself does not outrank a pronoun can bind that pronoun if O belongs to an operator complex that does outrank the pronoun.[28] This phenomenon is illustrated in (51) and (52), where the binder in the (a) examples does not outrank the pronoun it binds, but the complex it is contained in does.

(51) a. Everyone$_i$'s mother loves his$_i$ cute ways.

      b. Everyone's mother$_j$ loves her$_j$ free time.

---

[26]Lasnik and Stowell (1991) argue that only true quantifiers should count as operators in this domain. See Postal (1993) for qualifications.

[27]In Malayalam (Mohanan 1981), in Chinese (Higginbotham 1980), and in Hungarian (Kiss 1987), it appears that an operator complex is limited to the operator phrase itself.

[28]I will not explore the semantic basis for this phenomenon here. It is possible that *every*, *which*, and the other variable-binding operators are 'unselective' quantifiers or polyadic operators over all of the predicates in the operator complex:

(i) every man's mother: $(\forall x, y)((x \text{ a man})(y \text{ the mother of } x) \rightarrow \ldots)$

(52) a. Whose$_i$ mother loves his$_i$ cute ways?

b. Whose mother$_j$ loves her$_j$ free time?

The domain of an operator is thus defined by its operator complex, and its precedence restrictions are defined with respect to that complex as well:

(53) *Whose mother$_j$ is her$_j$ free time loved by?

In (53), her$_j$ does not f-precede *whose*, but it does f-precede the operator complex of *whose*, by virtue of preceding the gap of *whose mother$_j$*.

The conditions on pronominal binding can be generalized to operator complexes as follows:

(54) **Syntactic rank and operator binding (revised):**
The domain of O is restricted to the set of f-structures that O's operator complex outranks.

(55) **Linear order and operator binding (revised):**
The domain of a variable-binding operator O excludes all f-structure elements that f-precede O's operator complex.

Finally, note that if we define a topicalized constituent to be its own operator complex—

(56)

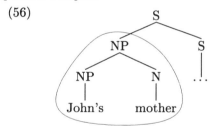

—we can explain contrasts such as the following observed by Wasow (1979) (see also Postal 1993):

(57) a. John$_i$'s mother, his$_i$ friends adore.

b. *Everyone$_i$'s mother, his$_i$ friends adore.

c. *Whose$_i$ mother do his$_i$ friends adore?

4.2 Control and Indirect Binding

There are cases in which a pronoun is interpreted as bound to an operator even though it is not in the domain of the operator as defined in (54) and (55):[29]

(58) a. *His$_i$ losing his$_i$ marbles irked every boy$_i$.

---

[29]Examples like (58b) are observed in Higginbotham (1980: 688).

b. Losing his$_i$ marbles irked every boy$_i$.

c. *Losing his$_i$ marbles irked every boy$_i$'s mother .

In (a), *every boy* does not outrank *his*, and binding is ill formed. The necessary syntactic rank relation is also lacking in (b), but binding is nevertheless possible, though it is ill formed again in (c). What is going on in (b) is anaphoric control (see the discussion of (9) above). Anaphoric control is not subject to c-command or rank, but to distinct functional and semantic factors, including the thematic role structure of the predicate (see Bresnan 1982, Mohanan 1983, Kroeger 1993, and the references cited in these). In (b) the object of the verb anaphorically controls the null subject of the gerund, and that subject binds the pronominal *his*. The operator thus binds the pronoun indirectly, through the control relation. In (c), there is no control relation between the operator and the pronoun, and binding is ill formed.

I believe that a similar phenomenon occurs in (59a), where the *of* phrase in this case is the semantic controller of the nominal subject: no matter how good a soldier you may be, someone else's devotion cannot be expected OF YOU. When this implicit control relation linking the operator to the nominal is absent, as in (59b) and (59c), the expected weak crossover violations appear.[30]

(59) a. Devotion to his$_i$ country is expected of every soldier$_i$.

b. ?*Devotion to his$_i$ country is expected of every soldier$_i$'s family.

c. *How devoted to his$_i$ country is every soldier$_i$?

Finally, (60a) illustrates the so-called 'functional' binding cases discussed by Engdahl (1986) and Chierchia (1991). These are good if we expect an answer such as *his first book*, which gives a general function from authors to books. It seems that in these cases, the pronoun is not directly bound by the operator but by the function which is the denotation of the NP containing it. Again the conditions on interpretation here differ from those on weak crossover considered earlier, as shown by (60b,c).

(60) a. Which of his$_i$ books does every author$_i$ like least?

b. ?*Which of his$_i$ books do every author$_i$'s parents like least?

c. *How proud of his$_i$ books does every author$_i$ seem?

A number of other factors affecting weak crossover have been discussed (see Postal 1993, Reinhart 1983b, and Williams 1994, among others).

---

[30]Examples of this type are due to Higginbotham (1980: 690). A similar analysis to that proposed here is given in Williams (1994).

I will not attempt to give a comprehensive treatment of these factors because they do not distinguish my proposal from others.[31]

5 Conclusion

In conclusion, weak crossover should not be used as a diagnostic for phrase structure configurations, because the syntactic asymmetries it reveals can be explained by syntactic rank independently of c-command relations, and because independently of syntactic rank, it is subject to linear order effects. This conclusion has interesting consequences for theories of extraction, scrambling, and null pronominals, suggesting that not all null pronominals and not all 'movements' of phrase structure categories are represented by empty categories in phrase structure. In particular, the weak crossover evidence shows that there are two kinds of null pronominals—those which (as in Palauan and Spanish) show precedence effects and those which (as in Malayalam and in English control constructions) do not. The first kind has an overt element in morphology that anchors them in c-structure and allows them to bear precedence relations; the second kind does not. Likewise, the evidence shows that there are two kinds of extractions or "movements"—those whose ordering relations for weak crossover can be read off of the overt positions of the "moved" items (as in clause-bound scrambling in Hindi and Malayalam), and those whose ordering relations must take into account the source position of the moved item (as in cross-clausal extractions in Hindi and English wh-movement). The first kind are traceless alternative orderings; the second kind are antecedent-gap extractions, where the gap is represented in c-structure.[32] This analysis captures a generalization across these two classes of "null elements": the ones that affect linear ordering relations are just the ones that are represented in c-structure under the Principle of Lexical Expression (4).

Finally, the fact that syntactic rank—a functional or relational property of syntax—can be independent of linear order—a structural, categorial property, is completely opposed to the reductionist trend of syntactic theory represented in work by Larson (1988), Mahajan (1990), Pesetsky (1992), and Kayne (1993), among others. But it is a rather natural result

---

[31]Both Reinhart (1983b) and Williams (1994) discuss theta role structure as a factor in weak crossover. In the present framework the relative prominence of different role relations is represented in the a-structure and could be formalized as a constraint on that dimension (cf. Bresnan 1994a, Dalrymple 1993, and the references cited in these sources).

[32]I assume that within LFG such antecedent-gap extractions have an empty category in c-structure which anchors an inside-out functional uncertainty equation (cf. Dalrymple 1993).

within an architecture of grammar based on parallel structures, each with its own formal elements and prominence relations, which simultaneously constrain the surface forms of language.

Acknowledgments

I am grateful to Mary Dalrymple, Elisabet Engdahl, Ron Kaplan, K. P. Mohanan, Tara Mohanan, and Tom Wasow for comments and discussion along the way on earlier versions of this work.

References

Alsina, Alex. 1993. A Theory of Complex Predicates: Evidence from Causatives in Bantu and Romance. Paper presented at the Complex Predicates Workshop, CSLI, Stanford University.

Andrews, III, Avery. 1990. Unification and Morphological Blocking. *Natural Language and Linguistic Theory* 8(4):507–557.

Andrews, III, Avery, and Chris Manning. 1993. Information Spreading and Levels of Representation in LFG. Technical Report CSLI-93-176. Stanford University: Center for the Study of Language and Information.

Austin, Peter, and Joan Bresnan. 1994. Non-configurationality in Australian aboriginal languages. Bundoora, Victoria (Australia) and Stanford, CA: LaTrobe University and Stanford University MS. To appear in Natural Language & Linguistic Theory.

Bach, Emmon, and Barbara Partee. 1980. Anaphora and Semantic Structure. In *Papers from the Parasession on Pronouns and Anaphora*, ed. Jody Kreiman and Almerindo E. Ojeda, 1–28. University of Chicago. Chicago Linguistic Society.

Barss, Andrew, and Howard Lasnik. 1986. A Note on Anaphora and Double Objects. *Linguistic Inquiry* 17(2):347–354.

Biloa, Edmond. 1990. Resumptive pronouns in Tuki. *Studies in African Linguistics* 12:211–236.

Bresnan, Joan. 1982. Control and Complementation. *Linguistic Inquiry* 13:343–434. Reprinted in Joan Bresnan, ed., *The Mental Representation of Grammatical Relations*, pages 282–390. Cambridge: The MIT Press.

Bresnan, Joan. 1984. Bound Anaphora on Functional Structures. Presented at the Tenth Annual Meeting of the Berkeley Linguistics Society, February 17, 1984.

Bresnan, Joan, and Sam A. Mchombo. 1986. Grammatical and Anaphoric Agreement. In *Papers from the Parasession on Pragmatics and Grammatical Theory at the Twenty-Second Regional Meeting of the Chicago Linguistic Society*, ed. Anne M. Farley, Peter T. Farley, and Karl-Erik McCullough, 278–297. University of Chicago. Chicago Linguistic Society.

Bresnan, Joan. 1994a. Locative Inversion and the Architecture of Universal Grammar. *Language* 70(1):72–131.

Bresnan, Joan. 1994b. Linear Order vs. Syntactic Rank: Evidence from Weak Crossover. In *CLS 30-I: Papers from the Thirtieth Regional Meeting of the Chicago Linguistic Society*, ed. Katie Beals, Jeannette Denton, Bob Knippen, Lynette Melnar, Hisami Suzuki and Erika Zeinfeld.

Bresnan, Joan, and Sam A. Mchombo. 1987. Topic, pronoun, and agreement in Chicheŵa. *Language* 63(4):741–782.

Bresnan, Joan, and Jonni M. Kanerva. 1989. Locative Inversion in Chicheŵa: A Case Study of Factorization in Grammar. *Linguistic Inquiry* 20(1):1–50. Also in E. Wehrli and T. Stowell, eds., Syntax and Semantics 26: Syntax and the Lexicon. New York: Academic Press.

Bresnan, Joan, and Annie Zaenen. 1990. Deep Unaccusativity in LFG. In *Grammatical Relations. A Cross-Theoretical Perspective*, ed. Katarzyna Dziwirek, Patrick Farrell, and Errapel Mejías-Bikandi. 45–57. Stanford University: Center for the Study of Language and Information.

Butt, Miriam. 1993a. Complex Predicates in Urdu. Paper presented at the Complex Predicates Workshop, CSLI, Stanford University.

Butt, Miriam. 1993b. *The Structure of Complex Predicates in Urdu*. Doctoral dissertation, Stanford University.

Chierchia, Gennaro. 1991. Functional WH and weak crossover. In *Proceedings of the Tenth West Coast Conference on Formal Linguistics*, ed. Dawn Bates, 75–90. Stanford University. Stanford Linguistics Association.

Choi, Hye-Won. 1994. Weak crossover in scrambling languages and optimality. MS, Stanford University, Stanford, California.

Chomsky, Noam. 1976. Conditions on Rules of Grammar. *Linguistic Analysis* 2:303–351.

Chomsky, Noam. 1981. *Lectures on Government and Binding*. Dordrecht: Foris Publications.

Dalrymple, Mary. 1993. *The Syntax of Anaphoric Binding*. CSLI Lecture Notes, No. 36. Stanford University: Center for the Study of Language and Information.

Dalrymple, Mary and Annie Zaenen. 1991. Modeling Anaphoric Superiority. *Proceedings of the International Conference on Current Issues in Computational Linguistics*, Penang, Malaysia, pp. 235–247.

Engdahl, Elisabet. 1986. *Constituent Questions*. Dordrecht: Kluwer Academic Publishers.

Farmer, Ann, Ken Hale, and Natsuko Tsujimura. 1986. A Note on Weak Crossover in Japanese. *Natural Language and Linguistic Theory* 4(1):33–42.

Georgopoulos, Carol. 1991a. *Syntactic variables: Resumptive pronouns and A′ binding in Palauan*. Dordrecht: Kluwer Academic Publishers.

Georgopoulos, Carol. 1991b. Canonical government and the specifier parameter: An ECP account of weak crossover. *Natural Language and Linguistic Theory* 9(1):1–46.

Grimshaw, Jane. 1991. Extended Projection. MS, Rutgers University.

Haider, Hubert. 1989. θ-Tracking Systems – Evidence from German. In *The Typology of Asymmetries*, ed. Lászlo Marácz and Pieter Muysken. 185–206. Dordrecht: Foris Publications.

Hale, Ken. 1983. Warlpiri and the grammar of non-configurational languages. *Natural Language and Linguistic Theory* 1:5–47.

Higginbotham, James. 1980. Pronouns and bound variables. *Linguistic Inquiry* 11:679–708.

Hoji, Hajime. 1985. *Logical Form Constraints and Configurational Structures in Japanese*. Doctoral dissertation, University of Washington.

Jackendoff, Ray S. 1990. On Larson's treatment of the double object construction. *Linguistic Inquiry* 21(3):427–456.

Jackendoff, Ray S. 1994. Lexical Insertion in a Post-Minimalist Theory of Grammar. MS, Brandeis University.

Jaeggli, Osvaldo, and Kenneth J. Safir. 1989. The Null Subject Parameter and Parametric Theory. In *The Null Subject Parameter*, ed. Osvaldo Jaeggli and Kenneth J. Safir. 1–44. Dordrecht: Kluwer Academic Publishers.

Jacobson, Pauline. 1977. The Syntax of Crossing Coreference Sentences. Doctoral dissertation, University of California, Berkeley.

Kac, Michael B. 1978. *Corepresentation of Grammatical Structure*. Minneapolis: University of Minnesota Press.

Kameyama, Megumi. 1985. *Zero Anaphora: The Case of Japanese*. Doctoral dissertation, Stanford University.

Kaplan, Ronald M., and Joan Bresnan. 1982. Lexical-Functional Grammar: A Formal System for Grammatical Representation. In *The Mental Representation of Grammatical Relations*, ed. Joan Bresnan. 173–281. Cambridge, MA: The MIT Press. Reprinted in Part I of this volume.

Kaplan, Ronald M. 1987. Three Seductions of Computational Psycholinguistics. In *Linguistic Theory and Computer Applications*, ed. Peter Whitelock, Harold Somers, Paul Bennett, Rod Johnson, and Mary McGee Wood. 149–188. London: Academic Press. Reprinted in Part V of this volume.

Kaplan, Ronald M., and Annie Zaenen. 1988. Functional Uncertainty and Functional Precedence in Continental West Germanic. In *Österreichische Artificial-Intelligence-Tagung, Proceedings*, ed. Harald Trost, 114–123. Berlin. Springer-Verlag.

Kaplan, Ronald M., and Annie Zaenen. 1989. Functional Precedence and Constituent Structure. In *Proceedings of ROCLING II*, ed. Chu-Ren Huang and Key-Jiann Chen, pp. 19–40. Taipei, Republic of China.

Kayne, Richard S. 1993. The antisymmetry of syntax. MS, Graduate Center, CUNY, New York.

Keenan, Edward L., and Bernard Comrie. 1977. Noun Phrase Accessibility and Universal Grammar. *Linguistic Inquiry* 8(1):63–99.

King, Tracy H. 1993. *Configuring topic and focus in Russian*. Doctoral dissertation, Stanford University.

É. Kiss, Katalin. 1987. *Configurationality in Hungarian*. Dordrecht: D. Reidel.

Koopman, Hilda, and Dominique Sportiche. 1983. Variables and the Bijection Principle. *The Linguistic Review* 2:139–160.

Kroeger, Paul. 1991. *Phrase Structure and Grammatical Relations in Tagalog.* Doctoral dissertation, Stanford University. Reprinted in the *Dissertations in Linguistics* series, CSLI Publications, Stanford, CA.

Langacker, Ronald W. 1969. On Pronominalization and the Chain of Command. In *Modern Studies in English*, ed. David A. Reibel and Sanford A. Schane. 160–186. Englewood Cliffs, NJ: Prentice-Hall.

Larson, Richard. 1988. The Double Object Construction. *Linguistic Inquiry* 19(3):335–391.

Larson, Richard. 1990. Double objects revisited: Reply to Jackendoff. *Linguistic Inquiry* 21(4):589–632.

Lasnik, Howard, and Tim Stowell. 1991. Weakest Crossover. *Linguistic Inquiry* 22(4):687–720.

Lee, Young-Suk. 1993. *Scrambling as case-driven obligatory movement.* Doctoral dissertation, University of Pennsylvania.

Mahajan, Anoop. 1990. *The A/A-bar distinction and movement theory.* Doctoral dissertation, MIT.

McCloskey, James. 1990. Resumptive Pronouns, A′ Binding, and Levels of Representation in Irish. In *Syntax and Semantics 23: The Syntax of the Modern Celtic Languages*, ed. Randall Hendrick. 199–256. New York: Academic Press.

Mohanan, K. P. 1981. On Pronouns and Their Antecedents. MS. dated March 1981. National University of Singapore.

Mohanan, K. P. 1982. Grammatical Relations and Clause Structure in Malayalam. In *The Mental Representation of Grammatical Relations*, ed. Joan W. Bresnan. 504–589. Cambridge, MA: The MIT Press.

Mohanan, K. P. 1983. Functional and Anaphoric Control. *Linguistic Inquiry* 14(4):641–674.

Mohanan, Tara. 1990. *Arguments in Hindi.* Doctoral dissertation, Stanford University. Also published in the Dissertation Series, CSLI Press, 1994.

Pesetsky, David. 1992. *Zero syntax. Volume I; Experiencers and cascades.* MS, MIT, Cambridge, Mass.

Pollard, Carl, and Ivan A. Sag. 1992. Anaphors in English and the Scope of the Binding Theory. *Linguistic Inquiry* 23(2):261–303.

Pollard, Carl, and Ivan A. Sag. 1994. *Head-Driven Phrase Structure Grammar.* Chicago: The University of Chicago Press.

Postal, Paul M. 1972. A Global Constraint on Pronominalization. *Linguistic Inquiry* 3(1):35–59.

Postal, Paul M. 1993. Remarks on Weak Crossover Effects. *Linguistic Inquiry* 24(3):539–556.

Reinhart, Tanya. 1976. *The Syntactic Domain of Anaphora.* Doctoral dissertation, MIT.

Reinhart, Tanya. 1983a. Coreference and bound anaphora: A restatement of the anaphora question. *Linguistics and Philosophy* 6:47–88.

Reinhart, Tanya. 1983b. *Anaphora and Semantic Interpretation.* Chicago: The University of Chicago Press.

Ross, John Robert. 1967. On the Cyclic Nature of English Pronominalization. In *To Honor Roman Jakobson.* 1669–82. The Hague: Mouton. Reprinted in *Modern Studies in English,* ed. David A. Reibel and Sanford A. Schane, 1969. Englewood Cliffs, NJ:Prentice-Hall.

Sadock, Jerrold M. 1991. *Autolexical Syntax: A Theory of Parallel Grammatical Representations.* Chicago: The University of Chicago Press.

Safir, Ken. 1984. Multiple Variable Binding. *Linguistic Inquiry* 15(4):603–638.

Sag, Ivan A. and Janet Dean Fodor. 1994. Extraction without Traces. *WCCFL* 13, to appear.

Saito, Mamoru, and Hajime Hoji. 1983. Weak Crossover and Move Alpha in Japanese. *Natural Language and Linguistic Theory* 1:245–259.

Sells, Peter. 1984. Resumptive Pronouns and Weak Crossover. In *Proceedings of the Third West Coast Conference on Formal Linguistics,* ed. Mark Cobler, Susannah MacKaye, and Michael Wescoat, 252–262. Stanford University. Stanford Linguistics Association.

Sells, Peter. 1987. Backwards Anaphora and Discourse Structure: Some Considerations. Technical Report CSLI-87-114. Stanford University: Center for the Study of Language and Information.

Shlonsky, Ur. 1992. Resumptive Pronouns as a Last Resort. *Linguistic Inquiry* 23(3):443–468.

Simpson, Jane. 1991. *Warlpiri Morpho-Syntax: A Lexicalist Approach.* Dordrecht: Kluwer Academic Publishers.

Speas, Margaret. 1990. *Phrase Structure in Natural Language.* Dordrecht: Kluwer Academic Publishers.

Wasow, Thomas. 1979. *Anaphora in Generative Grammar.* Ghent: E. Story.

Williams, Edwin. 1994. *Thematic Structure in Syntax.* Cambridge, MA: The MIT Press.

Zaenen, Annie. 1989. Nominal Arguments in Dutch and WYSIWYG LFG. MS, Xerox Palo Alto Research Center.

Part IV

Semantics and Translation

One of the principal advantages inherent in the architecture of LFG, noted in its earliest formulations, is the clear suitability of the f-structure as a syntactic basis for semantic analysis. F-structures provide a uniform format for stating the syntactic information that is most important for semantic composition. In fact, some semantic information is actually integrated into the f-structure; Kaplan and Bresnan (1982) observe that values of the attribute PRED, referred to as 'semantic forms', "govern the process of semantic interpretation." However, the earliest work on LFG concentrated primarily on syntactic issues, and issues of semantic representation and interpretation were not addressed in detail.

Halvorsen's 1983 article "Semantics for Lexical-Functional Grammar" presented the first thorough semantic analysis of a wide variety of syntactic constructions within the LFG framework. He pointed out the desirability of a universal system of semantic composition, which the use of the uniform f-structure format makes possible. His approach posited a set of translation principles making reference to certain f-structure configurations, and provided translations for control verbs, quantifiers, adjuncts, and more.

Halvorsen's use of translation rules which make reference to f-structure configurations is an example of *description by analysis*; the second paper in this section, "Projections and Semantic Description in Lexical-Functional Grammar" by Halvorsen and Kaplan, defines this as a "method of generating range descriptions by analyzing and matching the properties of domain structures." A different approach was adopted by Halvorsen and his colleagues in 1987, with the publication of *Situations, Language and Logic* by Fenstad, Halvorsen, Langholm, and van Benthem. This work described a means of simultaneously building up f-structures and semantic representations by means of constraint propagation; this general method is known as *codescription*. The result is an f-structure of the familiar sort together with a *situation schema*, a set of attribute-value pairs which was given a model-theoretic interpretation. The difference between the methods of description by analysis and codescription is discussed at greater length in Kaplan (1989), reprinted in Part I of this volume.

The first paper in this section, Halvorsen and Kaplan's "Projections and Semantic Description in Lexical-Functional Grammar", extends the insights of Fenstad et al. in an important way, by using *projection functions* to provide a piecewise correspondence between f-structures and semantic structures. The projection function between f-structures and semantic structures is analogous to the correspondence between c-structure nodes and f-structures. This crucial insight, also developed in detail by Kaplan (1987), has led to much other work on semantics and translation, including the other two papers in the section.

The second paper in this section, Halvorsen's "Situation Semantics and Semantic Interpretation in Constraint-Based Grammars", concentrates on the issue of compositionality: the use of the projection architecture enables an approach to semantic composition that is systematic without being compositional in the structure of the syntactic tree.

The third paper, Kaplan, Netter, Wedekind, and Zaenen's "Translation by Structural Correspondences", addresses problems arising in the context of machine translation, showing that the projection architecture provides a solution for many problems of translation, including syntactic mismatches between the source and target languages. Subsequent work by Sadler, Crookston, and Way (1989), Sadler, Crookston, Arnold, and Way (1990), and Sadler and Thompson (1991) observed certain difficulties with this approach, and considered whether some of these difficulties could be resolved by changing some of the architectural assumptions of the LFG framework.

An alternative solution was proposed in later LFG research. This alternative works by augmenting the description language of LFG rather than by altering the basic projection architecture. Kaplan and Wedekind (1991), in their paper "Restriction and Structure Misalignment", introduce the *restriction operator*, a descriptive device which allows reference to proper subsets of the full set of attribute-value pairs of an f-structure. These subsets can be assigned a semantic interpretation, and a translation procedure can be recursively defined. Wedekind and Kaplan provide such a definition in their 1993 paper "Type-Driven Semantic Interpretation of F-Structures", and Kaplan and Wedekind discuss the application to problems of translation in their 1993 paper "Restriction and Correspondence-Based Translation".

Other recent work within the LFG framework also relies crucially on the projection architecture to associate f-structures with their meanings.

In their paper "LFG Semantics Via Constraints", Dalrymple, Lamping, and Saraswat (1993) present a deductive approach to assembling meanings, based on reasoning with constraints. The use of *linear logic* as a 'glue' for assembling meanings also allows for a coherent treatment of modification and the requirements of completeness and coherence. An extension of the approach to a treatment of quantifiers and intensionality was presented by Dalrymple, Lamping, Pereira, and Saraswat in their 1995 papers "A Deductive Account of Quantification in LFG" and "Intensional Verbs Without Type-Raising or Lexical Ambiguity".

References

Dalrymple, Mary, John Lamping, Fernando C. N. Pereira, and Vijay Saraswat. 1995a. A Deductive Account of Quantification in LFG. In *Quantifiers, Deduction, and Context*, ed. Makoto Kanazawa, Christopher J. Piñón, and Henriette de Swart. Stanford, California: Center for the Study of Language and Information.

Dalrymple, Mary, John Lamping, Fernando C. N. Pereira, and Vijay Saraswat. 1995b. Intensional Verbs Without Type-Raising or Lexical Ambiguity. In *Information-Oriented Approaches to Logic, Language and Computation*, ed. Dag Westerståhl and Jerry Seligman. Stanford, California: Center for the Study of Language and Information.

Dalrymple, Mary, John Lamping, and Vijay Saraswat. 1993. LFG Semantics Via Constraints. In *Proceedings of the Sixth Meeting of the European ACL*. University of Utrecht, April. European Chapter of the Association for Computational Linguistics.

Fenstad, Jens Erik, Per-Kristian Halvorsen, Tore Langholm, and Johan van Benthem. 1987. *Situations, Language and Logic*. Dordrecht: D. Reidel.

Halvorsen, Per-Kristian. 1983. Semantics for Lexical-Functional Grammar. *Linguistic Inquiry* 14(4):567–615.

Kaplan, Ronald M., and Joan Bresnan. 1982. Lexical-Functional Grammar: A Formal System for Grammatical Representation. In *The Mental Representation of Grammatical Relations*, ed. Joan Bresnan. 173–281. Cambridge, MA: The MIT Press. Reprinted in Part I of this volume.

Kaplan, Ronald M. 1987. Three Seductions of Computational Psycholinguistics. In *Linguistic Theory and Computer Applications*, ed. Peter Whitelock, Mary McGee Wood, Harold L. Somers, Rod Johnson, and Paul Bennett. 149–188. London: Academic Press. Reprinted in Part V of this volume.

Kaplan, Ronald M. 1989. The Formal Architecture of Lexical-Functional Grammar. In *Proceedings of ROCLING II*, ed. Chu-Ren Huang and Keh-Jiann Chen, 1–18. Reprinted in Part I of this volume.

Kaplan, Ronald M., and Jürgen Wedekind. 1991. Restriction and Structure Misalignment. MS, Xerox Palo Alto Research Center.

Kaplan, Ronald M., and Jürgen Wedekind. 1993. Restriction and Correspondence-Based Translation. In *Proceedings of the Sixth Meeting of the European ACL*. University of Utrecht, April. European Chapter of the Association for Computational Linguistics.

Sadler, Louisa, Ian Crookston, Doug Arnold, and Andy Way. 1990. LFG and Translation. In *Third International Conference on Theoretical and Methodological Issues in Machine Translation*, 11–13. Linguistic Research Center, University of Texas–Austin.

Sadler, Louisa, Ian Crookston, and Andy Way. 1989. Co-description, Projection, and "Difficult" Translation. In *Working Papers in Language Processing*. Department of Languages and Linguistics, University of Essex.

Sadler, Louisa, and Henry Thompson. 1991. Structural Non-Correspondence in Translation. In *Proceedings of the Fifth Meeting of the European ACL*, 293–298. Berlin. European Chapter of the Association for Computational Linguistics.

Wedekind, Jürgen, and Ronald M. Kaplan. 1993. Type-driven Semantic Interpretation of F-Structures. In *Proceedings of the Sixth Meeting of the European ACL*. University of Utrecht, April. European Chapter of the Association for Computational Linguistics.

9

Projections and Semantic Description in Lexical-Functional Grammar

PER-KRISTIAN HALVORSEN AND RONALD M. KAPLAN

Abstract. In this paper we show how the rule language of Lexical-Functional Grammar (LFG) can be extended to permit the statement of semantic rules. This extension permits semantic structure and functional structure to be simultaneously characterized without requiring that the f-structures themselves be taken as input to the semantic component. This makes possible a simplification of functional representations as well as novel semantic analyses, such as a treatment of quantifier scope ambiguity based on functional uncertainty that avoids the need for any quantifier-storage mechanism. The proposals are based on a theory of projections that exploits the notion of structural correspondences to capture the informational dependencies between levels of linguistic form and meaning.

1 Introduction

The equality- and description-based organization of LFG (Kaplan and Bresnan 1982) and related unification-based formalisms (DCG (Pereira and Warren 1980), FUG (Kay 1979), PATR (Shieber et al. 1983), and HPSG (Pollard and Sag 1987)) have had easily discernible effects on syntactic theory and the practice of syntactic characterization. But the implications of this organization on architectures for semantic interpretation have not yet been carefully examined. As it turns out, the nature of

This paper originally appeared in *Proceedings of the International Conference on Fifth Generation Computer Systems* (Tokyo: Institute for New Generation Computer Technology, 1988), 1116–1122.

Formal Issues in Lexical-Functional Grammar
edited by
Mary Dalrymple
Ronald M. Kaplan
John T. Maxwell III
Annie Zaenen

semantic rules has to be radically altered in this new description-based paradigm as compared to Montague Grammar (Montague 1970). Indeed, some of the most appealing results of Montague's theory do not carry over, for example, compositionality of interpretation and the completeness of the interpretation process (see Halvorsen 1988). In this paper we show this by way of a case study of semantic interpretation in LFGs based on the notion of *structural correspondences* or *projections* (Kaplan 1987). We first consider what informational dependencies exist between constituent structure (c-structure), functional structure (f-structure), and semantic structure (s-structure). We present a version of the theory of projections where the s-structure is a direct projection of the c-structure and an indirect projection of the f-structure. The specification of these relations is formulated in an extension to the rule language for LFGs that accommodates the notion of multiple projections. In particular, this notation permits the statement of semantic rules on a par with rules for the characterization of functional structures. This theory does not take functional structures to be the sole input to semantic interpretation, and consequently, all semantically relevant information does not have to be funneled through the f-structure. Yet, it allows the dependencies between functional and semantic information to be captured by means of *codescription*—the association of functional and semantic annotations with nodes of the c-structure.

2 Structural Correspondences

A fundamental problem for linguistic theory is to account for the connection between the surface form of an utterance and its meaning. On our view of grammatical theory, this relationship is explicated in terms of *correspondences* between representation structures (Kaplan 1987; Kaplan and Bresnan 1982), rather than *derivation* (i.e. step-wise transformation of structures). We include in the grammar a statement of the informational dependencies between aspects of the linguistic form of the utterance and its meaning, rather than the prescription of an algorithm for step-wise derivation of the meaning of the utterance from its form.

We assume that the various levels of linguistic analysis (syntax, semantics, prosodic structure etc.) are autonomous and obey their own well-formedness conditions. Each level may also employ representations with different mathematical properties (e.g. trees for syntactic structure, finite functions or directed graphs for functional and semantic structures). Even though structures at two different levels may be of different types, we can set them in correspondence using a piecewise function from elements of one into elements of the other.

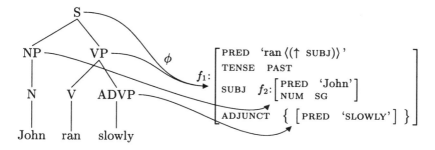

FIGURE 1 C-structure to f-structure correspondence

The original theory of Lexical-Functional Grammar focussed on the correspondence between c-structure trees, exhibiting the hierarchical organization of phrases, and f-structures, representing the grammatical relations holding in the sentence. This correspondence is given by the mapping ϕ, a piecewise function which may be many-to-one (as illustrated in Figure 1 where the S and VP node are both mapped to the same functional structure, f_1). Moreover, ϕ is not required to be onto (there may be elements of the f-structure which are not in the range of ϕ). This possibility has been used, for example, to provide an intuitive account of unexpressed pronouns (so-called null- or zero-anaphors) (see, for example, Kameyama 1989).

Functional structures (e.g. f_1 and f_2 in Figure 1) are finite monadic functions. Thus f_1 is the function which, when applied to the argument SUBJ, yields the function f_2; when applied to the argument TENSE its value is PAST, and so on. In LFG the information about the properties of f-structures that correspond to c-structure nodes is expressed in simple constraints expressing equality, set inclusion, or existence. A Boolean combination of such constraints is referred to as a *functional description*. Thus the simple functional description

(1) $(f_1 \text{ SUBJ}) = f_2$

states that the result of applying the function characterized by the f-structure corresponding to the S node n_1 (i.e. $f_1 = \phi(n_1)$) to the argument SUBJ is the function f_2 corresponding to the NP node, since $f_2 = \phi(n_2)$. Indeed, given the correspondence ϕ illustrated in Figure 1, the information in this equation can be equivalently formulated as:

(2) $(\phi(n_1) \text{ SUBJ}) = \phi(n_2)$

The structural correspondence view separates the statement of informational dependencies between levels of analysis from the process of computing one representation based on information about another. This perspective also opens up the possibility of there being equi-potent informational dependencies between *several* structures, as when viewing the language as consisting of a number of mutually constraining modules. This is the outlook invited by the observation underlying situation semantics (Barwise and Perry 1983) that the interpretation of an utterance depends not only on its syntactic form, but also on the circumstances in which it was uttered, the intonation with which it was uttered, etc.

From the linguistic point of view, the crucial question is which subset of all the conceivable informational dependencies do in fact obtain between the different levels of analysis of an utterance. Formally, a correspondence can be defined between any two levels, but a particular linguistic theory may assign meaning to only some of these possibilities. Thus, the theory of projections specializes the notion of structural correspondence and embodies particular claims about what levels of representation (e.g. c-structure and s-structure) are directly related through functional mappings, which levels are related through composite mappings, and which levels are related only by accident.

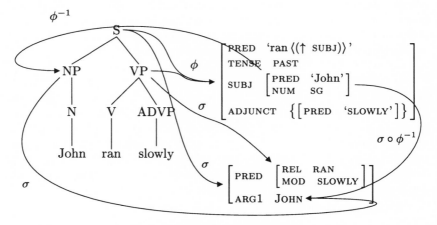

FIGURE 2 Functional and semantic structures

Figure 2 shows a semantic structure in addition to the functional structure associated with the syntactic tree. The s-structure is viewed as a projection of the c-structure tree through the correspondence function σ. With this configuration the s- and f-structures are not directly related to each other, but informational dependencies holding between them can still be expressed, albeit in an indirect fashion. In particular, informational dependencies between f-structures and s-structure can be specified through inversion and composition of the mappings ϕ and σ. Thus, given ϕ and σ both having a domain of c-structure nodes, we can define $\sigma' = \sigma \circ \phi^{-1}$ as a correspondence between functional and semantic structures. As we illustrate below, the fact that functional subjects (e.g. *John*) supply the semantic information associated with the agent-role of active agentive verbs (e.g. *run*) can be expressed in terms of σ'.[1]

Although grammatical relations represented in the f-structure are commonly aligned with semantic argument roles as in this example, this is not always the case. One instance of divergence between f- and s-structures arises in the analysis of adverbs. In order to provide an elegant account of subject-verb agreement as well as other phenomena, ϕ associates the same f-structure to both the S and VP nodes (as in Figure 2). However, there is a clear semantic distinction between adverbial phrases which modify sentences (e.g. *On several occasions*) and adverbials that modify verb-phrases (e.g. *slowly*) (see Thomason and Stalnaker 1973). If s-structures are projected directly from the f-structure, then the usual alignment of functional and semantic relations together with the conflation of information used for subject-verb agreement would obliterate the distinctions needed to characterize these differences. By projecting s-structure from the c-structure, the adverb distinctions can be maintained, while the convergence of f-structural and semantic information can still be captured through the composite projection σ' defined above.

3 Projections and CoDescription

Previous proposals for semantic interpretation of LFGs took functional structures as input to the semantic component. The semantic representations were described based on an analysis of the level of functional structure (what we now call *description by analysis*). The first examples of this approach were provided by Halvorsen (1982) and Halvorsen (1983). There, LFGs were interpreted with four interpretation principles which applied in any order to f-structure configurations that matched the pattern specified in the interpretation principle. The patterns picked out semantically significant aspects of the f-structure. These interpretation principles licensed the introduction of a set of semantic equations. The complete set of semantic equations had been found when all the semantically significant f-structure configurations had been matched by an interpretation principle. The semantic equations could be solved using the same unification algorithms as in the construction of the func-

---

[1]Since the f-structure projection ϕ is many-to-one, its inverse is a more general relation, not a single-valued function. This feature among others moves us outside the standard bounds of unification towards more general constraint-programming (Jaffar and Lassez 1987).

284 / Per-Kristian Halvorsen and Ronald M. Kaplan

tional structure itself. Other examples of semantic interpretation using the description-by-analysis approach are given by Frey and Reyle (1983) and Reyle (1988). They defined a set of *transfer rules* which mapped functional structures into semantic representations by means of a modified lambda-calculus. The mapping from c-structure to f-structure is the prototypical example of description-by-analysis—the functional description is produced by matching the context-free rules against the node-configurations in the c-structure.

Every interpretation scheme based on description-by-analysis requires that all semantically relevant information be encoded in the functional structure. This assumption rules out the possibility of writing semantic interpretation rules triggered by specific c-structure configurations unless otherwise unmotivated "diacritical" features are included in the f-structure. There are two reasons for this: (1) The connection between syntactic rules and interpretation principles is severed by stating the interpretation rules on f-structures; (2) No separate semantic rule language is provided.

Our proposal for semantic interpretation is not based on an analysis of the f-structure. Rather, it depends on *codescription*, on simultaneously associating functional and semantic constraints through a single analysis of the c-structure tree.

The objective of the theory of projections is to focus attention on the relationship between various aspects of linguistic form and the interpretation of utterances. It is useful to compare our proposal to other approaches that use *distinguished attributes* in a single level of representation to combine syntactic and semantic information (e.g. FSTRUC and SITSCHEMA as in Fenstad et al. (1985, 1987), or SYNTAX and SEMANTICS as in Karttunen (1986) and Pollard and Sag (1987)). Although equality over monadic functions and attribute-value unification are expressive enough formally to encode quite complex informational dependencies, they may not provide the best conceptual framework for understanding the connection between relatively independent modules. This requires a framework where modularity and interaction can comfortably coexist. The theory of projections is an attempt at providing such a framework.

Thus the present proposal is not a formal refutation of the approach to the specification of semantic structures in unification grammars using one or more distinguished attributes. The distinguished attributes approach can instead be viewed as an implementation technique for simple projection theories which do not utilize inversion and composition of functional mappings as we propose here.

4 Notational Conventions

The point of departure for our semantic rule notation is the syntactic rule formalism of LFG. As originally formulated by Kaplan and Bresnan (1982), context-free phrase-structure rules are annotated with constraints that are instantiated to form functional descriptions, as illustrated in this simple S rule:[2]

$$S \longrightarrow \quad \underset{(\uparrow \text{ SUBJ}) = \downarrow}{NP} \quad \underset{\uparrow = \downarrow}{VP}$$

In these annotations, $\uparrow$ and $\downarrow$ refer to functional structures corresponding to specific nodes of the phrase-structure tree. For a tree configuration matching the rule, $\uparrow$ denotes the f-structure that directly corresponds to the mother of the node that matches the rule-category it is annotated to, and $\downarrow$ denotes the f-structure corresponding to that rule-category. The annotation on the NP, for example, indicates that the SUBJ of the f-structure corresponding to the NP's mother, namely the S node, is the f-structure corresponding to the NP node. Kaplan (1987) gave a precise explication of this arrow notation in terms of the structural correspondence ϕ, the function $\mathcal{M}$ on c-structure nodes that takes a node into its mother, and a single special symbol $*$ that denotes the node matching the rule-element it is annotated to. With these primitives the symbol $\uparrow$ can be seen as a convenient abbreviation for the specification $\phi \mathcal{M}*$, $\downarrow$ abbreviates $\phi*$, and an equivalent formulation of the SUBJ constraint above is $(\phi \mathcal{M}* \text{ SUBJ}) = \phi*$.

As discussed above, ϕ is a structural correspondence relating two syntactic levels of representation. The function σ is another correspondence, and in the present theory it maps between the set of c-structure nodes and the units of s-structure that characterize the content of an utterance, or, following Barwise and Perry (1983), the *described situation*. Along with the names of other correspondences mentioned by Kaplan (1987), the symbol σ is introduced into the vocabulary of our constraint language so that descriptions of semantic structure can be specified.[3]

If the f-structure and semantic structure are both considered projections of the c-structure, either ϕ or σ can be prefixed to any expression denoting a c-structure node to denote the corresponding f- or s-structure

---

[2]In the following we will refer to these constraints as equations. This should not obscure the fact that LFG permits constraints other than purely equational ones to be expressed.

[3]We emphasize that we could also have chosen another formal configuration in which semantic structures correspond to some other level of representation (e.g. f-structure, as suggested by Halvorsen (1988) and Kaplan (1987)). Which configuration offers the best account of syntax/semantics interactions depends in part on what the linguistic facts are. The adverb facts briefly discussed above seem to favor σ as a mapping from c-structure.

unit. The following are all well-formed expressions of the extended rule language: $\phi\mathcal{M}*$, $\phi*$, $\sigma\mathcal{M}*$, and $\sigma*$. $\mathcal{M}$, ϕ, and σ are all right-associative. Consequently, $(\sigma\mathcal{M} * \text{ARG1})$ denotes the value of the ARG1 attribute in the semantic structure corresponding to the mother of the current node.

The inverse of the c-structure to f-structure projector, ϕ^{-1}, gives us the c-structure node, or set of c-structure nodes, corresponding to a given f-structure. ϕ^{-1} can be prefixed to any expression denoting a unit of f-structure. Thus $\phi^{-1}(\phi\mathcal{M} * \text{SUBJ})$ denotes the set of nodes that map to the SUBJ function in the f-structure corresponding to the mother of the matching node. Reverting to the abbreviatory arrow convention, this expression can be simplified to $\phi^{-1}(\uparrow \text{SUBJ})$.

The composition of the σ projection with the inverse of the ϕ correspondence can now be used to express the fact that the functional subject and the first argument (or agent) in an active sentence coincide even if the information about the subject/agent is scattered throughout the sentence, as is the case in sentences with extraposed relative clauses (*A man entered who was limping*). This is accomplished by letting the semantic structure of the agent correspond to the full set of c-structure nodes that map to the functional subject, e.g. $\phi^{-1}(\uparrow \text{SUBJ})$ if $\uparrow$ denotes the f-structure of the main clause. The semantic structure corresponding to the subject of the mother's f-structure is then denoted by $\sigma\phi^{-1}(\uparrow \text{SUBJ})$ or, using the definition of σ' above, $\sigma'(\uparrow \text{SUBJ})$.

The name of a projection can occur in any equation whether in the lexicon or on phrase-structure rules. Where a particular equation occurs depends on the nature of the semantic generalization it expresses. The following is a typical lexical item with semantic equations:

> *kick*   V $(\uparrow \text{PRED}) = \text{`kick}\langle(\uparrow \text{SUBJ}), (\uparrow \text{OBJ})\rangle\text{'}$
> $(\sigma\mathcal{M}* \text{REL}) = \text{KICK}$
> $(\sigma\mathcal{M}* \text{ARG1}) = \sigma'(\uparrow \text{SUBJ})$
> $(\sigma\mathcal{M}* \text{ARG2}) = \sigma'(\uparrow \text{OBJ})$

This lexical entry contains two kinds of equations. First, there is a pure functional description:

$$(\uparrow \text{PRED}) = \text{`kick}\langle(\uparrow \text{SUBJ}), (\uparrow \text{OBJ})\rangle\text{'}$$

Second, there are inter-module equations constraining the relationship between the semantic interpretation and the functional properties of the phrase. The inter-modular constraint

$$(\sigma\mathcal{M}* \text{ARG1}) = \sigma'(\uparrow \text{SUBJ})$$

asserts that the agent argument role (labeled ARG1) of the *kick* relation is filled by the interpretation which, by force of other equations, is associated (indirectly through the nodes given by ϕ^{-1}) with the functional subject.

The extended rule language permits a third type of equation as well. This is the pure semantic equation. The lexical entry for the past tense marker illustrates this type of equation (cf. any σ-equation in the entry below, which is adapted from Fenstad et al. (1987)).

-*ed*   AFF   ($\uparrow$ TENSE) = PAST
$(\sigma \mathcal{M}* \text{ LOC}) = \sigma*$
$(\sigma* \text{ IND ID}) = \text{IND-LOC}$
$(\sigma* \text{ COND RELATION}) = \prec$
$(\sigma* \text{ COND ARG1}) = (\sigma* \text{ IND})$
$(\sigma* \text{ ARG2}) = \text{LOC-D}$
$(\sigma* \text{ POL}) = 1$

The analyses this notation makes possible exhibit several improvements over earlier treatments.

First, we can now explicate in equational terms the mixture of functional and semantic information implicit in LFG's semantic forms, where the associations between functional entities (SUBJ, OBJ, etc.) and semantic roles are given by the order of arguments, as in the example below.

'kick$\langle(\uparrow \text{SUBJ}),(\uparrow \text{OBJ})\rangle$'

Our equational treatment of the functional and the semantic information that semantic forms encode consigns the different types of information to separate levels of representation while explicitly marking the cross-level dependencies.

Second, the correct assignment of interpretations to roles in passive constructions and other constructions involving lexical rules is also achieved without further stipulations and without modification of the lexical rules. The original version of the passive rule in LFG (Kaplan and Bresnan 1982):

SUBJ $\mapsto$ BY-OBJ;

OBJ $\mapsto$ SUBJ

can be applied directly to the lexical form for *kick* with the desired result. This contrasts with the proposals of Cooper (1985; 1986) and Gawron (1986), where more elaborate mechanisms are introduced to cope with the effects of relation changing rules, and with the analysis in Barwise and Perry (1983), where no allowances are made for the effects of such rules.

As a final example of the beneficial effects of our extended rule language, we examine a storage-free analysis of quantifier scope ambiguities.

5   The Treatment of Scope

The preferred mechanism for scope analysis both in formal linguistic treatments and in natural language systems based on them has long been the so-called Cooper-storage (Cooper 1976).[4] This approach combines a compositional interpretation of a syntax tree with the ability to pass around in the tree a pair consisting of the interpretation of the quantified noun phrase and an indexed variable which is eventually bound by the quantifier in the noun phrase. Different scope interpretations are achieved by discharging the quantifier expression at different points in the process of putting together the interpretation of the rest of the sentence. The theory of interpretation and the rule-language which is presented here makes it possible to handle scope ambiguities without recourse to a storage mechanism.

The generalization underlying the use of Cooper-storage is that the quantifier associated with a quantified noun phrase can take scope at any one of a number of different levels in the sentence. This is exemplified by sentences like (3), which has two interpretations, one non-specific (4) and one specific (5), depending on the scope of the existential quantifier relative to the verb *try*:

(3)   Bill is trying to find a pretty dog

(4)   [Bill is trying $\exists x$[Bill find a pretty dog(x)]]]

(5) $\exists x$[Bill is trying [Bill find a pretty dog(x)]]]

In our analysis, these semantic facts are captured by having a single functional structure associated with two semantic structures, as shown in Figure 3.

The quantifier phrase, QP, can occur on two levels, either in the semantic structure corresponding to the nodes that map to the f-structure VCOMP, or in the semantic structure corresponding to the top level sentence. Putting these observations in more general terms, we see that a noun phrase NP_k in a complement C_j, where j indicates the level of embedding of C_j, can be quantified into the semantic structure corresponding to the top-level sentence, S_0, or into the semantic structure corresponding to any of the verbal-complements, VCOMPs, induced by embedded complement-phrases, C_i, where $i \leq j$. Stated in this fashion one can see that the problem of scope ambiguity can be analyzed by a generalization of the *functional uncertainty* notation (Kaplan and Maxwell 1988).

Kaplan and Maxwell (1988) introduced what we can call outside-in uncertainty. Function-application expressions of the form $(f\ \alpha)$ were used

---

[4]A mechanism similar to Cooper-storage for use in interpretation of quantifiers in the LUNAR system was proposed much earlier by Woods et al. (1972).

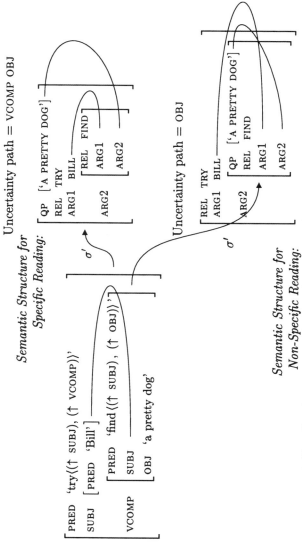

FIGURE 3   Functional structure and semantic structure for quantifier scope ambiguities

to designate a functional structure reachable from f via any path drawn from the regular set α. For example, ($\uparrow$ COMP* OBJ) could be used in the characterization of object relative clauses. We generalize this notion to allow inside-out uncertainty. We let expressions of the form (α f) denote functional structures from which f is reachable over some path in α. Thus the expression (VCOMP* OBJ $\uparrow$) denotes some f-structure from which there is a path to $\uparrow$ consisting of any number of VCOMPs followed by OBJ.

Now the generalization about scope possibilities stated above can be captured by adding the following annotation to any N which is the head of a quantified NP:[5]

$$(\sigma'(\text{VCOMP* GF } \uparrow) \text{ QP}) = \sigma\mathcal{M}*$$

The uncertainty expression (VCOMP* GF $\uparrow$) denotes functional structures f_i from which the f-structure of the NP containing the N can be reached following a path consisting of zero or more VCOMPs followed by a GF. The complete annotation states that the semantic structure of the NP, $\sigma\mathcal{M}*$, is the value of the QP attribute of the semantic structure corresponding to some node that f_i maps to through the σ' projection, ($\sigma'f_i$ QP).

Since our language for the statement of semantic rules is an extension of the language of functional descriptions, this descriptive possibility is immediately available to us. Functional uncertainty also has an efficient implementation based on an incremental decomposition of finite-state machines (Kaplan and Maxwell 1988).

6   Summary

We have shown how to formulate a semantic interpretation mechanism for LFGs based on structural correspondences and a theory of projections. We have also utilized a simple extension of the language for functional constraints to permit the treatment of multiple projections. While previous proposals have taken functional structures as input to the semantic interpretation component and thus have required all semantically relevant information to be reflected in the functional structure, our proposal uses codescription to coordinate the functional and semantic properties of a construction without imposing this requirement. This allows us to simplify functional representations by eliminating functionally irrelevant but semantically significant material. It also puts at our disposal the full power of the rule language of LFG, including functional uncertainty, and this, in its turn, makes it possible to formulate novel semantic analyses,

---

[5]Here GF stands for the set of governable grammatical functions (e.g. SUBJ, OBJ).

such as a treatment of quantifier scope ambiguities that avoids the use of any storage mechanism.

References

Barwise, Jon, and John Perry. 1983. *Situations and Attitudes*. Cambridge, MA: The MIT Press.

Cooper, Robin. 1976. *Montague's Semantic Theory and Transformational Syntax*. Doctoral dissertation, University of Massachusetts at Amherst.

Cooper, Robin. 1985. Meaning Representation in Montague Grammar and Situation Semantics. In *Proceedings of the Workshop on Theoretical Issues in Natural Language Processing*, 28–30. Halifax, Nova Scotia.

Cooper, Robin. 1986. Verb second—predication or unification? Delivered at the Workshop on Comparative Germanic Syntax, Reykjavik, Iceland.

Fenstad, Jens Erik, Per-Kristian Halvorsen, Tore Langholm, and Johan van Benthem. 1985. Equations, schemata and situations: A framework for linguistic semantics. Technical Report 29. Stanford University: Center for the Study of Language and Information.

Fenstad, Jens Erik, Per-Kristian Halvorsen, Tore Langholm, and Johan van Benthem. 1987. *Situations, Language and Logic*. Dordrecht: D. Reidel.

Frey, Werner, and Uwe Reyle. 1983. A PROLOG Implementation of Lexical-Functional Grammar. In *Proceedings of the Eighth International Joint Conference on Artificial Intelligence*, 727–729. Karlsruhe.

Gawron, Jean Mark. 1986. Types, Contents and Semantic Objects. *Linguistics and Philosophy* 9:427–476.

Halvorsen, Per-Kristian. 1982. Order-free semantic composition and Lexical-Functional Grammar. In *Proceedings of COLING-82*, 175–181. Prague, Czechoslovakia.

Halvorsen, Per-Kristian. 1983. Semantics for Lexical-Functional Grammar. *Linguistic Inquiry* 14(4):567–615.

Halvorsen, Per-Kristian. 1988. Situation Semantics and Semantic Interpretation in Constraint–Based Grammars. In *Proceedings of the International Conference on Fifth Generation Computer Systems, FGCS-88*, 471–478. Tokyo, Japan, November. Also published as CSLI Technical Report CSLI-TR-101, Stanford University, 1987. Reprinted in Part IV of this volume.

Jaffar, Joxan, and Jean-Louis Lassez. 1987. Constraint Logic Programming. In *Proceedings of the SIGACT-SIGPLAN Symposium on Principles of Programming Languages*, 111–119. ACM, January.

Kameyama, Megumi. 1989. Functional Precedence Conditions on Overt and Zero Pronominals. Unpublished MS, MCC, Austin, Texas.

Kaplan, Ronald M., and Joan Bresnan. 1982. Lexical-Functional Grammar: A Formal System for Grammatical Representation. In *The Mental Representation of Grammatical Relations*, ed. Joan Bresnan, 173–281. Cambridge, MA: The MIT Press. Reprinted in Part I of this volume.

Kaplan, Ronald M. 1987. Three Seductions of Computational Psycholinguistics. In *Linguistic Theory and Computer Applications*, ed. Peter Whitelock, Harold Somers, Paul Bennett, Rod Johnson, and Mary McGee Wood, 149–188. London: Academic Press. Reprinted in Part V of this volume.

Kaplan, Ronald M., and John T. Maxwell. 1988. An Algorithm for Functional Uncertainty. In *Proceedings of COLING-88*, Vol. 1, 297–302. Budapest. Reprinted in Part II of this volume.

Karttunen, Lauri. 1986. D-PATR: A Development Environment for Unification-Based Grammars. In *Proceedings of COLING-86*. Bonn. Also published as CSLI Report 61, Center for the Study of Language and Information, Stanford University, 1986.

Kay, Martin. 1979. Functional Grammar. In *Proceedings of the Fifth Annual Meeting of the Berkeley Linguistic Society*, ed. Christine Chiarello, John Kingston, Eve E. Sweetser, James Collins, Haruko Kawasaki, John Manley-Buser, Dorothy W. Marschak, Catherine O'Connor, David Shaul, Marta Tobey, Henry Thompson, and Katherine Turner, 142–158. The University of California at Berkeley. Berkeley Linguistics Society.

Montague, Richard. 1970. Universal Grammar. *Theoria* 36:373–398.

Pereira, Fernando C. N., and David H. D. Warren. 1980. Definite Clause Grammars for Natural Language Analysis — A Survey of the Formalism and a Comparison with Augmented Transition Networks. *Artificial Intelligence* 13:231–278.

Pollard, Carl, and Ivan A. Sag. 1987. *Information-Based Syntax and Semantics, Volume I*. No. 13 CSLI Lecture Notes. Stanford University: CSLI/The University of Chicago Press.

Reyle, Uwe. 1988. Compositional Semantics for LFG. In *Natural language parsing and linguistic theories*, ed. Uwe Reyle and Christian Rohrer. Dordrecht: D. Reidel.

Shieber, Stuart M., Hans Uszkoreit, Fernando C. N. Pereira, Jane J. Robinson, and Mabry Tyson. 1983. The Formalism and Implementation of PATR-II. In *Research on Interactive Acquisition and Use of Knowledge*. Menlo Park, CA. SRI International.

Thomason, Richmond H., and Robert C. Stalnaker. 1973. A Semantic Theory of Adverbs. *Linguistic Inquiry* 4(2):195–220.

Woods, William A., Ronald M. Kaplan, and Bonnie Nash-Webber. 1972. The Lunar Sciences Natural Language Information System: Final report. Technical Report 2378. Cambridge, MA: Bolt, Beranek, and Newman, Inc.

10

Situation Semantics and Semantic Interpretation in Constraint-Based Grammars

PER-KRISTIAN HALVORSEN

Abstract. This paper considers semantic interpretation, particularly in situation semantics, using constraint-based approaches to linguistic analysis (e.g. LFG, FUG, PATR, DCG, HPSG). We show how semantic representations can be arrived at by means of constraints on the relationship between the form of an utterance and its meaning. We examine previous proposals for semantic interpretation in unification grammars, and find that a construal of the semantic constraints as specifying operations in a semantic algebra (as in Montague Grammar), as opposed to constraints on the relationship between syntactic form and meaning representations, has prevented the emergence of simple and powerful methods for deriving semantic analyses in constraint-based frameworks. Using the language for stating semantic rules in LFG, we present examples of an approach to semantics that is systematic without being compositional in the structure of the syntactic tree.

1 The Problem of Semantic Interpretation

The integration of syntactic and semantic processing has prompted a number of different architectures for natural language systems, such as rule-by-rule interpretation (Thompson 1963), semantic grammars (Burton 1976), and cascaded ATNs (Woods 1980). The relationship between syntax and

This paper originally appeared in *Proceedings of the International Conference on Fifth Generation Computer Systems* (Tokyo: Institute for New Generation Computer Technology, 1988), 471–478, and as CSLI Technical Report CSLI-TR-101, Stanford University, 1987.

Formal Issues in Lexical-Functional Grammar
edited by
Mary Dalrymple
Ronald M. Kaplan
John T. Maxwell III
Annie Zaenen

semantics has also been of central concern in theoretical linguistics, particularly following Richard Montague's work, and with the recent rapprochement between theoretical and computational linguistics variations on Montague's interpretation scheme have been adopted and implemented in several syntactic theories with a significant following in computational linguistic circles. The first steps in this direction were taken by Hobbs and Rosenschein (1978). A parser for LFG was augmented with a Montagovian semantics by Halvorsen (1982, 1983). GPSG has been similarly extended by Gawron et al. (1982). Schubert and Pelletier (1982) followed with a compositional interpretation scheme using a first order logic rather than Montague's computationally intractable higher-order intensional logic.

The introduction of constraint- or unification-based mechanisms[1] for linguistic description has had obvious effects on syntactic theory and syntactic description. The transformational idiom for syntactic description has been eschewed in favor of lexical rules and declarative statements of constraints on the correspondences between different levels of analysis. Semantic analyses have been integrated with several of the unification-based syntactic theories at an early point (Pereira 1983; Halvorsen 1983). But the new possibilities they create for architectures for semantic interpretation or the consequences for the Montagovian view of compositionality have not been widely considered. These possibilities and the impact of situation semantics (Barwise and Perry 1983) is the focus of this paper. We present a view of semantic interpretation based on the notion of structural correspondences and the theory of projections (Kaplan 1987; Halvorsen and Kaplan 1988). Semantic rules which specify constraints on the correspondence between linguistic form and descriptions of meaning rather than operations on semantic (e.g. model-theoretic) objects are introduced. Meaning representations can then be determined in a systematic, yet not strictly compositional, manner.

2 Unification and Interpretation

We view unification as a technique for combining information given certain facts about how the individual pieces of information relate to each other. The task of semantic composition is exactly of this nature. It is concerned with the combination of semantic information based on the

---

[1] All existing constraint-based systems in linguistics rely heavily on unification for finding structural analyses. When the type of constraints considered is extended beyond equational constraints (as in LFG) other solution mechanisms might prove as fruitful as unification. There is a potentially interesting correspondence here with the move from unification-based logic programming towards *constraint logic programming* (Jaffar and Lassez 1987).

relationship between the constituents in a phrase-structure tree or some other syntactic representation. The method for combination of information used in Montague grammar (MG) was function application and set formation, or equivalently, the operations of the lambda-calculus. This choice imposes certain restrictions on the manner of combination of information in the interpretation step. Specifically, it requires that the informational substructures to be combined are contiguous in the structure being interpreted. Unification supplemented with the flexible addressing scheme usually associated with it in computational linguistics permits a loosening of this restriction of contiguity.

2.1 Compositionality

A clearly desirable trait of any interpretation mechanism is that it be *systematic*. By this we simply mean that the interpretation of the utterance should be mechanically derivable from the information available given the rules of the interpretation scheme. One would also like for the interpretation mechanism to be *complete*. This means that all meaningful utterances in the fragment described should have an interpretation.

Compositionality is an additional requirement often viewed as important (Partee 1983). Under a strict interpretation a *compositional semantics* is one where the interpretation algorithm is recursive on the syntactic tree assigned to the utterance, and the *meaning* of a constituent is required to be a function of the meaning of its immediate constituents. Strict compositionality is not necessarily entailed by systematicity and/or completeness as defined here. However, as long as function application and set formation, or the operations of the lambda-calculus, provide the mechanism for composition of information, strict compositionality does follow from the systematicity requirement. But with new methods for composition of partial information, such as unification or even more general constraint satisfaction techniques, non-compositional alternatives which do not necessarily sacrifice systematicity become available.

The utility of the strict version of the compositionality hypothesis is also brought into question when we turn our attention from *meanings* to *interpretations*, i.e. from the consideration of the semantic potential of sentences or utterance types (meaning), to the impact of an utterance in a specific context (interpretation). Determination of interpretations calls for integration of information from various kinds of sources (e.g. linguistic and non-linguistic context) for which the structured semantic objects of situation semantics and the unification-based constraint-satisfaction techniques we employ are well-suited.

Developments both in grammatical theory and in logic serve as enabling conditions for a shift towards an approach to interpretation reflecting the partiality of the information about meaning made available through discourse, and permitting a systematic, yet not strictly compositional, characterization of meaning. The use of highly typed logics, such as Montague's intensional logic, has been supplemented by investigations of many-sorted logics for natural language semantics (Fenstad et al. 1987). The highly typed semantics encouraged a hierarchical view of semantic composition to reflect the type structure. The use of many-sorted logics has promoted a flatter type-structure which eliminates this pull towards compositionality in the structure of the syntactic tree. Along another dimension, the focus on possible-worlds semantics has been expanded to include consideration of semantic systems with partial models, such as situation semantics (Barwise and Perry 1983, 1985). This corresponds well with the tendency in constraint-based systems to provide descriptions which are monotonically increasing in specificity. Situation semantics also provides structured semantic objects as interpretations for utterances (Gawron 1986). It is thus possible to refer to the constituent parts of interpretations, which enables us to explore other avenues to systematic interpretation than composition according to the syntactic phrase-structure.

3   Semantic Interpretation in Montague Grammar

Montague's theory of semantic interpretation is intriguingly elegant (Montague 1970). His model of language involved the construction of two algebras—a syntactic algebra and a semantic algebra.[2] The syntactic algebra provided a set of syntactic objects, i.e. the lexical items, and a set of syntactic operations (e.g. concatenation) defined over the union of the basic and derived syntactic objects. The semantic algebra consisted of a set of semantic objects (e.g. individuals and truth-values) and a set of semantic operations (e.g. function application and set formation) defined over the basic and derived semantic objects.

How, then, did Montague achieve such a successful statement of the relation between syntax and semantics, given the strict separation between the semantic and the syntactic domain, and given that the semantic rules themselves do not relate the syntactic and the semantic level? The answer lies in the structure of the syntactic and the semantic algebras. Montague demanded that there be a homomorphism from the syntactic algebra into the semantic algebra (see Figure 1).

---

[2]See Halvorsen and Ladusaw (1979) for a discussion of the relevant formal properties of Montague's theory of language and semantic interpretation.

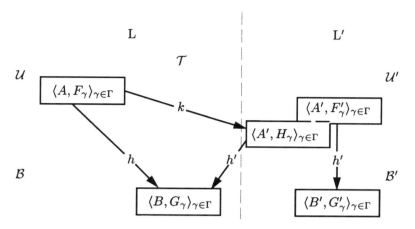

k   the translation function from L into L'
h' the meaning assignment determined for L' by B'
h the meaning assignment determined for L by B
      the interpretation induced by the translation base into L'.

FIGURE 1 Translation and interpretation through homomorphisms
in Montague Grammar (after Halvorsen and Ladusaw 1979)

This meant that for each of the syntactic operations there is a corresponding (possibly complex) semantic operation. The definition of the
homomorphism determines directly what semantic rule can serve to interpret constructions derived by a given syntactic rule. It also provides
an automatic "completeness"-proof for the interpretation system in that
every well-formed syntactic object is guaranteed to have a corresponding
well-formed semantic object (see Section 2.1). The result is the so-called
"rule-to-rule" approach to semantic interpretation: An analysis for a sentence consists of two analysis trees, one for the syntax and one for the
semantics. The application of a rule in the syntax is always mirrored by
the application of the same semantic rule.

In Montague's approach to compositional semantics, the number and
complexity of the operations in the semantic algebra are reflected directly in the operations in the syntactic algebra and the syntactic rules.
Montague's semantic rules involve the full range of semantic operations
admissible in the semantic algebra, and they each correspond to distinct
syntactic rules. In unification-based grammars there is, basically, only
one compositional operation: unification. This creates problems for Mon-

tague's method for coordinating syntax and semantics through homomorphisms. The establishment of a homomorphism between the syntax and the semantics becomes difficult since the operational vocabulary employed in the syntax of unification grammars has been greatly simplified relative to Montague's system, while no similar simplification of the underlying semantic algebra has been proposed. In this new type of grammar one cannot rely on homomorphisms to correlate syntax and semantics. We propose that the syntax/semantics interactions instead be related by rules which explicitly constrain the cooccurrence possibilities for structures on the different levels.

4 Semantic Interpretation in Constraint-based Grammars

It is important for the success of unification-based approaches to natural language processing that a semantic analysis can be provided using a restricted rule language, like the one employed for syntactic description, without loss of precision. In demonstrating this one cannot rely on the accomplishments of Montague grammar, since, as was shown in Section 3, Montague's coordination of syntax and semantics based on homomorphisms does not carry over to constraint-based frameworks. In this section we present a model for semantic composition and semantic interpretation which is better suited to constraint-based theories of linguistic processing. In the process, our constraint-based system is contrasted with the most prominent distinguishing features of Montague grammar.

Our model of semantic interpretation (Figure 2) is based on the view that there are several information sources which are of semantic relevance (e.g. constituent-structure and functional structure).[3]

We formalize the informational dependencies in terms of constraints on the *structural correspondences* (Kaplan 1987) between representations of the different formal aspects of the utterance and the interpretation. The theory of *projections* sets out the details of how information flows between the different levels of representation (Halvorsen and Kaplan 1988). Syntactic phrase-structure rules annotated with functional and semantic descriptions are used to express the connection between syntax and semantics (Figure 3). We are operating with a level of semantic representation intermediate between syntactic structure and interpretations, but these representations are different from phrase-structural and functional

---

[3]Prosodic structure, discourse context, as well as physical and pragmatic constraints in the situation being described are crucial for interpretation, but not considered here.

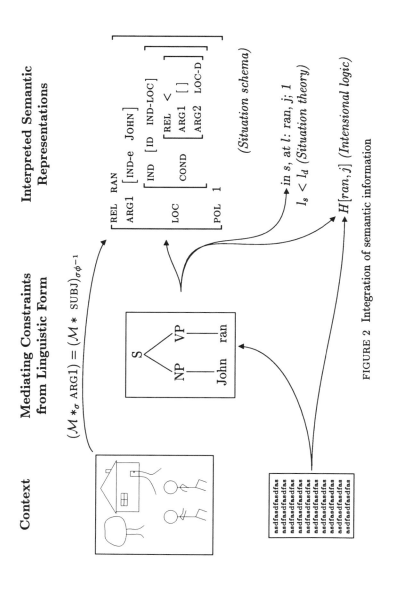

FIGURE 2 Integration of semantic information

$$S \longrightarrow \quad NP \qquad\qquad VP$$
$$(\phi\mathcal{M}* \text{ SUBJ}) = \phi* \qquad \phi\mathcal{M}* = \phi*$$
$$(\sigma\mathcal{M}* \text{ PRED}) = \sigma*$$
$$VP \longrightarrow \quad V \qquad\qquad ADVP$$
$$\phi* \in (\phi\mathcal{M}* \text{ ADJUNCTS})$$
$$\sigma* \in (\sigma\mathcal{M}* \text{ MOD})$$

FIGURE 3   Phrase-structure rules annotated with semantic and
functional descriptions

representations in that they are model-theoretically interpreted or have
associated proof-theories.[4]

4.1   Semantic Rules vs. Semantic Constraints

The *semantic constraints* (or *semantic equations*) which appear as annotations on the phrase-structure rule in Figure 3 are the constructs corresponding most closely to *semantic rules* in Montague grammars. But
Montague's semantic rules operate exclusively in the semantic domain:
They specify semantic operations (e.g. function application or abstraction) on semantic objects (e.g. sets). The semantic constraints in unification grammars, on the other hand, relate several levels of linguistic description. Consequently, the S-rule in Figure 3 performs several functions.
First, it admits a certain phrase-structure configuration: S dominating
an NP and a VP. Second, the association of elements of the rule with
annotations expresses constraints on the correspondence between phrase-
structure configurations and other levels of analysis (*projections*). The
annotations fall into two categories: The function ϕ maps from phrase-
structure nodes to functional structures. Semantic structures are related
to phrase-structure nodes by means of the function σ.[5] Finally, the σ-
equations themselves indicate how to combine partially specified semantic
structures in order to successively approximate an interpretation for the
entire sentence. The ϕ-equations do the same for the functional projection. In particular, the annotation on the NP states that this node
(denoted by *) has a mother ($\mathcal{M}*$, i.e. the S-node), which again has a
functional structure ($\phi\mathcal{M}*$), and the statement ($\phi\mathcal{M} * \text{ SUBJ}$) asserts that
this functional structure has a SUBJ attribute. The value of this attribute
is then asserted to be equal to the value of the functional structure of
the NP, ($\phi*$). The σ-equations on the VP node ensure that the content

---

[4]In our descriptive work we have utilized representations in Montague's higher order
intensional logic (Halvorsen 1982, 1983), situation schemata (Fenstad et al. 1985, 1987),
and PROSIT, a language for reasoning with situation theory (Nakashima et al. 1988).
[5]See Halvorsen and Kaplan (1988) for details.

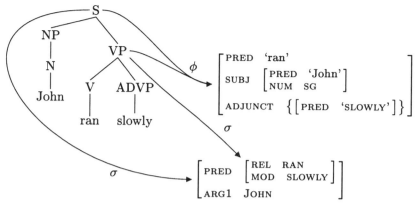

FIGURE 4   C-structure, semantic structure, and functional structure
related by constraints

$$VP \longrightarrow V\ ADVP \overset{h}{\Rightarrow} [\![\ ADVP\ ]\!]([\![\ V\ ]\!])$$

FIGURE 5   Montague grammar rule for VP adverbs

of the VP is accessible under the semantic PRED attribute as a subpart
of the content of the S node. Together the rules in Figure 3 serve to
relate the three structures in Figure 4 to give a syntactic and semantic
analysis for the sentence *John ran slowly*. Notice that in Figure 4 the
functional structure attribute ADJUNCT and the semantic structure attribute MODifier are introduced in the same rule and associated with the
same phrase, but the ADJUNCT is located at the sentence level, while the
semantic MODifier is on the VP level. This illustrates that the semantic
structure is not a simple image of the functional structure.

4.2   Description vs. Construction

The perspective prevalent in constraint-based systems draws a distinction between *description* of structures and the *construction* of structures.
Montague's semantic rules specify how to *construct* the semantic objects
which are the interpretations of sentences by telling us what semantic
operations to apply to what semantic objects. In particular, the MG rule
in Figure 5 states that the semantic object which is the meaning of the
VP is constructed by applying the function which is the interpretation of
the ADVP constituent to the meaning of the V constituent. In contrast,
the semantic descriptions of the annotated phrase-structure rules specify *properties* of the semantic objects which can serve as interpretations

for the syntactic configurations they are associated with, but they do not constitute a step-by-step algorithm for construction of the interpretations. Unification is not an operation on the objects in an underlying semantic algebra. Unification is simply used to combine *descriptions* of semantic objects. The annotated phrase structure rules in Figure 3 express that the [V ADVP]$_{VP}$ configuration in the domain of phrase-structures is *correlated* with the occurrence of a semantic structure which has a PRED attribute associated with the semantic structure of the VP and where the interpretation of the adverb is the value of the MODifier attribute which is encapsulated in the PREDicate together with the semantic structures of other elements of the VP, e.g. the verb *run* (cf. Figure 4). Any semantic representation, however constructed, which satisfies this description (and possibly other more specific descriptions), satisfies the semantic constraints of the annotated rules in Figure 3.

4.3 Partiality and Non-compositionality

Semantic interpretation in unification grammar typically has the property that the information that is associated with a constituent at any one point in the analysis only provides a partial description of the interpretation of the constituent. Moreover, information relating to the interpretation of a phrase can originate not only from its immediate constituents, but from non-contiguous phrases, as well as from context and other levels of analysis. This entails a divergence from a strictly compositional approach to semantic interpretation, but not an abandoning of a systematic algorithm for interpretation.

5 Other Views of Semantic Interpretation in Unification Grammars

Cooper has taken another approach to interpretation in unification grammars (Cooper 1985, 1986). Cooper views what we are calling semantic constraints as specifying semantic operations on semantic objects. Since unification is the only operation available in the constraint language in the grammatical theory he is using, it follows that unification takes on the role as the single most important semantic operation. This contrasts with our view where unification only functions to combine *descriptions* of semantic objects. According to Cooper's theory, the semantic equations of the PATR-style rule below imply an instruction to unify the interpretation of the S node with the interpretation of the VP node, and to unify the interpretation of the (subject) NP with the second argument role of the VP, which is an unsaturated state of affairs.[6]

(S NP VP
          (((0 SYNTAX) (2 SYNTAX))
          ((2 SYNTAX FORM) FINITE)
          ((0 SEMANTICS) (2 SEMANTICS))
          ((1 SEMANTICS) (2 SEMANTICS ARG1))))

If one restricts one's attention to a small fragment of English, it is possible to maintain that the only semantic operation needed is akin to unification. This is the case if the semantic operations involved only have the effect of (a) introducing (possibly unsaturated) states of affairs; or (b) filling argument positions in states of affairs. But if one wants to utilize the full range of semantic operations available in situation theory, this parallel between the operations available in the language of semantic descriptions and the operations in the semantic algebra breaks down. Specifically, situation theory allows the formation of conditions from collections of parameterized states of affairs and the formation of types from collections of conditions. The standard treatment of VPs in situation semantics provides them with types as interpretations. Thus, the interpretation of the phrase *kiss Mary* in Cooper (1985) is the following type:

(1) $[\mathbf{s}|\langle l, kiss, \mathbf{s}, Mary, 1\rangle]$

While the semantic operations involved in filling argument positions can be viewed as a natural extension to the notion of unification as used in the propagation of information in the syntactic derivation, the operation of type formation does not fit into this mold equally well. Some flexibility can be achieved by defining the unification operation to give different results when applied to different types of semantic objects, but this flexibility is not enough to allow us to hold forth unification as the only semantic operation in the semantic algebra.

We maintain that the constraints on the syntactic rules licensing the verb phrase *kiss Mary* should be understood as characterizing properties of the type which can serve as the interpretation for the VP by reference to the different parts of the description of the type (i.e. its parameter, s, its body, $\langle l, kiss, \mathbf{s}, Mary, 1\rangle$, and the identical labelling of the parameter and the kisser-role of the relation). Unification does play an important role in semantic interpretation in constraint-based grammars, but not because unification necessarily is an operation in the semantic algebra.

---

[6] A state of affairs contains a relation, its arguments, and a polarity: $\langle walk, John; 1\rangle$. An unsaturated state of affairs is a state of affairs with one or more of its arguments (or the polarity) left unspecified.

Rather, unification serves to combine the constraints on the relationship between syntactic structure and meaning representations provided by the annotated phrase-structure rules.

6 Grammatical Relations and Interpretation

If the coordination between syntax and semantics is not automatically achieved by virtue of a general correspondence (e.g. homomorphism in Montague grammar), we have to introduce some additional mechanism for correlating predicates and arguments with verbs and phrases in the syntactic tree. Simple heuristics based on order of occurrence in the surface string are not reliable. Other proposals for semantic interpretation in situation semantics make reference in the semantic objects themselves to grammatical relations. The objective is to attain the correct predicate-argument relations in the face of relation-changing linguistic rules such as passivization (*John kicked Pluto* vs. *Pluto was kicked by John*). These rules complicate the relationship between surface order of phrases and their argument roles. In an active sentence with the verb *kick*, the first NP denotes the kicker (agent), but in the corresponding passive sentence, the first NP denotes the thing which was kicked. Cooper (1985, 1986) suggests the use of different indeterminates for the various grammatical functions (e.g. **s**, a subject indeterminate; **o** an object indeterminate). In (1) this device is used to express the restriction that the meaning which is to be unified with the **s** indeterminate in the meaning for *kiss Mary* has to derive from a phrase carrying the grammatical relation of *subject* in an utterance. Similarly, Gawron (1986) makes use of semantic objects, so called labelled indeterminates, where grammatical relations label argument roles (Figure 6).[7]

The argument roles of a verb like *hand* can be filled in different ways. The role of the recipient can either be filled by the object as in *The boy handed the girl the toy*, or by a prepositional phrase (a so called OBL$_{\text{TO}}$) as in *The boy handed the toy to the girl*. These two possibilities correspond to the differently labelled indeterminates, y and z, in Figure 6. Gawron proposes a set of semantic rules operating on the labelled objects. One of these rules, the QI (Quantifying In) Rule (see (2)) is used in the composition of NP meanings (which are parametric indeterminates) with the situation types (i.e. labelled indeterminates) associated with verbs, verb-phrases and sentences.

---

[7] Here and in the following we will identify the argument roles of *hand* with argument positions: The hander-role is associated with the first argument position; the recipient-role is associated with the second argument position; and the object-transferred role is associated with the third argument position.

$$\$y = \{\langle \quad \begin{array}{ll} \text{LOC} & \$\text{LOC}0 \\ \text{REL} & \text{HAND} \\ \text{SUBJECT} & \$\text{IND}0 \\ \text{OBJECT} & \$\text{IND}1 \\ \text{OBJ2} & \$\text{IND}2 \\ \text{POL} & \$\text{POL}0 \end{array} \rangle\}$$

$$\$z = \{\langle \quad \begin{array}{ll} \text{LOC} & \$\text{LOC}0 \\ \text{REL} & \text{HAND} \\ \text{SUBJECT} & \$\text{IND}0 \\ \text{OBL}_{\text{TO}} & \$\text{IND}1 \\ \text{OBJECT} & \$\text{IND}2 \\ \text{POL} & \$\text{POL}0 \end{array} \rangle\}$$

FIGURE 6 Labelled indeterminates: *hand* (Gawron 1986)

(2) QI([XP] FUN [HEAD]) =
    ∪[XP] B([XP] : ARG FUN[HEAD])

The QI rule takes an indeterminate [XP], a label FUN, and a second indeterminate [HEAD]. It produces another labelled indeterminate which consists of the union of the indeterminate [XP] and a new labelled indeterminate which results from substituting the ARG value of [XP] for the value of FUN in [HEAD]. Gawron points out that the effect of applying QI to labelled indeterminates expressing the same content, but labelled differently, produces semantic objects with clearly different contents. His examples are (3) and (4), where $\$y$ and $\$z$ are the labelled indeterminates in Figure 6. $\$y$ and $\$z$ are labelled indeterminates both expressing the same content and differing only in their labelling.

(3) QI([*the girl*] OBJECT [$\$y$])

(4) QI([*the girl*] OBJECT [$\$z$])

In (3) *the girl* will be associated with the recipient role of *hand*, whereas in (4) *the girl* becomes the transferred object. This means that the meaning (here content) of a constituent is no longer a *function* of the meanings (contents) of its parts. The meaning function also depends on the labelling of the contents. Based on this, Gawron concludes that *direct interpretation* in Montague's sense is not possible in his theory: The labelled semantic objects are a crucial intermediate stage in the interpretation process.

The approach which is advocated here makes it unnecessary to allow reference to grammatical relations in the semantic objects. By limiting the use of grammatical relations to the constraints expressing conditions on the correspondence *between* the phrasal, functional and semantic structures, we avoid the problems pointed out by Gawron (1986). In our approach, the correlation of grammatical relations and semantic argument roles is accomplished in the annotations on the lexical items, and these annotations express constraints on the relationship between functional structures and semantic structures. We do not need to import concepts from the analysis of grammatical relations into the semantic analysis. Consider the lexical item for *hand* as it occurs in the sentence *The boy handed the toy to the girl*:

hand   V $(\phi\mathcal{M}*$ PRED$) = $ 'hand'
$(\sigma\mathcal{M}*$ REL$) = $ HAND
$(\sigma\mathcal{M}*$ ARG1$) = \sigma(\phi^{-1}(\phi\mathcal{M}*$ SUBJ$))$
$(\sigma\mathcal{M}*$ ARG2$) = \sigma(\phi^{-1}(\phi\mathcal{M}*$ OBL$_{\mathrm{TO}}))$
$(\sigma\mathcal{M}*$ ARG3$) = \sigma(\phi^{-1}(\phi\mathcal{M}*$ OBJ$))$

We use the theory of projections to relate information about grammatical relations and semantic roles (Halvorsen and Kaplan 1988). Recall that the ϕ-projection maps c-structure into f-structure and the σ-projection maps c-structure into semantic structure. We can use the composition of the σ-projection with the inverse of the ϕ-projection, $\sigma \circ \phi^{-1}$, to express the fact that the subject of *hand* fills the first argument (giver) role. Thus $(\sigma\mathcal{M}*$ ARG1$) = \sigma(\phi^{-1}(\phi\mathcal{M}*$ SUBJ$))$ states that the semantic structure of the first argument of the verb *hand*, $(\sigma\mathcal{M}*$ ARG1$)$, is the semantic structure corresponding to the node, or set of nodes, associated with the functional subject of the verb $\sigma(\phi^{-1}(\phi\mathcal{M}*$ SUBJ$))$. Similarly, the last two lines of equations in the lexical entry for *hand* relate the recipient role in the semantic structure to the OBL$_{\mathrm{TO}}$ and the transferred object to the OBJ. The relation changing rules of LFG, such as Dative Alternation, can apply without modification to the entry above and give the correct predicate argument associations for sentences like *The boy handed the girl the toy*.

Reference to grammatical features, such as grammatical relations, belong in the *inter-module* constraints which characterize the relationship between the phrase-structure, the functional structure and the semantic representation of a sentence. On the other hand, semantic operations, such as quantification (cf. the QI rule), may properly be a part of the semantic algebra, but they need not figure in the statement of the semantic constraints.

7 Conclusions

Adoption of a constraint-based approach to semantic composition invites a perspective on interpretation where partial information about the interpretation of phrases originates in the lexical items, in the constituent structure and in the functional structure, as well as in other modules of linguistic analysis. Descriptions of the interpretation of phrases are accumulated incrementally and the interpretation associated with a constituent can be affected by non-local context. This contrasts with the derivational (or constructive) and strictly compositional approach to interpretation advocated in Montague grammar.

The rule language of unification grammars is strongly limiting in the operations it makes available. Most theories of natural language semantics, on the other hand, make use of a rich arsenal of semantic operations. This difference is a source of problems for Montague's homomorphism-based strategy for interpretation if one takes semantic constraints in unification grammars to specify semantic operations. We have sketched a different view of semantic interpretation in unification grammars where unification of descriptions of semantic representations is used to characterize the class of objects that can serve as interpretations for an utterance. Through a simple extension to the rule language used for syntactic analysis in LFG, we are able to express semantic constraints that are sensitive to a combination of phrasal, functional and, potentially, other properties of the utterance.

Acknowledgments

I wish to thank Stanley Peters, Ron Kaplan, Meg Withgott, John Maxwell, Jens Erik Fenstad and the STASS working group at CSLI for useful discussions.

References

Barwise, Jon, and John Perry. 1983. *Situations and Attitudes*. Cambridge, MA: The MIT Press.

Barwise, Jon, and John Perry. 1985. Shifting Situations and Shaken Attitudes: An Interview with Barwise and Perry. *Linguistics and Philosophy* 8:105–161.

Burton, Richard R. 1976. Semantic Grammar: An Engineering Technique for Constructing Natural Language Understanding Systems. Technical Report 3453. Bolt Beranek and Newman, Inc.

Cooper, Robin. 1985. Meaning Representation in Montague Grammar and Situation Semantics. In *Proceedings of the Workshop on Theoretical Issues in Natural Language Processing*, 28–30. Halifax, Nova Scotia.

Cooper, Robin. 1986. Verb second — predication or unification? Delivered at the Workshop on Comparative Germanic Syntax, Reykjavik.

Fenstad, Jens Erik, Per-Kristian Halvorsen, Tore Langholm, and Johan van Benthem. 1985. Equations, schemata and situations: A framework for linguistic semantics. Technical Report 29. Stanford University: Center for the Study of Language and Information.

Fenstad, Jens Erik, Per-Kristian Halvorsen, Tore Langholm, and Johan van Benthem. 1987. *Situations, Language and Logic*. Dordrecht: D. Reidel.

Gawron, Jean Mark, John Paul King, John Lamping, Egon Loebner, Anne Paulson, Geoff Pullum, Ivan Sag, and Tom Wasow. 1982. Processing English with a Generalized Phrase Structure Grammar. Technical report, Computer Science Laboratory, Hewlett-Packard, Palo Alto, CA.

Gawron, Jean Mark. 1986. Types, Contents and Semantic Objects. *Linguistics and Philosophy* 9:427–476.

Halvorsen, Per-Kristian. 1982. Order-free semantic composition and Lexical-Functional Grammar. In *Proceedings of COLING-82*, 175–181. Prague, Czechoslovakia.

Halvorsen, Per-Kristian, and William A. Ladusaw. 1979. Montague's 'Universal Grammar': An Introduction for the Linguist. *Linguistics and Philosophy* 3:185–223.

Halvorsen, Per-Kristian. 1983. Semantics for Lexical-Functional Grammar. *Linguistic Inquiry* 14(4):567–615.

Halvorsen, Per-Kristian, and Ronald M. Kaplan. 1988. Projections and Semantic Description in Lexical-Functional Grammar. In *Proceedings of the International Conference on Fifth Generation Computer Systems*, 1116–1122. Tokyo, Japan. Institute for New Generation Systems. Reprinted in Part IV of this volume.

Hobbs, Jerry R., and Stanley Rosenschein. 1978. Making Computational Sense of Montague's Intensional Logic. *Artificial Intelligence* 9:287–306.

Jaffar, Joxan, and Jean-Louis Lassez. 1987. Constraint Logic Programming. In *Proceedings of the SIGACT-SIGPLAN Symposium on Principles of Programming Languages*, 111–119. ACM, January.

Kaplan, Ronald M. 1987. Three Seductions of Computational Psycholinguistics. In *Linguistic Theory and Computer Applications*, ed. Peter Whitelock, Harold Somers, Paul Bennett, Rod Johnson, and Mary McGee Wood, 149–188. London: Academic Press. Reprinted in Part V of this volume.

Montague, Richard. 1970. Universal Grammar. *Theoria* 36:373–398.

Nakashima, Hideyuki, Hiroyuki Suzuki, Per-Kristian Halvorsen, and Stanley Peters. 1988. Towards a Computational Interpretation of Situation Theory. In *Proceedings of the International Conference on Fifth Generation Computer Systems, FGCS-88*. Tokyo, Japan, November.

Partee, Barbara. 1983. Compositionality. In *Groningen-Amsterdam Studies in Semantics*. Foris Publications.

Pereira, Fernando C. N. 1983. Logic for Natural Language Analysis. Technical report. Menlo Park, CA: SRI International.

Schubert, Lenhart K., and Francis Jeffry Pelletier. 1982. From English to Logic: Context-Free Computation of 'Conventional' Logical Translations. *American Journal of Computational Linguistics* 10:165–176.

Thompson, F. B. 1963. The Semantic Interface in Man-Machine Communication. Technical Report 63TMP-35. Santa Barbara, CA: General Electric Co.

Woods, William A. 1980. Cascaded ATN grammars. *American Journal of Computational Linguistics* 6(1):1–12.

11

Translation by Structural Correspondences

Ronald M. Kaplan, Klaus Netter, Jürgen Wedekind and Annie Zaenen

Abstract. We sketch and illustrate an approach to machine translation that exploits the potential of simultaneous correspondences between separate levels of representation, as formalized in the LFG notation of codescriptions. The approach is illustrated with examples from English, German and French where the source and the target language sentences show noteworthy differences in linguistic analyses.

1 Introduction

In this paper we sketch an approach to machine translation that offers several advantages compared to many of the other strategies currently being pursued. We define the relationship between the linguistic structures of the source and target languages in terms of a set of correspondence functions instead of providing derivational or procedural techniques for converting source into target. This approach permits the mapping between source and target to depend on information from various levels of linguistic abstraction while still preserving the modularity of linguistic components and of source and target grammars and lexicons. Our conceptual framework depends on notions of structure, structural description, and structural correspondence. In the following sections we outline these

This paper originally appeared in *Proceedings of the Fourth Conference of the European Chapter of the Association for Computational Linguistics* (University of Manchester, 1989), 272–281. Used by permission of the Association for Computational Linguistics; copies of the publication from which this material is derived can can be obtained through Priscilla Rasmussen, ACL Office Manager, P.O. Box 6090 Somerset, NJ 08875, USA.

Formal Issues in Lexical-Functional Grammar
edited by
Mary Dalrymple
Ronald M. Kaplan
John T. Maxwell III
Annie Zaenen

basic notions and show how they can be used to deal with certain interesting translation problems in a simple and straightforward way. In its emphasis on description-based techniques, our approach shares some fundamental features with the one proposed by Kay (1984), but we use an explicit projection mechanism to separate out and organize the intra- and inter-language components.

Most existing translation systems are either interlingua-based or transfer-based. Transfer-based systems usually specify a single level of representation or abstraction at which transfer is supposed to take place. A source string is analyzed into a structure at that level of representation, a transfer program then converts this into a target structure at the same level, and the target string is then generated from this structure. Interlingua-based systems on the other hand require that a source string has to be analyzed into a structure that is identical to a structure from which a target string has to be generated.

Without further constraints, each of these approaches could in principle be successful. An interlingual representation could be devised, for example, to contain whatever information is needed to make all the appropriate distinctions for all the sentences in all the languages under consideration. Similarly, a transfer structure could be arbitrarily configured to allow for the contrastive analysis of any two particular languages. But it seems unlikely that systems based on such an undisciplined arrangement of information will ever succeed in practice. Indeed, most translation researchers have based their systems on representations that have some more general and independent motivation. The levels of traditional linguistic analysis (phonology, morphology, syntax, semantics, discourse, etc.) are attractive because they provide structures with well-defined and coherent properties, but a single one of these levels does not contain all the information needed for adequate translation. The D-structure level of Government-Binding theory, for example, contains information about the predicate-argument relations of a clause but says nothing about the surface constituent order that is necessary to accurately distinguish between old and new information or topic and comment. As another example, the functional structures of Lexical-Functional Grammar do not contain the ordering information necessary to determine the scope of quantifiers or other operators.

Our proposal, as it is set forth below, allows us to state simultaneous correspondences between several levels of source-target representations, and thus is neither interlingual nor transfer-based. We can achieve modularity of linguistic specifications by not requiring conceptually different kinds of linguistic information to be combined into a single structure. Yet that diverse information is still accessible to determine the set of target strings that adequately translate a source string. We also achieve modularity of a more basic sort: our correspondence mechanism permits contrastive transfer rules that depend on but do not duplicate the specifications of independently motivated grammars of the source and target languages (Isabelle and Macklovitch 1986; Netter and Wedekind 1986).

2 A General Architecture for Linguistic Descriptions

Our approach uses the equality- and description-based mechanisms of Lexical-Functional Grammar. As introduced by Kaplan and Bresnan (1982), Lexical-Functional Grammar assigns to every sentence two levels of syntactic representation, a constituent structure (c-structure) and a functional structure (f-structure). These structures are of different formal types—the c-structure is a phrase-structure tree while the f-structure is a hierarchical finite function—and they characterize different aspects of the information carried by the sentence. The c-structure represents the ordered arrangement of words and phrases in the sentence while the f-structure explicitly marks its grammatical functions (subject, object, etc.). For each type of structure there is a special notation or description-language in which the properties of desirable instances of that type can be specified. Constituent structures are described by standard context-free rule notation (augmented with a variety of abbreviatory devices that do not change its generative power), while f-structures are described by Boolean combinations of function-argument equalities stated over variables that denote the structures of interest. Kaplan and Bresnan assumed a correspondence function mapping between the nodes in the c-structure of a sentence and the units of its f-structure, and used that piecewise function to produce a description of the f-structure (in its equational language) by virtue of the mother-daughter, order, and category relations of the c-structure.

The formal picture developed by Kaplan and Bresnan, as clarified by Kaplan (1987), is illustrated in the following structures for sentence (1):

(1) a. The baby fell.

b.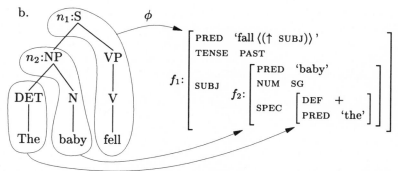

The c-structure appears on the left, the f-structure on the right. The c-structure to-f-structure correspondence, ϕ, is shown by the linking lines. The correspondence ϕ is a many-to-one function taking the S, VP, V nodes all into the same outermost unit of the f-structure, f_1.

The node-configuration at the top of the tree satisfies the statement S → NP VP in the context-free description language for the c-structure. As suggested by Kaplan (1987), this is a simple way of defining a collection of more specific properties of the tree, such as the fact that the S node (labeled n_1) is the mother of the NP node (n_2). These facts could also be written in equational form as $M(n_2) = n_1$, where M denotes the function that takes a tree-node into its mother. Similarly, the outermost f-structure satisfies the assertions $(f_1 \text{ TENSE}) = \text{PAST}$, $(f_1 \text{ SUBJ}) = f_2$, and $(f_2 \text{ NUM}) = \text{SG}$ in the f-structure description language. Given the illustrated correspondence, we also know that $f_1 = \phi(n_1)$ and $f_2 = \phi(n_2)$. Taking all these propositions together, we can infer first that

$$(\phi(n_1) \text{ SUBJ}) = \phi(n_2)$$

and then that

$$(\phi(M(n_2)) \text{ SUBJ}) = \phi(n_2)$$

This equation identifies the subject in the f-structure in terms of the mother-daughter relation in the tree.

In LFG the f-structure assigned to a sentence is the smallest one that satisfies the conjunction of equations in its functional description. The functional description is determined from the trees that the c-structure grammar provides for the string by a simple matching process. A given tree is analyzed with respect to the c-structure rules to identify particular nodes of interest. Equations about the f-structure corresponding to those nodes (via ϕ) are then derived by substituting those nodes into equation-patterns or schemata. Thus, still following Kaplan (1987), if * appears in a schema to stand for the node matching a given rule-category, the functional description will include an equation containing that node (or an expression such as n_2 that designates it) instead of $*$. The equation $(\phi(M(n_2))\ \text{SUBJ}) = \phi(n_2)$ that we inferred above also results from instantiating the schema $(\phi(M(*))\ \text{SUBJ}) = \phi(*)$ annotated to the NP element of the S rule in (2a) when that rule-element is matched against the tree in (1b). Kaplan observes that the $\uparrow$ and $\downarrow$ metavariables in the Kaplan/Bresnan formulation of LFG are simply convenient abbreviations for the complex expressions $\phi(M(*))$ and $\phi(*)$, respectively, thus explicating the traditional, more palatable formulation in (2b).

(2) a. S $\longrightarrow$ $\qquad$ NP $\qquad\qquad\qquad$ VP
$\qquad\qquad\qquad (\phi(M(*))\ \text{SUBJ}) = \phi(*)\quad \phi(M(*)) = \phi(*)$

$\quad$ b. S $\longrightarrow$ $\qquad$ NP $\qquad$ VP
$\qquad\qquad\qquad (\uparrow\ \text{SUBJ}) = \downarrow \quad \uparrow = \downarrow$

This basic conception of descriptions and correspondences has been extended in several ways. First, this framework has been generalized to additional kinds of structures that represent other subsystems of linguistic information (Kaplan 1987; Halvorsen 1988). These structures can be related by new structural correspondences that permit appropriate descriptions of more abstract structures to be produced. Halvorsen and Kaplan (1988), for example, discuss a level of semantic structure that encodes predicate-argument relations and quantifier scope, information that does not enter into the kinds of syntactic generalizations that the f-structure supports. They point out how the semantic structure can be set in correspondence with both c-structure and f-structure units by means of related mappings σ and σ'. Kaplan (1987) raises the possibility of further distinct structures and correspondences to represent anaphoric dependencies, discourse properties of sentences, and other *projections* of the same string.

Second, Kaplan (1988) and Halvorsen and Kaplan (1988) discuss other methods for deriving the descriptions necessary to determine these abstract structures. The arrangement outlined above, in which the description of one kind of structure (the f-structure) is derived by analyzing or matching against another one, is an example of what is called *description-by-analysis*. The semantic interpretation mechanisms proposed by Halvorsen (1983) and Reyle (1988) are other examples of this descriptive technique. In this method the grammar provides general patterns to compare against a given structure and these are then instantiated if the analysis is satisfactory. One consequence of this approach is that the structure in the range of the correspondence, the one whose description is being developed, can only have properties that are derived from information explicitly identified in the domain structure.

Another description mechanism is possible when three or more structures are related through correspondences. Suppose the c-structure and f-structure are related by ϕ as in (2a) and that the function σ then maps the f-structure units into corresponding units of semantic structure of the sort suggested by Fenstad et al. (1987). The formal arrangement is shown in Figure 1. This configuration of cascaded correspondences opens

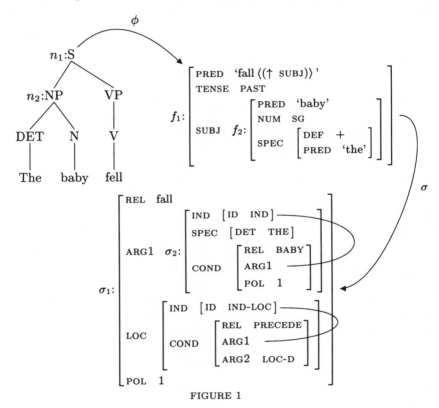

FIGURE 1

up a new descriptive possibility. If σ and ϕ are both structural correspondences, then so is their composition $\sigma \circ \phi$. Thus, even though the units of the semantic structure correspond directly only to the units of the f-structure and have no immediate connection to the nodes of the c-structure, a semantic description can be formulated in terms of c-structure relations. The expression $\sigma(\phi(M(*)))$ can appear on a c-structure rule-element to designate the semantic-structure unit corresponding to the f-structure that corresponds to the mother of the node that matches that rule-element. Since projections are monadic functions, we can remove the uninformative parentheses and write $(\sigma\phi M^* \text{ ARG1}) = \sigma(\phi M^* \text{ SUBJ})$, or, using the $\uparrow$ metavariable, $(\sigma\uparrow \text{ ARG1}) = \sigma(\uparrow \text{ SUBJ})$. Schemata such as this can be freely mixed with LFG's standard functional specifications in lexical entries and c-structure rules. For example, the lexical entry for *fall* might be given as follows:

(3)   *fall*   V $(\uparrow \text{ PRED}) = $ 'fall $\langle(\uparrow \text{ SUBJ})\rangle$'
                   $(\sigma\uparrow \text{ REL}) = \text{FALL}$
                   $(\sigma\uparrow \text{ ARG1}) = \sigma(\uparrow \text{ SUBJ})$

Descriptions formulated by composing separate correspondences have a surprising characteristic: they allow the final range structure (e.g. the semantic structure) to have properties that cannot be inferred from any information present in the intermediate (f-) structure. But those properties can obtain only if the intermediate structure is derived from an initial (c-) structure with certain features. For example, Kaplan and Maxwell (1988a) exploit this capability to describe semantic structures for coordinate constructions which necessarily contain the logical conjunction appropriate to the string even though there is no reasonable place for that conjunction to be marked in the f-structure. In sum, this method of description, which has been called *codescription,* permits information from a variety of different levels to constrain a particular structure, even though there are no direct correspondences linking them together. It provides for modularity of basic relationships while allowing certain necessary restrictions to have their influence.

The descriptive architecture of LFG as extended by Kaplan and Halvorsen provides for multiple levels of structure to be related by separate correspondences, and these correspondences allow descriptions of the various structures to be constructed, either by analysis or composition, from the properties of other structures. Earlier researchers have applied these mechanisms to the linguistic structures for sentences in a single language. In this paper, we extend this system one step further: we introduce correspondences between structures for sentences in different languages that stand in a translation relation to one another. The description of the target language structures are derived via analysis and codescription from the source language structures, by virtue of additional annotations in c-structure rules and lexical entries. Those descriptions are solved to find satisfying solutions, and these solutions are then the input to the target generation process.

In the two language arrangement sketched below, we introduce the τ correspondence to map between the f-structure units of the source language and the f-structure units of the target language. The σ correspondence maps from the f-structure of each language to its own corresponding semantic structure, and a second transfer correspondence τ' relates those structures.

(4)

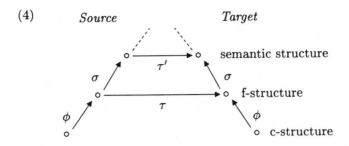

This arrangement allows us to describe the target f-structure by composing ϕ and τ to form expressions such as $\tau(\phi M^* \text{COMP}) = (\tau \phi M^* \text{XCOMP})$ or simply $\tau(\uparrow \text{COMP}) = (\tau \uparrow \text{XCOMP}))$. This maps a COMP in the source f-structure into an XCOMP in the target f-structure. The relations asserted by this equation are depicted in the following source-target diagram:

(5)

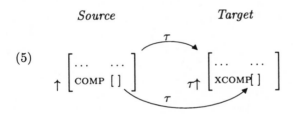

As another example, the equation $\tau'(\sigma \uparrow \text{ARG1}) = (\sigma \tau \uparrow \text{ARG1})$ identifies the first arguments in the source and target semantic structures. The equation $\tau' \sigma(\uparrow \text{SUBJ}) = \sigma(\tau \uparrow \text{TOPIC})$ imposes the constraint that the semantics of the source SUBJ will translate via τ' into the semantics of the target TOPIC but gives no further information about what those semantic structures actually contain.

Our general correspondence architecture thus applies naturally to the problem of translation. But there are constraints on correspondences specific to translation that this general architecture does not address. For instance, the description of the target-language structures derived from the source-language is incomplete. The target structures may and usually will have grammatical and semantic features that are not determined by the source. It makes little sense, for example, to include information about grammatical gender in the transfer process if this feature is exhaustively determined by the grammar of the target language. We can formalize the relation between the information contained in the transfer component and an adequate translation of the source sentence in the target sentence as follows: for a target sentence to be an adequate translation of a given source sentence, it must be the case that a minimal structure assigned to that sentence by the target grammar is subsumed by a minimal solution to the transfer description. One desirable consequence of this formalization is that it permits two distinct target strings for a source string whose meaning in the absence of other information is vague but not ambiguous.

Thus this conceptual and notational framework provides a powerful and flexible system for imposing constraints on the form of a target sentence by relating them to information that appears at different levels of source-language abstraction. This apparatus allows us to avoid many of the problems encountered by more derivational, transformational or procedural models of transfer. We will illustrate our proposal with some examples that have posed challenges for some other approaches.

3 Examples

3.1 Changes in Grammatical Function

Some quite trivial changes in structure occur when the source and the target predicate differ in the grammatical functions that they subcategorize for. We will illustrate this with an example in which a German transitive verb is translated with an intransitive verb taking an oblique complement in French:

(6) a. Der Student beantwortet die Frage.
    b. L'étudiant répond à la question.

We treat the oblique preposition as a PRED that itself takes an object. Ignoring information about tense, the lexical entry for *beantworten* in the German lexicon looks as follows:

(7) *beantworten*   V $(\uparrow \text{PRED}) = $ 'beantworten$\langle(\uparrow \text{SUBJ}), (\uparrow \text{OBJ})\rangle$'

while the transfer lexicon for *beantworten* contains the following mapping specifications:

(8) $(\tau\uparrow \text{PRED FN}) = $ répondre
    $(\tau\uparrow \text{SUBJ}) = \tau(\uparrow \text{SUBJ})$
    $(\tau\uparrow \text{AOBJ OBJ}) = \tau(\uparrow \text{OBJ})$

We use the special attribute FN to designate the function-name in semantic forms such as 'beantworten$<(\uparrow \text{SUBJ})(\uparrow \text{OBJ})>$'. In this transfer equation it identifies *répondre* as the corresponding French predicate. This specification controls lexical selection in the target, for example, selecting the following French lexical entry to be used in the translation:

(9) répondre V $(\uparrow \text{PRED}) = $ 'répondre$<(\uparrow \text{SUBJ})(\uparrow \text{AOBJ})>$'

With these entries and the appropriate but trivial entries for *der Student* and *die Frage* we get the following f-structure in the source language and associated f-structure in the target language for the sentence in (6a):

(10)

$$
f_1 \begin{bmatrix}
\text{PRED} & \text{'beantworten} \langle (\uparrow \text{SUBJ}), (\uparrow \text{OBJ}) \rangle \text{'} \\
\text{TENSE} & \text{PRES} \\
\text{SUBJ} \quad f_2 & \begin{bmatrix}
\text{PRED} & \text{'Student'} \\
\text{NUM} & \text{SG} \\
\text{GEND} & \text{MASC} \\
\text{SPEC} & \begin{bmatrix} \text{DEF} & + \\ \text{PRED} & \text{'der'} \end{bmatrix}
\end{bmatrix} \\
\text{OBJ} \quad f_3 & \begin{bmatrix}
\text{PRED} & \text{'Frage'} \\
\text{NUM} & \text{SG} \\
\text{GEND} & \text{FEM} \\
\text{SPEC} & \begin{bmatrix} \text{DEF} & + \\ \text{PRED} & \text{'die'} \end{bmatrix}
\end{bmatrix}
\end{bmatrix}
$$

$$
\tau_1 \begin{bmatrix}
\text{PRED} & \text{'répondre} \langle (\uparrow \text{SUBJ}), (\uparrow \text{AOBJ}) \rangle \text{'} \\
\text{TENSE} & \text{PRES} \\
\text{SUBJ} \quad \tau_2 & \begin{bmatrix}
\text{PRED} & \text{'étudiant'} \\
\text{NUM} & \text{SG} \\
\text{GEND} & \text{MASC} \\
\text{SPEC} & \begin{bmatrix} \text{DEF} & + \\ \text{PRED} & \text{'le'} \end{bmatrix}
\end{bmatrix} \\
\text{AOBJ} & \begin{bmatrix}
\text{PRED} & \text{'á} \langle (\uparrow \text{OBJ}) \rangle \text{'} \\
\text{PCASE} & \text{AOBJ} \\
\text{OBJ} \quad \tau_3 & \begin{bmatrix}
\text{PRED} & \text{'question'} \\
\text{NUM} & \text{SG} \\
\text{GEND} & \text{FEM} \\
\text{SPEC} & \begin{bmatrix} \text{DEF} & + \\ \text{PRED} & \text{'la'} \end{bmatrix}
\end{bmatrix}
\end{bmatrix}
\end{bmatrix}
$$

The second structure is the f-structure the grammar of French assigns to the sentence in (6b). This f-structure is the input for the generation process. Other examples of this kind are 'like'/ 'plaire' and 'help'/ 'helfen'.

In the previous example the effects of the change in grammatical function between the source and target language are purely local. In other cases there is a non-local dependency between the subcategorizing verb and a dislocated phrase. This is illustrated by the relative clause in (11):

(11) a. ...der Brief, den der Student zu beantworten scheint.
   b. ...la lettre, à laquelle l'étudiant semble répondre.
   ...the letter, that the student seemed to answer.

The within-clause functions of the relativized phrases in the source and target language are determined by predicates which may be arbitrarily deeply embedded, but the relativized phrase in the target language must correspond to the one in the source language.

Let us assume that relative clauses can be analyzed by the following slightly simplified rules, making use of functional uncertainty (see Kaplan and Maxwell 1988b for a technical discussion of functional uncertainty) to capture the non-local dependency of the relative phrase (equations on the head NP are ignored):

$$(12) \quad NP \longrightarrow NP \qquad S'$$
$$(\uparrow \text{RELADJ}) = \downarrow$$

$$S' \longrightarrow XP \qquad S$$
$$(\uparrow \text{REL-TOPIC}) = \downarrow \quad \uparrow = \downarrow$$
$$(\uparrow \text{XCOMP}^* \text{GF}) = \downarrow$$

We can achieve the desired correspondence between the source and the target by augmenting the first rule with the following transfer equations:

$$(13) \quad NP \longrightarrow NP \qquad S'$$
$$(\uparrow \text{RELADJ}) = \downarrow$$
$$\tau(\uparrow \text{RELADJ}) = (\tau\uparrow \text{RELADJ})$$
$$\tau(\downarrow \text{REL-TOPIC}) = (\tau\downarrow \text{REL-TOPIC})$$

The effect of this rule is that the τ value of the relativized phrase (REL-TOPIC) in the source language is identified with the relativized phrase in the target language. However, the source REL-TOPIC is also identified with a within-clause function, say OBJ, by the uncertainty equation in (12). Lexical transfer rules such as the one given in (8) independently establish the correspondence between source and target within-clause functions. Thus, the target within-clause function will be identified with the target relativized phrase. This necessary relation is accomplished by lexically and structurally based transfer rules that do not make reference to each other.

3.2 Differences in Control

A slightly more complex but similar case arises when the infinitival complement of a raising verb is translated into a finite clause, as in the following:

(14) a. The student is likely to work.

b. Il est probable que l'étudiant travaillera.

In this case the necessary information is distributed in the following way over the source, transfer, and target lexicons:

(15) *likely* A ($\uparrow$ PRED) = 'likely$\langle(\uparrow$ XCOMP$)\rangle(\uparrow$ SUBJ)' (source)
($\uparrow$ SUBJ) = ($\uparrow$ XCOMP SUBJ)

($\tau\uparrow$ PRED FN) = probable (transfer)
($\tau\uparrow$ COMP) = $\tau(\uparrow$ XCOMP)

probable A ($\uparrow$ PRED) = 'probable$\langle(\uparrow$ COMP$)\rangle(\uparrow$ SUBJ)'
($\uparrow$ SUBJ FORM) = IL
($\uparrow$ COMP COMPL) = QUE (target)
($\uparrow$ COMP TENSE) = FUTURE

Here the transfer projection builds up an underspecified target structure, to which the information given in the entry of *probable* is added in the process of generation. Ignoring the contribution of *is*, the f-structure for the English sentence identifies the nonthematic SUBJ of *likely* with the thematic SUBJ of *work* as follows:

(16)

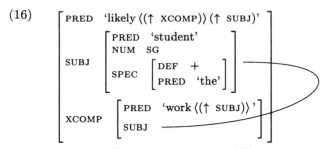

The corresponding French structure in (17) contains an expletive SUBJ, *il*, for *probable* and an overtly expressed SUBJ for *travailler*. The latter is introduced by the transfer entry for *work*:

(17)

$$
\begin{bmatrix}
\text{PRED} & \text{'probable} \langle (\uparrow \text{ COMP}) \rangle (\uparrow \text{ SUBJ})\text{'} \\
\text{SUBJ} & [\text{FORM} \quad \text{IL}] \\
\text{COMP} & \begin{bmatrix}
\text{PRED} & \text{'travailler} \langle (\uparrow \text{ SUBJ}) \rangle \text{'} \\
\text{COMPL} & \text{QUE} \\
\text{TENSE} & \text{FUTURE} \\
\text{SUBJ} & \begin{bmatrix}
\text{PRED} & \text{'étudiant'} \\
\text{GEND} & \text{MASC} \\
\text{NUM} & \text{SG} \\
\text{SPEC} & \begin{bmatrix} \text{DEF} & + \\ \text{PRED} & \text{'le'} \end{bmatrix}
\end{bmatrix}
\end{bmatrix}
\end{bmatrix}
$$

Again this f-structure satisfies the transfer description and is also assigned by the French grammar to the target sentence.

3.3   The Use of Multiple Projections

There is one detail about the example in (14) that needs further discussion. Simplifying matters somewhat, there is a requirement that the temporal reference point of the complement has to follow the temporal reference point of the clause containing *likely*, if the embedded verb is a process verb. Basically the same temporal relations have to hold in French with *probable*. The way this is realized will depend on what the tense of *probable* is, which in turn is determined by the discourse up to that point. A sentence similar to the one given in (14b) but appearing in a narrative in the past would translate as the following:

(18)   Il était probable que l'étudiant travaillerait.

In the general case the choice of a French tense does not depend on the tense of the English sentence alone, but is also determined by information that is not part of the f-structure itself. We postulate another projection, the temporal structure, reached from the f-structure through the correspondence χ (from $\chi\rho o\nu\iota\kappa o\varsigma$, temporal). It is not possible to discuss here the specific characteristics of such a structure. The only thing that we want to express is the constraint that the event in the embedded clause follows the event in the main clause. We assume that the temporal structure contains the following information for *likely-to-V*, as suggested by Fenstad et al. (1987):

(19)   *likely*   V $(\chi\uparrow \text{ COND REL}) = \text{precede}$
$(\chi\uparrow \text{ COND ARG1}) = (\chi \uparrow \text{ IND})$
$(\chi\uparrow \text{ COND ARG2 ID}) = \text{IND-LOC2}$

This is meant to indicate that the temporal reference point of the event denoted by the embedded verb extends after the temporal reference point of the main event. The time of the main event is in part determined by the tense of the verb *be*, which we ignore here. The only point we want to make is that aspects of these different projections can be specified in different parts of the grammar. We assume that French and English have the same temporal structure but that in the context of *likely* it is realized in a different way. This can be expressed by the following equation:

(20) $\chi\uparrow = \chi\tau\uparrow$

Here the identity between χ and $\chi\tau$ provides an interlingua-like approach to this particular subpart of the relation between the two languages. This is diagrammed in Figure 2.

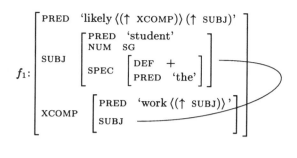

f_1:

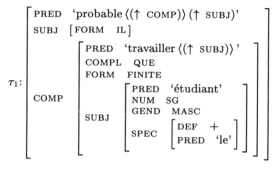

τ_1:

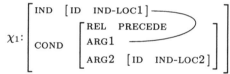

χ_1:

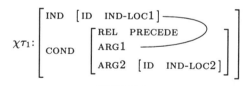

$\chi\tau_1$:

FIGURE 2

Allowing these different projections to simultaneously determine the surface structure seems at first blush to complicate the computational problem of generation, but a moment of reflection will show that that is not necessarily so. Although we have split up the different equations among several projections for conceptual clarity, computationally we can consider them to define one big attribute value structure with χ and τ as special attributes, so the generation problem in this framework reduces to the problem of generating from attribute-value structures which are formally of the same type as f-structures (see Halvorsen and Kaplan 1988, Wedekind 1988, and Momma and Dörre 1987, for discussion).

3.4 Differences in Embedding

The potential of the system can also be illustrated with a case in which we find one more level of embedding in one language than we find in the other. This is generally the case if a modifier-head relation in the source language is reversed in the target structure. One such example is the relation between the sentences in (21):

(21) a. The baby just fell.
b. Le bébé vient de tomber.

One way to encode this relation is given in the following lexical entry for *just* (remember that all the information about the structure of *venir* in French will come from the lexicon and grammar of French itself):

(22) *just*   ADV $(\uparrow \text{PRED}) = \text{`just}\langle(\uparrow \text{ARG})\rangle\text{'}$
$(\tau\uparrow \text{PRED FN}) = \text{venir}$
$(\tau\uparrow \text{XCOMP}) = \tau(\uparrow \text{ARG})$

This assigns to *just* a semantic form that takes an ARG function as its argument and maps it into the French *venir*. This lexical entry is combined with phrase-structure rule (23). This rule introduces sentence adverbs and makes the f-structure corresponding to the S node fill the ARG function in the f-structure corresponding to the ADV node.

(23)   S $\longrightarrow$ NP $\begin{pmatrix} \text{ADV} \\ \uparrow = (\downarrow \text{ARG}) \end{pmatrix}$ VP
        $(\uparrow \text{SUBJ}) = \downarrow$

Note that the f-structure of the ADV is not assigned a function within the S-node's f-structure, which is shown in (24). This is in keeping with the fact that the adverb has no functional interactions with the material in the main clause.

(24)
$$\begin{bmatrix} \text{PRED} & \text{`fall}\langle(\uparrow \text{SUBJ})\rangle\text{'} \\ \text{TENSE} & \text{PAST} \\ \text{SUBJ} & \begin{bmatrix} \text{PRED} & \text{`baby'} \\ \text{NUM} & \text{SG} \\ \text{SPEC} & \begin{bmatrix} \text{DEF} & + \\ \text{PRED} & \text{`the'} \end{bmatrix} \end{bmatrix} \end{bmatrix}$$

The relation between the adverb and the clause is instead represented only in the f-structure associated with the ADV node:

(25)

$$
\begin{bmatrix}
\text{PRED} & \text{`just}\langle(\uparrow\ \text{ARG})\rangle\text{'} \\[4pt]
\text{ARG} &
\begin{bmatrix}
\text{PRED} & \text{`fall}\langle(\uparrow\ \text{SUBJ})\rangle\text{'} \\
\text{TENSE} & \text{PAST} \\
\text{SUBJ} &
\begin{bmatrix}
\text{PRED} & \text{`baby'} \\
\text{NUM} & \text{SG} \\
\text{SPEC} &
\begin{bmatrix}
\text{DEF} & + \\
\text{PRED} & \text{`the'}
\end{bmatrix}
\end{bmatrix}
\end{bmatrix}
\end{bmatrix}
$$

In the original formulation of LFG, the f-structure of the highest node was singled out and assigned a special status. In our current theory we do not distinguish that structure from all the others in the range of ϕ: the grammatical analysis of a sentence includes the complete enumeration of ϕ-associations. The S-node's f-structure typically does contain the f-structures of all other nodes as subsidiary elements, but not in this adverbial case. The target structures corresponding to the various f-structures are also not required to be integrated. These target f-structures can then be set in correspondence with any nodes of the target c-structure, subject to the constraints imposed by the target grammar. In this case, the fact that *venir* takes an XCOMP which corresponds to the ARG of *just* means that the target f-structure mapped from the ADV's f-structure will be associated with the highest node of the target c-structure. This is shown in (26).

(26)

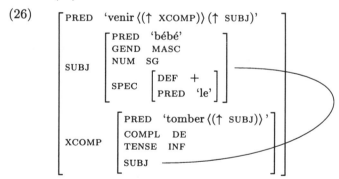

The above analysis does not require a single integrated source structure to map onto a single integrated target structure. An alternative analysis can handle differences of embedding with completely integrated structures. If we assign an explicit function to the adverbial in the source sentence, we can reverse the embedding in the target by replacing (23) with (27):

(27) S $\longrightarrow$ NP $\begin{pmatrix} \text{ADV} \\ (\uparrow \text{ SADJ}) = \downarrow \\ \tau\uparrow = (\tau\downarrow \text{ XCOMP}) \end{pmatrix}$ VP

In this case the embedded f-structure of the source adverb will be mapped onto the f-structure that corresponds to the root node of the target c-structure, whereas the f-structure of the source S is mapped onto the embedded XCOMP in the target. The advantages and disadvantages of these different approaches are being investigated further.

4   Conclusion

We have sketched and illustrated an approach to machine translation that exploits the potential of simultaneous correspondences between different levels of linguistic representation. This is made possible by the equality and description based mechanisms of LFG. This approach relies mainly on codescription, and thus it is different from other LFG-based approaches that use a description-by-analysis mechanism to relate the f-structure of a source language to the f-structure of a target language (see for example Kudo and Nomura 1986). Our proposal allows for partial specifications and multi-level transfer. In that sense it also differs from strategies pursued, for example, in the Eurotra project (Arnold and des Tombe 1987), where transfer is based on one level of representation obtained by transforming the surface structure in successive steps.

We see it as one of the main advantages of our approach that it allows us to express correspondences between separate pieces of linguistically motivated representations and in this way allows the translator to exploit the linguistic descriptions of source and target language in a more direct way than is usually proposed.

Acknowledgments

Thanks to P.-K. Halvorsen, H. Kamp, M. Kay and C. Rohrer for discussion and comments.

References

Arnold, Douglas J., and Louis des Tombe. 1987. Basic theory and methodology in Eurotra. In *Machine Translation: Theoretical and methodological issues*, ed. S. Nirenburg. 114–135. Cambridge, England: Cambridge University Press.

Fenstad, Jens Erik, Per-Kristian Halvorsen, Tore Langholm, and Johan van Benthem. 1987. *Situations, Language and Logic*. Dordrecht: D. Reidel.

Halvorsen, Per-Kristian. 1983. Semantics for Lexical-Functional Grammar. *Linguistic Inquiry* 14(4):567–615.

Halvorsen, Per-Kristian. 1988. Situation Semantics and Semantic Interpretation in Constraint–Based Grammars. In *Proceedings of the International Conference on Fifth Generation Computer Systems, FGCS-88*, 471–478. Tokyo, Japan, November. Also published as CSLI Technical Report CSLI-TR-101, Stanford University, 1987. Reprinted in Part IV of this volume.

Halvorsen, Per-Kristian, and Ronald M. Kaplan. 1988. Projections and Semantic Description in Lexical-Functional Grammar. In *Proceedings of the International Conference on Fifth Generation Computer Systems*, 1116–1122. Tokyo, Japan. Institute for New Generation Systems. Reprinted in Part IV of this volume.

Isabelle, Pierre, and Elliott Macklovitch. 1986. Transfer and MT Modularity. In *Proceedings of COLING-86*, 115–117. Bonn.

Kaplan, Ronald M., and Joan Bresnan. 1982. Lexical-Functional Grammar: A Formal System for Grammatical Representation. In *The Mental Representation of Grammatical Relations*, ed. Joan Bresnan, 173–281. Cambridge, MA: The MIT Press. Reprinted in Part I of this volume.

Kaplan, Ronald M. 1987. Three Seductions of Computational Psycholinguistics. In *Linguistic Theory and Computer Applications*, ed. Peter Whitelock, Harold Somers, Paul Bennett, Rod Johnson, and Mary McGee Wood, 149–188. London: Academic Press. Reprinted in Part V of this volume.

Kaplan, Ronald M. 1988. Correspondences and their inverses. Paper presented at the Syntax and Semantics Workshop, April, Titisee, FRG.

Kaplan, Ronald M., and John T. Maxwell. 1988a. Constituent Coordination in Lexical-Functional Grammar. In *Proceedings of COLING-88*, Vol. 1, 303–305. Budapest. Reprinted in Part II of this volume.

Kaplan, Ronald M., and John T. Maxwell. 1988b. An Algorithm for Functional Uncertainty. In *Proceedings of COLING-88*, Vol. 1, 297–302. Budapest. Reprinted in Part II of this volume.

Kay, Martin. 1984. Functional Unification Grammar: A Formalism for Machine Translation. In *Proceedings of COLING-84*, 75–78. Stanford, CA.

Kudo, Ikuo, and Hirosato Nomura. 1986. Lexical-Functional Transfer: A Transfer Framework in a Machine Translation System based on LFG. In *Proceedings of COLING-86*, 112–114. Bonn.

Momma, Stefan, and Jochen Dörre. 1987. Generation from f-structures. In *Categories, Polymorphism, and Unification*, ed. Ewan Klein and Johan van Benthem, 147–167. Edinburgh: Centre for Cognitive Science.

Netter, Klaus, and Jürgen Wedekind. 1986. An LFG-based Approach to Machine Translation. In *Proceedings of IAI-MT 86*. Saarbrücken.

Reyle, Uwe. 1988. Compositional Semantics for LFG. In *Natural language parsing and linguistic theories*, ed. Uwe Reyle and Christian Rohrer. Dordrecht: D. Reidel.

Wedekind, Jürgen. 1988. Generation as Structure-Driven Derivation. In *Proceedings of COLING-88*, 732–737. Budapest.

Part V

Mathematical and Computational Issues

The original design of the LFG formalism was guided by a combination of different goals. In keeping with the *Competence Hypothesis* (Bresnan and Kaplan 1982; Kaplan and Bresnan 1982), it was intended to permit the statement of linguistic generalizations in a notation that would allow simple, psychologically plausible processing mechanisms to be defined. The notation was also intended to be mathematically tractable and to admit interpretation by simple and efficient processing algorithms.

The concern with mathematical and computational issues was an important way in which the LFG approach was distinguished from other popular formalisms of the 1970's. Transformational grammars, for example, had been shown by Peters and Ritchie (1973) to generate all recursively enumerable sets, and the major computational formalisms, including Augmented Transition Networks (Woods, 1970), Definite Clause Grammars (Pereira and Warren 1980), and Kay's (1967) Powerful Parser formalism, also were known to have that generative capacity. Mathematical analysis sheds little light on the scientifically interesting properties of systems with such descriptive power, and for many computational problems there are no complete and efficient algorithms.

The LFG formalism was set up from the start to provide a direct characterization of the phrasal and functional levels of linguistic representation through a simple composition of two well-known mathematical systems, context-free rewriting grammars and quantifier-free constraints on attribute-value structures. When it was first formulated, this arrangement seemed to be appropriately limited in its expressive power, but a series of later studies was needed to provide a rigorous understanding of its formal properties. At the outset it was obvious that the system had at least the generative capacity of context-free grammars, since context-free devices were properly included in the formalism. At a workshop at Stanford University, Maling and Zaenen (1980) raised the problem of Dutch cross-serial dependencies as a formal challenge for LFG and other nontransformational theories of syntax. Providing the first demonstration that LFG had more than context-free power, the solution to this empirical problem stimulated an initial round of formal investigations.

Kaplan and Bresnan (1982) reported the results of these early studies. They observed that the functional description language was equivalent to the quantifier-free theory of equality, and noted that the equational constraints could be used to code very complex dependencies among different parts of a phrase structure tree. Many of the classical non-context-free formal languages could thus be given very simple grammatical characterizations. Bresnan et al. (1982) made use of these descriptive mechanisms to provide a very simple account of the Dutch phenomena.

Kaplan and Bresnan also worked to establish an upper bound on the power of the system. They showed that the simple composition of context-free and equational systems was very powerful indeed: it could characterize all the recursively enumerable sets. They located the source of this excessive power in the fact that the context-free component could assign an unbounded number of phrase structures to a given string, and each of these might have to be checked for functional validity before the grammaticality of the string could be determined. They proposed a natural restriction on the number of grammatically relevant phrase structures and showed that this condition was necessary and sufficient to guarantee the recursiveness of the overall system and hence the decidability of its recognition problem. Kaplan and Bresnan called this the "nonbranching dominance" condition, but it has become better known in the literature as the condition of "off-line parsability".

A much better understanding of the mathematical properties of LFG emerged from the work of Kelly Roach, then a student at Stanford University. In two papers that were unfortunately never completed or published, Roach examined the LFG notation from the perspective of formal language theory. He showed (Roach 1985) that the class of languages generated by lexical-functional grammars shares many properties with the class of context-free languages. The LFG languages are closed under the operations of union, concatenation, and positive Kleene closure, for example. Also, every LFG language can be characterized by an LFG grammar whose c-structure rules are in Chomsky Normal Form. He also proved a far more interesting normal-form theorem: Every LFG language can be characterized by an LFG grammar with a single c-structure rule in left-linear form (essentially, 'S → (S) word'). Since a c-structure grammar of this form generates only regular languages, Roach's theorem establishes the surprising fact that hierarchical phrase-structure configurations add nothing to the weak generative capacity of the system. As an immediate corollary, Roach showed that the LFG languages, unlike the context-free languages, are closed under intersection.

In another partial manuscript, Roach (1983) proved some other notable propositions. Generalizing on the method of counting f-structures used first by Kaplan and Bresnan (1982), he showed that certain arithmetic operations and their compositions can be simulated by the lengths of the sentences in lexical-functional languages over a one-letter alphabet. These operations include addition, multiplication, and exponentiation, so that, for example, a grammar can be constructed for a language whose strings are of length 2^n for all $n \geq 1$. Roach draws two important consequences from this peculiar construction. Given these operations, it is possible to provide for any Diophantine equation an LFG grammar whose language will be non-empty if and only if that equation has an integer solution. This problem (Hilbert's Tenth) is known to be undecidable, and the emptiness problem for LFGs must therefore be undecidable too. Nishino (1991) later provided another proof of this result using a reduction to Post's Correspondence Problem. Roach's arithmetic operations are also sufficient to produce languages that violate the pumping lemma for the Indexed Languages, indicating that the lexical-functional languages are not contained within that other well-known class.

Mark Johnson's work has also helped to set LFG and related formalisms on a firm mathematical foundation. In his thesis (Johnson 1988), he provided a very precise translation of LFG's functional description language from its somewhat idiosyncratic notation into a more carefully defined 'attribute-value logic'. This brings out more clearly the connection between the LFG formalism and the more standard notation of the first-order quantifier-free theory of equality. It also enables alternative and more rigorous proofs for some previously known properties (for example, decidability with off-line parsability) and leads to a number of new and interesting results. Johnson shows that the attribute-value logic is sound, complete, and compact, and that certain restrictions and extensions of the logic and its models do not affect satisfiability or validity. In later work, represented by his paper in this section "Logic and feature structures", Johnson continues his work on grounding grammatical formalisms in standard mathematical systems. He discusses the Schönfinkel-Bernays subset of first-order logic, pointing out that this class of formulas is rich enough to express the attribute-value specifications found in LFG and other unification formalisms as well as a large family of formal extensions. It immediately follows that the satisfiability problem for all such extensions is decidable.

Another line of research has led to a clearer understanding of the computational properties of LFG. Kaplan and Bresnan (1982) showed that the recognition problem—determining whether or not a given string belongs to the language generated by a given (off-line parsable) LFG grammar— is decidable. They outlined a straightforward algorithm that applies a simple equation solver to functional descriptions instantiated on the trees produced by any context-free parser. They did not analyze the computational complexity either of this particular algorithm or of the recognition problem in general. Berwick (1982) did perform a more careful analysis and demonstrated that LFG recognition belongs to the class of $\mathcal{NP}$-complete problems. This means that LFG recognition is equivalent in its worst-case complexity to a large number of other problems that can be solved very quickly (that is, in $\mathcal{P}$olynomial time) on a $\mathcal{N}$ondeterministic Turing machine. Intuitively, these problems have in common the fact that the correctness of candidate solutions is easy to verify, but a correct candidate may be hidden among an exponentially large number of incorrect possibilities. A nondeterministic Turing machine is a mathematical fiction that operates very quickly because it is charged only for the time it takes to verify correct solutions. A deterministic Turing machine is a more realistic model of computation, but it is charged for the time it takes to search for the candidate solutions as well as for the time to verify each one. There are no known algorithms for solving $\mathcal{NP}$-complete problems on a deterministic Turing machine in less than exponential time.

Exponential algorithms are generally regarded as computationally impractical, and this result suggests that the original goal of obtaining simple and efficient LFG processing algorithms is unattainable. It also raises questions about the likelihood that LFG grammars can be embedded in plausible models of psycholinguistic performance, given the apparent ease with which people can produce and comprehend sentences.

It is important to keep in mind, however, that this result does not take into account other information that might be available in practical or psychological situations to guide the search for solutions. The Competence Hypothesis proposes that a formal grammar comprises only one component of a complete model of performance, and that the behavior of such a model would also be determined by other, nongrammatical processing parameters. Indeed, as Kaplan (1982) observed, the search-with-fast-verify paradigm presents a particular advantage in psycholinguistic modeling. Nongrammatical parameters such as frequency and semantic or pragmatic context can act as imperfect oracles that heuristically influence the search process, as Ford et al. (1982) suggested. This reduces the number of solutions offered for verification while the computational cost of testing each one remains polynomially bounded. Thus, the decomposability of LFG recognition into search and verify processes may aid in constructing performance models that naturally account for the interplay between heuristic guidance and grammatical constraints. The first paper in this section, "Three Seductions of Computational Psycholinguistics", discusses a number of conceptual issues that arise in the attempt to construct computationally explicit performance models, especially ones that incorporate the competence specifications of a formal linguistic theory such as LFG.

It is also important to note that Berwick's $\mathcal{NP}$-completeness result concerns only the worst-case complexity of the formalism. It indicates that for *some* LFG grammar there may be *some* sentence that takes exponential time to recognize. But it may be the case that grammars of actual natural languages lie in a (perhaps difficult to characterize) subset of all possible lexical-functional grammars, and that grammars in this class are in fact amenable to efficient processing. Indeed, Nishino (1991), Seki et al. (1993), and Ando et al. (1994) have identified formal subclasses of the lexical-functional languages that are recognizable in polynomial time, but it is still unknown whether these subclasses provide the necessary degree of linguistic expressiveness. Even if natural languages do not lie in such a restricted subclass, it may be that the sentences that are particularly difficult to process occur quite infrequently and have very unusual structural properties. If either of these possibilities holds true, then it may be possible to discover processing algorithms that operate in polynomial time for usual grammars and usual sentences, exhibiting worst-case complexity only in very rare circumstances.

This section includes two papers that address these computational issues. In "A Method for Disjunctive Constraint Satisfaction", Maxwell and Kaplan examine one major source of exponential behavior, the fact that the functional description language allows simple equations to be embedded in arbitrary Boolean expressions. The most straightforward way of determining the satisfiability of such a formula is first to transform the Boolean expression to disjunctive normal form (DNF) and then to use any of the well-known, fast methods to solve the resulting conjoined sets of equations. The exponential behavior comes from the DNF transformation; this can generate an exponential number of candidate conjunctions to be processed by the polynomial equation solver. Maxwell and Kaplan suggest an alternative processing strategy that defers the disjunctive expansion until after the equation solver has detected possible incompatibilities. If for typical sentences and typical grammars conflicting equations tend to come from nearby substructures, the amount of disjunctive expansion is drastically reduced. Kasper (1987) and Eisele

and Dörre (1988) offer different approaches to the problem of disjunctive expansion.

The second paper by Maxwell and Kaplan, "The Interface between Phrasal and Functional Constraints," considers a potential source of exponential computation that remains even if Boolean combinations of basic equations can be solved quite rapidly, say, by disjunctive unification. The context-free component can generate exponentially many trees for a given string, and the satisfiability of the functional description for each of them must be tested. One particular strategy, bottom-up pruning, for mediating between the phrasal and functional constraint systems is commonly used in implementations of LFG and of other feature-based syntactic formalisms. Maxwell and Kaplan explore a family of other configurations and provide arguments and evidence to suggest that the conventional technique is not the optimal one.

Research on the mathematical and computational properties of LFG and related formalisms is still ongoing. One recent result concerns the generation problem: the problem of determining whether or not, given a particular grammar and a particular functional structure, there exists a string in the language of that grammar that would be assigned that functional structure. Wedekind (1995) has provided an answer to this question, showing that this problem is decidable even, surprisingly, when the condition on off-line parsability is not respected. Other recent work by Blackburn and Gardent (1995) has drawn a connection between the structural correspondence architecture of LFG and formal notions that are currently being explored in modal logic.

References

Ando, S., R. Nakanishi, H. Seki, and T. Kasami. 1994. A polynomial-time recognizable subclass of Lexical-Functional Grammars. *IEICE Transactions on Information and Systems*. Conditionally accepted.

Berwick, Robert. 1982. Computational complexity and Lexical Functional Grammar. *American Journal of Computational Linguistics* 8:20–23.

Blackburn, Patrick, and Claire Gardent. 1995. A specification language for Lexical-Functional Grammars. In *Proceedings of the Seventh Meeting of the European ACL*, 39–44. Dublin. European Chapter of the Association for Computational Linguistics.

Bresnan, Joan, and Ronald M. Kaplan. 1982. Introduction: Grammars as Mental Representations of Language. In *The Mental Representation of Grammatical Relations*. xvii–lii. Cambridge, MA: The MIT Press. Reprinted in Part I of this volume.

Bresnan, Joan, Ronald M. Kaplan, Stanley Peters, and Annie Zaenen. 1982. Cross-serial Dependencies in Dutch. *Linguistic Inquiry* 13:613–635.

Eisele, Andreas, and Jochen Dörre. 1988. Unification of Disjunctive Feature Descriptions. In *Proceedings of the Twenty-Sixth Annual Meeting of the ACL*, 286–294. Buffalo, NY. Association for Computational Linguistics.

Ford, Marilyn, Joan Bresnan, and Ronald M. Kaplan. 1982. A Competence-Based Theory of Syntactic Closure. In *The Mental Representation of Grammatical Relations*, ed. Joan Bresnan. 727–796. Cambridge, MA: The MIT Press.

Johnson, Mark. 1988. *Attribute-Value Logic and the Theory of Grammar*. Doctoral dissertation, Stanford University. Published in the CSLI Lecture Notes series, number 16. 1988. Stanford, CSLI Press.

Kaplan, Ronald M. 1982. Determinism and nondeterminism in modelling psycholinguistic processes. Paper presented to the conference on Linguistic Theory and Psychological Reality Revisited, Princeton University.

Kaplan, Ronald M., and Joan Bresnan. 1982. Lexical-Functional Grammar: A Formal System for Grammatical Representation. In *The Mental Representation of Grammatical Relations*, ed. Joan Bresnan. 173–281. Cambridge, MA: The MIT Press.

Kasper, Robert T. 1987. A Unification Method for Disjunctive Feature Descriptions. In *Proceedings of the Twenty-Fifth Annual Meeting of the ACL*, 235–242. Stanford, CA. Association for Computational Linguistics.

Kay, Martin. 1967. Experiments with a Powerful Parser. In *Proceedings of the Second International Conference on Computational Linguistics*. Grenoble.

Maling, Joan, and Annie Zaenen. 1980. Notes on base-generation and unbounded dependencies. Paper presented to the Sloan Workshop on Alternatives to Transformational Grammar, Stanford University.

Nishino, Tetsuro. 1991. Mathematical analysis of Lexical-Functional grammars. *Language Research* 27(1):119–141.

Pereira, Fernando C. N., and David H. D. Warren. 1980. Definite Clause Grammars for Natural Language Analysis — A Survey of the Formalism and a Comparison with Augmented Transition Networks. *Artificial Intelligence* 13:231–278.

Peters, Stanley, and R. W. Ritchie. 1973. On the Generative Power of Transformational Grammars. *Information Sciences* 6:49–83.

Roach, Kelly. 1983. LFG languages over a 1-letter alphabet. MS, Cognitive and Instructional Sciences Group, Xerox Palo Alto Research Center.

Roach, Kelly. 1985. The Mathematics of LFG. MS, Xerox Palo Alto Research Center.

Seki, H., R. Nakanishi, Y. Kaji, S. Ando, and T. Kasami. 1993. Parallel multiple context-free grammars, finite state translation systems, and polynomial-time recognizable subclasses of Lexical-Functional Grammars. In *Proceedings of the 31st Annual Meeting of Association for Computational Linguistics*, 130–139.

Wedekind, Jürgen. 1995. Some remarks on the decidability of the generation problem in LFG- and PATR-style unification grammars. In *Proceedings of the Seventh Meeting of the European ACL.* Dublin. European Chapter of the Association for Computational Linguistics.

Woods, William A. 1970. Transition Network Grammars for Natural Language Analysis. *Communications of the ACM* 13(10):591–606.

12

Three Seductions of Computational Psycholinguistics

RONALD M. KAPLAN

1 Introduction

Descriptive linguists, computational linguists, and psycholinguists have traditionally been concerned with different aspects of the formal study of language. Linguists want explicit grammatical formulations to characterize the well-formed sentences of a language and to indicate in some systematic way how the sequence of elements that makes up an utterance encodes that utterance's meaning. They don't particularly care about specific processing algorithms that might be used to identify well-formed sentences or to associate them with their meanings, but this is a central concern of computational linguists. Computational linguists are interested in discovering the feasible algorithms that can interpret grammatical descriptions to recognize or produce utterances, and in understanding how the performance of these algorithms depends on various properties of grammars and machine architectures. Psycholinguists are also concerned with processes and algorithms, but not just with ones that are feasible within conventional computational architectures. They focus on algorithms and architectures that model or elucidate the language processing capabilities of human speakers and listeners.

These differences in concern have been the source of much debate over the years, and in some cases, suspicion, misunderstanding and confusion.

This paper is a slightly edited transcript of a talk presented to the workshop on Linguistic Theory and Computer Applications, University of Manchester Institute of Science and Technology, September 1985. It originally appeared in *Linguistic Theory and Computer Applications*, ed. P. Whitelock, M. M. Wood, H. L. Somers, R. Johnson, and P. Bennett (London: Academic Press, 1987), 149–181.

Formal Issues in Lexical-Functional Grammar
edited by
Mary Dalrymple
Ronald M. Kaplan
John T. Maxwell III
Annie Zaenen

The formalisms and methods of one approach have often seemed counterintuitive, if not totally inappropriate, for addressing the problems of the others. But it also happens that what seem like obvious and intuitive strategies for a given approach are actually inappropriate even for addressing its own problems. For each discipline there are certain compelling temptations or seductions that practitioners typically and frequently fall into. In the metaphysical remarks at the beginning of my talk I want to review some of the errors that have come from paying too much attention to intuitions that come from any of these domains. These are temptations that lead you into doing things that you wouldn't really want to do if you understood what was really going on. I have picked out three particular seductions that might spark some discussion later.

Having outlined some of the ways in which one can get off the track, I want to tell you a little bit about Lexical Functional Grammar and how it is organized to avoid some of these seductions. I'll present some fundamental formal concepts that we use in LFG but which I think can be abstracted away from the details of our formalism. I think these mechanisms are common to a variety of formalisms and perhaps represent the right level at which to define a linguistic meta-language.

2 The Procedural Seduction: A Computational Temptation

The first seduction is what I call the procedural seduction, the mistaken belief that you know what to do next and that you can gain computational efficiency by saying what it is. This comes from your intuitions about computation, about how you would actually go about recognizing and generating utterances with specific, concrete algorithms and programs. This kind of seduction had a valid justification in its day. Starting out in the sixties, everybody thought that non-procedural formalisms, such as context-free grammars, were too weak. You couldn't express the generalizations you wanted to express about natural languages in a context-free formalism. If you tried, you would end up with thousands of incomprehensible rules, and merely storing such a grammar would take a major amount of the available memory. You were running on a 1620 that had approximately 2 bytes of memory and this was very important.

Despite the general appeal of declarative systems, there was widespread acceptance in the computational community, if not also the linguistic community, of Chomsky's (1963) arguments that context-free grammars were too weak to support either natural language descriptions or computations. But what the noncomputational linguists were using at the time—transformational grammar—did not seem to offer a reasonable computational alternative. Transformational grammar was neither fish nor fowl: though developed by noncomputational linguists with what we might now call a declarative orientation, the formalism nonetheless relied on an implicit sequential ordering of operations to define valid deep-structure/surface-structure correspondences. This implicit derivation procedure was not regarded as crucial to the theory of grammar—any mathematically equivalent technique for enumerating valid correspondences would do just as well—but in point of fact it was extremely difficult to devise alternative procedures that accurately computed the proper results. Nobody could do any reasonable computations with the transformational grammars that the linguists were actually using. A number of restricted forms of transformational grammar, more or less in the spirit of Chomsky's proposals, were implemented and explored in some detail, but they were not really accepted as serious candidates by a large number of computational linguists.

The solution to that kind of thing was to add more general operations to a simple declarative base. That's what the ATN (Woods 1970) was. Take a very simple thing like a context-free grammar or recursive transition network and add on a way of managing more information by virtue of registers containing information that persisted across a rule or network. You didn't just have a feature value or category value that you could test against some literal locally in the grammar, but you could actually carry information through a network and even up and down the tree. As we saw this morning, Woods did this in the obvious way, given that he was working in LISP. He said 'let's put a list of forms on the arc and we'll simply EVAL them'. He defined a list of primitive forms that you could use—SETR and GETR, etc., but of course everybody who wrote ATN grammars realized that he had provided an escape hatch, a route to arbitrary LISP evaluations. This also provided a seduction to go out and write your own functions, to explore alternative ways of manipulating grammatical, and frequently, process-control information.

Initially people would write actions that were compositions of the primitive functions. But then of course people starting using other random woolly types of computations. It was a reasonable move at the time but it led down the slippery slope (see Figure 1).

Richer formalisms basically allow outputs to be determined by intermediate process steps, intermediate operations and intermediate data that are not theoretically committed. In any linguistic system there are certain kinds of structures that really have some theoretical significance, that you'd like to argue about with somebody and say that that's the way language is, that that's what's in somebody's head or that's what

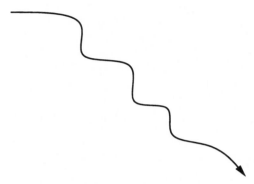

FIGURE 1 The slippery slope

a possible human language can have. Those are the things that you are theoretically committed to.

But in these richer procedural formalisms you get the possibility of determining inputs and outputs by things that you don't really care about, that have to do with particular details, either of your specification or your implementation. You have various combinations of indexing, caches, strategies, extra registers, and the ability to look at the internal implementation state of the parser. You can control what sentences get recognized and what structures can be associated with them by virtue of information that you really don't have a good theoretical grasp on.

The outputs begin to depend on the details of a particular, usually complicated, implementation or interpreter. Complexity is really the key here. The ATN parser in the LUNAR system (Woods, Kaplan, and Nash-Webber 1972), for example, was a 40-page LISP function, each line of which had some particular motivation—perhaps some argument that somebody had made, a process-control feature that somebody might take advantage of, or an accident that somebody left in the code. Because it was trying to allow for various kinds of information flow upwards and downwards through the tree, it was very difficult to understand what the formalism actually meant. The same is true of other powerful procedural systems. The only way you could figure out the input/output behavior of the formalism was to run the one particular program that implemented it. As a scientist, you couldn't get an independent grasp on it, and I regard this as a serious theoretical, if not practical, problem.

The major computational motivation for this was to obtain some degree of fine process control. Let's enrich our grammatical notation a little bit more so that we can actually say, 'do this under these situations but not under those situations', or appeal to pragmatics and say 'we've been going on long enough on this path and it's not worth it, let's cut it off'. By letting process-control specifications into the grammar, you thought you were going to get something that ran more efficiently—you thought you as a grammar writer knew enough about the global parsing situation to give detailed instructions about what to do next. If you looked at ATN grammars you saw people beginning to invent new ways of doing that kind of thing—suggesting constructs for splitting configurations and merging them back together, having exclusive OR instead of inclusive OR, etc.

The reason I claim that this approach is seductive is because it doesn't get you where you want to go, whether you're a linguist or a computer scientist. In hindsight it seems that whenever the sequential, procedural facilities of the ATN formalism were used, some sort of linguistic error was being committed, in the sense that generalizations were not being expressed. You ended up with a grammar which could be correctly describing all the sentences of the language but would have replication and redundancy, would be patched all over the place to make up for some basic deficiencies.

To give you just one example of that, take the interaction between passive and tag questions. The traditional way of doing passive in an ATN is to find the initial noun phrase and call it the subject as a first guess. Then as you go from left to right, if you later discover that there is a form of the verb *be* and a passive participle, you swap the registers around. You take what was the subject and make it be the object and then if you later find an animate by-phrase you make that the subject. That was seen as a smooth move in those days and became, in fact, one of the intuitive successes that ATN advocates (including Woods 1970; Woods, Kaplan, and Nash-Webber 1972; and Kaplan 1972) could point to.

One of the reasons was that the only alternative that people could conceive of was to say 'active and passive are nondeterministic alternatives; you take the one that corresponds to active and if that doesn't work out then you fail all the way back to the beginning. Starting again at the initial state, you go off on another path corresponding to passive'. The procedural perception of the way a parser would behave with a grammar of this sort is that it would have done a lot of work recognizing that initial noun phrase, which could have been a complicated, elaborate structure. Upon determining that the sentence isn't active, all the information about the initial noun phrase is thrown away, and the parser goes off on a completely separate nondeterministic path, rediscovering exactly the same internal structure of that initial noun phrase.

Thus register swapping was the canonical technique for doing the active and passive in the ATN. The problem with this strategy is that it loses track of the surface subject. When you consider tag questions, such as

(1) a. John saw the girl, didn't he?
     b. The girl was seen by John, wasn't she?

you see that the tag pronoun agrees with the surface subject, not the deep subject, and the identity of the surface subject was lost in the passive register swapping. The grammar would have to be expanded, either by listing separate transitions for passive-tags and active-tags, or by also keeping track of the surface subject in addition to the deep one. But then the intuitive advantages of the ATN analysis begin to disappear. This is not the only example where register swapping is associated with a loss of generalization—in fact, in retrospect I think that all instances of register swapping in my original LUNAR grammar suffered from linguistic defects of this sort.

Process-control specifications in the grammar also cause you to lose what I call an 'ideal-convergent language characterization'. This is discussed briefly in Bresnan and Kaplan (1982) and is really a separate talk, so I'll say just a few words about it now. The basic idea is that you can evaluate theories of grammar-based processing as to whether their behavior corresponds to the behavior of an ideal native speaker in the limit as the amount of available processing resources goes to infinity. Of course, the behavior of an ideal native speaker, one who knows his language perfectly and is not affected by restrictions of memory or processing time, lapses of attention, and so forth, is difficult to observe. But as psycholinguistic methods and technologies improve, we can imagine doing experiments in which we somehow vary the cognitive resources of real speakers and hearers, by removing distractions, giving them scratch-pad memories, etc. We can then take the limiting, asymptotic behavior of real speakers as approximations to the behavior of the ideal. A grammar-based processing model which, when given more and more computational resources, more and more accurately simulates the behavior of the ideal has the 'ideal-convergent' property. But when you have things like cutting off paths and heuristically destroying options in the grammar you lose the ability to converge on this fiction of the ideal native speaker. Similarly, Marcus' deterministic parsing system is also not ideal-convergent: if the grammar explicitly indicates how many buffer cells to use, the behavior of the system will not change if more memory resources are added.

More seriously from the perspective of natural language processing, just when you think that you're getting computational efficiency, in fact you might be losing it. This is because you're committing yourself to more specific details of implementation by letting constraints on the step-by-step order of execution sneak out into your grammar specification. So you lose the ability to have alternative implementations that might be suitable for some purposes but not for others. A case in point is island-driving with an ATN (Bates 1976). The idea is that in speech recognition you might not want to start at the beginning of a sentence but instead start processing outward in both directions from an island of reliability, a word in a speech wave that's easily and reliably identified, and use that as a pivot point for your analysis. The order of computation thus differs markedly from the order defined by the canonical interpretation of left-to-right register-setting operations and top-down sending and lifting. It's possible but very difficult to vary the order of execution and still get the correct results. John Carroll (1983), one of Karen Sparck Jones' students at Cambridge, did an implementation, and it was also tried in the BBN speech system. Martin Kay and I looked at the problem and decided there has to be a different way of thinking about things. The ability to tune an implementation to take advantage of heuristically available information is drastically reduced if your grammatical specifications are committed to particular execution orders, as was the ATN.

You can also get a loss of efficiency, because your specification language now is so complex and is trying to describe so much about the process that you lose the ability to have automatic compile-time and run-time optimizations. You're really relying on the grammar writer to put in the optimization. But in many cases the grammar writer really doesn't know what's going on, doesn't have a sense of the global structure of the grammar. But there may be algorithms that can systematically reorganize the grammar in various ways, compile it in various ways, if there's a lot of freedom of implementation and not a lot of overspecification of exactly what the flow of control should be. If the flow of control is overspecified then rearranging it can change the input-output relations in ways that a compiler can't figure out. So you can actually lose the possibility of performing significant compile-time optimizations.

One kind of run-time optimization that you lose in the ATN is the use of a well-formed substring table that can save exactly the work that the grammar writer was trying to save in doing the passive as outlined above. With a well-formed substring table, that initial noun phrase would be remembered as a noun phrase, independent of the role it plays in the larger sentential context. But because the ATN formalism allows information to be passed around in such complex ways, it was difficult and costly to simulate even a simple well-formed substring table in the original ATN, and there were no net efficiency advantages.

In sum, it's not necessarily the case that when you want to get ef-

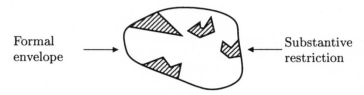

FIGURE 2 The shape of a linguistic theory

ficiency you should allow yourself more procedural specification. That's the point of the first seduction.

3 The Substance Seduction: A Linguistic Temptation

The substance seduction is the mistaken belief that you know what you're talking about. This is a typical pitfall of linguistic approaches. We had some discussion of this yesterday, that linguists are interested in restrictions, imposing substantive constraints. They take the driving meta-theoretical goal to be to characterize all and only the possible human languages.

But the problem is that, at least in the current state of the art, they don't know which generalizations and restrictions are really going to be true and correct, and which are either accidental, uninteresting or false. The data just isn't in; indeed, the definitive data may in fact be psychological and not linguistic in nature. So if we try to restrict our formalisms by taking substance into account, what we think is true of possible languages, we're apt to make a number of mistakes, some of which have undesirable consequences. Premature identification of substantive generalizations may lead to grammatical descriptions that complicate, or even defy, formal specification. I have a little picture here to illustrate the point (Figure 2).

A formal theory might have a relatively smooth outline and be easy to implement, well-behaved mathematically, and so forth. Then you start taking chunks out of it (shown shaded) because you claim that no human language or no grammar has such and such a property. The functional locality restriction that was proposed for LFG is an example. This stipulates that no functional designator can be specified with more than two function applications, and thus introduces a notational complication into the formalism. But it doesn't really restrict the kinds of sentences that can be accepted or the kinds of structures that can be assigned to them. It is thus a theoretical complication for which direct empirical support is difficult, if not impossible, to come up with.

With restrictions like these, you may end up with a formalism that has very bizarre and irregular contours, that is very difficult to understand mathematically or to implement correctly. This is because it has all sorts of special 'don't do this in this situation, do do this in that situation' conditions that are not directly visible in the grammar itself. By imposing restrictions on the basis of what you think can or cannot happen, you're in effect adding special conditions to the notation's interpretation, complicating its definition. Often these restrictions turn out to be computationally or mathematically inconsequential, in that they impose no true restriction on what may be computed, as in the case of functional locality. Substantive hypotheses about the nature of human language, even inconsequential ones that complicate our formalisms, are important to pay attention to if they have some convincing empirical support. But I don't think we should regard three examples in one language or one example in each of three languages as particularly convincing, and this exaggerates only slightly the kind of evidence behind many constraints that linguists have proposed.

It's a mistake to carry premature and unjustified substantive hypotheses into our computational and mathematical work, especially if that leads to mathematically complex, even if more restrictive, theories. We should let considerations of mathematical and computational simplicity have higher priority in defining the formal envelope in which to do our work. Until we can more clearly recognize the true substantive generalizations, we should be wary of the seduction of substance.

4 The Interaction Seduction:
A Psycholinguistic/Computational Temptation

People have been proving the obvious for years now, that people don't process modularly. If you look at very fine time grains in human sentence processing, one way or another, you will likely find out that pragmatic information is being processed while you're still trying to figure out what the first phoneme is, before you've figured out the noun phrase, before you figure out what the predicate is and so forth. Many studies have been done to demonstrate this unsurprising point. The conclusion that computational linguists and psycholinguists have often drawn from these demonstrations is that no modular theory, no theory that, for example, separates out syntax and semantics or morphology and syntax, can possibly provide an accurate psychological model. This is the interaction seduction: the mistaken belief that just because information from all linguistic levels can be shown to interact in human language processing, modular theories of that process should be rejected as incorrect and undesirable.

As computational linguists you might or might not care about having an accurate psychological model. But whether or not you're interested in psychology, your intuitions about what's good and what's bad are informed by your psychological world-view, your own intuitions about how you process. You might also conclude that reasonable computational frameworks must therefore have syntactic specifications and processes mixed up and integrated with, for example, phonetic and semantic specifications and processes. This kind of intermixing of constraints from what are typically thought of as different linguistic levels is just what you find in so-called semantic grammars. These grammars embody the view that different kinds of linguistic constraints must be intermixed because the information that they deal with can be shown to interact in observable language processing behavior.

But this is a confusion of two quite separate issues, simulation and explanation. As scientists, we are not merely interested in simulating human behavior—in constructing a black box that behaves exactly as people behave, has the same profiles of complexity and so forth. What we're really interested in as scientists is explanation—in developing models that help us understand how it is that people behave that way, not merely demonstrating that we can build an artifact that behaves similarly. We don't want to replace one black box, namely a person, by another black box, namely the artifact that we've built. We should look for modular theories that account for the observed interactions in terms of the interleaving of information from separate, scientifically comprehensible subsystems.

In the interaction seduction we fail to distinguish the static specification of a system from its execution behavior. It should be an obvious point that in principle you can have separate specification of syntax and semantics and pragmatics and still, at run-time, have those operations interleaved and depend on one another in a very intricate way. But it has been difficult to come up with modular formalisms and theories that have enough descriptive power and yet also allow for run-time integration of constraints.

I think this is sometimes confounded with the procedural seduction. If your syntactic theory is very very complex—because it has lots of procedural specifications or its interpretation is basically a complex procedure— then it's going to be very difficult to see how interleaving can take place. You have to be able to understand in a kind of abstract and mathematical way, in a manipulable way, the structure of your formalism in order to be able to use compilation techniques or even run-time interpretation techniques that will interleave the syntax and semantics.

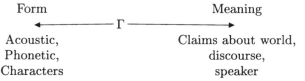

FIGURE 3 Grammatical mapping between form and meaning

Those are some of the issues that I think have been confused, and are confusing, in the development of computational and linguistic theories. There are many many more. What I want to do for the remainder of my time is to get a little bit more concrete about the strategy that we took in developing the LFG theory, to try to get at the primitive mechanisms that I think are implicit in many, if not all, linguistic theories.

5 The Grammatical Mapping Problem

The basic problem that we are confronting is what I call 'the grammatical mapping problem'—the problem of characterizing and computing the mapping Γ between the surface form of an utterance and its meaning (the claims that it makes about the world, the discourse, the speaker, and so forth) (Figure 3).

This is a very simple and abstract view—that what linguistics is about, what we're trying to do in computational linguistics, is to be able to map back and forth between form (the external representation) and meaning.

It is an obvious observation that the external forms vary. They vary from language to language. The same thing said in different languages is totally different. Even within a language you have different ways of saying basically the same thing. Internal representations from language to language presumably are the same, they have a universal character that doesn't vary. Moreover, it seems that this mapping is in some sense simple and transparent, since, by virtue of perceiving an external form, human beings seem able to quickly and easily discover what its meaning is. Yet it also seems that the mapping is quite complex. There are ambiguities and paraphrase relations and dependencies that operate over long stretches of an utterance, and these have defied clear and simple specifications in any number of explicit theories over the years. The challenge for linguistic theories is to give a transparent account of these mapping complexities.

Once you characterize how forms and meanings relate to each other, there's something else that you want as well. You want effective procedures for mapping back and forth between form and meaning, both for practical purposes—natural language processing—but also for the theoretical purposes, to account for the fact that people can do this kind of thing. If you have a formal system that describes what the relationship is, but it's not computable, you haven't really approached the psychological question of how it is that people can do this sort of thing.

We suggest that the fundamental computational linguistic problem is what we call 'structure mapping'. Generative linguistics tends to think of generation as the thing that grammars are supposed to do—generate all and only the acceptable sentences of a language. I don't think that's right, particularly if you take the view that grammatical mapping is what we're after. What we really need to be concerned with is not the generation of structures but the correspondences or mappings between structures. What I claim is that there is a nice way of thinking about structure mappings that, to use the terms that came up in discussion yesterday, is not only simple and general but also useful, and that it's common to all the various theories and formalisms that Stuart [Shieber] talked about and some others as well. (Henry [Thompson] observed that the notions of generality and usefulness are distinct and there has been some confusion about that. But Turing machines are simple and general but not useful, that is they don't really illuminate the problems that we would like to solve.)

The notion of structure mapping also gives us a basis for comparing theories at a more refined level. Theories can differ in the kinds of mathematical structures—trees, strings, functions, etc.—that they allow, the kinds of mappings between structures that they support, and the empirical interpretation they give to these structures and mappings. You can have mappings between similar kinds of structures—trees to trees as in transformational grammar and for which there's a fair amount of technology. But you can also have mappings between dissimilar structures, between strings and trees as in context-free grammars, or between trees and functions, strings and functions, and so on.

Theories can also differ in the kinds of specifications of these mappings that they provide. You can have procedural specifications that tell you how to construct the output from the input by a particular sequence of operations, but you can also have declarative specifications that tell you what the output is given the input but don't necessarily say what you should do to compute it. If somebody gives you an input and says 'I think this is an output', then you can verify whether or not that's the case. But given the input you can't necessarily go and construct the output. That's what I take to be the major difference between procedural and declarative specifications.

6   Lexical-Functional Grammar

I'm going to use LFG as an example of these things but again I think that
the ideas generalize beyond that. Basically what we have is very simple—
the formal notions of structure in the abstract, of structural description
and of structural correspondence. Those are the three aspects of this
notion of structure mapping that I want to get at.

Now I'm going to make it a bit more concrete. In LFG there are at
least three kinds of structures, levels of representation, for a sentence.
There's the word string that makes up the external form of the sentence,
for example (2). There's the constituent phrase structure, which varies
across languages, where you have traditional surface structure (3) and
parts of speech labeling categories, perhaps a feature system on those
categories (although in the case of LFG if there is one it's a very weak
one).

(2)   I saw the girl.

(3)

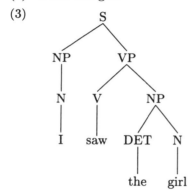

The third kind of structure is the 'functional structure' (f-structure).
We claim this is nearly invariant across languages and is a formal representation of notions like subject and object and case and so forth (4).

(4)
$$
\begin{bmatrix}
\text{PRED} & \text{'see} \langle (\uparrow \text{ SUBJ}), (\uparrow \text{ OBJ}) \rangle \text{'} \\
\text{TENSE} & \text{PAST} \\
\text{SUBJ} & \begin{bmatrix} \text{PRED} & \text{'pro'} \\ \text{PERS} & 1 \\ \text{NUM} & \text{SG} \end{bmatrix} \\
\text{OBJ} & \begin{bmatrix} \text{PRED} & \text{'girl'} \\ \text{DEF} & + \\ \text{PERS} & 3 \\ \text{NUM} & \text{SG} \end{bmatrix}
\end{bmatrix}
$$

Structure (4) is a mathematical function that takes atomic attributes into values that might also be functions, structure (3) is a tree, structure (2) is a string. Here are three kinds of structure, and the reason why LFG illustrates the issues of structure mapping better than transformational grammar is that we really are consciously mapping between structures of different formal types. You can't rely on the same kinds of predicates being applicable both to the input and the output.

7 Structures and Structural Descriptions

Well, very abstractly and simply, what is a structure? The simplest mathematical notion of a structure is a set of elements with some defined relations and properties. Strings are one example: for a string like *abc*, the elements are the set of words and the only relation is the linear precedence relationship. For trees (or 'c-structures') you have (5): the elements are a set of nodes N, you have a mother function M that takes nodes into nodes, a precedence relation < and a labeling function λ that takes nodes into some other finite labeling set L.

(5) N: set of nodes
   M: N $\rightarrow$ N
   < $\subseteq$ N $\times$ N
   λ: N $\rightarrow$ L

And for f-structures you have (6), where F, the set of f-structures is defined as the solution to these recursive domain equations. Something is an f-structure, it belongs to the set, if it's a symbol or if it's a function from symbols into that set.

(6) S: set of symbols
   F = S + (S $\rightarrow$ F)

Basically, the set of f-structures is the set of hierarchical finite tabular functions—sets of ordered pairs satisfying a uniqueness condition where the value itself can be a set of ordered pairs also satisfying a uniqueness condition, and so on. The only defining relation for these structures is function application. A function f applied to a symbol s has some value v if and only if the pair <s,v> is in that set f, as in (7) (using LISP parenthetic notation).

(7) (f s) = v iff <s v> $\in$ f

So those are some examples of structures. They happen to be, as I said, the ones that we use in LFG.

We next observe that structures can be described in terms of the properties and relations by which they are defined. So if I have a tree (8):

(8)

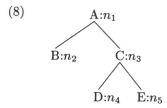

I can write down a description of that tree (having given the nodes some sort of names, n_1, n_2, etc.): the mother of n_2 is n_1, the label of n_1 is A, and so forth. A complete description of this tree is provided by the set of equations (9):

(9)
$$M(n_2) = n_1 \quad M(n_4) = n_3$$
$$\lambda(n_1) = A \quad M(n_5) = n_3$$
$$\lambda(n_2) = B \quad \lambda(n_4) = D$$
$$M(n_3) = n_1 \quad \lambda(n_5) = E$$
$$\lambda(n_3) = C \quad n_4 < n_5$$
$$n_2 < n_3$$

Given a tree I can write down a set of propositions that that tree satisfies. I can also write down a set of propositions that a given f-structure satisfies. For the f-structure in (10), where the names f_i are marked on the opening brackets, I can write f_1 applied to q is the value f_2, f_2 applied to s is t, and so forth (11).

(10)
$$f_1: \begin{bmatrix} q & f_2: \begin{bmatrix} s & t \\ u & v \end{bmatrix} \\ w & x \end{bmatrix}$$

(11)
$$(f_1 \ q) = f_2$$
$$(f_2 \ s) = t$$
$$(f_2 \ u) = v$$
$$(f_1 \ w) = x$$

Structures can thus be described by their properties and relations. Conversely, given a consistent description, the structures that satisfy it may be discovered—but not always. It depends on the complexity of the description language. For the simple functional domain of f-structures descriptions that involve only equality and function application can be solved by an attribute-value merging or unification operator (e.g. Kaplan and Bresnan 1982). But one could imagine algebraic systems with complex uninvertible operators where the algebraic descriptions are just not solvable. One would like to know when one crosses into that kind of space, or at least when one would cross into it so that one doesn't. It's not always obvious. But in the simple domains that seem to appear in linguistic work it is decidable whether any structures exist that satisfy a given description and there are algorithms for producing these satisfying structures.

A set of propositions in a given structural description is usually satisfied by many structures. The description (9) is satisfied by the tree (8) but it is also satisfied by an infinite number of larger trees (e.g. (12)). It is true of this tree that the mother of n_2 is n_1 and, indeed, all the equations in (9) are true of it. But this tree has nodes beyond the ones described in (9) and it satisfies additional propositions that the tree in (8) does not satisfy.

(12)

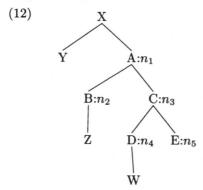

Similarly, for the description (11) of the f-structure (10), there are infinitely many larger f-structures, such as (13), that also satisfy the same set of equations.

(13)
$$f_1: \begin{bmatrix} q & f_2: \begin{bmatrix} s & t \\ u & v \\ a & b \end{bmatrix} \\ w & x \\ c & f_3 \begin{bmatrix} d & e \\ g & h \end{bmatrix} \end{bmatrix}$$

In general, structures that satisfy descriptions form a semi-lattice that is partially ordered by the amount of information they contain. The minimal structure satisfying the description may be unique if the description itself is determinate, if there are enough conditions specified, enough equations and not too many unknowns. The notion of minimality figures in a number of different ways within the LFG theory, to capture some intuitions of restriction and constraint, but unless there are questions I don't think I'll go into that. Minimality also enters into LFG's definition of grammaticality: we reject a string as ungrammatical if its functional description does not have a unique minimal solution.

8 Structural Correspondences

Having made some straightforward observations about structures and structural descriptions, we now turn to the last important idea, the concept of a structural correspondence. Structures of different types can be set in correspondence by a piecewise function. If you have structures of any two types, it doesn't matter what they are, then you can define a piecewise function that goes from the elements of one of the structures into the elements of the other structure. In (14) I've given the example of a function ϕ that goes from the nodes of a tree into f-structure space.

(14) ϕ: N → F

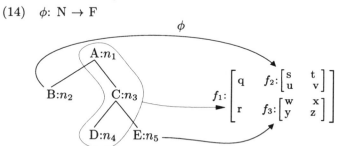

Node n_1 maps onto f_1 and node n_2 maps onto f_2, and so forth. You have two structures and a function that connects them, that sets them in correspondence. This is just a mathematical function, there's no procedure attached to it. But once you assume this sort of correspondence, then the descriptions of elements in its range can be defined in terms of the elements and relations of its domain. Previously we described an f-structure by specifying only f-structure properties and elements. Now, with the f-structure elements assumed to correspond to tree nodes, we can describe the f-structure in terms of the mother-daughter relationships in the tree.

In (14), for example, if we take the mother of node n_2 in the tree and take its functional structure and apply it to q, then we get the functional structure corresponding to node n_2. If we take the functional structure of node n_2 and apply it to s we get t, the functional structure of node n_5 applied to y is z, and so forth in (15).

(15) $((\phi \; (M \; n_2)) \; q) = (\phi \; n_2)$
$((\phi \; n_2) \; s) = t$
$((\phi \; n_5) \; x) = z$

Thus the f-structure is characterized in terms of function-application in the f-structure description language, but also in terms of the mother function and possibly other relations in the tree. Our notions of structural description and structural correspondence combine in this way so that the description of a range structure can involve both its own native relations but also the properties of a corresponding domain structure.

A structural correspondence set up in this way has to be a function but it doesn't have to be one-to-one. We can have several nodes in the tree that map onto the same f-structure; the correspondence ϕ in (14) maps the nodes n_1, n_3, and n_4 all onto the same f-structure f_1. When we have several nodes mapping onto the same f-structure, that f-structure in some sense becomes an equivalence class or quotient of nodes induced by the correspondence. It represents the folding together or normalization of information carried jointly by the individual nodes that map onto it.

A structural correspondence also may not be 'onto'. This is illustrated by (16), which shows the c-structure and f-structure that might be appropriate for a sentence containing a gerund with a missing subject.

(16)

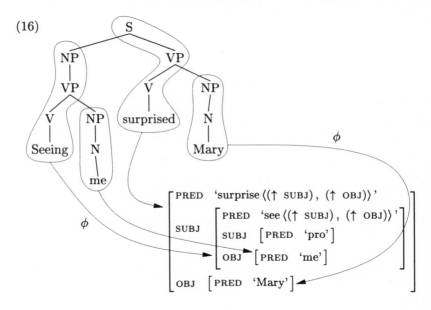

In most phrasally-based theories you would postulate an empty node on the tree side in order to represent the fact that there is an understood subject, a dummy subject, because subjects (and predicate-argument relations) are represented in those theories by particular node configurations. In LFG, given that the notion of subject is defined in the range of the correspondence, we don't need the empty node in the tree. Instead, the f-structure's description, derived from the tree relations of the gerund c-structure, can have an equation that specifies directly that the subject's predicate is an anaphoric pronoun, with no node in the tree that it corresponds to. This account of so-called null anaphors in terms of the non-onto nature of the structural correspondence has a number of interesting mathematical consequences, but I won't go into them here.

I have been presenting some very very simple ideas. I want to keep coming back to this notion of simplicity because if it's simple you can see alternative implementations, you can begin to understand some mathematical properties. Yet I want to claim that this is a basis for much of what we do, not only in LFG but in other theories as well.

Continuing on, we note that a correspondence may induce non-native relationships in its range. For example, the precedence relation is a native relationship in the constituent structure—it is a defining condition of c-structure that nodes may be linearly ordered. But f-structures are functions, they don't have a precedence relationship defined on them. But we can construct an f-structure precedence relationship as a natural image of c-structure precedence. For two f-structures, f_1 and f_2, f_1 f-precedes f_2 if and only if for all nodes n_1 in the inverse image of f_1 and for all nodes n_2 in the inverse image of f_2, those nodes are in the proper c-structure relationship (17).

(17)　$f_1 <_f f_2$ iff
　　　for all $n_1 \in \phi^{-1}(f_1)$ and for all $n_2 \in \phi^{-1}(f_2)$,
　　　$n_1 <_c n_2$

We have already seen that there is a deformation of the distinctions in the domain structure as you go through the many-to-one mappings to get into the range quotient classes. Defining relations also get deformed in the same way—you get quotients of the relations as well. That turns out also to be useful—it seems that f-precedence as a degraded image of c-precedence gives a nice account of certain constraints on anaphoric relations (Bresnan 1984).

Let me now summarize the formal architecture of LFG. In LFG the c-structure trees are the external syntactic structures representing surface phrase configurations. They are very concrete, highly constrained by the actual words in the string, in contrast to the more abstract phrase-structures of some other theories. There are no empty nodes in LFG c-structures, for example. The f-structures represent the abstract, internal grammatical relations, the notions of subject and object and predicate and so forth. There is a structural correspondence that maps the c-structure nodes to f-structure units. This mapping is many to one, and this fact gives us a way of accounting for intuitions of control, headedness, and some cases of feature propagation. It is also not onto, and that's how we represent zero anaphora.

The allowable c-structures for a sentence are specified by a context-free grammar. The grammar doesn't generate the f-structures directly: it generates a functional description, and the minimal f-structures, if any, that satisfy it represent that sentence's grammatical relations. Thus we have a generative system for descriptions of f-structures based on an independent, context-free way of describing c-structures. This way of looking at things differs conceptually, even if not in mathematical power, from other approaches in which, intuitively, the internal structures, not descriptions of them, are directly generated.

Notation is a very important issue in the design of a linguistic theory, particularly if what you're trying to do is to get other people to use it. If you just want to use it yourself then perhaps it's not such a big deal because you know what you mean.

In LFG, the way descriptions of the f-structure are derived is this: you start with an ordinary context-free rule such as (18) which tells you what phrase structure you can have—it defines allowable phrase structure configurations. This can be used to generate nodes in an acceptable tree or to match against nodes of an existing tree to verify that it is acceptable. We let the symbol * stand for the node that is generated by or matches against a particular element in the right-side of the rule. Then, using that symbol, the mother function, and the structural correspondence, we can write general propositions about the f-structures that correspond to the nodes in any tree configuration that satisfies this rule. In (18) we specify that the f-structure corresponding to the NP's mother applies to SUBJ to give the f-structure corresponding to the NP, and that the f-structure corresponding to the mother of the VP, namely the S node, is also the f-structure corresponding to the VP. The terms of this notational system are category-equation pairs.

(18) S $\longrightarrow$ NP VP
$$((\phi \circ M \ *) \ \text{SUBJ}) = (\phi \ *) \qquad (\phi \circ M \ *) = (\phi \ *)$$

We then simplify to a more convenient notation. We use up-arrow ($\uparrow$) to stand for the composition of the structural correspondence with the mother function, and down-arrow ($\downarrow$) to stand for the structural correspondence applied to the current node *. This reduces the annotation on the NP to (19), which you can read as 'my mother's f-structure's subject is my f-structure'.

(19) $(\uparrow \ \text{SUBJ}) = \downarrow$

Having such an intuitive natural language paraphrase is very important, if what you're trying to do is to export a notation or formalism.

This brings up a point that I was talking about to Karen [Sparck Jones] at lunch and that she said I should mention: the 'Trojan horse' theory of computational linguistics. This relates to what Gerald [Gazdar] said [in his presentation]. Linguists don't really design formalisms, or at least, they don't seem to design very good ones. It is the business of computational linguists to do this, and this is what we're skilled at. But we've got to design formalisms that linguists will use, to make sure that they don't come up and start using formalisms that are unimplementable. Then they'll do all their work finding out all these wonderful facts about language, even writing them down, in a way that we can't deal with. We want to come up with formalisms that we can get linguists to adopt, as a Trojan horse, to attract them to what we believe is the right way of doing things, to ways which will help us to do our work. It takes a fair amount of care and attention to design appealing formalisms; we actually spend a lot of time worrying about these issues as we developed the LFG framework.

(20) is just to give you an example of a little bit more of an LFG grammar. This shows that the equations that describe the f-structure in terms of the c-structure come not only from rules in the grammar but also from entries in the lexicon, and these have exactly the same interpretation. We don't make a distinction between the syntax and the lexicon in a theory like this. If you have a language like Eskimo where all the work is done in the lexicon and the morphology, you can do it within this framework just as well as you can handle a language like English.

(20) *the*   DET $(\uparrow$ SPEC$) =$ DEF

     man   N $(\uparrow$ PRED$) =$ 'man'
                    $(\uparrow$ PERS$) = 3$
                    $(\uparrow$ NUM$) =$ SG

     walks   V $(\uparrow$ PRED$) =$ 'walk $\langle(\uparrow$ SUBJ$)\rangle$ '
                    $(\uparrow$ SUBJ NUM$) =$ SG
                    $(\uparrow$ SUBJ PERS$) = 3$
                    $(\uparrow$ TENSE$) =$ PRES

The LFG notation is thus based on the simple notions of structure, structural description, and structural correspondence.

9 Extensions and Variations

There are various extensions, generalizations and restrictions that one might consider once you have this as the space you're working in. You can think about extending the structural domain, that is, allowing in structures that have more properties, more kinds of relations. In the original version of LFG (Kaplan and Bresnan 1982) we allowed slightly richer structures than I've discussed so far in this talk. We also allowed sets of f-structures to be values in f-structure ordered pairs. That was done originally so that we could have a representation for multiple adjuncts, but we mentioned in a footnote that if we only understood how to do conjuncts we would do it that way too. Since then we've actually done a lot of work on conjunction and in fact do use sets to represent the conjoined items. It is worth noting that there is no obvious encoding of membership relations in the PATR formalism, which goes against Shieber's claim (Shieber 1987) that LFG is reducible to PATR.

You can fiddle around with the description language without actually changing the domain that you're describing. Take the set of trees as your structures and the description language that I gave in (5) which had a mother function and a precedence relation. You can say 'look, what we want is the left daughter function, that's the thing that we want to use to describe trees'. Or 'we want to take the closure of the mother function' to express some long-distance dependencies. You want to be able to refer to some node arbitrarily far above some other node, as Mitch [Marcus] has been doing in his D-theory (Marcus 1987). You invent some new notation to be part of the description language but it's describing structures that are the same sort as you had originally. This is different than the set-membership case, where new kinds of elements were added to the structural domain.

As another example of changing the description language, we are now proposing to allow regular expressions over attribute names in our function application specifications, thus formalizing a notion of *functional uncertainty*. Under this proposal you can specify the result of applying an f-structure to COMP* OBJ, where the Kleene * indicates that you can go down through an arbitrary chain of complements to get to one with an object that you can then say something about. This provides an alternative to the LFG account of long-distance dependencies given in Kaplan and Bresnan (1982, 231 ff.). Originally we did it in terms of the M* relationship—this was implicit in the double-up and double-down metavariables—but I now believe it was a mistake to define long-distance dependencies in terms of c-structure configurations. We were misled by our phrasal, transformational linguistic upbringing. If you look carefully at the old data and also at some new data, you find that a much better account can be given in terms of a long-distance relationship on f-structures, specified in this regular extension to the language of functional descriptions. It's a question of which side of ϕ you have the long-distance relation on. I now think you should have long-distance relations in the range of ϕ instead of its domain. This makes the claim that properties of the c-structure, such as category, that don't carry through the structural correspondence are irrelevant to long-distance dependencies.

You can also fool around with the way that descriptions of structures can be generated. To a certain extent I think this is what Mitch [Marcus] is doing in D-theory. We can think of a context-free grammar, for example, as involving a structural correspondence between strings and trees. We can write it down in terms of the concatenation relationship and perhaps lexical information about the words, which carry descriptions of tree relations like the mother of the mother of this node is the mother of that node, and so forth. You can take a context-free grammar and re-represent it in that kind of descriptive language, although the notation would probably be quite inconvenient. What I think Mitch is saying is 'if you think of descriptions as the thing that you're operating with, there are other ways of generating descriptions than the full set of context-free rule formalisms'. He introduces templates and other new notational conventions (e.g. the expression i → p v is to be interpreted as allowing p* v*). He's exploring the space of description generation mechanisms and how they might be restricted or constrained from other ways that you might think of for mapping between strings and trees.

You can also think about multiple levels of representation related by multiple correspondences. Clearly you can have a correspondence between any two levels of structure, but each of those can correspond to other kinds of structures by means of other correspondence functions. You might have correspondences among c-structures, f-structures, anaphoric structures, semantic structures, island structures, structures to represent the sharing of any kind of information among the elements of the word-string. If the range of one correspondence is the domain of another, the composition of the two correspondence functions might have interesting properties. If two correspondences are defined on the same domain, you have independent mappings representing notionally different equivalence classes of information. Either way, it is possible to give modular specifications of different kinds of linguistic information with interactions encoded implicitly by the requirement that the different structural descriptions be mutually or simultaneously satisfied. If no collection of related structures exists with all the specified properties, that might be reason to mark the sentence as ungrammatical.

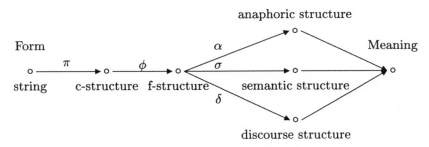

FIGURE 4 Decomposition of Γ

This is what we do in LFG, of course. The f-structure description mechanism serves as a filter because the described f-structure does not exist if the description is inconsistent. This would be the case if you said the subject's number was singular on the noun phrase node and the subject's number was plural on the verb phrase node. The verb phrase's f-structure is the same as the sentence's f-structure, so you're talking about the same attribute. You would have an inconsistency. There is no function that has subject with number with value singular and number with value plural, because f-structures are functions and functions have a uniqueness condition. So there is no f-structure that can satisfy that description and that is one of the formal characterizations of ungrammaticality.

I'll illustrate the use of multiple correspondences by going back to the problem I started out with, the problem of characterizing the grammatical mapping between form and meaning. We can use multiple correspondences to get a decomposition of the grammatical mapping Γ into hopefully coherent and illuminating sub-mappings between linguistically interesting structures. One hypothetical arrangement of structural correspondences is shown in Figure 4. Starting out with the word string, we assume a structural correspondence π that takes us to the constituent structure. The c-structure is then mapped by φ to the functional structure, in the usual LFG way. We might then postulate a further correspondence σ from f-structure to units of a semantic structure of the sort that Halvorsen (1983) has proposed. This is much closer to a meaning representation: it explicitly marks predicate-argument relationships, quantifier scope ambiguities, and so forth—dependencies and properties that don't enter into syntactic generalizations (at least as we currently believe and recognize) but do enter into meaning. We might also include another correspondence α defined on f-structures that maps them onto anaphoric structures: two f-structure units map onto the same element of anaphoric structure just in case they are coreferential; this is how the intuition of coreference is formalized under this view. The figure also shows a mapping δ from f-structure to a level of discourse structure, which would give a separate formal account of discourse notions such as topic and focus. The patterns of correspondences would indicate how these are related to the grammatical functions, nodes in the phrase structure, and words in the string. The anaphoric and discourse structures, like the semantic structure, also contribute to meaning representations. By fitting these other systems of linguistic information into the same conceptual framework of description and correspondence, we can make use of the already existing mathematical and computational techniques and rich notations for structure specification. If we further defined a transfer component between source and target f-structures in terms of a correspondence, we might get the same conceptual advantages in configuring a machine translation system.

Although the structures related by multiple correspondences might be descriptively or linguistically motivated levels of representation, justified by sound theoretical argumentation, they are formally and mathematically, and also computationally, eliminable. The mathematical point is trivial: suppose we have a level of constituent structure and a structural correspondence that goes from the string to the constituent structure, and another correspondence that goes from c-structure to f-structure. Obviously there is a structural correspondence that goes from the word string directly to the f-structure, namely the composition of π with ϕ. It's a function that's not one-to-one, it's not onto, it has all the expected properties. So as a kind of formal, mathematical trick, you can say 'Those intermediate levels of representation are not real, they are just linguistic fictions, useful for stating the necessary constraints'.

This arrangement provides for some somewhat surprising descriptive possibilities. Looking at the mapping between f-structure and semantic structure, it might seem that the semantic structure may only contain information that is derivable from attributes and values present in the f-structure. This is what you would expect if you thought of the correspondence σ as an interpretation function operating on the f-structure to produce the semantic structure. The semantic structure, for example, could not reflect category and precedence properties in the c-structure that don't show up in the f-structure. But σ, as a piecewise correspondence, does not interpret the f-structure at all. It is merely a device for encoding descriptions of the semantic structure in terms of f-structure relations. And since the f-structure is described in terms of ϕ and c-structure properties, we can take the composition $\sigma \circ \phi$ and use it to assert properties of semantic structure also in terms of c-structure relations, even though the correspondence isn't direct. Descriptions generated by the context-free grammar can use designators such as $(\sigma\uparrow)$ along with $\uparrow$ to characterize f-structure and semantic structure simultaneously. This compositional arrangement of correspondences permits the *codescription* of separate levels of representation. One effect of this codescription possibility is that semantic structure might contain certain attributes and values that are contingent on c-structure properties that have no f-structure correlates.

This organization also has some surprising computational consequences: cascaded correspondences and the intermediate structures they pass through can be constructively eliminated. One of many theorems that Kelly Roach (1985) has proved is that for any LFG grammar that associates f-structure and c-structures with a string, you can construct algorithmically another LFG grammar that assigns f-structures that are homomorphically related to the first ones, but the second grammar has essentially a finite-state base instead of a context-free base. For this second grammar there is no notion of phrase structure as a separate level with interesting properties. Instead, it enforces all the constraints that the first grammar's c-structure component imposes by additional attributes and values in the f-structure in addition to those needed to carry the original functional information. But you never have a phase of context-free parsing, you never actually construct the c-structure as a separate, coherent level of representation. This result may have important practical consequences, since the conditions that must be evaluated to analyze or produce a sentence can now be stated in a uniform description system. Though constraints come from independent, modular specifications involving notionally different kinds of linguistic information, this construction permits interleaving them in online computation, to take heuristic advantage of the most reliable sources of information. It thus provides an answer to the interaction seduction; you can construct, say, a semantic grammar, as the compile-time composition of syntactic and semantic correspondences.

It is also a very illuminating result, because it answers a basic question about where the power of this kind of description system comes from. The recursive nesting property of the context-free component may give rise to nicer linguistic formulations, but it is not essential to the expressive power of these systems. From a strictly formal perspective, function-application and equality give rise to the full power of the system. This result also has a rhetorical use: when we're being attacked, as sometimes we are, for having too many levels of representation, we can say 'You're right, we do have too many levels of representation, there's really no need for c-structure (or, carrying the argument further along, for f-structure)'.

This proposed use of multiple correspondences to get the interaction of modular specifications can be compared to Bill Woods' (1980) cascaded

ATN. The generalization that Woods made to handle multiple levels of representation was to consider a collection of ATNs as left-to-right procedures feeding each other on some intermediate tapes. What we do here is to set structures in compositional relationships to each other. We don't have any left- or right-ness, we're not inheriting any of the procedural properties of the ATN, all we have is transparent descriptions.

I want to finish up with an example to illustrate one other formal possibility. We have had some discussion of defaults, and whether default specifications should be procedural or declarative. In the spirit of the declarative, description-oriented approach I have been presenting, I propose handling defaults by adding an operator to the f-structure description language. The description language that we have so far is a very simple algebra, an algebra that has no operators in it. All it has is function application, equality, and set-membership. It doesn't have any devices, analogous to the plus or times of arithmetic, for combining two f-structures to get a third. But why should we confine ourselves to such a restrictive system? Maybe there are some operators that can be linguistically useful. One interesting possibility is what I've called 'priority union' (21):

(21) $/: (F \times F) \rightarrow F$

Priority union takes a pair of f-structures into an f- structure, and is defined the following way. For two f-structures A and B, 'A/B' is their priority union, perhaps read as A given B, or A in the context of B. It is the set of pairs $<s\ v>$ such that v is equal to the value of the attribute s in the f-structure A, if s is in the domain of A, otherwise the value of s in the f-structure B. The operator gives priority to the values in A but anything that A doesn't include gets filled in from B. (22) shows what the priority union would be for a particular pair of operand f-structures:

$$(22) \quad A = \begin{bmatrix} q & r \\ s & t \\ u & v \end{bmatrix} \quad B = \begin{bmatrix} q & m \\ s & t \\ p & l \end{bmatrix} \quad A/B = \begin{bmatrix} q & r \\ s & t \\ u & v \\ p & l \end{bmatrix}$$

A/B gets $<q\ r>$ from A, ignoring what would be the inconsistent value of q in B, not even noticing it. $<s\ t>$ is common to both so A/B includes that. It also has $<u\ v>$ from A and $<p\ l>$ from B.

The basic idea is that values found in A override the values found in B, and B supplies the defaults. Note that this is not done as a procedure, it's done as an operator. It's simply a characterization of satisfactory structures.

This operator might be applied to specify default or unmarked values for morphological features. It might also be used in the description of various kinds of ellipsis constructions, for example, to assign proper interpretations for gapping constructions. A basic rule for sentence coordination is given in (23):

(23) S $\longrightarrow$ S and S
         $\downarrow \in \uparrow$ $\downarrow \in \uparrow$

This has statements that involve membership instead of equality, indicating that the f-structures of the daughter nodes are members of the set that corresponds to the mother node. For ordinary conjunction the same statement appears on both daughter categories. A simple variation of this basic rule provides for gapping in the second conjunct. Instead of saying that the second daughter simply contributes its corresponding f-structure to the mother set, we can say that the mother set will contain the priority union of the second daughter's f-structure with defaults taken from the first daughter's f-structure. If, as is independently needed to handle English Aux-inversion, a verb is allowed to be optional in the VP that expands the second S, the predicate for the second f-structure will be inherited from the first if it is not carried by an explicit verb in the usual string position.

Now there are a lot of technical issues, as Stuart [Shieber] has and, I'm sure, will remind me of, concerning this particular operator and what its algebraic properties are. These are important questions that I at least have not yet worked on, and it may turn out that this is not the operator that we actually want. But the point here is to illustrate the spirit of this approach, that you can formalize notions like default, what you might think of as procedural notions, by thinking of operators that produce new structures, structures that are not directly in the image of the structural correspondence.

Acknowledgments

I am indebted to Peter Whitelock for reducing my talk to its initial written form.

References

Bates, Madeleine. 1976. Syntax in Automatic Speech Understanding. *American Journal of Computational Linguistics*. Microfiche 45.

Bresnan, Joan, and Ronald M. Kaplan. 1982. Introduction: Grammars as Mental Representations of Language. In *The Mental Representation of Grammatical Relations*. xvii–lii. Cambridge, MA: The MIT Press.

Bresnan, Joan. 1984. Bound Anaphora on Functional Structures. Presented at the Tenth Annual Meeting of the Berkeley Linguistics Society.

Carroll, John A. 1983. An island parsing interpreter for the full augmented transition network formalism. In *Proceedings of the First Meeting of the European ACL*, 101–105. University of Manchester. European Chapter of the Association for Computational Linguistics.

Chomsky, Noam. 1963. Formal Properties of Grammars. In *Handbook of Mathematical Psychology*, ed. R. Duncan Luce, Robert R. Bush, and Eugene Galanter. 323–418. New York: Wiley.

Halvorsen, Per-Kristian. 1983. Semantics for Lexical-Functional Grammar. *Linguistic Inquiry* 14(4):567–615.

Kaplan, Ronald M. 1972. Augmented transition networks as psychological models of sentence comprehension. *Artificial Intelligence* 3:77–100.

Kaplan, Ronald M., and Joan Bresnan. 1982. Lexical-Functional Grammar: A Formal System for Grammatical Representation. In *The Mental Representation of Grammatical Relations*, ed. Joan Bresnan, 173–281. Cambridge, MA: The MIT Press. Reprinted in Part I of this volume.

Marcus, Mitchell P. 1987. Deterministic Parsing and Description Theory. In *Linguistic Theory and Computer Applications*, ed. Peter Whitelock, Harold Somers, Paul Bennett, Rod Johnson, and Mary McGee Wood. 69–112. London: Academic Press.

Roach, Kelly. 1985. The mathematics of LFG. Unpublished MS, Xerox Palo Alto Research Center.

Shieber, Stuart M. 1987. Separating Linguistic Analyses from Linguistic Theories. In *Linguistic Theory and Computer Applications*, ed. Peter Whitelock, Harold Somers, Paul Bennett, Rod Johnson, and Mary McGee Wood. 1–36. London: Academic Press.

Woods, William A. 1970. Transition Network Grammars for Natural Language Analysis. *Communications of the ACM* 13(10):591–606.

Woods, William A. 1980. Cascaded ATN grammars. *American Journal of Computational Linguistics* 6(1):1–12.

Woods, William A., Ronald M. Kaplan, and Bonnie Nash-Webber. 1972. The Lunar Sciences Natural Language Information System: Final report. Technical Report 2378. Cambridge, MA: Bolt, Beranek, and Newman, Inc.

13

Logic and Feature Structures

MARK JOHNSON

Abstract. Feature structures play an important role in linguistic knowledge representation in computational linguistics. Given the proliferation of different feature structure formalisms it is useful to have a "common language" to express them in. This paper shows how a variety of feature structures and constraints on them can be expressed in predicate logic (except for the use of *circumscription* for non-monotonic devices), including sorted feature values, subsumption constraints and the non-monotonic *ANY* values and "constraint equations". Many feature systems can be completely axiomatized in the *Schönfinkel-Bernays class* of first-order formulae, so the decidability of the satisfiability problem for these systems follows immediately.

1 Introduction

The number of different feature structure devices and formalisms proposed in the "unification grammar" literature is growing so fast that it is important to find a "common language" in which they can be expressed. This paper shows how a variety of different types of feature structures and constraints on them can be expressed in predicate logic (or standard non-monotonic extensions thereof), including:

- (parameterized) sorts,
- subsumption constraints, and
- non-monotonic constraints (specifically LFG "constraint equations").

These were chosen merely to give a feeling for the ease with which fairly complex constructions can be described in predicate logic; they by no

An earlier version of this paper appeared in *Proceedings of the Twelfth International Joint Conference on Artificial Intelligence* (Sydney, Australia, August 1991), 992–996.

Formal Issues in Lexical-Functional Grammar
edited by
Mary Dalrymple
Ronald M. Kaplan
John T. Maxwell III
Annie Zaenen

means exhaust the class of feature structures and constraints that can be given first-order axiomatizations. This suggests that instead of requiring radically new types of interpretations, even complex feature structures and constraints on them can be described using standard techniques. Not all these extensions have to be used in an implementation, of course; a reasonable policy might be to only implement the decidable extensions described below, for example. Since feature structures are a kind of frame representation, the results presented here should be of interest to the wider A.I. community.

The results in this paper extend those presented in earlier work, especially Johnson (1988, 1990, 1991), Smolka (1988, 1989), with which (due to space limitations) familiarity is presupposed.

2 The Schönfinkel-Bernays Class

One advantage of axiomatizing feature structures in first-order predicate logic is that its proof-theoretic, model-theoretic and computational properties are well-known. This paper exploits some of the results on *decidable classes* of first-order logic (Dreben and Goldfarb 1979, Guerevyich 1976) to show that the satisfiability problem for certain types of feature structure constraints is decidable. We show that a variety of such structures and constraints can be axiomatized using formulae from the Schönfinkel-Bernays class, (called *SB* below); since the satisfiability of any formula in *SB* is decidable, the satisfiability problem for these feature structure constraints must be decidable too.

A formula is in *SB* iff it is a closed formula of the form

$$\exists x_1, \ldots, x_m \, \forall y_1, \ldots, y_n \, \phi$$

where ϕ is a formula containing no function or quantifier symbols.[1] *SB* formulae possess the *finite model property*, i.e. if a formula has a model then it has a finite model (Lewis and Papadimitriou 1981). Lewis (1980) investigated the computational complexity of the decision problem for such formulae and showed that the satisfiability problem for *SB* formulae is PSPACE-complete, and (by Proposition 3.2 of Lewis 1980) that the satisfiability problem for SB_n is NP-complete, where SB_n is the class of *SB* formulae containing n or fewer universal quantifiers.

The conjunction (and disjunction) of two *SB* formulae is itself an *SB* formulae (after quantifiers have been moved outward). This means that *SB* axiomatizations of different kinds of feature structures can be conjoined, and the satisfiability of the composite system is also decidable.

---

[1] Because ϕ can always be expanded to disjunctive normal form, Schönfinkel-Bernays formulae are a generalization of Datalog clauses that allow disjunctive consequents. I hope to explore this more fully in later work.

For example, Johnson (1991) axiomatizes 'set values' using *SB* formulae, and these axioms can be combined with e.g. the *SB* axioms for sorts given below to yield a system with both 'set-valued' and 'sorted' objects completely axiomatized in *SB*, and hence with a decidable satisfiability problem.

3   Attribute-value features

Attribute-value features, popularized in the work of Shieber (1986) and others, are the most common type of features used in computational linguistics. The treatment here is effectively the same as that in Johnson (1991), Smolka (1988, 1989), so it is only summarized here.

Attribute-value features are in effect *partial functions* (see Kaplan and Bresnan 1982, Johnson 1988), and they can be formalized in first-order logic either

- as relations that obey functionality axioms (as is done here), or
- as "total" functions over a domain that includes a designated element that is interpreted as an "undefined" value (see Johnson 1988, 1990).

These two different formalizations reduce the satisfiability problem for attribute-value feature structure constraints to different classes of first-order formulae, and lead to different insights about the original problem.

Here, we conceptualize "pure" attribute-value features as instances of an "arc" relation, where $arc(x, a, y)$ is true iff there is an arc labelled a from x to y. (In some expositions the elements x and y are called *nodes* and a is called an *attribute*). The following axioms express the constraints that the *arc* relation must satisfy for it to be an attribute-value structure. The predicate *con* is true of the attribute-value constants.

The first axiom requires that the *arc* relation is functional. (Used as an inference rule in a forward chaining system, it requires the "unification" of the "destinations" of a pair of arcs labelled with the same attribute leaving the same node; see Johnson 1990, 1991 for details).

(1) $\forall x, a, y, z \; arc(x, a, y) \land arc(x, a, z) \longrightarrow y = z.$

The second axiom requires that attribute-value constants have no attributes. (This axiom is responsible for "constant-compound clashes").

(2) $\forall c, a, y \; \neg(con(c) \land arc(c, a, y))$

The attribute-value constants have special properties expressed by the next two axiom schema. These schema stipulate properties of the entities that the attribute-value constants, a subset of the constant symbols of the first-order language, denote. Not every constant symbol will be an attribute-value constant, since it is useful to have constant symbols that refer to other entities as well.

The first schema requires that every attribute-value constant have the property *con*.

(3)   For all attribute-value constants c, $con(c)$.

The second axiom schema requires that distinct attribute-value constants have distinct denotations. (This is sometimes called a "unique name assumption").

(4)   For all pairs of distinct attribute-value constants c_1 and c_2,
$$c_1 \neq c_2.$$

This axiomatization is quite permissive, in that it allows

- cyclic structures,
- infinite structures,
- intensional structures (i.e., different elements may share the same attributes and values),
- disconnected structures, and
- allows values to be used as attributes.

Additional axioms could have been added to prohibit such structures, but because there seems to be no linguistic or computational motivation for such additional stipulations they are not made here. (Axioms prohibiting cyclic structures and attributes from being values can be formulated in *SB*, an *extensionality requirement* can be axiomatized using a first-order formula not in *SB*, while an axiom prohibiting infinite structures cannot be expressed in first-order logic).

Each node in a syntactic parse tree is associated with an element (different nodes can be associated with the same element; see Chapter 3 of Johnson 1988 for full details). Lexical entries and syntactic rules constrain the elements associated with parse-tree nodes. Following Kaplan and Bresnan (1982) we represent these constraints by formulae containing no universal quantifiers.

For example, a (simplified) lexical entry for the English verb *swim* might require that:

- the attribute-value element u associated with a node dominating the terminal item *swim* have a *semantics* attribute whose value is *swim'* (which abbreviates the verb's "semantic value"),
- that u have an *agreement* attribute whose value is, say, v, and
- that the value of v's *number* and *person* attributes (representing the verb's agreement features) *not* be *singular* and *3rd* respectively (these are the features of the inflected form *swims*).

These constraints might be expressed in an extended PATR-II notation (see Shieber 1986) as

$$\langle u\ semantics \rangle = swim' \wedge$$
$$\neg(\langle u\ agreement\ number \rangle = singular \wedge$$
$$\langle u\ agreement\ person \rangle = 3rd\ )$$

and in FDL notation (see Smolka 1988, 1989) as

$$semantics : swim' \wedge$$
$$\neg(agreement : number : singular \wedge$$
$$agreement : person : 3rd\ )$$

This paper takes no position on what *notation* such feature constraints should be written in, but simply suggests that whatever notation is used to express this constraint it should *mean* the same thing as the following formula.

$$\exists v\ \ arc(u, semantics, swim') \wedge$$
$$arc(u, agreement, v) \wedge$$
$$\neg(arc(v, number, singular) \wedge$$
$$arc(v, person, 3rd))$$

(In this formula u is a constant that is not an attribute-value constant, while *semantics*, *swim'*, *number*, *singular*, *person* and *3rd* are attribute-value constants). Arbitrary boolean combinations (including negation) of attribute-value constraints can be expressed in this manner.[2]

Note that the axioms defining attribute-value features and formulae expressing attribute-value constraints are all in SB, so their conjunction is also (equivalent to) a SB formula, and hence the satisfiability of such systems of constraints is decidable. Further, the only quantifiers appear in the axioms 1 and 2 so this conjunction is in fact in SB_7, and hence the satisfiability problem for systems of feature constraints is in NP.[3] Since the satisfiability problem for arbitrary conjunctions and disjunctions of atomic feature structure constraints (here, *arc* atoms) is NP-complete (Kasper and Rounds 1990), the satisfiability problem for the system described here is NP-complete.

---

[2]The proper treatment of negation in "feature logics" has been the subject of considerable discussion (Moshier and Rounds 1987, Pereira 1987, Dawar and Vijay-Shanker 1990, Johnson 1988, 1990, 1991): however I know of no linguistic application in which a classical interpretation of negation yields intuitively "incorrect" results.

[3]The axioms 1 and 2 can be replaced with an equivalent axiom that "shares" the universally quantified variables, so systems of attribute-value constraints can be expressed as formulae in SB_4.

4 Sorts

The term "sort" is used to mean different things by different authors. We sketch here how two common interpretations of sorts can be axiomatized by considering some simple examples, and follow Smolka (1988, 1989) in modelling sorts by unary predicates (*parameterized* sorts are modelled by predicates of higher arity).

First, suppose that sorts are taken to restrict the possible attributes of an element, so that e.g. something of sort *agr* can only have the attributes *number* or *person* (with perhaps restrictions on the values of these attributes that for simplicity are not dealt with here). The following axiom defines this notion of sort.

(5)
$$\forall x \; agr(x) \longrightarrow$$
$$\forall a, y \; arc(x, a, y) \to a = person \lor a = number.$$

(This one-place predicate *agr* could be used in a more refined lexical entry for *swim* that requires $agr(v)$, i.e. that v be of sort *agr*.)

Second, suppose that sorts are also to require that certain attributes *must* have a value, so that e.g. something of sort *agr'* must have values for the attributes *number* or *person*. (Axiom 5 only prevents anything satisfying *agr* from having any attributes other than *person* and *number*.) The following axiom defines this sort.

(6)
$$\forall x \; agr'(x) \longrightarrow$$
$$\exists y, z \; arc(x, person, y) \land arc(x, number, z).$$

Both kinds of sorts can be optionally augmented by an *extensionality requirement*, which stipulates that no two distinct elements in the same sort have identical values for their attributes. For example, the following axiom requires that no two elements of sort *agr* can have the same values for their *person* and *number* attributes.

(7)
$$\forall x, y, u, v \quad (agr(x) \land arc(x, number, u) \land$$
$$arc(x, person, v) \land agr(y) \land$$
$$arc(y, number, u) \land$$
$$arc(y, person, v))$$
$$\to x = y$$

Because axioms of the form of 5 and 7 are in SB, the satisfiability of attribute-value systems augmented with sort constraints of the first type is decidable, and (given a fixed set of sorts and hence a fixed number of universal quantifiers) is NP-complete. On the other hand, axioms of the form of 6 are not in SB. While this does not imply undecidability, Smolka (1988, 1989) has shown that for systems that allow *parameterized sorts* (i.e. sort predicates with arity greater than one) this is in fact the case.

Of course, there is no reason to restrict attention to unary predicates. For example, assuming that lists are represented in the standard attribute-value formulation using *first* and *rest* attributes (see Shieber 1986 or Johnson 1988 for details), the following axioms define the predicate $member(x, l)$, which is true iff x appears somewhere in the proper list represented by l.[4]

(8)
$$
\begin{aligned}
\forall x, l \ arc(l, \mathit{first}, x) &\longrightarrow member(x, l) \\
\forall x, l, l' \ arc(l, \mathit{rest}, l') \land & \\
member(x, l') &\longrightarrow member(x, l) \\
\forall x, l, l' \ member(x, l) &\longrightarrow arc(l, \mathit{first}, x) \lor \\
& \quad (arc(l, \mathit{rest}, l') \to \\
& \quad \ member(x, l'))
\end{aligned}
$$

Again, since the axioms in 8 are in SB, they can be conjoined with any other SB axioms and the system remains decidable.

5 Subsumption Constraints

This section and the next focuses on some of the most difficult aspects of the theory of feature structures. Subsumption constraints are notoriously tricky to formulate. Partly, this is because the term 'subsumption' is used to refer to two different notions in the feature structure literature.

First, subsumption can be construed as a relation between a pair of systems of constraints. ϕ *subsumes* ψ iff every feature structure that satisfies ψ also satisfies ϕ. (This notion of subsumption is used in the prediction step of generalized Earley and LR parsing algorithms for feature structure grammars; see Shieber (1989, 1985) for details.) In a pure "unification-based grammar" framework, ϕ and ψ are both quantifier-free formulae (e.g. boolean combinations of *arc* atoms), so ϕ subsumes ψ iff

$$ A \models \psi \to \phi $$

where A is the relevant feature-structure axiomatization. Clearly, if A is in SB then this notion of subsumption is decidable.

Second, subsumption can be construed as a relation between elements within a feature structure, where e subsumes e', written $e \sqsubseteq e'$ iff there is a partial endomorphism h such that $h(e) = e'$, that preserves attribute-value constants and attributes and their values (and possibly sorts). (This notion of subsumption is needed to describe the agreement properties of conjoined phrases; see Shieber 1989 for details.) It is straightforward

---

[4]The axioms in 8 do not require that l be (an attribute-value encoding of) a list. A unary 'sort' predicate that does require this is easily formulated, however. Among other things, this predicate should require that the "empty list" constant *nil* has neither *first* nor *last* arcs leaving it. (This could also be achieved by treating *nil* as an attribute-value constant.)

to axiomatize this in second-order predicate logic by treating the partial endomorphism h as a functional relation (i.e. $h(x, y)$ iff $h(x)$ is defined and equal to y).

$$\forall e, e' \ e \sqsubseteq e' \ \longleftrightarrow$$
$$\exists h \ (\ \forall x, y, z \ h(x, y) \wedge h(x, z) \rightarrow y = z \ \wedge$$
$$h(e, e') \ \wedge$$
$$\forall c \ con(c) \rightarrow h(c, c) \ \wedge$$
$$\forall x, y, a, u \ h(x, y) \wedge arc(x, a, u) \ \rightarrow \ \exists v \, arc(y, a, v) \wedge h(u, v) \ )$$

Dörre and Rounds (1989) have shown the undecidability of conjunctions of subsumption and attribute-value constraints, so clearly this notion of subsumption cannot be axiomatized in SB. Perhaps surprisingly, *positively occurring* subsumption constraints[5] can be axiomatized quite directly in first-order logic in a manner discovered jointly with John Maxwell.

As just formulated, subsumption seems to rely on an existential quantification over partial endomorphisms h, but by

- replacing the bi-conditional with an implication (which does not affect satisfiability if all subsumption constraints occur positively), and
- skolemizing the embedded existential quantification

we obtain an equivalent first order (but not SB) formulation in terms of a four-place relation h', where $h'(e, e', x, y)$ iff $h(x, y)$, where h is the partial endomorphism whose existence is asserted by the existential in the definition of $e \sqsubseteq e'$. The first axiom has the same effect as requiring that $h(e, e')$.

$$(9) \qquad\qquad \forall e, e' \ e \sqsubseteq e' \ \longrightarrow \ h'(e, e', e, e').$$

The second axiom requires that h' preserve attributes and their values.

$$(10) \qquad \begin{aligned} \forall e, e', x, y, a, z \ & h'(e, e', x, y) \wedge arc(x, a, z) \\ &\longrightarrow \exists v \ arc(y, a, v) \wedge h'(e, e', z, v). \end{aligned}$$

The third axiom requires that h' preserve constants.

$$(11) \qquad\qquad \forall e, e', y \ h'(e, e', c, y) \ \longrightarrow \ c = y.$$

The fourth axiom requires that h' is functional.

$$(12) \qquad \forall e, e', x, y, z \ h'(e, e', x, y) \wedge h'(e, e', x, z) \ \longrightarrow \ y = z.$$

---

[5]A subformula occurs positively iff it is in the scope of an even number of negation symbols. The simplification of a biconditional to an implication when the relation defined by the biconditional appears elsewhere only positively is described and proved not to alter satisfiability in Johnson (1991).

6 Constraint equations and *ANY* values

Finally, we turn to perhaps the most thorny problem for any theoretical account of feature structures: default values and other non-monotonic constructions. This section shows how these notions can be formalized by using *circumscription* to require satisfying models to be *minimal models*.[6] This approach has two major advantages over other approaches:

- expansion to disjunctive normal form is not required, and
- a single notion of satisfiability is defined which treats the monotonic and non-monotonic constructions simultaneously.

Several versions of circumscription are discussed in the literature; for an introduction see e.g. Genesereth and Nilsson (1987). The *parallel circumscription formula* ϕ' for relations $R_1, \ldots, R_n$ in ϕ has the property that a model $\mathcal{M}$ satisfies $\phi \wedge \phi'$ iff $\mathcal{M}$ is an $R_1, \ldots, R_n$-minimal model of ϕ. (In general ϕ' is a second-order formula.)

An important intuition guiding early work in unification grammar (especially that of Kaplan and Bresnan 1982 and Kay 1985) is that only the *minimal* feature structures satisfying the constraints are of linguistic interest, and that lexical entries and syntactic rules may impose additional conditions that a minimal model has to satisfy in order to be well-formed. This section shows how these intuitions can be formalized using circumscription.

For example, most current theories of natural language syntax posit a requirement that all noun-phrases must be *assigned* a 'case feature' by some syntactic rule or lexical entry. This could be implemented in a feature-structure based system by adding a constraint to all lexical entries for nouns that a *minimal* model is well-formed only if the associated feature element has a *case* attribute; this is sometimes called an *ANY*-value constraint on the *case* attribute. Similarly, a *constraint equation* between two entities $x =_c y$ is satisfied iff $x = y$ in a minimal model of the attribute-value formulae. (See the discussion on pages 108–110 of Johnson (1988) for a more detailed explanation of such constraints.)

"Constraint equations" and *ANY* values can be treated in the following way. We represent the constraint that an attribute a must be defined on an element x in a minimal model by $any(x, a)$, and constraint equations by $x =_c y$. Now let ϕ be the conjunction of the equality axioms, the attribute-value axioms and all of the (formulae corresponding to) feature structure constraints from a given parse, and let ϕ' be the parallel circumscription formula for *arc*, *con* and $=$ in ϕ. We circumscribe precisely

---

[6]Fernando Pereira suggested to me that circumscription could be used to provide a formal account of non-monotonic feature structure constraints.

these relations because a minimal model is one which possesses as few arcs as possible, specifies attribute-value constants as the denotation of as few variables as possible, and identifies as equal or "unified" as few pairs of variables as possible (see the definition of the subsumption ordering on attribute-value models in Johnson 1988).

Then a model $\mathcal{M}$ satisfies all of the constraints (including the so-called "defining equations", the "constraint equations" and the ANY constraints) iff

$$
\begin{aligned}
(13) \quad \mathcal{M} \;\models\; & \phi \wedge \phi' \wedge \\
& \forall x, a \; any(x, a) \leftrightarrow \exists y \; arc(x, a, y) \wedge \\
& \forall x, y \; x =_c y \leftrightarrow x = y.
\end{aligned}
$$

The circumscription of equality requires that two constants denote the same entity (i.e. are "unified") in a model iff interpreting them as denoting distinct entities would result in the violation of some axiom or constraint. The circumscription of arc and con requires that these relations are also minimal.

Note that this formulation restricts attention to "classical" minimal models. However, for some applications this seems to be too strong. For example, the constraint attached to the NP child in the LFG rule (Kaplan and Bresnan 1982)

$$
\begin{array}{ccc}
\text{VP} \longrightarrow & \text{V} & \text{NP} \\
& \uparrow = \downarrow & (\uparrow \text{OBJ}) = \downarrow \\
& & ((\downarrow \text{CASE}) = \text{ACC})
\end{array}
$$

includes an *optional* feature structure constraint, which would be represented in the framework described here as

$$
arc(vp, \text{OBJ}, np) \;\wedge\; (arc(np, \text{CASE}, \text{ACC}) \vee true)
$$

Now, the left-hand disjunct contributes nothing to the truth conditions if disjunction is interpreted classically (since $\phi \vee true \equiv true$), so this is clearly not the intended interpretation. Rather, Kaplan and Bresnan seem to interpret disjunction as a kind of non-deterministic choice operator, so that all of the minimal models of both ϕ and ψ are also minimal models of $\phi \vee \psi$.

7 Conclusion

This paper has shown how a wide variety of different types of feature structures and constraints on them can be described using predicate logic. The decidability of the satisfiability problem of many interesting feature structure systems follows directly from the fact that they can be axiomatized in the Schönfinkel-Bernays class. Further, axiomatizing feature structures in first-order logic allows us to apply standard techniques to the formalization of non-monotonic feature structure constraints.

Acknowledgments

The research described here was conducted while I was a Gastprofessor at the Institut für maschinelle Sprachverarbeitung, Universität Stuttgart, which I would like to thank for providing a supportive environment in which to get this work done. Robert Carpenter, Jochen Dörre, Andreas Eisele, Harry Lewis, John Maxwell, Michael Moorreau, Ron Kaplan, Fernando Pereira, and Gert Smolka have all made insightful comments on the work reported here. I would like to especially thank Tore Langholm for pointing out several errors and omissions from the earlier version of this paper. Naturally all responsibility for errors remains my own.

References

Dawar, A., and K. Vijay-Shanker. 1990. An Interpretation of Negation in Feature Structures. *Computational Linguistics* 16(1):11–21.

Dörre, Jochen, and William C. Rounds. 1989. On Subsumption and Semiunification in Feature Algebra. Technical Report 97. IBM Deutschland.

Dreben, Burton, and Warren D. Goldfarb. 1979. *The Decision Problem: Solvable Classes of Quantificational Formulas*. Reading, MA: Addison-Wesley.

Genesereth, Michael R., and Nils J. Nilsson. 1987. *Logical Foundations of Artificial Intelligence*. Los Altos, CA: Morgan Kaufmann Publishers, Inc.

Guerevyich, Y. 1976. The Decision Problem for Standard Classes. *The Journal of Symbolic Logic* 41(2):460–464.

Johnson, Mark. 1988. *Attribute-Value Logic and the Theory of Grammar*. CSLI Lecture Notes, No. 16. Stanford University: CSLI/The University of Chicago Press.

Johnson, Mark. 1990. Expressing Disjunctive and Negative Feature Constraints in Classical First-order Logic. In *Proceedings of the Twenty-Eighth Annual Meeting of the ACL*. Pittsburgh, PA. Association for Computational Linguistics.

Johnson, Mark. 1991. Features and Formulae. *Computational Linguistics* 17(2):131–151.

Kaplan, Ronald M., and Joan Bresnan. 1982. Lexical-Functional Grammar: A Formal System for Grammatical Representation. In *The Mental Representation of Grammatical Relations*, ed. Joan Bresnan. 173–281. Cambridge, MA: The MIT Press. Reprinted in Part I of this volume.

Kasper, Robert T., and William C. Rounds. 1990. The Logic of Unification in Grammar. *Linguistics and Philosophy* 13(1).

Kay, Martin. 1985. Unification in Grammar. In *Natural Language Understanding and Logic Programming*, ed. Veronica Dahl and Patrick Saint-Dizier. Amsterdam: North Holland.

Lewis, Harry R. 1980. Complexity Results for Classes of Quantificational Formulae. *Journal of Computer and System Sciences* 21:317–353.

Lewis, Harry R., and Christos H. Papadimitriou. 1981. *Elements of the theory of computation.* Englewood Cliffs, NJ: Prentice-Hall.

Moshier, Drew, and William C. Rounds. 1987. A Logic for Partially Specified Data Structures.In *The ACM Symposium on the Principles of Programming Languages.* Munich, Germany. Association for Computing Machinery.

Pereira, Fernando C. N. 1987. Grammars and Logics of Partial Information. In *Proceedings of The International Conference on Logic Programming.* Melbourne, Australia.

Shieber, Stuart M. 1985. Using restriction to extend parsing algorithms for complex feature-based formalisms. In *Proceedings of the 23rd Annual Meeting of the ACL,* 145–152. Chicago. Association for Computational Linguistics.

Shieber, Stuart M. 1986. *An Introduction to Unification-Based Approaches to Grammar.* CSLI Lecture Notes, No. 4. Stanford University: CSLI/The University of Chicago Press.

Shieber, Stuart M. 1989. *Parsing and Type Inference for Natural and Computer Languages.* Doctoral dissertation, Stanford University.

Smolka, Gert. 1988. A Feature Logic with Subsorts. Technical report. IBM Deutschland. LILOG Report 33, IWBS.

Smolka, Gert. 1989. Feature Constraint Logics for Unification Grammars. Technical report. IBM Deutschland. IWBS Report 93.

14

A Method for Disjunctive Constraint Satisfaction

JOHN T. MAXWELL III AND RONALD M. KAPLAN

1 Introduction

A distinctive property of many current grammatical formalisms is their use of feature equality constraints to express a wide variety of grammatical dependencies. Lexical-Functional Grammar (Kaplan and Bresnan 1982), Head-Driven Phrase-Structure Grammar (Pollard and Sag 1987), PATR (Karttunen 1986), FUG (Kay 1979, Kay 1982), and the various forms of categorial unification grammar (Karttunen 1989, Uszkoreit 1986, Zeevat et al. 1987) all require an analysis of a sentence to satisfy a collection of feature constraints in addition to a set of conditions on the arrangement of words and phrases. Conjunctions of equality constraints can be quickly solved by standard unification algorithms, so they in themselves do not present a computational problem. However, the equality constraints derived for typical sentences are not merely conjoined together in a form that unification algorithms can deal with directly. Rather, they are embedded as primitive elements in complex disjunctive formulas. For some formalisms, these disjunctions arise from explicit disjunction operators that the constraint language provides for (e.g. LFG) while for others disjunctive constraints are derived from the application of alternative phrase structure rules (e.g. PATR). In either case, disjunctive specifications help to simplify the statement of grammatical possibilities. Alternatives expressed locally within individual rules and lexical entries can appeal to

This paper originally appeared under the title "An Overview of Disjunctive Constraint Satisfaction" in *Proceedings of the International Workshop on Parsing Technologies* (Pittsburgh, PA, 1989), 18–27 and with the current title in *Current Issues in Parsing Technology*, ed. Masaru Tomita (Dordrecht: Kluwer, 1991), 173–190.

more general disjunctive processing mechanisms to resolve their global interactions.

The computational problem, of course, is that processing disjunctive specifications is exponentially difficult in the worst case, even if conjunctions of primitive propositions can be solved very quickly, as is the case with equality. For example, the most direct way of dealing with a disjunctive formula is to convert it to disjunctive normal form and then separately solve each of the conjunctive subformulas in the result. There are in general exponentially many such subformulas to consider, hence the overall exponential complexity of the whole process. Despite its computational cost, the DNF strategy does have the significant advantage that it decouples the processing of disjunctions from any details of the primitive constraint formalism or of the conjunctive method for solving them. Grammatical constraint formulas can be solved by merely composing well-known DNF algorithms with equally well-known unification algorithms in a simple, modular implementation that is easy to understand and easy to prove correct.

The exponential time-bound does not reflect our naive intuitions about the intrinsic complexity of the natural language parsing problem. The number of alternatives that remain consistent for any given sentence is typically much, much smaller than the number that a DNF parsing algorithm would explore, and traces of such algorithms typically show enormous amounts of repetitive and irrelevant computation. Although disjunctive constraint satisfaction is known to be worst-case exponential, we and others have suspected that the disjunctive configurations that emerge from grammatical specifications may conform to certain restricted patterns that admit of more rapid solution algorithms. Karttunen (1984) observed that many grammatical disjunctions can be resolved locally among a limited number of morphological feature values and do not usually have the more global interactions that the DNF algorithm is optimized to handle. Kasper (1987a, 1987b) suggested that many grammatical constraints lead to immediate inconsistencies and proposed an algorithm that noticed some of these inconsistencies before expanding to disjunctive normal form.

We have developed a contrasting set of intuitions. Working with Lexical-Functional Grammars, we have noticed that, as a grammar increases in its coverage, the number of disjunctions to be processed grows in rough proportion to the number of words in a sentence. However, we have not observed that elements of these disjunctions typically are mutually inconsistent. Rather, the most striking pattern is that disjunctions arising from words and phrases that are distant from each other in the string tend not to interact. A disjunction representing an ambiguity in the person or number of a sentence's subject, for example, tends to be independent of any ambiguities in, say, the complement's complement's object. That is, the constraint system is globally satisfiable no matter what choices are made from the two distant disjunctive branches. If disjunctions are independent, or free, of each other, it is not necessary to explore all combinations of their branches to determine the satisfiability of the entire system.

The algorithm we propose in this paper is optimized for this common pattern of free disjunctions. Natural languages seem to have a certain locality property in that distant words and phrases usually contribute information about different grammatical functions and features. Distant disjunctions therefore tend to relate to different branches of the attribute-value matrix (functional structure in LFG terminology) that is characterized by the set of equality constraints. In essence, instead of multiplying disjunctions in advance of running a purely conjunctive unification algorithm, our algorithm embeds disjunctions underneath the particular attributes they are concerned with. Equality processing is then carried out on this disjunctive structure. Our method retains the important advantage of the DNF strategy of directly referencing the axioms of the conjunctive equality theory, and thus remains easy to understand and prove correct.

There are four main steps in our algorithm for processing disjunctive systems:

1. turn the disjunctive system into an equi-satisfiable flat conjunction of contexted constraints
2. normalize the contexted constraints using extensions of standard techniques
3. extract and solve a propositional 'disjunctive residue'
4. produce models for satisfiable systems

Intuitively, the disjunctive residue represents the satisfiable combinations of disjuncts in a simple propositional form. Each of the transformations above preserves satisfiability, and so the original disjunctive system is satisfiable if and only if the disjunctive residue is satisfiable. If the disjunctions are relatively independent, then the disjunctive residue is significantly easier to solve than the original system.

The first four sections of this paper cover the steps outlined above. The next section compares this approach with some other techniques for dealing with disjunctive systems of constraints. The last section discusses some of the things that we learned along the way.

2   Turning Disjunctions into Contexted Constraints

2.1   Basic Lemma

Our method depends on a simple lemma for converting a disjunction into a conjunction of implications:

Lemma 1 $\phi_1 \vee \phi_2$ *is satisfiable iff* $(p \rightarrow \phi_1) \wedge (\neg p \rightarrow \phi_2)$ *is satisfiable, where p is a new propositional variable.*

Proof:

1.   If $\phi_1 \vee \phi_2$ is satisfiable, then either ϕ_1 is satisfiable or ϕ_2 is satisfiable. Suppose that ϕ_1 is satisfiable. Then if we choose p to be true, then $p \rightarrow \phi_1$ is satisfiable because ϕ_1 is satisfiable, and $\neg p \rightarrow \phi_2$ is vacuously satisfiable because its antecedent is false. Therefore $(p \rightarrow \phi_1) \wedge (\neg p \rightarrow \phi_2)$ is satisfiable.

2.   If $(p \rightarrow \phi_1) \wedge (\neg p \rightarrow \phi_2)$ is satisfiable, then both clauses are satisfiable. One clause will be vacuously satisfiable because its antecedent is false and the other will have a true antecedent. Suppose that $p \rightarrow \phi_1$ is the clause with the true antecedent. Then ϕ_1 must be satisfiable for $p \rightarrow \phi_1$ to be satisfiable. But if ϕ_1 is satisfiable, then so is $\phi_1 \vee \phi_2$. Q.E.D.

Intuitively, the new variable p is used to encode the requirement that at least one of the disjuncts be true. In the remainder of the paper we use lower-case p to refer to a single propositional variable, and upper-case P to refer to a boolean combination of propositional variables. We call $P \rightarrow \phi$ a *contexted* constraint, where P is the *context* and ϕ is called the *base* constraint.

(Note that this lemma is stated in terms of *satisfiability*, not logical equivalence. A form of the lemma that emphasized logical equivalence would be: $\phi_1 \vee \phi_2 \leftrightarrow \exists p : (p \rightarrow \phi_1) \wedge (\neg p \rightarrow \phi_2)$.)

2.2   Turning a Disjunctive System into a Conjunctive System

The lemma given above can be used to convert a disjunctive system of constraints into a flat conjunction of contexted constraints in linear time. The resulting conjunction is satisfiable if and only if the original system is satisfiable. The algorithm for doing so is as follows:

Algorithm 1

(a) *push all of the negations down to the literals*

(b) *convert the disjunctions into conjunctions using Lemma 1 above*

(c) *flatten nested contexts with:*

$$(P_i \rightarrow (P_j \rightarrow \phi)) \Leftrightarrow (P_i \wedge P_j \rightarrow \phi)$$

(d) *separate conjoined constraints with:*

$$(P_i \rightarrow \phi_1 \wedge \phi_2) \Leftrightarrow (P_i \rightarrow \phi_1) \wedge (P_i \rightarrow \phi_2)$$

This algorithm is a variant of the reduction used to convert disjunctive systems to an equi-satisfiable formula in conjunctive normal form in the proof that the satisfiability problem for CNF is NP-complete (Hopcroft and Ullman 1979). In effect, we are simply converting the disjunctive system to an implicational form of CNF (since $P \rightarrow \phi$ is logically equivalent to $\neg P \vee \phi$). CNF has the desirable property that if any one clause can be shown to be unsatisfiable, then the entire system is unsatisfiable.

2.3 Example

The functional structure f of an uninflected English verb has the following constraints in the formalism of Lexical-Functional Grammar (Kaplan and Bresnan 1982):

(1)
$$((f \text{ INF}) = - \wedge (f \text{ TENSE}) = \text{PRES} \wedge \neg[(f \text{ SUBJ NUM}) = \text{SG} \wedge$$
$$(f \text{ SUBJ PERS}) = 3])$$
$$\vee (f \text{ INF}) = +$$

(In LFG notation, a constraint of the form $(f\,a) = v$ asserts that $f(a) = v$, where f is a function, a is an attribute, and v is a value. $(f\,a\,b) = v$ is shorthand for $f(a)(b) = v$.) These constraints say that either an un-inflected English verb is a present tense verb which is not third person singular, or it is infinitival. In the left column below this system has been reformatted so that it can be compared with the results of applying Algorithm 1 to it, shown on the right:

reformatted: *converts to:*

(	$(f \text{ INF}) = -$	$(p_1 \rightarrow$	$(f \text{ INF}) = -) \wedge$
$\wedge$	$(f \text{ TENSE}) = \text{PRES}$	$(p_1 \rightarrow$	$(f \text{ TENSE}) = \text{PRES}) \wedge$
$\wedge \neg [$	$(f \text{ SUBJ NUM}) = \text{SG}$	$(p_1 \wedge p_2 \rightarrow$	$(f \text{ SUBJ NUM}) \neq \text{SG}) \wedge$
	$\wedge (f \text{ SUBJ PERS}) = 3])$	$(p_1 \wedge \neg p_2 \rightarrow$	$(f \text{ SUBJ PERS}) \neq 3) \wedge$
$\vee$	$(f \text{ INF}) = +$	$(\neg p_1 \rightarrow$	$(f \text{ INF}) = +)$

3 Normalizing the Contexted Constraints

A conjunction of contexted constraints can be put into an equi-satisfiable normalized form that makes it easy to identify all unsatisfiable combinations of constraints. The basic idea is to start with algorithms that determine the satisfiability of purely conjunctive systems and extend each rule of inference or rewriting rule so that it can handle contexted constraints. We illustrate this approach by modifying two conventional satisfiability algorithms, one based on deductive expansion and one based on rewriting.

3.1 Deductive Expansion

Deductive expansion algorithms work by determining all the deductions that could lead to unsatisfiability given an initial set of clauses and some rules of inference. The key to extending a deductive expansion algorithm to contexted constraints is to show that for every rule of inference that is applicable to the base constraints, there is a corresponding rule of inference that works for contexted constraints. The basic observation is that base constraints can be conjoined if their contexts are conjoined:

Lemma 2 $(P_1 \to \phi_1) \wedge (P_2 \to \phi_2) \Rightarrow (P_1 \wedge P_2 \to \phi_1 \wedge \phi_2)$

If we know from the underlying theory of conjoined base constraints that $\phi_1 \wedge \phi_2 \to \phi_3$, then the transitivity of implication gives us:

$$(2) \qquad (P_1 \to \phi_1) \wedge (P_2 \to \phi_2) \Rightarrow (P_1 \wedge P_2 \to \phi_3)$$

Equation (2) is the contexted version of $\phi_1 \wedge \phi_2 \to \phi_3$. Thus the following extension of a standard deductive expansion algorithm works for contexted constraints:

Algorithm 2

For every pair of contexted constraints $P_1 \to \phi_1$ and $P_2 \to \phi_2$ such that:

(a)   *there is a rule of inference $\phi_1 \wedge \phi_2 \to \phi_3$*
(b) $P_1 \wedge P_2 \neq \text{FALSE}$
(c)   *there are no other clauses $P_3 \to \phi_3$ such that $P_1 \wedge P_2 \to P_3$*

add $P_1 \wedge P_2 \to \phi_3$ to the conjunction of clauses being processed.

Condition (b) is based on the observation that any constraint of the form $\text{FALSE} \to \phi$ can be discarded since no unsatisfiable constraints can ever be derived from it. This condition is not necessary for the correctness of the algorithm, but may have performance advantages. Condition (c) corresponds to the condition in the standard deductive expansion algorithm that redundant constraints must be discarded if the algorithm is to terminate. We extend this condition by noting that any constraint of the form $P_i \to \phi$ is redundant if there is already a constraint of the form

$P_j \to \phi$, where $P_i \to P_j$. This is because any unsatisfiable constraints derived from $P_i \to \phi$ will also be derived from $P_j \to \phi$. Our extended algorithm terminates if the standard algorithm for simple conjunctions terminates. When it terminates, an equi-satisfiable disjunctive residue can be easily extracted, as described in Section 4 below.

3.2 Rewriting

Rewriting algorithms work by repeatedly replacing conjunctions of constraints with logically equivalent conjunctions until a normal form is reached. This normal form usually has the property that all unsatisfiable constraints can be determined by inspection. Rewriting algorithms use a set of rewriting rules that specify what sorts of replacements are allowed. These are based on logical equivalences so that no information is lost when replacements occur. Rewriting rules are interpreted differently from logical equivalences, however, in that they have directionality: whenever a logical expression matches the left-hand side of a rewriting rule, it is replaced by an instance of the logical expression on the right-hand side, but not vice-versa. To distinguish the two, we will use $\leftrightarrow$ for logical equivalence and $\Leftrightarrow$ for rewriting rules. (This corresponds to our use of $\to$ for implication and $\Rightarrow$ for deduction above.)

A rewriting algorithm for contexted constraints can be produced by showing that for every rewrite rule that is applicable to the base constraints, there is a corresponding rewrite rule for contexted constraints. Suppose that $\phi_1 \wedge \phi_2 \Leftrightarrow \phi_3$ is a rewriting rule for base constraints. An obvious candidate for the contexted version of this rewrite rule would be to treat the deduction in (2) as a rewrite rule:

$$(3) \quad (P_1 \to \phi_1) \wedge (P_2 \to \phi_2) \Leftrightarrow (P_1 \wedge P_2 \to \phi_3) \quad \text{(incorrect)}$$

This is incorrect because it is not a logical equivalence: the information that ϕ_1 is true in the context $P_1 \wedge \neg P_2$ and that ϕ_2 is true in the context $P_2 \wedge \neg P_1$ has been lost as the basis of future deductions. If we add clauses to cover these cases, we get the logically correct:

$$(4) \quad \begin{aligned} (P_1 \to \phi_1) \wedge (P_2 \to \phi_2) \Leftrightarrow \\ (P_1 \wedge \neg P_2 \to \phi_1) \wedge (P_2 \wedge \neg P_1 \to \phi_2) \wedge (P_1 \wedge P_2 \to \phi_3) \end{aligned}$$

This is the contexted equivalent of $\phi_1 \wedge \phi_2 \Leftrightarrow \phi_3$. Note that the effect of this is that the contexted constraints on the right-hand side have unconjoinable contexts (that is, the conjunction of the contexts is tautologically false). Thus, although the right-hand side of the rewrite rule has more conjuncts than the left-hand side, there are fewer implications to be derived from them.

Loosely speaking, a rewriting algorithm is constructed by iterative application of the contexted versions of the rewriting rules of a conjunctive theory. Rather than give a general outline here, let us consider the particular case of attribute value logic.

3.3 Application to Attribute-Value Logic

Attribute-value logic is used by both LFG and unification-based grammars. We will start with a simple version of the rewriting formalism given in Johnson (1987). For our purposes, we only need two of the rewriting rules that Johnson defines (Johnson 1987, 38-39):

(5) $t_1 \approx t_2 \Leftrightarrow t_2 \approx t_1$ when $\|t_1\| < \|t_2\|$
($\|t_i\|$ is Johnson's norm for terms.)

(6) $(t_2 \approx t_1 \wedge \phi) \Leftrightarrow (t_2 \approx t_1 \wedge \phi[t_2/t_1])$
where ϕ contains t_2 and $\|t_2\| > \|t_1\|$

($\phi[t_2/t_1]$ denotes ϕ with every occurrence of t_2 replaced by t_1.)

We turn equation (6) into a contexted rewriting rule by a simple application of (4) above:

(7) $(P_1 \rightarrow t_2 \approx t_1) \wedge (P_2 \rightarrow \phi) \Leftrightarrow$
$(P_1 \wedge \neg P_2 \rightarrow t_2 \approx t_1) \wedge (\neg P_1 \wedge P_2 \rightarrow \phi) \wedge (P_1 \wedge P_2 \rightarrow (t_2 \approx t_1 \wedge \phi[t_2/t_1]))$

We can collapse the two instances of $t_2 \approx t_1$ together by observing that

$$(P \rightarrow A \wedge B) \Leftrightarrow (P \rightarrow A) \wedge (P \rightarrow B)$$

and that

$$(P_i \rightarrow A) \wedge (P_j \rightarrow A) \Leftrightarrow (P_i \vee P_j \rightarrow A)$$

giving the simpler form:

(8) $(P_1 \rightarrow t_2 \approx t_1) \wedge (P_2 \rightarrow \phi) \Leftrightarrow$
$(P_1 \rightarrow t_2 \approx t_1) \wedge (P_2 \wedge \neg P_1 \rightarrow \phi) \wedge (P_2 \wedge P_1 \rightarrow \phi[t_2/t_1])$

Formula (8) is the basis for a very simple rewriting algorithm for a conjunction of contexted attribute-value constraints:

Algorithm 3

For each pair of clauses $P_1 \rightarrow t_2 \approx t_1$ and $P_2 \rightarrow \phi$:

(a) *if $\|t_2\| > \|t_1\|$, then set x to t_1 and y to t_2, else set x to t_2 and y to t_1*

(b) *if ϕ mentions y and $\|P_2 \wedge P_1\| > 0$ then replace $P_2 \rightarrow \phi$ with $(P_2 \wedge \neg P_1 \rightarrow \phi) \wedge (P_2 \wedge P_1 \rightarrow \phi[y/x])$*

Notice that since $P_1 \rightarrow t_2 \approx t_1$ is carried over unchanged in (8), we only have to replace $P_2 \rightarrow \phi$ in step (b). Note also that if $P_2 \wedge P_1$ is FALSE, there is no need to actually add the clause $(P_2 \wedge P_1 \rightarrow \phi[t_2/t_1])$ since no unsatisfiable constraints can be derived from it. Similarly if $P_2 \wedge \neg P_1$ is FALSE there is no need to add $P_2 \wedge \neg P_1 \rightarrow \phi$.

3.4 Proof of Termination

We can prove that the contexted version of Johnson's algorithm terminates by extending his proof of termination (Johnson 1987, 38-40) to include contexted constraints. Johnson defines a norm on terms $\|t\|$ such that if $\|t_1\| < \|t_2\|$ and ϕ uses t_2, then $\|\phi[t_2/t_1]\| < \|\phi\|$ for all ϕ. We do not need to know the details of this norm, except to note that $\|\phi_1 \wedge \phi_2\| = \|\phi_1\| \cdot \|\phi_2\|$.

We now define $\|P \to \phi\|$ to be $\|\phi\|^{\|P\|}$, where $\|P\|$ is the number of solutions that P has in the truth table for all the propositional variables in the entire system. (In terms of a Venn diagram, $\|P\|$ is the size of the area covered by P.) One consequence of this definition is that $\|P_i\| = \|P_i \wedge P_j\| + \|P_i \wedge \neg P_j\|$ for all P_i and P_j.

Using this definition, the norm for the left hand side of (8) is:

$$\|(P_1 \to t_2 \approx t_1) \wedge (P_2 \to \phi)\|$$
$$(9) \qquad = \quad \|(P_1 \to t_2 \approx t_1)\| \cdot \|(P_2 \to \phi)\|$$
$$= \quad \|t_2 \approx t_1\|^{\|P_1\|} \cdot \|\phi\|^{\|P_2\|}$$

and the norm for the right hand side is:

$$(10) \quad \|((P_1 \to t_2 \approx t_1) \wedge (P_2 \wedge \neg P_1 \to \phi) \wedge (P_2 \wedge P_1 \to \phi[t_2/t_1]))\|$$
$$= \quad \|((P_1 \to t_2 \approx t_1)\| \cdot \|(P_2 \wedge \neg P_1 \to \phi)\| \cdot \|(P_2 \wedge P_1 \to \phi[t_2/t_1])\|$$
$$= \quad \|t_2 \approx t_1\|^{\|P_1\|} \cdot \|\phi\|^{\|P_2 \wedge \neg P_1\|} \cdot \|\phi[t_2/t_1]\|^{\|P_2 \wedge P_1\|}$$

We now show that (10) < (9) whenever $\|t_1\| < \|t_2\|$:

$$\|t_1\| < \|t_2\|$$
$$\to \quad \|\phi[t_2/t_1]\| < \|\phi\| \qquad \text{(by Johnson's definition)}$$
$$\to \quad \|\phi[t_2/t_1]\|^{\|P_2 \wedge P_1\|} < \|\phi\|^{\|P_2 \wedge P_1\|} \quad \text{(because } \|P_2 \wedge P_1\| \text{ is always} > 0\text{)}$$
$$\to \quad \|\phi[t_2/t_1]\|^{\|P_2 \wedge P_1\|} \cdot \|\phi\|^{\|P_2 \wedge \neg P_1\|} < \|\phi\|^{\|P_2 \wedge P_1\|} \cdot \|\phi\|^{\|P_2 \wedge \neg P_1\|}$$
$$\to \quad \|\phi[t_2/t_1]\|^{\|P_2 \wedge P_1\|} \cdot \|\phi\|^{\|P_2 \wedge \neg P_1\|} < \|\phi\|^{\|P_2 \wedge P_1\| + \|P_2 \wedge \neg P_1\|}$$
$$\to \quad \|\phi[t_2/t_1]\|^{\|P_2 \wedge P_1\|} \cdot \|\phi\|^{\|P_2 \wedge \neg P_1\|} < \|\phi\|^{\|P_2\|} \quad \text{(by our definition of } \|P\|\text{)}$$
$$\to \quad \|t_2 \approx t_1\|^{\|P_1\|} \cdot \|\phi[t_2/t_1]\|^{\|P_2 \wedge P_1\|} \cdot \|\phi\|^{\|P_2 \wedge \neg P_1\|} < \|t_2 \approx t_1\|^{\|P_1\|} \cdot \|\phi\|^{\|P_2\|}$$

We can conclude from this that each application of (8) in Algorithm 3 will monotonically reduce the norm of the system as a whole, and hence the algorithm must terminate.

3.5 Example

The following example illustrates how this algorithm works. Suppose that (12) is the contexted version of (11):

(11)
$$[f_2 = f_1 \vee (f_1 \, a) = c_1] \wedge [(f_2 \, a) = c_2 \vee (f_1 \, a) = c_3]$$
$$\text{where } c_i \neq c_j \text{ for all } i \neq j$$

(12)
a. $\quad p_1 \rightarrow f_2 = f_1$
b. $\quad \neg p_1 \rightarrow (f_1 \, a) = c_1$
c. $\quad p_2 \rightarrow (f_2 \, a) = c_2$
d. $\quad \neg p_2 \rightarrow (f_1 \, a) = c_3$

(For clarity, we omit the $\wedge$'s whenever contexted constraints are displayed in a column.) There is an applicable rewrite rule for constraints (12a) and (12c) that produces three new constraints:

(13)
$$\begin{array}{lll} p_1 \rightarrow f_2 = f_1 & \Leftrightarrow & p_1 \rightarrow f_2 = f_1 \\ p_2 \rightarrow (f_2 \, a) = c_2 & & \neg p_1 \wedge p_2 \rightarrow (f_2 \, a) = c_2 \\ & & p_1 \wedge p_2 \rightarrow (f_1 \, a) = c_2 \end{array}$$

Although there is an applicable rewrite rule for (12d) and the last clause of (13), we ignore it since $p_1 \wedge p_2 \wedge \neg p_2$ is FALSE. The only other pair of constraints that can be rewritten are (12b) and (12d), producing three more constraints:

(14)
$$\begin{array}{lll} \neg p_1 \rightarrow (f_1 \, a) = c_1 & \Leftrightarrow & \neg p_1 \rightarrow (f_1 \, a) = c_1 \\ \neg p_2 \rightarrow (f_1 \, a) = c_3 & & p_1 \wedge \neg p_2 \rightarrow (f_1 \, a) = c_3 \\ & & \neg p_1 \wedge \neg p_2 \rightarrow c_1 = c_3 \end{array}$$

Since no more rewrites are possible, the normal form of (12) is thus:

(15)
a. $\quad p_1 \rightarrow f_2 = f_1$
b. $\quad \neg p_1 \rightarrow (f_1 \, a) = c_1$
c. $\quad \neg p_1 \wedge p_2 \rightarrow (f_2 \, a) = c_2$
d. $\quad p_1 \wedge \neg p_2 \rightarrow (f_1 \, a) = c_3$
e. $\quad p_1 \wedge p_2 \rightarrow (f_1 \, a) = c_2$
f. $\quad \neg p_1 \wedge \neg p_2 \rightarrow c_1 = c_3$

4 Extracting the Disjunctive Residue

When the rewriting algorithm is finished, all unsatisfiable combinations of base constraints will have been derived. But more reasoning must be done to determine from base unsatisfiabilities whether the disjunctive system is unsatisfiable. Consider the contexted constraint $P \rightarrow \phi$, where ϕ is unsatisfiable. In order for the conjunction of contexted constraints to be satisfiable, it must be the case that $\neg P$ is true. We call $\neg P$ a *nogood*, following TMS terminology (de Kleer 1986). Since P contains propositional variables indicating disjunctive choices, information about which conjunctions of base constraints are unsatisfiable is thus back-propagated into information about the unsatisfiability of the conjunction of the disjuncts that they come from. The original system as a whole is satisfiable just in case the conjunction of all its nogoods is true. We call the conjunction of all of the nogoods the *residue* of the disjunctive system.

For example, clause (15f) asserts that $\neg p_1 \wedge \neg p_2 \rightarrow c_1 = c_3$. But $c_1 = c_3$ is unsatisfiable, since we know that $c_1 \neq c_3$. Thus $\neg(\neg p_1 \wedge \neg p_2)$ is a nogood. Since $c_1 = c_3$ is the only unsatisfiable base constraint in (15), this is also the disjunctive residue of the system. Thus (11) is satisfiable because $\neg(\neg p_1 \wedge \neg p_2)$ has at least one solution (e.g. p_1 is true and p_2 is true).

Since each nogood may be a complex boolean expression involving conjunctions, disjunctions and negations of propositional variables, determining whether the residue is satisfiable may not be easy. In fact, the problem is NP complete. However, we have accomplished two things by reducing a disjunctive system to its residue. First, since the residue only involves propositional variables, it can be solved by propositional reasoning techniques (such as de Kleer's ATMS (de Kleer 1986)) that do not require specialized knowledge of the problem domain. Second, we believe that for the particular case of linguistics, the final residue will be simpler than the original disjunctive problem. This is because the disjunctions introduced from different parts of the sentence usually involve different attributes in the feature structure, and thus they tend not to interact.

Another way that nogoods can be used is to reduce contexts while the rewriting is being carried out, using identities like the following:

(16) $\neg P_1 \wedge (\neg P_1 \wedge P_2 \rightarrow \phi) \Leftrightarrow \neg P_1 \wedge (P_2 \rightarrow \phi)$

(17) $\neg P_1 \wedge (P_1 \wedge P_2 \rightarrow \phi) \Leftrightarrow \neg P_1$

(18) $P_1 \wedge \neg P_1 \Leftrightarrow \text{FALSE}$

Doing this can improve the performance since some contexts are simplified and some constraints are eliminated altogether. However, the overhead of comparing the nogoods against the contexts may outweigh the potential benefit.

4.1 Complexity Analysis

The first part of our algorithm (converting the original constraints into contexted constraints) is linear in the number of constraints, since the number of transformations in Algorithm 1 is directly proportional to the number of operators in the original formula. In the particular case of unification, the second part (normalizing the constraints) can be made to run in polynomial time (although we have not given a proof of this). The third part, solving the disjunctive residue, contains the exponential that cannot be avoided. However, if the nogoods are mostly independent, then the complexity of this part will be closer to $k2^m$ than 2^n, where $m \ll n$. This is because the disjunctive residue will break down into a number of independent problems each of which is still exponential, but with much smaller exponents.

4.2 Example

Let us assume that the following constraints represent the German words *die* and *Koffer*:

die: $((f \text{ CASE}) = \text{NOM} \lor (f \text{ CASE}) = \text{ACC})$
$\land([[(f \text{ GEND}) = \text{FEM} \land (f \text{ NUM}) = \text{SG}] \lor (f \text{ NUM}) = \text{PL})$

Koffer: $(f \text{ GEND}) = \text{MASC} \land (f \text{ PERS}) = 3\land$
$([[(f \text{ NUM}) = \text{SG} \land (f \text{ CASE}) \neq \text{GEN}]$
$\lor[(f \text{ NUM}) = \text{PL} \land (f \text{ CASE}) \neq \text{DAT}])$

If we convert to contexted constraints and sort by attributes we get the following:

(19)

a.	$p_1 \rightarrow$	$(f \text{ CASE}) = \text{NOM}$
b.	$\neg p_1 \rightarrow$	$(f \text{ CASE}) = \text{ACC}$
c.	$p_3 \rightarrow$	$(f \text{ CASE}) \neq \text{GEN}$
d.	$\neg p_3 \rightarrow$	$(f \text{ CASE}) \neq \text{DAT}$
e.	$p_2 \rightarrow$	$(f \text{ GEND}) = \text{FEM}$
f.	$true \rightarrow$	$(f \text{ GEND}) = \text{MASC}$
g.	$p_2 \rightarrow$	$(f \text{ NUM}) = \text{SG}$
h.	$\neg p_2 \rightarrow$	$(f \text{ NUM}) = \text{PL}$
i.	$p_3 \rightarrow$	$(f \text{ NUM}) = \text{SG}$
j.	$\neg p_3 \rightarrow$	$(f \text{ NUM}) = \text{PL}$
k.	$true \rightarrow$	$(f \text{ PERS}) = 3$

Normalizing the constraints produces the following nogoods:

(20)

a.	p_2	(e and f)
b.	$p_2 \land \neg p_3$	(g and j)
c.	$\neg p_2 \land p_3$	(h and i)

The conjunction of these nogoods has the solutions: $p_1 \land \neg p_2 \land \neg p_3$ and $\neg p_1 \land \neg p_2 \land \neg p_3$.

5 Producing the Models

Assuming that there is a method for producing a model for a conjunction of base constraints, we can produce models from the contexted system. Every assignment of truth values to the propositional variables introduced in Lemma 1 corresponds to a different conjunction of base constraints in the original system, and each such conjunction is an element of the DNF of the original system. Rather than explore the entire space of assignments, we need only enumerate those assignments for which the disjunctive residue is true.

Given an assignment of truth values that is consistent with the disjunctive residue, we can produce a model from the contexted constraints by assigning the truth values to the propositional variables in the contexts, and then discarding those base constraints whose contexts evaluate to false. The minimal model for the remaining base constraints can be determined by inspection if the base constraints are in normal form, as is the case for rewriting algorithms. (Otherwise some deductions may have to be made to produce the model, but the system is guaranteed to be satisfiable.) This minimal model will satisfy the original disjunctive system.

5.1 Example

The residue for the system given in (19) is $\neg p_2 \wedge \neg[p_2 \wedge \neg p_3] \wedge \neg[\neg p_2 \wedge p_3]$. This residue has two solutions: $p_1 \wedge \neg p_2 \wedge \neg p_3$ and $\neg p_1 \wedge \neg p_2 \wedge \neg p_3$. We can produce models for these solutions by extracting the appropriate constraints from (19), and reading off the models. Here are the solutions for this system:

solution:	constraints:	model:
$p_1 \wedge \neg p_2 \wedge \neg p_3$	$(f \text{ CASE}) = \text{NOM} \wedge$ $(f \text{ GEND}) = \text{MASC} \wedge$ $(f \text{ NUM}) = \text{PL} \wedge$ $(f \text{ PERS}) = 3$	$f = \begin{bmatrix} \text{CASE} & \text{NOM} \\ \text{GEND} & \text{MASC} \\ \text{NUM} & \text{PL} \\ \text{PERS} & 3 \end{bmatrix}$
$\neg p_1 \wedge \neg p_2 \wedge \neg p_3$	$(f \text{ CASE}) = \text{ACC} \wedge$ $(f \text{ GEND}) = \text{MASC} \wedge$ $(f \text{ NUM}) = \text{PL} \wedge$ $(f \text{ PERS}) = 3$	$f = \begin{bmatrix} \text{CASE} & \text{ACC} \\ \text{GEND} & \text{MASC} \\ \text{NUM} & \text{PL} \\ \text{PERS} & 3 \end{bmatrix}$

6 Comparison with Other Techniques

In this section we compare disjunctive constraint satisfaction with some of the other techniques that have been developed for dealing with disjunction as it arises in grammatical processing. These other techniques are framed in terms of feature-structure unification and a unification version of our approach would facilitate the comparisons. Although we do not provide a detailed specification of context-extended unification here, we note that unification can be thought of as an indexing scheme for rewriting. We start with a simple illustration of how such an indexing scheme might work.

6.1 Unification Indexing

Regarding unification as an indexing scheme, the main question that needs to be answered is where to index the contexts. Suppose that we index the contexts with the values under the attributes. Then the attribute-value (actually, attribute-*context*-value) matrix for (21a) would be (21b):

(21)   *a.* $(f\,a) = c_1 \vee [(f\,b) = c_2 \vee (f\,a) = c_3]$

$$b. \quad \begin{bmatrix} a & \begin{bmatrix} p_1 & c_1 \\ \neg p_1 \wedge \neg p_2 & c_3 \end{bmatrix} \\ b & \begin{bmatrix} \neg p_1 \wedge p_2 & c_2 \end{bmatrix} \end{bmatrix}$$

Since the contexts are indexed under the attributes, two disjunctions will only interact if they have attributes in common. If they have no attributes in common, their unification will be linear in the number of attributes, rather than multiplicative in the number of disjuncts. For instance, suppose that (22b) is the attribute value matrix for (22a):

(22)   *a.* $(f\,c) = c_4 \vee [(f\,d) = c_5 \vee (f\,e) = c_6]$

$$b. \quad \begin{bmatrix} c & [p_3 & c_4] \\ d & [\neg p_3 \wedge p_4 & c_5] \\ e & [\neg p_3 \wedge \neg p_4 & c_6] \end{bmatrix}$$

Since these disjunctions have no attributes in common, the attribute-value matrix for the conjunction of (21a) and (22a) will be simply the *concatenation* of (21b) and (22b):

(23)
$$\begin{bmatrix} a & \begin{bmatrix} p_1 & c_1 \\ \neg p_1 \wedge \neg p_2 & c_3 \end{bmatrix} \\ b & [\neg p_1 \wedge p_2 & c_2] \\ c & [p_3 & c_4] \\ d & [\neg p_3 \wedge p_4 & c_5] \\ e & [\neg p_3 \wedge \neg p_4 & c_6] \end{bmatrix}$$

The DNF approach to this problem would produce nine f-structures with eighteen attribute-value pairs. In contrast, our approach produces one f-structure with eleven attribute-value and context-value pairs. In general, if disjunctions have independent attributes, then a DNF approach is exponential in the number of disjunctions, whereas our approach is linear. This independence feature is very important for language processing, since, as we have suggested, disjunctions from different parts of a sentence usually constrain different attributes.

6.2 Karttunen's Disjunctive Values

Karttunen (1984) introduced a special type of value called a "disjunctive value" to handle certain types of disjunctions. Disjunctive values allow simple disjunctions such as:

(24) $\qquad (f \text{ CASE}) = \text{ACC} \lor (f \text{ CASE}) = \text{NOM}$

to be represented in the unification data structure as:

(25) $\qquad \left[\text{CASE} \quad \{ \text{NOM ACC} \} \right]$

where the curly brackets indicate a disjunctive value. Karttunen's disjunctive values are not limited to atomic values, as the example he gives for the German article *die* shows:

(26) $\qquad die = \left[\text{INFL} \left[\begin{array}{ll} \text{CASE} & \{ \text{NOM ACC} \} \\ \text{AGR} & \left\{ \begin{array}{l} \left[\begin{array}{ll} \text{GEND} & \text{FEM} \\ \text{NUM} & \text{SG} \end{array} \right] \\ \left[\text{NUM} \quad \text{PL} \right] \end{array} \right\} \end{array} \right] \right]$

The corresponding attribute-context-value matrix for our scheme would be:

(27) $\qquad die = \left[\text{INFL} \left[\begin{array}{ll} \text{CASE} & \left[\begin{array}{ll} p_1 & \text{NOM} \\ \neg p_1 & \text{ACC} \end{array} \right] \\ \text{AGR} & \left[\begin{array}{ll} \text{GEND} & \left[p_2 \quad \text{FEM} \right] \\ \text{NUM} & \left[\begin{array}{ll} p_2 & \text{SG} \\ \neg p_2 & \text{PL} \end{array} \right] \end{array} \right] \end{array} \right] \right]$

The advantage of disjunctive constraint satisfaction is that it can handle all types of disjunctions, whereas disjunctive values can only handle atomic values or simple feature-value matrices with no external dependencies. Furthermore, disjunctive constraint satisfaction can often do better than disjunctive values for the types of disjunctions that they can both handle. This can be seen in (27), where disjunctive constraint satisfaction has pushed a disjunction further down the AGR feature than the disjunctive value approach in (26). This means that if AGR were given an attribute other than GEND or NUM, this new attribute would not interact with the existing disjunction.

However, disjunctive values may have an advantage of reduced overhead, because they do not require embedded contexts and they do not have to keep track of nogoods. It may be worthwhile to incorporate disjunctive values in our scheme to represent the very simple disjunctions, while disjunctive constraint satisfaction is used for the more complex disjunctions.

6.3 Kasper's Successive Approximation

Kasper (1987a, 1987b) proposed that an efficient way to handle disjunctions is to do a step-wise approximation for determining satisfiability. Conceptually, the step-wise algorithm tries to find the inconsistencies that come from fewer disjuncts first. The algorithm starts by unifying the non-disjunctive constraints together. If the non-disjunctive constraints are inconsistent, then there is no need to even consider the disjunctions. If they are consistent, then the disjuncts are unified with them one at a time, where each unification is undone before the next unification is performed. If any of these unifications are inconsistent, then its disjunct is discarded. Then the algorithm unifies the non-disjunctive constraints with all possible pairs of disjuncts, and then all possible triples of disjuncts, and so on. (This technique is called "k-consistency" in the constraint satisfaction literature (Freuder 1978).) In practice, Kasper noted that only the first two steps are computationally useful, and that once bad singleton disjuncts have been eliminated, it is more efficient to switch to DNF than to compute all of the higher degrees of consistency.

Kasper's technique is optimal when most of the disjuncts are inconsistent with the non-disjunctive constraints, or the non-disjunctive constraints are themselves inconsistent. His scheme tends to revert to DNF when this is not the case. Although simple inconsistencies are prevalent in many circumstances, we believe they become less predominant as grammars are extended to cover more and more linguistic phenomena. The coverage of a grammar increases as more options and alternatives are added, either in phrasal rules or lexical entries, so that there are fewer instances of pure non-disjunctive constraints and a greater proportion of inconsistencies involve higher-order interactions. This tendency is exacerbated because of the valuable role that disjunctions play in helping to control the complexity of broad-coverage grammatical specifications. Disjunctions permit constraints to be formulated in local contexts, relying on a general global satisfaction procedure to enforce them in all appropriate circumstances, and thus they improve the modularity and manageability of the overall grammatical system. We have seen this trend towards more localized disjunctive specifications particularly in our developing LFG grammars, and have observed a corresponding reduction in the number of disjuncts that can be eliminated using Kasper's technique. On the other hand, the number of independent disjunctions, which our approach does best on, tends to go up as modularity increases.

One other aspect of LFG grammatical processing is worth noting. Many LFG analyses are ruled out not because they are inconsistent, but rather because they are incomplete. That is, they fail to have an attribute that a predicate requires (e.g. the object is missing for a transitive verb). Since incomplete solutions cannot be ruled out incrementally (an incomplete solution may become complete with the addition of more information), completeness requirements provide no information to eliminate disjuncts in Kasper's successive approximation. These requirements can only be evaluated in what is effectively a disjunctive normal form computation. But our technique avoids this problem, since independent completeness requirements will be simply additive, and any incomplete contexts can be easily read off of the attribute-value matrix and added to the nogoods before solving the residue.

Kasper's scheme works best when disjuncts can be eliminated by unification with non-disjunctive constraints, while ours works best when disjunctions are independent. It is possible to construct a hybrid scheme that works well in both situations. For example, we can use Kasper's scheme up until some critical point (e.g. after the first two steps), and then switch over to our technique instead of computing the higher degrees of consistency.

Another, possibly more interesting, way to incorporate Kasper's strategy is to always process the sets of constraints with the fewest number of propositional variables first. That is, if $P_3 \wedge P_4$ had fewer propositional variables than $P_1 \wedge P_2$, then the rewrite rule in (29) should be done before (28):

(28) $\qquad (P_1 \rightarrow \phi_1) \wedge (P_2 \rightarrow \phi_2) \Rightarrow (P_1 \wedge P_2 \rightarrow \phi_5)$

(29) $\qquad (P_3 \rightarrow \phi_3) \wedge (P_4 \rightarrow \phi_4) \Rightarrow (P_3 \wedge P_4 \rightarrow \phi_6)$

This approach would find smaller nogoods earlier, which would allow combinations of constraints that depended on those nogoods to be ignored, since the contexts would already be known to be inconsistent.

6.4 Eisele and Dörre's techniques

Eisele and Dörre (1988) developed an algorithm for taking Karttunen's notion of disjunctive values a little further. Their algorithm allows disjunctive values to be unified with reentrant structures. The algorithm correctly detects such cases and "lifts the disjunction due to reentrancy".

They give the following example:

(30)
$$
\left[a: \left\{ \begin{bmatrix} b: & + \\ c: & - \end{bmatrix}, \begin{bmatrix} b: & - \\ c: & + \end{bmatrix} \right\} \right] \sqcup \left[a: \begin{bmatrix} b: & \langle d \rangle \\ d: & [\ ] \end{bmatrix} \right] =
$$

$$
\left\{ \begin{bmatrix} a: & \begin{bmatrix} b: & \langle d \rangle \\ c: & - \end{bmatrix} \\ d: & + \end{bmatrix}, \begin{bmatrix} a: & \begin{bmatrix} b: & \langle d \rangle \\ c: & + \end{bmatrix} \\ d: & - \end{bmatrix} \right\}
$$

Notice that the disjunction under the "a" attribute in the first matrix is moved one level up in order to handle the reentrancy introduced in the second matrix under the "b" attribute.

This type of unification can be handled with embedded contexts without requiring that the disjunction be lifted up. In fact, the disjunction is moved down one level, from under "a" to under "b" and "c":

(31)
$$
\left[a: \begin{bmatrix} b: & \begin{bmatrix} p_1 & + \\ \neg p_1 & - \end{bmatrix} \\ c: & \begin{bmatrix} p_1 & - \\ \neg p_1 & + \end{bmatrix} \end{bmatrix} \right] \sqcup \left[a: \begin{bmatrix} b: & \langle d \rangle \\ d: & [\ ] \end{bmatrix} \right] =
$$

$$
\left[a: \begin{bmatrix} b: & \langle d \rangle \\ c: & \begin{bmatrix} p_1 & - \\ \neg p_1 & + \end{bmatrix} \end{bmatrix} \right] \\ d: & \begin{bmatrix} p_1 & + \\ \neg p_1 & - \end{bmatrix}
$$

6.5 Overall Comparison

The major cost of using disjunctive constraint satisfaction is the overhead of dealing with contexts and the disjunctive residue. Our technique is quite general, but if the only types of disjunction that occur are covered by one of the other techniques, then that technique will probably do better than our scheme. For example, if all of the nogoods are the result of singleton inconsistencies (the result of unifying a single disjunct with the non-disjunctive part), then Kasper's successive approximation technique will work better because it avoids our overhead. However, if many of the nogoods involve multiple disjuncts, or if some nogoods are only produced from incomplete solutions, then disjunctive constraint satisfaction will do better than the other techniques, sometimes exponentially so. We also believe that further savings can be achieved by using hybrid techniques if the special cases are sufficiently common to warrant the extra complexity.

7 Concluding Remarks

We set out to exploit a particular property of parsing (namely that constraints under different attributes tend not to interact) in order to obtain better average time performance for constraint satisfaction. Along the way, we have discovered a few strategies that we did not anticipate but in retrospect seem quite useful.

The first strategy is to *use the conjunctive theory to drive the disjunctive theory*. This is useful because in our case the conjunctive theory is polynomial and the disjunctive theory is exponential. Since the conjunctive theory can reduce the search space of the disjunctive theory in polynomial time, this saves the disjunctive theory exponential time. In general, it makes sense to use the more constrained theory to drive the less constrained theory. This is one of the major ways in which we differ from the ATMS (de Kleer 1986) work; the ATMS uses disjunctive information to guide the conjunctive theory, whereas we do it the other way around. We believe that it may be possible to gain more benefits by going even further in this direction.

The second strategy is to *use CNF rather than DNF*. This is because CNF allows for a compact representation of ambiguity. That is, a conjunction of independent disjunctions is much smaller than the equivalent formula expressed as a disjunction of conjunctions. This is particularly important for processing modular linguistic descriptions. In modular systems with separate specifications of syntax, semantics, pragmatics, etc., the syntactic component alone does not include all the constraints needed to determine the ultimately correct analysis of a sentence. It usually provides a set of possible outputs that are then filtered by the constraints of the more abstract modules, and these outputs are typically enumerated as a (possibly large) set of separate alternative structures. But in the absence of semantic or pragmatic constraints, many of the residual syntactic ambiguities appear as free or independent disjunctions, and these can be encoded efficiently using CNF. Thus, our approach to disjunction has the added advantage of reducing the performance penalty frequently associated with modular characterizations of linguistic information.

Acknowledgments

The approach described in this paper emerged from discussion and interaction with a number of our colleagues. We are particularly indebted to John Lamping, who suggested the initial formulation of Lemma 1, and to Bill Rounds for pointing out the relationship between our conversion algorithm and the NP completeness reduction for CNF. We are also grateful for many helpful discussions with Dan Bobrow, Johan de Kleer, Jochen Dörre, Andreas Eisele, Pat Hayes, Mark Johnson, Lauri Karttunen, and Martin Kay.

References

de Kleer, Johan. 1986. An Assumption-based TMS. *Artificial Intelligence* 28:127–162.

Eisele, Andreas, and Jochen Dörre. 1988. Unification of Disjunctive Feature Descriptions. In *Proceedings of the Twenty-Sixth Annual Meeting of the ACL*, 286–294. Buffalo, NY. Association for Computational Linguistics.

Freuder, E. C. 1978. Synthesizing Constraint Expressions. In *Communications of the ACM*, Vol. 21, 958–966.

Hopcroft, John E., and Jeffrey D. Ullman. 1979. *Introduction to Automata Theory, Languages and Computation.* Reading, MA: Addison-Wesley.

Johnson, Mark. 1987. *Attribute-Value Logic and the Theory of Grammar.* Doctoral dissertation, Stanford University. Also published as CSLI Lecture Notes, No. 16. Stanford University: CSLI/The University of Chicago Press. 1988.

Kaplan, Ronald M., and Joan Bresnan. 1982. Lexical-Functional Grammar: A Formal System for Grammatical Representation. In *The Mental Representation of Grammatical Relations*, ed. Joan Bresnan, 173–281. Cambridge, MA: The MIT Press. Reprinted in Part I of this volume.

Karttunen, Lauri. 1984. Features and values. In *Proceedings of COLING-84*, 28–33. Stanford, CA.

Karttunen, Lauri. 1986. D-PATR: A Development Environment for Unification-Based Grammars. In *Proceedings of COLING-86*. Bonn. Also published as CSLI Report 61, Center for the Study of Language and Information, Stanford University, 1986.

Karttunen, Lauri. 1989. Radical Lexicalism. In *Alternative Conceptions of Phrase Structure*, ed. Mark Baltin and Anthony Kroch. Chicago University Press.

Kasper, Robert T. 1987a. *Feature Structures: A Logical Theory with Application to Language Analysis.* Doctoral dissertation, University of Michigan.

Kasper, Robert T. 1987b. A Unification Method for Disjunctive Feature Descriptions. In *Proceedings of the Twenty-Fifth Annual Meeting of the ACL*, 235–242. Stanford, CA. Association for Computational Linguistics.

Kay, Martin. 1979. Functional Grammar. In *Proceedings of the Fifth Annual Meeting of the Berkeley Linguistic Society*, ed. Christine Chiarello, John Kingston, Eve E. Sweetser, James Collins, Haruko Kawasaki, John Manley-Buser, Dorothy W. Marschak, Catherine O'Connor, David Shaul, Marta Tobey, Henry Thompson, and Katherine Turner, 142–158. The University of California at Berkeley. Berkeley Linguistics Society.

Kay, Martin. 1982. Parsing in Functional Unification Grammar. In *Natural Language Parsing*, ed. David R. Dowty, Lauri Karttunen, and A. Zwicky, 251–278. Cambridge, England: Cambridge University Press.

Pollard, Carl, and Ivan A. Sag. 1987. *Information-Based Syntax and Semantics, Volume I*. No. 13 CSLI Lecture Notes. Stanford University: CSLI/The University of Chicago Press.

Uszkoreit, Hans. 1986. Categorial Unification Grammars. In *Proceedings of COLING-86*. Bonn.

Zeevat, Henk, Ewan Klein, and Jo Calder. 1987. Unification categorial grammar. In *Categorial Grammar, Unification Grammar, and Parsing*, ed. N. Haddock, Ewan Klein, and Glyn Morrill. Edinburgh, Scotland: University of Edinburgh.

15

The Interface between Phrasal and Functional Constraints

JOHN T. MAXWELL III AND RONALD M. KAPLAN

Abstract. Many modern grammatical formalisms divide the task of linguistic specification into a context-free component of phrasal constraints and a separate component of attribute-value or functional constraints. Conventional methods for recognizing the strings of a language also divide into two parts so that they can exploit the different computational properties of these components. This paper focuses on the interface between these components as a source of computational complexity distinct from the complexity internal to each. We first analyze the common hybrid strategy in which a polynomial context-free parser is modified to interleave functional constraint solving with context-free constituent analysis. This strategy depends on the property of monotonicity in order to prune unnecessary computation. We describe a number of other properties that can be exploited for computational advantage, and we analyze some alternative interface strategies based on them. We present the results of preliminary experiments that generally support our intuitive analyses. A surprising outcome is that under certain circumstances an algorithm that does no pruning in the interface may perform significantly better than one that does.

1 Introduction

A wide range of modern grammatical formalisms divide the task of linguistic specification either explicitly or implicitly into a context-free com-

This paper originally appeared in *Computational Linguistics* 19(4): 571–590. 1993. Used by permission of the Association for Computational Linguistics; copies of the publication from which this material is derived can can be obtained through Priscilla Rasmussen, ACL Office Manager, P.O. Box 6090 Somerset, NJ 08875, USA.

Formal Issues in Lexical-Functional Grammar
edited by
Mary Dalrymple
Ronald M. Kaplan
John T. Maxwell III
Annie Zaenen
Copyright © 1995, Stanford University

403

ponent of phrasal constraints and a separate component of attribute-value or functional constraints. Lexical-Functional Grammar (Kaplan and Bresnan 1982), for example, is very explicit in assigning both a phrase-structure tree and an attribute-value functional structure to every sentence of a language. Generalized Phrase Structure Grammar (Gazdar et al. 1985) assigns a phrase-structure tree whose categories are attribute-value structures. For Functional Unification Grammar (Kay 1979) and other unification formalisms that evolved from it (such as HPSG (Pollard and Sag 1987)), the phrase structure is more implicit, showing up as the record of the control strategy that recursively re-instantiates the collection of attribute-value constraints from the grammar. For Definite Clause Grammars (Pereira and Warren 1980) the phrase-structure is implicit in the unification of the concealed string-position variables and the recursive re-instantiation of the additional logic variables that carry functional information.

The computational problem of recognizing whether a given string belongs to the language of a grammar also divides into two parts, since it must be determined that the string satisfies both the phrasal and functional constraints. These two types of constraints have different computational properties. It is well known that context-free phrase structure constraints can be solved in time polynomial in the length of the input sentence, whereas all known algorithms for solving Boolean combinations of equality or unification constraints in the worst-case run in time exponential in size of the constraint system.

There have been a number of approaches for implementing such hybrid constraint systems. In one approach the context-free constraints are converted to the form of more general functional constraints so that a general purpose constraint satisfaction method can uniformly solve all constraints. While this has the advantage of simplicity and elegance, it usually gains no advantage from the special properties of the context-free subsystem. The original implementation for DCGs (Pereira and Warren 1980) followed this strategy by translating the grammar into equivalent Prolog clauses and using the general Prolog interpreter to solve them.

On the other hand, functional constraints of a sufficiently restricted kind can be translated into context-free phrasal constraints and solved with special purpose mechanisms. This is true, for example, of all GPSG feature constraints. In the extreme, a GPSG grammar could be completely converted to an equivalent context-free one and processed with only phrasal mechanisms, but the fast polynomial bound may then be overwhelmed by an enormous grammar-size constant, making this approach computationally infeasible for any realistic grammar (Barton et al. 1987).

More common approaches involve hybrid implementations that attempt to take advantage of the special computational properties of phrasal constraints while also handling the general expressiveness of arbitrary feature constraints. Although this sounds good in principle, it turns out to be hard to accomplish in practice. An obvious first approach, for example, is to solve the context-free constraints first using familiar polynomial algorithms (Earley 1970, Kaplan 1973, Younger 1967), and then to enumerate the resulting phrase-structure trees. Their corresponding functional constraints are solved by converting to disjunctive normal form (DNF) and using also well-known general purpose constraint algorithms (Nelson and Oppen 1980, Knight 1989).

This configuration involves a simple composition of well-understood techniques but has proven to be a computational disaster. The phrasal mechanisms compute in polynomial time a compact representation of all possible trees, each of which presents a potentially exponential problem for the constraint solver to solve. If the phrasal component is not properly restricted, there can be an infinite number of such trees and the whole system is undecidable (Kaplan and Bresnan 1982). But even with an appropriate restriction on valid phrase structures, such as LFG's prohibition against nonbranching dominance chains, the number of such trees can be exponential in the length of the sentence. Thus, even though a context-free parser can very quickly determine that those trees exist, if the grammar is exponentially ambiguous then the net effect is to produce an exponential number of potentially exponential functional constraint problems.

This is an important observation. There have been several successful efforts in recent years to develop solution algorithms for Boolean combinations of functional constraints that are polynomial for certain special, perhaps typical, cases (Kasper 1987, Maxwell and Kaplan 1989, Dörre and Eisele 1990, Nakano 1991). But even if the functional constraints could always be solved in polynomial time (for instance, if there were no disjunctions), the simple composition of phrasal constraints and functional constraints would still in the worst case be exponential in sentence length. This exponential does not come from either of the components independently; rather, it lies in the interface between them.

Of course, simple composition is not the only strategy for solving hybrid constraint systems. A typical approach involves interleaving phrasal and functional processing. The functional constraints associated with each constituent are incrementally solved as the constituent is being constructed, and the constituent is discarded if those constraints prove to be unsatisfiable. Although this interface strategy avoids the blatant excesses of simple composition, we show below that in the worst case it is also exponential in sentence length. However, it is too early to conclude that there is no sub-exponential interface strategy, since the computational properties of this interface have not yet been extensively investigated. This paper maps out a space of interface possibilities, describes alternative strategies that can provide exponential improvements in certain common situations, and suggests a number of areas for further exploration.

2 Interleaved Pruning

We begin by examining in more detail the common hybrid strategy in which a polynomial context-free parser is modified to interleave functional constraint solving with context-free constituent analysis. All known polynomial parsers make essentially equivalent use of a well-formed substring table (Sheil 1976), so we can illustrate the computational properties of interleaved strategies in general by focusing on the familiar operations of active-chart parsing (Kaplan 1973, Kay 1986 (1980), Thompson 1983). There are, of course, other popular parsers, such as the generalized LR(k) parser (Tomita 1986); however in the worst-case these are known not to be polynomial (Johnson 1989) unless a chart-like mechanism is added (Schabes 1991), and so they raise no new interface issues. Here and in the remainder of this paper we assume the restriction against nonbranching dominance chains to guarantee termination of the parsing computation.

2.1 The Active Chart Parser

Recall that the chart in an active-chart parser contains edges that record how various portions of the input string match the categorial sequences specified by different rules. An inactive edge spans a substring that satisfies all the categorial requirements of a rule and thus represents the fact that a constituent has been completely identified. An active edge spans a substring that matches only part of a rule and represents a constituent whose daughters have only been partially identified. An active edge may span an empty substring at a particular string position and indicate that no rule categories have yet been matched; such an edge represents the unconfirmed hypothesis that a constituent of the rule's type starts at that string position.

The chart is initialized by adding inactive edges corresponding to the lexical items and at least one empty active edge before the first word. The active edge represents the hypothesis that an instance of the root category starts at the beginning of the input string. The computation proceeds according to the following fundamental rules: First, whenever an active edge is added to the chart, then a new edge is created for each of the inactive edges to its right whose category can be used to extend the rule-match one step further. The new edge records the extended match and spans the combined substrings of the active and inactive edges. Also, for each category that can extend the active edge, a new empty edge is created to hypothesize the existence of a constituent of that type beginning to the right of the active edge. Second, whenever an inactive edge is added to the chart, a new edge is similarly created for each active edge to its left whose rule-match can be extended by the category of the inactive edge. Newly created edges are added to the chart and spawn further computations only if they are not equivalent to edges that were added in previous steps. Thus, in Figure 1, only one new edge n is created for the four different ways of combining the active edges a_x with the inactive edges i_y.

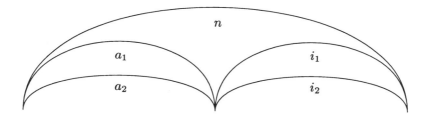

FIGURE 1 Context-Free Edge Creation

The polynomial behavior of this algorithm for a context-free grammar depends crucially on the fact that equivalent edges are proscribed and that the number of distinct edges is polynomial in sentence length. In the context-free case, two edges are equivalent if they span the same substring and impose exactly the same requirements for further matching of the same rule. The polynomial bound on the number of distinct edges comes from the fact that equivalence does not depend on the internal substructure of previously matched daughter constituents (Sheil 1976). The chart data structures are carefully organized to make equivalent edges easy to detect.

Conceptually, the chart is only used for determining whether or not a string belongs to the language of a context-free grammar, and by itself does not give any trees for that string. A *parse-forest* variation of the chart can be created by annotating each edge with all of the combinations of active and inactive edges that it could come from (these annotations are ignored for the purpose of equivalence). This representation can be used to read out quickly each of the trees that are allowed by the grammar. Note that a parse-forest representation still only requires space polynomial in sentence length since there are only a polynomial number of ways for each of the edges to be constructed out of edges with the same termination points.

2.2 Augmenting the Active Chart Parser with Functional Constraints

The main benefit of the chart algorithm is that subtrees are not recomputed when they are incorporated as daughters in alternative trees. It is possible to retain this benefit while also allowing functional constraints to be processed as constituents are being analyzed. Edges are augmented so that they also record the functional constraints associated with a constituent. The constraints associated with lexical items are stored in the initial inactive edges that correspond to them. Whenever a new edge is created from an active and an inactive, its constraints are formed by conjoining together the constraints of those edges with the constraints specified on the rule-category that matches the inactive edge. Having collected the constraints for each edge in this way, we know that the input string is grammatical if it is spanned by a root-category edge whose constraints are satisfiable. Note that for this to be the case, the notion of equivalence must also be augmented to take account of the constraints: two edges are equivalent now if, in addition to satisfying the conditions specified above, they have the same constraints (or perhaps only logically equivalent ones).

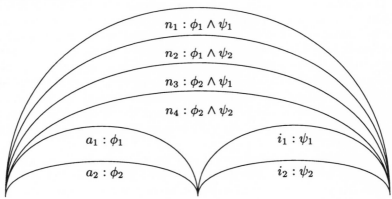

FIGURE 2 Augmented Edge Creation

These augmentations impose a potentially serious computational burden, as illustrated in Figure 2. Here, ϕ_x and ψ_y represent the constraints associated with a_x and i_y, respectively. Although we are still carrying out the steps of the polynomial context-free algorithm, the behavior is no longer polynomial. The constraints of an edge include those from the particular rule-categories that match against its daughter edges, with different daughter matches resulting in different constraints. The net effect is that there can be a different set of constraints for every way in which a particular category can be realized over a given substring. If the phrase-structure grammar is exponentially ambiguous, there will be exponentially many ways of building at least one constituent, and there will be exponentially many edges in the chart (distinguished by their constraints). Thus we retain the time benefit of avoiding subtree recomputation but the algorithm becomes exponential in the worst-case.

2.3   The Advantage of Pruning

This strategy has proved to be very appealing, however, because it does offer computational advantages over the simple composition approach. Under this regime every edge, not just the spanning roots, has its own constraints, and we can therefore determine the satisfiability of every edge as it is being constructed. If the constraint system is monotonic and the constraints for a particular edge are determined to be unsatisfiable, then that edge is discarded. The effect of this is to prune from the search space all edges that might otherwise have been constructed from unsatisfiable ones. This is illustrated in Figure 3, where S[ϕ] denotes the solution of ϕ, and X indicates that a solution is unsatisfiable. Since ϕ_1 is unsatisfiable, n_1 and n_2 never get built. Pruning n_1 and n_2 does not eliminate any valid solutions, since we know that their constraints would also have been unsatisfiable. Thus, by incrementally gathering and solving functional constraints, we can potentially eliminate from later consideration a number of trees exponential in sentence length. In some cases it may only take a polynomial amount of work to determine all solutions even though the phrasal constraints are exponentially ambiguous.

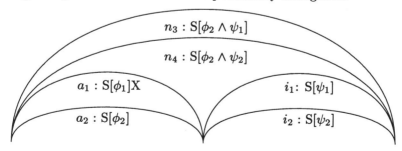

FIGURE 3 The Advantage of Pruning

A familiar variation on the pruning strategy is to use the solutions associated with daughter constituents when computing a solution for a mother's constraints. This can have a significant effect, since it avoids recomputing the solutions to the daughters' constraints in the process of solving those of the mother. However, there is a technical issue that needs to be addressed. Since a daughter edge may be used by more than one mother, its solution cannot be changed destructively without the risk of introducing cross-talk between independent mothers. One way to avoid this is to copy the daughter solutions before merging them together, but this can be expensive. In recent years, there has been a great deal of attention devoted to this problem, and a number of different techniques have been advanced to reduce the amount of copying (Karttunen 1986, Wroblewski 1987, Godden 1990, Tomabechi 1991).

2.4 Still Exponential

Although pruning can eliminate an exponential number of trees, this strategy is still exponential in sentence length in the worst case when the grammar is exponentially ambiguous with few constituents that are actually pruned. There are two cases where few constituents are actually pruned. One is true ambiguity, such as occurs with unrestricted prepositional phrase attachment. The grammar for PPs in English is well-known to be exponentially ambiguous (Church and Patil 1982). If there are no functional or semantic restrictions on how the PPs attach, then none of the possibilities will be pruned and the interleaved pruning strategy, just like simple composition, will produce an exponential number of constituents spanning a string of prepositional phrases.

The other case where few constituents are actually pruned is when most candidate solutions are eliminated high in the tree, for example, because they are incomplete rather than inconsistent. In LFG (Kaplan and Bresnan 1982) functional constraints are incomplete when a predicate requires grammatical functions that are not realized in the string. (The requirement that predicate argument frames be completely filled is encoded in different but equivalent ways in other formalisms.) This can occur when, say, a verb requires a SUBJ and an OBJ, but the tree only provides a SUBJ. Since edges constructed from an incomplete edge may themselves be complete, incomplete edges cannot be discarded from the chart.

In sum, although the interleaved bottom-up strategy does permit some edges to be discarded and prunes the exponentially many trees that might be built on top of them, it does not in general eliminate the exponential explosion at the phrasal-functional interface. In fact, some researchers have observed that an augmented chart, even with interleaved pruning, may actually be worse than general constraint satisfaction algorithms because of the exponential space required to cache intermediate results [Varile, Damas, and van Noord, personal communications].

3   Exploitable Properties

Monotonicity is one of several constraint system properties that can be exploited to produce different interface strategies. Other properties include independence, conciseness, order invariance and constraint system overlap. In the remainder of this section we discuss these properties and outline some techniques for exploiting them. In the following sections we give examples of interface algorithms that incorporate some of these techniques. Finally, we compare the performance of these algorithms on a sample grammar and some sample sentences.

3.1   Monotonicity

A system of constraints is *monotonic* if no deduction is ever retracted when new constraints are conjoined. This means that if ψ is unsatisfiable, then $\psi \wedge \phi$ is also unsatisfiable for arbitrary ϕ, so that ϕ can be completely ignored. This property is exploited, for instance, in unification algorithms which terminate as soon as an inconsistency is detected. In order for this to be a useful heuristic, it must be easy to determine that ψ is unsatisfiable and hard to solve $\psi \wedge \phi$. In the interleaved pruning strategy, determining that a constituent's constraints are unsatisfiable can be expensive, but this cost is often offset by the exponential number of edges that may be eliminated when a constituent is discarded. In general, the usefulness of the interleaved pruning strategy is determined by the fraction of edges that are pruned.

3.2   Independence

Two systems of constraints are *independent* if no new constraints can be deduced when the systems are conjoined. In particular, two disjunctions $\bigvee_i \phi_i$ and $\bigvee_j \psi_j$ are independent if there are no i, j and atomic formula χ such that $\phi_i \wedge \psi_j \rightarrow \chi$ and $\neg(\phi_i \rightarrow \chi)$ and $\neg(\psi_j \rightarrow \chi)$. If two systems of constraints are independent, then it can be shown that their conjunction is satisfiable if and only if they are both satisfiable in isolation. This is because there is no way of deriving false from the conjunction of any sub-constraints if false was not already implied by one of those subconstraints by itself. Independence is most advantageous when the systems contain disjunctions, since there is no need to multiply into disjunctive normal form in order to determine the satisfiability of the conjunction. This can save an amount of work exponential in the number of disjunctions, modulo the cost of determining or producing independence.

One example of an algorithm that exploits independence is the context-free chart parser. Since sister constituents are independent of each other, their satisfiability can be determined separately. This is what makes a context-free chart parser polynomial instead of exponential. There are also several disjunctive unification algorithms that exploit independence, such as constraint unification (Hasida 1986, Nakano 1991), contexted unification (Maxwell and Kaplan 1989), and unification based on disjunctive feature logic (Dörre and Eisele 1990).

We say that a system of constraints is in *free-choice form* if it is a conjunction of independent disjunctions and all of the disjuncts are satisfiable. This means that we can freely choose one disjunct from each disjunction and the result of conjoining these disjuncts together is guaranteed to be satisfiable. If recursively all of the disjuncts are also in free-choice form, then we have a *nested free-choice form*. The parse-forest representation for the chart discussed earlier is an example of a nested free-choice form. The advantage of such a form is that an exponential number of solutions (trees) can be represented in polynomial space. In general, any system of constraints in free-choice form can produce a number of solutions exponential in the size of the system. Each solution only requires a polynomial number of disjunctive choices to produce.

3.3   Conciseness

We say that a constraint system (or solution) is *concise* if its size is a polynomial function of the input that it was derived from. Most systems of constraints that have been converted to DNF are not concise, since in general converting a system of constraints to DNF produces a system that is exponential in the size of the original. Free-choice systems may or may not be concise. However, the constraint systems that tend to arise in solving grammatical descriptions are often concise when kept in free-choice form.

It is an important but often overlooked property of parse-forest representations of context-free charts that they are concise. All of the solutions of even an exponentially ambiguous context-free grammar can be represented in a structure whose size is cubic in the size of the input string and quadratic in the size of the grammar. So far, there has been little attention to the problem of developing algorithms for hybrid systems that exploit this property of the chart.

A constraint system may be made concise by *factoring* the constraints. A disjunction can be factored if there is a common part to all of its disjunctions. That is, the disjunction $(A \wedge \phi_1) \vee (A \wedge \phi_2) \vee ...(A \wedge \phi_n)$ can be reduced to $A \wedge (\phi_1 \vee \phi_2 \vee ...\phi_n)$. Another advantage of factoring is that under certain circumstances it can improve the effectiveness of the pruning and partitioning techniques mentioned above. For instance, suppose that two disjunctions are conjoined, one with factor A and the other with factor B, and that $A \wedge B \rightarrow$ FALSE. Then if A and B are factored out and processed before the residual disjunctions, then the disjunctions don't have to be multiplied out. In a similar manner, if A and B are independent of the residual disjunctions, and the residual disjunctions are also independent of each other, then factoring A and B out first would allow the problem to be partitioned into three independent sub-problems and again the disjunctions would not have to be multiplied out. Thus under some circumstances, factoring can save an exponential amount of work. In Section 5 we discuss an interface algorithm based on factoring.

3.4 Order Invariance

Phrasal constraint systems and functional constraint systems commonly used for linguistic description have the property that they can be processed in any order without changing the final result. Although the order that the constraints are processed doesn't change the result in any way, it can have a dramatic impact on how quickly solutions can be found or non-solutions discarded. Unfortunately, we do not know in advance which order will find solutions or discard non-solutions in the shortest amount of time, and so we depend on heuristics that choose an order that is thought more likely to evaluate solutions quickly. The question of processing order can be broken down into three parts: the order in which functional constraints are processed, the order in which phrasal constraints are processed, and the order in which functional and phrasal constraints are processed relative to one another.

There has been a lot of effort directed towards finding the best order for processing functional constraints. Kasper observed that separating constraints into disjunctive and non-disjunctive parts and processing the non-disjunctive constraints first can improve performance when the non-disjunctive constraints are unsatisfiable (Kasper 1987). It has also been observed that the order in which features are unified can have an effect, and that it is better to unify morpho-syntactic features before structural features. Both of these approaches reorder the constraints so that pruning is more effective, taking advantage of the monotonicity of functional constraints.

Research in context-free parsing has led to methods that can process phrasal constraints in any order and still maintain a polynomial time bound (e.g. Sheil 1976). However, in an interleaved strategy the order in which phrasal constraints are evaluated can make a substantial performance difference. This is because it determines the order in which the functional constraints are processed. The particular interleaved strategy discussed above effectively builds constituents and thus solves functional constraints in a bottom-up order. An alternative strategy might build constituents top-down and prune daughters whenever the collection of top-down functional constraints are unsatisfiable. It is also possible to process constituents in a head-driven order (Kay 1989) or to utilize an opportunistic islands-of-certainty heuristic (Stock et al. 1988).

The relative processing order of phrasal and functional constraints is not as well-studied. There has been relatively uncritical acceptance of the basic interleaved arrangement. Another possibility might be to process all of the functional constraints before the phrasal constraints. An example of this kind of strategy is a semantic-driven algorithm, where subjects and objects are chosen from the string for their semantic properties, and then phrasal constraints are checked to determine whether the connection makes sense syntactically. In Section 4 we describe still another algorithm in which all of the phrasal constraints are processed before any of the functional constraints and discuss the advantages of this order.

3.5 Constraint System Overlap

As we mentioned in the introduction, the division between phrasal and functional constraints is somewhat fluid. All phrasal constraints can be converted into functional constraints, and some functional constraints can be converted into phrasal constraints. Turning all of the phrasal constraints into functional constraints obscures their special computational properties. On the other hand, turning all of the functional constraints into phrasal constraints is impractical even when possible because of the huge grammar that usually results. So it seems that the ideal is somewhere in between, but where? In Section 7, we observe that moving the boundary between phrasal and functional constraints can have a striking computational advantage in some cases.

4   Non-Interleaved Pruning

We now consider a pruning strategy that does not interleave the processing of phrasal and functional constraints. Instead, all of the phrasal constraints are processed first, and then all of the functional constraints are collected and processed. This takes advantage of the fact that our constraint systems are order invariant. In the first step, an unmodified context-free chart parser processes the phrasal constraints and produces a parse-forest representation of all the legal trees. In the second step, the parse-forest is traversed in a recursive descent starting from the root spanning edge. At each edge in the parse forest the solutions of the daughter edges are first determined recursively and then combined to produce solutions for the mother edge. For each way that the edge can be constructed, the daughter solutions of that way are conjoined and solved. If a daughter edge has no solutions, then there is no need to extract the solutions of any remaining sisters. The resulting set of solutions is cached on the mother in case the mother is also part of another tree. This process is illustrated in Figure 4. Note that this strategy differs from simple composition in that the functional component operates on edges in the chart rather than individually enumerated trees.

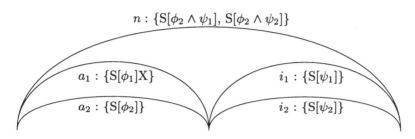

$$n : \{S[\phi_2 \wedge \psi_1], S[\phi_2 \wedge \psi_2]\}$$

$$a_1 : \{S[\phi_1]X\}$$

$$a_2 : \{S[\phi_2]\}$$

$$i_1 : \{S[\psi_1]\}$$

$$i_2 : \{S[\psi_2]\}$$

FIGURE 4 Non-Interleaved Pruning

The first step of this strategy is polynomial in sentence length since we can use a context-free algorithm that does not accumulate constraints for each constituent. The second step may be exponential since it does accumulate constraints for each edge and the constraints can encode all possible sub-trees for that edge. However, this method filters the functional computation using the global well-formedness of the phrase structure constraints. The performance can be significantly better than an interleaved approach if an exponentially ambiguous sub-tree fits into no complete parse tree. The disadvantage of this approach is that edges that might have been eliminated by the functional constraints have to be processed by the chart parser. However, this can at most add a polynomial amount of work, since the chart parser is in the worst case polynomial. Of course, this approach still incurs the overhead of copying, since it caches solutions on each edge.

5   Factored Extraction

We now examine an interface algorithm that is very different from both interleaved and non-interleaved pruning. Instead of focusing on pruning, this strategy focuses on factoring. We call this strategy a *factored extraction* strategy because it extracts a concise set of functional constraints from a chart and then passes the constraints to a constraint solver. Unlike the pruning strategies, constraints are not solved on an edge-by-edge basis: only the constraints for the spanning root edge are solved. Thus this is a non-interleaved strategy.

As with the non-interleaved pruning strategy, the first step is to build a chart based on the context-free grammar alone. This can be done in polynomial time using the active chart parser, and has the advantage of filtering constituents that are not part of some spanning tree for the sentence.

The second step is to extract the system of constraints associated with the spanning root edge. Consider the parse forest for the sentence *Bill saw the girl with the telescope* given in Figure 5. All of the constituents that are not part of a spanning tree have already been eliminated (for instance, the S that spans *Bill saw the girl*). The letters *a* through *v* represent lexical and grammatical constraints. For instance, *a* stands for the lexical constraints for *Bill* as an NP, and *u* stands for the grammatical constraint $(f_S \text{ SUBJ}) = f_{NP(Bill)}$, indicating that the NP that dominates *Bill* is the subject of S. Structural ambiguity is represented by a bracket over the ambiguous constituents. In this case, there is only one structural ambiguity, the one between the VPs that span the string *saw the girl with the telescope*. They represent two different ways of attaching the PP; the first attaches it to *saw*, and the second attaches it to *girl*.

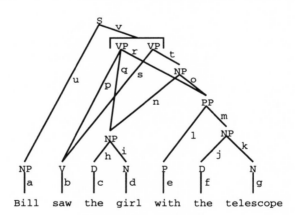

FIGURE 5 Parse Forest

We extract the system of constraints for this sentence by starting from the S at the top and conjoining the result of recursively extracting constraints from its daughters. For constituents that are ambiguous, we *disjoin* the result of extracting the constraints of the ambiguous constituents. In addition, we cache the constraints of each node that we encounter, so that even if a node can be incorporated in more than one parse, we need only extract its constraints once. Note that since we are not caching solved constraints, there can be no cross-talk between constituents and copying is therefore not required. The result of this process is a re-entrant structure that is polynomial in the length of the string. If the re-entrant structure were expanded, it would produce the following:

$$a \wedge u \wedge [(b \wedge p \wedge c \wedge h \wedge d \wedge i \wedge q \wedge e \wedge l \wedge f \wedge j \wedge g \wedge k \wedge m \wedge r) \vee (b \wedge s \wedge c \wedge h \wedge d \wedge i \wedge n \wedge e \wedge l \wedge f \wedge j \wedge g \wedge k \wedge m \wedge o \wedge t)] \wedge v$$

However, instead of expanding the constraints, we make them smaller by factoring common elements out of the disjunctions. For instance, the b constraint is common to both disjuncts, and hence can be factored into the conjunctive part. Also, since the p and s constraints identically encode the relationship between the verb and the VP, they can also be factored. In general, we factor disjunctions on a node by node basis and cache the results on each node, to avoid repeating the factoring computation. Although a straight-forward implementation for factoring two sets of constraints would be quadratic in the number of edges, a linear factoring algorithm is possible if the constraints are sorted by string position and height in the tree (as they are in the example above). Factoring produces the following system of constraints:

$$a \wedge u \wedge b \wedge c \wedge h \wedge d \wedge i \wedge e \wedge l \wedge f \wedge j \wedge g \wedge k \wedge m \wedge p \wedge [(q \wedge r) \vee (n \wedge o \wedge t)] \wedge v$$

We can make factoring even more effective by doing some simple constraint analysis. In LFG, for example, the head of a constituent is usually annotated with the constraint $\uparrow = \downarrow$. This equality means that the head can be substituted for the mother without affecting satisfiability. This substitution tends to increase the number of common constraints, and thus increases the potential for factoring. In this example, q and t become the same since the NPs have the same head and n becomes tautologically true since its only function is to designate the head. This means that the disjunction can be reduced to just $r \vee o$:

$$a \wedge u \wedge b \wedge c \wedge h \wedge d \wedge i \wedge e \wedge l \wedge f \wedge j \wedge g \wedge k \wedge m \wedge p \wedge q \wedge (r \vee o) \wedge v$$

Thus the resulting system of constraints is completely conjunctive except for the question of where the PP attaches. This is the ideal functional characterization for this sentence. This approach produces an effect similar to Bear and Hobbs (1988), only without requiring special mechanisms.

It also avoids the objections that Wittenburg and Barnett (1988) raise to a canonical representation for PP attachment, such as always attaching low. The only point at which special linguistic knowledge is utilized is the last step, where constraint analysis depends on the fact that heads can be substituted for mothers in LFG. Similar head-dependent analyses may also be possible for other grammatical theories, but factoring can make the constraint system substantially smaller even without this refinement.

Factoring is advantageous whenever a node participates in all of the sub-trees of another node. For example, this occurs frequently in adjunct attachment, as we have seen. It also occurs when a lexical item has the same category in all the parses of a sentence, which permits all the constraints associated with that lexical item to be factored out to the top level. Another advantage of the extraction algorithm comes from the fact that it does not solve the constraints on a per-edge basis, so that copying is not an issue for the phrasal-functional interface (although it still may be an issue internal to some functional constraint solvers).

The major disadvantage of factored extraction is that no pruning is done in the interface. This is left for the functional constraint solver, which may or may not know how to prune constraints based on their dependencies in the chart. Without pruning, the solver may do an exponential amount of futile work. In the next two sections we describe ways to get both pruning and factoring in the same algorithm.

6 Factored Pruning

It is relatively easy to add factoring to the non-interleaved pruning strategy. Remember that in that strategy the result of processing an edge is a disjunction of solutions, one for each alternative sequence of daughter edges. We can factor these solutions before any of them are used by higher edges (note that this is easier to do in a non-interleaved strategy than an interleaved one). That is, if there are any common sub-parts, then the result will be a conjunction of these sub-parts with a residue of disjunctions. This is very similar to the factoring in factored extraction, except that we are no longer able to take advantage of the phrasally motivated groupings of constraints to rapidly identify large common sub-parts. Instead we must factor at the level of individual constraints, since the solving process tends to destroy these groupings.

The advantage of factored pruning over factored extraction is that we can prune, although at the cost of having to copy solutions. In the next section we will describe a complementary strategy that has the effect of adding pruning to factored extraction without losing its non-copying character.

7   Selective Feature Movement

So far we have examined how the properties of monotonicity, independence, conciseness, and order invariance can be exploited in the phrasal-functional interface. To conclude our discussion of interface strategies, we now consider how constraint system overlap can be exploited. As we have noted, many functional constraints can in principle be converted to phrasal constraints. Although converting all such functional constraints is a bad idea, it can be quite advantageous to convert some of them, namely, those constraints that would enable the context-free parser to prune the space of constituents.

Consider a grammar with the following two rules (using LFG notation (Kaplan and Bresnan 1982)):

$$
S \longrightarrow \begin{pmatrix} S' \\ \downarrow \in (\uparrow \text{ADJUNCT}) \\ (\downarrow \text{COMPL}) = + \end{pmatrix} \quad \begin{matrix} NP \\ (\uparrow \text{SUBJ}) = \downarrow \end{matrix} \quad \begin{matrix} VP \\ \uparrow = \downarrow \end{matrix}
$$

$$
S' \longrightarrow \left\{ \begin{matrix} \text{COMP} \\ (\uparrow \text{COMPL}) = + \\ \\ e \\ (\uparrow \text{COMPL}) = - \end{matrix} \right\} \quad \begin{matrix} S \\ \uparrow = \downarrow \end{matrix}
$$

The first rule says that an S consists of an NP and a VP optionally preceded by an S'. The functional constraints assert that the functional structure corresponding to the NP is the SUBJ of the one corresponding to the S, the VP's f-structure is the head, and the f-structure of the S' is an adjunct whose COMPL feature is +. According to the second rule, an S' consists of an S optionally preceded by a COMP (the e stands for the empty string). If the COMP is present, then the COMPL feature will be +, otherwise it will be −. These rules allow for sentences such as *Because John kissed Sue, Mary was jealous* but exclude sentences such as **John kissed Sue, Mary was jealous.*

The difficulty with these rules is that they license the context-free parser to postulate an initial S' for a sentence such as *Bill drank a few beers*. This S' will eventually be eliminated when its functional constraints are processed, because of the contradictory constraints on the value of the COMPL feature. An interleaved strategy would avoid building any edges on top of this spurious constituent (for example, an S with an initial adjunct). However, a non-interleaved strategy may build an exponential number of unnecessary trees on top of this S', especially if such a string is the prefix of a longer sentence. If we convert the COMPL functional requirements into equivalent phrasal ones, the context-free parser will not postulate an initial S' for sentence like these. This can be done by splitting the S' rule into distinct categories S'_{COMPL+} and S'_{COMPL-} as follows:

$$S \longrightarrow \begin{pmatrix} S'_{COMPL+} \\ \downarrow \in (\uparrow \text{ ADJUNCT}) \\ (\downarrow \text{ COMPL}) = + \end{pmatrix} \quad \begin{matrix} NP \\ (\uparrow \text{ SUBJ}) = \downarrow \end{matrix} \quad \begin{matrix} VP \\ \uparrow = \downarrow \end{matrix}$$

$$S'_{COMPL+} \longrightarrow \quad \begin{matrix} COMP \\ (\uparrow \text{ COMPL}) = + \end{matrix} \quad \begin{matrix} S \\ \uparrow = \downarrow \end{matrix}$$

$$S'_{COMPL-} \longrightarrow \quad \begin{matrix} e \\ (\uparrow \text{ COMPL}) = - \end{matrix} \quad \begin{matrix} S \\ \uparrow = \downarrow \end{matrix}$$

With these rules the context-free parser would fail to find an S'_{COMPL+} in the sentence *Bill drank a few beers*. Thus the S with an initial adjunct and many otherwise possible trees would never be built. In general, this approach notices local inconsistencies in the grammar and changes the categories and rules to avoid encountering them.

Moving features into the constituent space has the effect of increasing the number of categories and rules in the grammar. In the worst case, the size of the chart grows linearly with the number of categories, and computation time grows quadratically in the size of the grammar (Younger 1967, Earley 1970). Just considering the cost of phrasal processing, we have increased the grammar size and therefore have presumably made the worst case performance worse. However, if features are carefully selected so as to increase the amount of pruning done by the chart, the net effect may be that even though the grammar allows more types of constituents, the chart may end up with fewer instances.

It is interesting to compare this technique to Shieber's restriction proposal (Shieber 1985). Both approaches select functional features to be moved forward in processing order in the hope that some processing will be pruned. Shieber's approach changes the processing order of functional constraints so that some of them are processed top-down instead of bottom-up. Our approach takes a different tack, actually converting some of the functional constraints into phrasal constraints. Thus Shieber's does its pruning using functional mechanisms whereas our approach prunes via standard phrasal operations.

8   Some Performance Measures

In the foregoing sections we outlined a few specific interface strategies, each of which incorporates a different combination of techniques for exploiting particular constraint system properties. We argued that each of these techniques can make a substantial performance difference under certain circumstances. In this section we report the results of some preliminary computational comparisons that we conducted to determine whether these techniques can make a practical difference in parsing times. Our results are only suggestive because the comparisons were based on a single grammar and a small sample of sentences. Nevertheless, the patterns we observed are interesting in part because they reinforce our intuitions but also because they lead to a deeper understanding of the underlying computational issues.

We conducted our comparisons by first fixing a base grammar and 20 test sentences and then varying along three different dimensions. The LFG grammar was developed by Jeff Goldberg and Annie Zaenen for independent purposes and came to our attention because of its poor performance using previously implemented algorithms. The test sentences were derived from a compiler text book and are given in the appendix. One dimension that we explored was selective feature movement. We produced a descriptively equivalent variation of the base grammar by choosing certain functional constraints to move into the phrasal domain. A second dimension was the choice of strategy. We compared the interleaved pruning, non-interleaved pruning, factored pruning, and factored extraction strategies discussed above. As a final dimension we compared two different unification algorithms.

8.1 Grammar Variants

The Goldberg-Zaenen base grammar was designed to have broad coverage over a set of complex syntactic constructions involving predicate-argument relations. It does not handle noun-noun compounds, and so these are hyphenated in the test sentences. The grammar was written primarily to capture linguistic generalizations and little attention was paid to performance issues. We measured performance on the 20 test sentences using this grammar in its original form. We also measured performance on a variant of this grammar produced by converting certain functional requirements into phrasal constraints. We determined which constraints to move by running the interleaved pruning strategy on the base grammar and identifying which constraints caused constituents to be locally unsatisfiable. We then modified the grammar and lexicon by hand so that those constraints were reflected in the categories of the constituents. Examination of the results prompted us to split five categories:

- VP was split into VP_{INF+} and VP_{INF-}, where $(\uparrow INF) = +$ is true of VP_{INF+}, and $(\uparrow INF) \neq +$ is true of VP_{INF-}.

- V was split into V_{AUX}, V_{OBL}, V_{TRANS}, and V_{OTHER}, where V_{AUX} is an auxiliary verb, V_{OBL} is a verb with an oblique argument, V_{TRANS} is a transitive verb, and V_{OTHER} is anything else.
- N was split into N_{OBL+} and N_{OBL-}, where N_{OBL+} takes an oblique argument and N_{OBL-} does not.
- COMP was split into $COMP_{COMPL+}$ and $COMP_{COMPL-}$, where $COMP_{COMPL+}$ has $(\uparrow COMPL) = +$ and $COMP_{COMPL-}$ has $(\uparrow COMPL) = -$.
- PP was split into PP_{PRED} and PP_{PCASE}, where PP_{PRED} has a predicate and PP_{PCASE} has a PCASE (is used as an oblique argument).

All of these splits were into mutually exclusive classes. For instance, in the PP case every use of a preposition in the grammar had either a PCASE or a predicate but not both.

8.2 Strategy Variants

Table 1 summarizes the combination of techniques used in the strategies we have mentioned in this paper. The simple composition strategy is the naive first implementation discussed in the introduction; it is included in the table only as a point of reference. Factored extraction is the only other interface strategy that does not do per-edge solving and caching, and therefore does not require a special copying algorithm. Obviously, the listed strategies do not instantiate all possible combinations of the techniques we have outlined. In all the strategies we use an active chart parser for the phrasal component.

TABLE 1 Strategies and Techniques

Strategy	Interleave	Solve Per Edge	Prune	Factor
Simple composition	–	–	–	–
Interleaved pruning	yes	yes	yes	–
Non-interleaved pruning	–	yes	yes	–
Factored pruning	–	yes	yes	yes
Factored extraction	–	–	–	yes

8.3 Unifier Variants

Unification is a standard technique for determining the satisfiability of and building attribute-value models for systems of functional constraints with equality. In recent years there has been a considerable amount of research devoted to the development of unification algorithms that perform well when confronted with disjunctive constraint systems (Hasida 1986, Maxwell and Kaplan 1989, Dörre and Eisele 1990, Nakano 1991). Some of these unifiers take advantage of the same properties of constraint systems that we have discussed in this paper. For example, Kasper's algorithm takes advantage of monotonicity and order invariance to achieve improved performance when pruning is possible. It works by first determining the satisfiability of the conjunctive constraints, and then checking disjuncts one at a time to find those that are inconsistent with the conjunctive part. Finally, the disjuncts that remain are multiplied into DNF. Our contexted unification algorithm (Maxwell and Kaplan 1989) also allows for pruning but in addition takes advantage of independence to achieve its performance. It works by objectifying the disjunctions so that the constraints can be put into conjunctive normal form (CNF). This algorithm has the advantage that if disjunctions are independent, they do not have to be multiplied out. These unifiers depend on different properties, so we have included both variants in our comparisons to see whether there are any interactions with the different interface strategies. In the discussion below, we call the unifier that we implemented based on Kasper's technique the "benchmark" unifier.

8.4   Results and Discussion

We implemented each of the four strategies and two unifiers in our computational environment, except that, because of resource limitations, we did not implement factored pruning for the benchmark unifier. We then parsed the 20 test sentences using the two grammars for each of these configurations. We measured the compute time for each parse and averaged these across all the sentences. The results are shown in Table 2. To make comparisons easier, the mean times in this table have been arbitrarily scaled so that the mean for the interleaved pruning strategy with the benchmark unifier is 100.

TABLE 2   Mean Scaled Computation Time

Grammar	Strategy	Benchmark	Contexted
Base	Interleaved pruning	100	42
	Non-interleaved pruning	71	25
	Factored pruning	—	23
	Factored extraction	>1000	>1000
Modified	Interleaved pruning	38	26
	Non-interleaved pruning	29	19
	Factored pruning	—	13
	Factored extraction	21	7

The most striking aspect of this table is that it contains a wide range of values. We can conclude even from this limited experiment that the properties and techniques we have discussed do in fact have practical significance. The strategy in the fourth line ran much longer than we were willing to measure, while every other combination behaved in a quite reasonable way. Since the fourth line is the only combination that does neither functional nor phrasal pruning, this demonstrates how important pruning is.

Looking at the grammar variants, we see that in all cases performance is substantially better for the modified grammar than for the base grammar. This is in agreement with Nagata's (1992) finding that a medium grain phrase-structure grammar performs better than either a coarse-grain or fine-grain grammar. The modified grammar increases the amount of pruning that is done by the chart because we carefully selected features for this effect. The fact that this improves performance for even the pruning strategies is perhaps surprising, since the same number of inconsistencies are being encountered. However, with the modified grammar the inconsistencies are being encountered earlier, and hence prune more. This effect is strongest for the factored extraction algorithm since inconsistencies are never detected by the interface; they are left for the unifier to discover.

Turning to the interface strategies, we see that non-interleaved pruning is always better than interleaved pruning. This is also as expected, because the non-interleaved strategy has the benefit of global phrasal pruning as well as incremental functional pruning. Nagata (1992) reports similar results with early and late unification. Non-interleaved pruning is not as efficient as factored pruning, however. This shows that factoring is an important technique once the benefits of pruning have been obtained. The factored extraction strategy exhibits the most interesting pattern of results, since it shows both the worst and best performance in the table. It gives the worst performance with the base grammar, as discussed above. It gives the overall best performance for the modified grammar with the contexted unifier. This takes advantage of the best arrangement for pruning (in the chart), and its contexted unifier can best operate on its factored constraints. The next best performance is the combination of factored pruning with the modified grammar and the contexted unifier. Although both strategies take advantage of factoring and pruning, factored pruning does worse because it must pay the cost of copying the solutions that it caches at each edge.

Finally, the type of unifier also made a noticeable difference. The contexted unifier is always faster than the benchmark one when they can be compared. This is to be expected because, as mentioned above, the contexted unifier both prunes and takes advantage of independence. The benchmark unifier only prunes.

Average computing time is one way of evaluating the effects of these different combinations, since it gives a rough performance estimate across a variety of different sentences. However, the degree of variability between sentences is also important for many practical purposes. A strategy with good average performance may be unacceptable if it takes an unpredictably large amount of time on some sentences. Table 3, which shows the computing time of the worst sentence in each cell, gives a sense of the inter-sentence variability. These values use the same scale as Table 2.

TABLE 3   Maximum Scaled Computation Time

Grammar	Strategy	Benchmark	Contexted
Base	Interleaved pruning	691	314
	Non-interleaved pruning	421	182
	Factored pruning	—	135
	Factored extraction	>20000	>20000
Modified	Interleaved pruning	112	104
	Non-interleaved pruning	101	74
	Factored pruning	—	43
	Factored extraction	126	15

This table supports roughly the same conclusions as Table 2. There is a wide range of values, the modified grammar is better than the base, and the contexted unifier is faster than the benchmark one. In many cells, the maximum values are substantially larger than the corresponding means, thus indicating how sensitive these algorithms can be to variations among sentences. There is an encouraging result, however. Just as the lowest mean value appears for factored extraction with the modified grammar and contexted unifier, so does the lowest maximum. Moreover, that cell has the lowest ratio of maximum to mean, almost 2. Thus, not only is this particular combination the fastest, it is also much less sensitive to variations between sentences. However, factored extraction is very sensitive to the amount of pruning done by the phrasal constraints, and thus may not be the best strategy when it is impractical to perform appropriate grammar modifications. In this situation, factored pruning may be the best choice because it is almost as fast as factored extraction but much less sensitive to grammar variations.

9 Concluding Remarks

As we discussed in the introduction, the interleaved pruning strategy is substantially better than simple composition and so it is no surprise that it is a widely used and little questioned interface strategy. However, it is only one point in a complex and multi-dimensional space of possibilities, and not necessarily the optimal point at that. We outlined a number of alternative strategies, and presented preliminary measurements to suggest that factored extraction may give better overall results, although it is very sensitive to details of the grammar. Factored pruning also gives good results and is less sensitive to the grammar. The good results of these two strategies show how important it is to take advantage of both monotonicity and independence and of the polynomial nature of the phrasal constraints.

The investigations summarized in this paper suggest several directions for future research. One direction would aim at developing a grammar compiler that automatically selects and moves the best set of features. A compiler could hide this transformation from the grammar developer or end user, so that it would be considered merely a performance optimization and not a change of linguistic analysis. Another research direction might focus on a way of adding functional pruning to the factored extraction algorithm so that it would be less sensitive to variations in the grammar.

At a more general level, our explorations have illustrated the richness of the space of phrasal-functional interface possibilities, and the potential value of examining these issues in much greater detail. Of course, further experimental work using other grammars and larger corpora are necessary to confirm the preliminary results we have obtained. We also need more formal analyses of the computation complexity of interface strategies to support the intuitive characterizations that we have presented in this paper. We believe that the context-free nature of phrasal constraints has not yet been fully exploited in the construction of hybrid constraint processing systems and that further research in this area can still lead to significant performance improvements.

Appendix: Test Sentences

1. These normally include syntactic analyses.
2. The phases are largely independent of the target-machine.
3. Those phases depend primarily on the source-language.
4. Code-optimization is done by the front-end as well.
5. However there has been success in this direction.
6. Often the phases are collected into a front-end.

7. Generally these portions do not depend on the source-language.
8. The front-end consists of those phases that depend primarily on the source-language.
9. If the back-end is designed carefully it may not be necessary to redesign the back-end.
10. It produces a compiler for the same source-language on a different machine.
11. It has become fairly routine to take the front-end of a compiler.
12. It is not even necessary to redesign much of the back-end.
13. The front-end consists of those phases that depend primarily on the source-language.
14. It is also tempting to compile several different languages into the same intermediate language.
15. The back-end also includes those portions of the compiler that depend on the target-machine.
16. This matter is discussed in Chapter-9.
17. The front-end also includes the error-handling that goes along with these phases.
18. It is tempting to use a common back-end for the different front-ends.
19. Because of subtle differences in the viewpoints of the different languages there has been only limited success in that direction.
20. It has become routine to redo its associated back-end to produce a compiler for the same source-language on a different machine.

References

Barton, G. Edward, Robert C. Berwick, and Eric Sven Ristad. 1987. *Computational Complexity and Natural Language*. Cambridge, Massachusetts: MIT Press.

Bear, John, and Jerry R. Hobbs. 1988. Localizing Expression of Ambiguity. In *Second Conference on Applied Natural Language Processing*, 235–241.

Church, Kenneth W., and Ramesh Patil. 1982. Coping with syntactic ambiguity or how to put the block in the box on the table. *Computational Linguistics* 8(3-4):139–149.

Dörre, Jochen, and Andreas Eisele. 1990. Feature Logic with Disjunctive Unification. In *Proceedings of COLING 90*.

Earley, J. 1970. An Efficient Context-Free Algorithm. *Communications of the ACM* 13:94–102.

Gazdar, Gerald, Ewan Klein, Geoffrey Pullum, and Ivan Sag. 1985. *Generalized Phrase Structure Grammar*. Cambridge, Massachusetts: Harvard University Press.

Godden, K. 1990. Lazy Unification. In *Proceedings of the 28th Annual Meeting of the ACL.*

Hasida, K. 1986. Conditioned Unification for Natural Language Processing. In *Proceedings of COLING 86*, 85–87.

Johnson, Mark. 1989. The Computational Complexity of Tomita's Algorithm. In *Proceedings of the International Workshop on Parsing Technologies*, 203–208.

Kaplan, Ronald M. 1973. A multi-processing approach to natural language. In *Proceedings of the 1973 National Computer Conference*, 435–440. Montvale, N. J. AFIPS Press.

Kaplan, Ronald M., and Joan Bresnan. 1982. Lexical-Functional Grammar: A Formal System for Grammatical Representation. In *The Mental Representation of Grammatical Relations*, ed. Joan Bresnan. 173–281. Cambridge, MA: The MIT Press. Reprinted in Part I of this volume.

Karttunen, Lauri. 1986. D-PATR: A Development Environment for Unification-Based Grammars. In *Proceedings of COLING 1986*. Bonn, Germany.

Kasper, Robert T. 1987. A Unification Method for Disjunctive Feature Descriptions. In *Proceedings of the 25th Annual Meeting of the ACL.*

Kay, Martin. 1979. Functional Grammar. In *Proceedings of the 5th Annual Meeting of the Berkeley Linguistic Society*, ed. C. Chiarello et al.

Kay, Martin. 1986 (1980). Algorithm schemata and data structures in syntactic processing. In *Readings in Natural Language Processing*, ed. Barbara J. Grosz, Karen Sparck-Jones, and Bonnie Lynn Webber. 35–70. Los Altos, Calif.: Morgan Kaufmann.

Kay, Martin. 1989. Head-Driven Parsing. In *Proceedings of the International Workshop on Parsing Technologies*, 52–62.

Knight, Kevin. 1989. Unification: A Multidisciplinary Survey. *ACM Computing Surveys* 21(1):93–124.

Maxwell, III, John T., and Ronald M. Kaplan. 1989. An Overview of Disjunctive Constraint Satisfaction. In *Proceedings of the International Workshop on Parsing Technologies*. (Also published as "A method for disjunctive constraint satisfaction" in M. Tomita, editor, *Current Issues in Parsing Technology*, Kluwer Academic Publishers, 1991.) Reprinted in Part V of this volume.

Nagata, Masaaki. 1992. An Empirical Study on Rule Granularity and Unification Interleaving Toward an Efficient Unification-Based Parsing System. In *Proceedings of COLING 92*, 177–183.

Nakano, Mikio. 1991. Constraint Projection: An Efficient Treatment of Disjunctive Feature Descriptions. In *Proceedings of the 29th Annual Meeting of the ACL*, 307–314.

Nelson, Greg, and Derek C. Oppen. 1980. Fast Decision Procedures Based on Congruence Closure. *Journal of the ACM* 27(3):356–364.

Pereira, Fernando C. N., and David H. D. Warren. 1980. Definite clause grammars for language analysis – a survey of the formalism and a comparison with augmented transition networks. *Artificial Intelligence* 13(3):231–278.

Pollard, Carl, and Ivan Sag. 1987. *Information-Based Syntax and Semantics*. CSLI Lecture Notes, Vol. 13. Stanford: CSLI.

Schabes, Yves. 1991. Polynomial Time and Space Shift-Reduce Parsing of Arbitrary Context-free Grammars. In *Proceedings of the 29th Annual Meeting of the ACL*, 106–113.

Sheil, Beau. 1976. Observations on Context-Free Parsing. In *Proceedings of COLING 76*.

Shieber, Stuart M. 1985. Using restriction to extend parsing algorithms for complex feature-based formalisms. In *Proceedings of the 23rd Annual Meeting of the ACL*.

Stock, Oliviero, Rino Falcone, and Patrizia Insinnamo. 1988. Island Parsing and Bidirectional Charts. In *Proceedings of COLING 88*, 636–641.

Thompson, Henry. 1983. MCHART: a Flexible, Modular Chart Parsing System. In *Proceedings of AAAI-83*, 408–410.

Tomabechi, Hideto. 1991. Quasi-Destructive Graph Unification. In *Second International Workshop on Parsing Technology*, 164–171.

Tomita, Masaru. 1986. *Efficient Parsing for Natural Language*. Boston, Mass.: Kluwer.

Wittenburg, Kent, and Jim Barnett. 1988. Canonical Representation in NLP Systems Design. In *Second Conference on Applied Natural Language Processing*, 253–259.

Wroblewski, David A. 1987. Nondestructive Graph Unification. In *Proceedings of AAAI87*.

Younger, D. H. 1967. Recognition and Parsing of Context-Free Languages in Time n^3. *Information and Control* 10:189–208.

Name Index

431

Subject Index

A′-position, 253
A-position, 253
A-structure, *see* Argument structure
Across-the-board constraint, 132, 208, 223
Adjunct, *see also* Brace notation, ADJUNCTS value; F-description solution operators, Include; Long-distance dependencies, adjuncts vs. arguments; Object, oblique, and adjuncts; Prepositional phrases, adjunct vs. argument; Prepositional phrases, adjunct vs. argument; Set value notation; Sets, 19, 67–70, 74, 201, 275, 360
Adverbs, 283
Affix hopping, 59
Agreement, xiii
  number, 59
Ambiguity
  structural, *see also* Prepositional phrases, attachment, 416–418
Anaphor, *see also* Anaphoric binding; Antecedent; Coreference, 94n, 167
  null, *see also* Empty category; Subject, null, 17, 21, 226, 281, 357
Anaphoric binding, x, 134, 167–173, 212, 258

constraints, 168–172, 174
  domain path f-structure (DPF), 171
Anaphoric binding domain, *see also* PathOut, 168, 171–172
Anaphoric structure, 23, 362
Angle bracket notation (⟨ ⟩), 33, 34n
Annotations, *see* Schemata
Antecedent, *see also* Anaphor; Anaphoric binding; Coreference; PathIn, 167, 170
ANY-value constraint, 377–378
Arabic, xiv
Arc relation, *see also* Attribute-value, features, 371, 377–378
Argument position, *see* A-position
Argument structure (a-structure), 242n, 269n
Arguments
  oblique, 255
Asterisk notation, *see* Kleene closure operator, *
ATN, *see* Augmented Transition Network
Attribute, 32, 45, 46n, 125
  distinguished, 284
  FORM vs. PRED, 66
Attribute-value
  constants, *see also* *Con* predicate, 371–372

437

interlingua-based, 312, 324
transfer-based, 312
Malay, xiv
Malayalam, xiv, 213, 248, 254, 258–
263, 266n, 269
Mapping, *see also* Codescription; Correspondence functions; Structural correspondence, 349–350
Mapping theory, xi–xiii
Marathi, xiv, 172
Membership
operator ($\in$), 19, 68
problem, *see also* Verification problem, 114, 148, 180
Merge, *see* F-description solution operators, Merge
Metaform, *see also* Semantic form, 77
Metavariable, 39–45
bounded domination (long-distance), *see also* Binding, syntactic; Constituent controllee; Constituent controller; Long-distance dependency, 39, 85, 131, 360
category requirements, 91–92, 142–143, 154
immediate domination, *see also* Down-arrow notation; Up-arrow notation, 39, 44n, 85, 315
ordering, 110
Metavariable category subscript notation, 92
MG, *see* Montague grammar
Middle field, 233–238
Minimality condition, *see also* Functional description, minimal solution, 14, 56, 149, 354, 377
Modal logic, 336
Model, *see also* Functional structure, 2, 392–393
acyclic, *see also* Functional structure, acyclic, 189
cyclic, *see also* Functional structure, cyclic, 184, 189
minimal, *see also* Functional description, minimal solution; Minimality condition; Subsumption, 184, 189, 191, 377–378, 393
Modern Irish, xiv
Mohawk, 121
Montague grammar, 280, 293, 295–302
semantic interpretation in, 296–298
Movement rules, 32

Natural language parsing, *see* Natural language processing
Natural language processing, 4, 347–349, 382
Negation, 133
in feature logics, 373n
Nested dependencies, *see also* Crossing, 96, 110–113
nearly, 111
strictly, 111
Nogood, *see also* Disjunctive residue, 390–392
Non-local dependency, *see* Long-distance dependency
Nonbranching dominance constraint, 116, 190, 222, 224, 230, 332, 333, 405, 406
Noncoreference, *see also* Disjoint reference, 168, 247, 260
Normal form
conjunctive, 385, 399
disjunctive, 335, 382, 396, 399, 405
Norwegian, xiv, 85, 169–170, 173
Null object, *see* Empty category; Pronoun, null

Object
double, 254
instantiation of, 40
oblique, 51, 54–55, 69–70, 156n, 319–320
and adjuncts, 74